FROM COLONY TO NATION

THE JOHNS HOPKINS SYMPOSIA IN
COMPARATIVE HISTORY

The Johns Hopkins Symposia in Comparative History are occasional volumes sponsored by the Department of History at The Johns Hopkins University and The Johns Hopkins University Press. Each considers, from a comparative perspective, an important topic of current historical interest and comprises essays by leading scholars in the United States and other countries. The present volume is the sixth.

FROM COLONY
TO NATION

Essays on the Independence of Brazil

A. J. R. Russell-Wood	Stuart B. Schwartz
Emília Viotti da Costa	Richard M. Morse
Maria Odila Silva Dias	Manoel da Silveira Cardozo
Stanley E. Hilton	E. Bradford Burns

Edited by
A. J. R. Russell-Wood

THE JOHNS HOPKINS UNIVERSITY PRESS
Baltimore and London

Manufactured in the United States of America

The Johns Hopkins University Press, Baltimore, Maryland 21218
The Johns Hopkins University Press Ltd., London

Library of Congress Catalog Card Number 74–24381
ISBN 0–8018–1665–3

Library of Congress Cataloging in Publication data
will be found on the last printed page of this book.

Contents

Foreword by Jack P. Greene   vii

Preface by A. J. R. Russell-Wood   ix

Abbreviations and Orthography   xi

COLONIAL ROOTS OF INDEPENDENCE

Preconditions and Precipitants of the Independence
Movement in Portuguese America   3
A. J. R. RUSSELL-WOOD

POLITICAL ASPECTS

The Political Emancipation of Brazil   43
EMÍLIA VIOTTI DA COSTA

The Establishment of the Royal Court in Brazil   89
MARIA ODILA SILVA DIAS

The United States and Brazilian Independence   109
STANLEY E. HILTON

SOCIAL ASPECTS

Elite Politics and the Growth of a Peasantry in Late
Colonial Brazil   133
STUART B. SCHWARTZ

Brazil's Urban Development: Colony and Empire   155
RICHARD M. MORSE

CULTURAL ASPECTS

The Modernization of Portugal and the Independence of Brazil   185
MANOEL DA SILVEIRA CARDOZO

The Intellectuals as Agents of Change and the Independence
of Brazil, 1724–1822   211
E. BRADFORD BURNS

Chronological Table   247

Glossary   251

Notes on Contributors   253

Index   255

Foreword

The gaining of independence by Brazil in 1822 seems to have attracted, more especially in the English-speaking world, far less attention than the earlier and more dramatic struggles for independence in British and Hispanic America. At least in part to remedy this neglect, this volume presents a wide-ranging exploration of the background to Brazilian independence. It contains eight penetrating and authoritative essays, each by a distinguished student of colonial Brazil. The editor, A. J. R. Russell-Wood, to whose indefatigable and often inspired labors we owe both this volume and the conference from which it emerged, opens the book with a lucid and comprehensive overview of the preconditions and precipitants of the movement for Luso-American independence. The seven independent essays that follow explore selected aspects of that movement: those by Emília Viotti da Costa, Maria Odila Silva Dias, and Stanley E. Hilton, the political; those by Stuart B. Schwartz and Richard M. Morse, the social; and those by Manoel da Silveira Cardozo and E. Bradford Burns, the cultural.

Although each of these essays stands on its own, collectively they make it clearer than ever before both that the relative ease with which Brazil obtained independence provides a useful counterpoint to the embattled—and protracted—struggles for separate status by the British and Spanish colonies and that a close scrutiny of the Brazilian experience is necessary for any comprehensive understanding of the early—and the first modern—struggle for political decolonization that took place in the Americas during the half-century beginning in 1776. This volume, like *Neither Slave nor Free*, its predecessor in a projected series of book-length publications growing out of symposia sponsored by the Atlantic History and Culture Program at The Johns Hopkins University, also serves to illuminate a significant part of the experience of the broader Atlantic world over the past five centuries.

Jack P. Greene
Director, Atlantic History and
Culture Program

Preface

On September 7, 1822, Dom Pedro made his historic declaration, "Independence or death. We are separate from Portugal," on the banks of the Ypiranga River in the State of São Paulo. The events leading to this declaration and the delicate interweave of political, economic, social, cultural, and emotional factors in the years preceding the movement toward independence in Brazil have been the subject of a number of historical treatises. Some have questioned the importance of 1822 itself and point to the opening of the ports (1808), the raising of the state of Brazil to the status of a kingdom (1815), or more distant events such as the numerous conspiracies and uprisings of the late eighteenth century as being of greater significance. Such historical debate can in no way detract from the very real achievement of the Brazilian people in celebrating the sesquicentenary of independence in 1972. This was the occasion for festivities and celebrations in Brazil and for official ceremonies and lectures in scholarly groups in Brazil, in Europe, and in the United States. The Department of History of The Johns Hopkins University resolved to hold a symposium to which would be invited distinguished scholars of Brazilian history. This meeting was held in conjunction with the newly established interdisciplinary Atlantic History and Culture Program for the training of undergraduate and graduate students.

The object of the conference was twofold. Invitations were sent to established scholars with personal research experience in the archives and repositories of Brazil but whose breadth of vision transcended the frontiers of Brazil. By their papers it was hoped they would contribute to our understanding of Brazil before independence and also enable us to view Brazilian independence within the broader framework of colonialism and the movement toward independence throughout the Americas. It was also the hope of the organizer that such papers would not only stimulate interest in Brazil but lead to a more critical evaluation of the nature of the colonial pacts from a comparative perspective. The result would be an increase in our appreciation of the multiplicity of factors inherent to the transition from colony to independent nation and a critical evaluation of the achievement of independence per se.

The symposium was held at The Evergreen House on October 18 and 19, 1972, and was attended by some thirty speakers and panelists. The historians who delivered papers were Professors Richard M. Morse (Yale

University), E. Bradford Burns (University of California at Los Angeles), Stuart B. Schwartz (University of Minnesota), Richard Graham (University of Texas at Austin), Manoel da Silveira Cardozo (Catholic University), and Dr. Leslie Bethell (University of London). Those who presented papers also served as moderators of the open discussions that followed, and they were joined in this role by Professors David W. Cohen, Jack P. Greene, and A. J. R. Russell-Wood, all of The Johns Hopkins University.

Each historian had been asked to write on a general aspect (cultural, political, social, intellectual, economic) of the years preceding the independence movement, but the actual choice of topic was left to him. In all cases, the scholars based their papers on the results of previously unpublished research and examined areas which they felt were neglected or inadequately understood. Financial considerations restricted the number of invitations to speakers from abroad. In this volume, this limitation has in part been remedied by papers by Professors Emília Viotti da Costa, Maria Odila Silva Dias, and Stanley E. Hilton, whose topics complemented those of the participants.

The symposium was held under the auspices of the Department of History of The Johns Hopkins University. The Charles Del Mar Foundation and The Maryland Foundation for Latin American Affairs under its executive director Mrs. Geraldina Weintraub provided generous assistance from the time of inception to the successful outcome of the meeting and contributed toward the cost of publication. To Mrs. Weintraub and Major General Roland H. Del Mar (U.S.A., ret.) must go much of the credit for providing encouragement and moral support at times of stress, particularly when it appeared pressures might result in the cancellation of the symposium. Numerous people within and without the Johns Hopkins community contributed time and effort unstintingly and of their own accord: these included Miss Linda van Reuth, Miss Elaine Ewing, Mrs. Mary Jane Hall, Mrs. Ria Stewart, Miss Terry Wozniak, and a corps of departmental secretaries and university telephonists who performed a thankless task gallantly and graciously.

A. J. R. Russell-Wood

Abbreviations and Orthography

In the interest of concision, citations to the more commonly used archives, to manuscript and printed collections, and to journals have been abbreviated and standardized throughout the footnotes in conformity with the following list.

ABNRJ	*Anais da Biblioteca Nacional,* Rio de Janeiro.
ANRJ	Arquivo Nacional, Rio de Janeiro.
AHU	Arquivo Histórico Ultramarino, Lisbon.
BNRJ	Biblioteca Nacional, Rio de Janeiro.
DHBNRJ	*Documentos Históricos,* Biblioteca Nacional, Rio de Janeiro.
HAHR	*Hispanic American Historical Review.*
RIAHGP	*Revista do Instituto Archeológico, Histórico e Geográfico Pernambucano.*
RIGHBahia	*Revista do Instituto Geográfico e Histórico da Bahia.*
RIHGB	*Revista do Instituto Histórico e Geográfico Brasileiro,* Rio de Janeiro.

The Portuguese language as spoken and written in the mother country and overseas colonies has been characterized by its conservatism in morphology and syntax, but it presents problems of orthography. Orthographic reforms have done little to resolve inconsistencies of accentuation and transliteration in modern Portuguese and Brazilian. Older forms persist alongside modern forms and provide a wide range of lexical variants, especially in proper names, e.g., Annaes-anais, geográphico-geografico, arquivo-archivo, Antonio-António-Antônio, Baía-Bahia, Vasconcellos-Vasconcelos. Variants in the text have been standardized, but references in footnotes have been left in original form. In general, English forms of common place names have been used, e.g., Oporto, not Pôrto, and Lisbon, not Lisbôa; but occasionally the Portuguese forms have been maintained to avoid possible ambiguity.

Colonial Roots of
Independence

A . J . R . RUSSELL-WOOD

Preconditions and Precipitants of the Independence Movement in Portuguese America

Europe and the Americas: The Colonial Pacts

The years from 1775 to 1825 in the Americas witnessed a radical upheaval in the New World, which had begun to show the fruits of two and a half centuries of discovery, exploration, settlement, and colonization. Much had been achieved in terms of social consolidation and economic progress, but the story of success had been tempered and soured by the increasing realization on the part of the colonists that the reins of power lay not in the Americas but in the courts and council chambers of Europe. Angered by the iniquities of commercial exploitation, frustrated by the imbalance of power and authority, and victims of pressures exerted by political events in Europe as well as from within the Americas, the colonists had become increasingly disenchanted with the colonial pacts. In Spanish America, in the French colonies in North America and the Caribbean, in the Dutch islands of the Caribbean and on the mainland of South America, in the North American colonies of Great Britain, and in the Portuguese colony of Brazil, European-born and American-born colonists alike had espoused with decreasing reluctance the option which independence represented. The success of the struggle by the British colonies in North America against the mother country exerted an osmotic influence, created an awareness and consciousness of independence, and even acted as a direct stimulant to dissentient groups elsewhere in the American continent.

There was no single stereotyped path towards independence in the Americas. The British colonists in North America chose the route of outright defiance, resulting in violence and bloodshed before a final settlement by the Treaty of Paris in 1783. Even among the "kingdoms" of Spanish America, there was no unified course or single solution. The Central American area from present-day Guatemala to Costa Rica

3

gained independence peacefully, but the Spanish colonies of South America saw pitched battles. The Caribbean islands only gained their independence at a late date. The Spanish colonies in the Americas achieved their independence not by a single unified revolution but by a series of revolutions. There was no common design, intent, or execution. The initial result was not one but seven new nations, soon to be further divided. Nor was there any unity of ideological aspiration. Mexico had a short-lived flirtation with a monarchical solution, but elsewhere royalist sentiment was finally overcome by an all-embracing but little-understood republicanism.

Brazil achieved its independence relatively peacefully and expeditiously. On September 7, 1822, the prince regent, Dom Pedro, while on a visit to the captaincy of São Paulo, defiantly declared, "It is time! Independence or death. We are separate from Portugal." He had informed the city council of Rio de Janeiro on January 9 that he would "remain for the good of all and for the general happiness of the nation," thereby defying an order of the Portuguese Côrtes, or government, that he return to Lisbon. On May 26, 1824, President James Monroe of the United States recognized Brazil as an independent nation, and his lead was soon followed by the European powers. Finally, in 1825, under severe pressure from the United Kingdom, which had acted as an intermediary in the diplomatic negotiations between colony and mother country, Portugal recognized the independence of the richest colony of her seaborne empire.

Despite considerable disparity in content and emphasis in the policies of the European nations toward their colonies in the Americas, there were certain aspects common to all. Of paramount importance was the precise nature of the relationship between mother country and colony. This relationship was not constant, nor did it possess the internal strength to remain inviolate. It was highly susceptible (one might almost say vulnerable) to new developments or shifts of power on the international level; to new directives taken by the mother country, either on its own initiative or in response to internal or external social, political, and economic pressures; to new economic developments in the colonies; to new social aspirations or ideological awarenesses on the part of the colonists; or to the interaction of factors present in the mother country and in the colonies none of which alone would have been of sufficient importance or strength to affect the relationship. The colonial pact was both as strong and as fragile as any relationship between two persons one of whom sees himself or herself as determining the destiny of the other.

The colonial pact was a balance between dependence and independence. It was alternately well defined or tenuous, respected or resented, a pillar of strength or a progenitor of weakness. It was a historic act on an emotionally charged tightrope woven of political, economic, social, and cultural strands. At one end were the colonists, imbued with hopes, aspiring and striving to play a more significant role in the empires of which they were but one part, or at least to have some say in determining governmental policies which would directly affect their lives. At the other end was the metropolitan government, intent not only on preserving but also on strengthening the authority of the mother country over the colony and on keeping the colony in a state of dependence. Given the differences of attitude, it was inevitable that the relationship between the European mother countries and the American colonies should be characterized by mutual distrust. Reforms enacted by the mother countries stimulated a gamut of colonial responses ranging from reluctant compliance and recognition of imperial authority to disbelief, apathy, scorn, and, in some cases, outright refusal to obey the new regulations. At no time was the response uniform throughout the colonies, and only on rare occasions and by coincidence did identical administrative measures taken by governments in Europe for enactment in the American colonies evoke identical responses. Indeed, in no colony was the response uniform in every sector of society or geographical region. It is in the very differences of the colonial reaction throughout the Americas that historians have found a fertile ground for study, but it is unfortunate that this focus should have resulted in a lack of attention to the similarities of the colonists' experience in the Americas, be they French, Portuguese, Spanish, British, Dutch, or Scandinavian in origin or descent.

In recent years historians have borrowed with increasing frequency, but not always with a corresponding increase in understanding, from the social sciences. All too often the borrowing has been limited to a transfer of epithets and slogans from one discipline to another, with no serious attempt to analyze or appreciate the concepts behind the terminology. The prolific use of such terms as "creolization," "cultural divergence," "acculturation," and "culture contact" has been matched only by the no less indiscriminate emphasis on an approach described variously as "intercultural," "transcultural," "interdisciplinary," "interface," etc. A certain *frisson* is imparted to the spine of the reader or the participant at academic gatherings whenever these words are spoken. It is ironic that the result of such transpositions and such emphases should have been to limit our understanding to certain areas rather than to enhance our appreciation of the colonization of the Americas as a whole. This tunnel vision has been the result of changing academic fashions, the linguistic shortcomings of individual researchers, and the fact that existing archival and documentary resources are limited and cannot provide full coverage on a chosen theme.

It is high time for scholars to recognize that the transoceanic experience did not divide Dutch from French, British from Portuguese, or Spaniards from Danes. Migrants all viewed the Atlantic passage with trepidation and shared an equal range of unfounded superstitions and unbounded aspirations. On arrival in the New World, the challenges to survival faced by a Yorkshireman in North America did not differ in substance from those faced by an Azorean peasant in Brazil. Common to all were clearing of land for agriculture, establishing the first settlement, sowing of the first crops, conquest of or coexistence with indigenous peoples, and acclimatization to new environments, new foods, and new life styles. Whatever the religion, whatever the language, whatever the climate, throughout the Americas the dedication of the first place of worship, the harvesting of the first crops, and the establishment of the first township were cause for celebration. With the passage of time, animal and crop husbandry were developed, people moved away from the first landfall, settlements developed into towns and towns into cities, communications were improved, labor pools were established, certain crops were found to be more suitable than others, and an economy developed. The band of settlers became a regimented and defined society. Prosperity, demographic increase, and conflicts of interest demanded the creation of administrative entities of local government. To be sure, the aspirations of a Cortés could not have been fulfilled in the political and social ambience of the British colonies in North America; the British West Indian expedient of adopting the parish as an unit of local government would not have been feasible in Minas Gerais; the approaches to the sedentary Amerindian population were not identical in all cases; and the Dutchman of Curaçao did not look on a black person with the same eyes as his Spanish, British, French, or Portuguese counterparts. Differences there were, but these were usually more of emphasis or of degree than of substance.

This point also applies to the relationship between the metropolitan governments and their American colonies. It cannot be overemphasized that with some few exceptions there was no consistent common policy formulated by the European powers toward the colonies. Shifting spheres of influence in Western Europe and internal national considerations determined the adoption of policies which varied from nation to nation at any given time and were subject to modifications at different periods. The personal whims of a sovereign, the demands of an alliance, external pressures, and national interests contributed to modifications, amendments, innovations, and even total reversals in colonial policies. Nevertheless, certain factors were common to all the colonial pacts. Given actions provoked broad reactions, ranging from indifference to direct confrontation between colony and mother country. In the earlier years of the colonial pacts metropolitan governments felt themselves sufficiently strong to adopt an essentially exploitative policy toward their colonies without fear of open challenge or reprisal from the colonists. Metropolitan reforms did not usually meet with ready compliance by the colonists, but comply they did, at least on the surface. Pockets of resistance were extinguished, but no metropolitan government succeeded in eradicating the growing trend in the eighteenth century toward self-examination and self-assessment on the part of the American colonists. In large part introspective, this was an ill-defined blending of emotionalism and pragmatism. Sometimes it surfaced in the form of an act of resistance, but more frequently it could be seen only in apathy and a general malaise at the nature of the colonial pact. On occasions it culminated in the taking of a more defined and determined stand by the colonists, who were able to force a compromise on the metropolitan government.

Once the relationship between colony and metropolis ceased to be a delicate balancing act and took on the appearance of a tug-of-war, compromises became less possible. The hardening of the positions of the two parties provided no alternative to direct confrontation between mother country and colony. And yet, for the most part, the colonists only embarked on the road to independence with considerable reluctance and often without the complete support of their fellow Americans. Introspection, indecision, apathy, reversals, and a willingness to reach for an "ultimate solution" short of separation characterized independence movements in the Americas. It is difficult, if not impossible, to define preconditions for such independence movements. To attribute a pattern to such trends would be to endow them with a stereotyped and structured quality which none possessed. Nevertheless, there was a certain rhythm in the move toward independence throughout the Americas by colonists of different nationalities, different religions, and different languages. The essays collected in this volume examine the nature of this rhythm as exemplified by the move toward independence on the part of Portuguese crown subjects in Brazil, and my task here is to place the independence movement in the broader economic, social, and political context of colonial Brazil.

Portuguese America: The Economic, Social, and Political Context

The chance discovery of Brazil by Pedro Álvares Cabral in 1500 had evoked little interest in Portugal. Soon to be consumed by the glitter of "Golden Goa" and the apparently unlimited resources of the East, Dom Manuel (king of Portugal, 1495–1521) had faced the fact that it was impossible to enlarge to the Americas an empire already overextended in Africa and Asia. Manpower and financial resources had made such New World involvement as speculative as it was impossible. Only under the threat of foreign interest had Dom João III (1521–57) been induced to establish an ill-fated donatory system in Portuguese America. Not until 1549, a full half-century after its discovery, was royal government established in Brazil, with the capital at Salvador. During the later sixteenth and seventeenth centuries sugar became the dominant product of an export economy which depended on the slave markets of West Africa for its pool of labor. The prosperity of Brazil awoke the unwelcome attentions of the Dutch West India Company, which successfully occupied a large part of the northeast from 1630 to 1654. An economic depression in the sugar industry in the 1670s and 1680s was offset to some degree by the development of a free range cattle industry in the interior of the northeast and the export of hides. Similarly, it was in the early years of the eighteenth century that the cultivation of tobacco, especially in the fertile Recôncavo of Bahia, was to become a major export commodity not only to Europe and Asia but also to West Africa. It is a question of the chicken-and-egg variety as to whether or not it was the expanding prosperity of the northeast which demanded an ever larger number of slaves or whether the West African demand for the sweetened cord tobacco acted as a stimulus to agriculture. The major event in the economic history of Brazil was the discovery of placer mines in Minas Gerais in the 1690s and later in Cuiabá, Goiás, and Bahia. This event alone guaranteed renewed crown interest in the colony, which was to be enhanced by the discovery of diamonds in Tijuco in the 1720s.

These two occurrences polarized public opinion, disrupted the colonial economy and society, resulted in a hardening of crown policy, and had profound effects not only on Portugal but on the economies of Western Europe. With the decline in mineral production (noticeable in the 1730s and obvious from the third quarter of the century on), the result of technological inadequacy rather than the exhaustion of deposits, Brazil turned to the land once again. The sugar industry had recovered from its earlier depressed state. The cattle industry was proving successful in Minas Gerais and the southern captaincies as well as in the northeast. By the third quarter of the eighteenth century the captaincies of the Maranhão and Pará were assuming greater economic importance with the establishment of cocoa plantations, and increasing importance was being given to the production of cotton as an export corp. Coffee had been planted in the captaincy of São Paulo, but it was only after the colonial period ended that it became a major factor in Brazilian agriculture.

Before the establishment of the donatory system by Dom João III, the colonization of Brazil had been uncontrolled. Amerindians, French, Portuguese, and adventurers of different nationalities had coexisted with little strife in isolated coastal settlements. The establishment of a capital and crown government offered a degree of security to potential migrants, but their response was slow. Only in the seventeenth century, with the decline of Portuguese interests in the East, and in the eighteenth century, in the wake of mineral discoveries, did migration from Portugal and the Atlantic islands to Brazil show any significant increases. Such colonization was almost exclusively male throughout much of the colonial period, and laments about the shortage of white women of marriageable age in Brazil were a constant theme in the reports of governors and viceroys to the crown. It must also be acknowledged that the Portuguese crown gave little incentive to migrants. Its colonization policy, if indeed there were such a policy, was restricted to sponsoring married couples, primarily from the Azores, for settlement in Pará from the 1660s onward. More successful and of more far-reaching importance was the implementation of this policy in the eighteenth century for the settlement of Rio Grande do Sul and Santa Catarina. The number of non-Portuguese subjects in colonial Brazil was small, and it would appear that the quotas of English and Dutch permitted by the treaties of the late seventeenth century were not filled. Nevertheless, even at the end of the colonial period, the distribution of settlers had been predominantly along the littoral in isolated clusters, with a noticeable imbalance between the coastal zones and the interior. Despite penetration of the interior in the seventeenth and eighteenth centuries, notably by the *bandeirantes,* cattle ranchers, and miners, to say nothing of Catholic missionaries in the north, much of the interior remained at best sparsely and spasmodically populated at the beginning of the nineteenth century.

The settlement of Brazil was to bring the Portuguese into contact with peoples of other civilizations. The result was a truly multiracial, intercultural, and polyglot society in the Americas. Such contacts among peoples of European, Amerindian, and African descent have proved a fascinating and fertile ground for scholars of all disciplines, and it is greatly to be hoped that more comparative studies of colonial attitudes will be forthcoming. In the early stages of colonization there had been amicable contacts between settlers and the native Amerindians. Relations rapidly deteriorated however, and the Amerindians were ousted from those areas on the coast surrounding the major nuclei of Portuguese settlement. Although they ceased to be a major factor in the mainstream of the life of the colony, their presence was real in the Amazon, Mato Grosso, Goiás, the Maranhão, southern Bahia, Pôrto Seguro, Espírito Santo, Minas Gerais, and São Paulo. Unlike the Amerindians of Central America at the time of the Spanish invasion, those of Brazil were predominantly nomadic. The victims of war waged by the settlers, enslavement, and exposure to previously unknown bacteria, they withdrew rather than suffer the fate of their counterparts in the Spanish American empire. Indeed, such was the strength and warlike nature of the

Amerindian population at the beginning of the nineteenth century that on May 3, 1808, Dom João VI declared war on the Botocudos of Minas Gerais, and military expeditions were dispatched in Espírito Santo, Pôrto Seguro, Bahia, and São Paulo to "pacify" savage Indians.

Portuguese crown policy toward its Amerindian subjects ranged from patronizing tolerance for much of the colonial period to hostility in the early nineteenth century. In this regard it differed markedly from the policies adopted by the crowns of England, France, and Spain toward the indigenous population of the Americas. In part this divergence may have been the result of contacts with Amerindian civilizations at dissimilar stages of evolution and with varying degrees of stability or mobility, but the answer does not lie in the varying characteristics of the indigenous populations alone. The French and English in North America saw the Amerindian tribes as bargaining tools or temporary allies in their own disputes. Attempts to organize the Amerindians as a labor pool had proven tentative, temporary, and unrewarding. The trade in furs amounted to little more than a commercial understanding between suppliers, entrepreneurs, and consumers. However, from the outset the Portuguese (with varying degrees of intensity) had attempted to incorporate the more tractable of the Amerindian tribes into a greater society. The Jesuits played a major role in Luso-Amerindian relations in Brazil before they won the enmity of king and colonist alike over the use and abuse of Amerindians as a labor source. Pombal's measures (from 1750 to 1777) remedied some of these abuses by encouraging miscegenation, abolishing the enslavement of the Amerindians, outlawing the *resgates,* and establishing the directorate system. In the Amazon area the result was the creation of a pool of free Amerindian labor in the nineteenth century, but elsewhere many of the Pombaline measures were either amended or repealed by the crown or were ignored by the colonists, causing a violent anti-Amerindian reaction at that very time when Brazil was seeking its independence from Portuguese dominance.

Whereas the Amerindian in Brazil was to be the cause of soul-searching on the part of the Portuguese crown, an instrument for Jesuit economic imperialism, and the object of hatred on the part of the colonists, no such ambiguity of role or moral and religious considerations surrounded the colored person of African origin or descent. The presence of the African in Portuguese America was a direct response to the demand for a larger source of labor of a type which the Amerindian population was unable to supply. Slaves were intended initially merely to supplement Amerindian labor, and in fact worked alongside Amerindians in the building of the first capital, but within half a century (1550–1600) the economy of colonial Brazil had become wholly dependent on Africa as a source of labor. If this was true of the sugar industry, it was no less true of the exploitation of mineral resources in the early eighteenth century and the cultivation of cotton in the second half of the century in the Maranhão. The only two major export crops not dependent on African slave labor were tobacco cultivation and cattle raising. However, the latter could count the presence of some mulatto cowboys and herders, and the prosperity of tobacco was inextricably interwoven with the slave trade. In general, the flux and reflux in the slave trade reflected the ebb and flow in the economic fortunes of Brazil.

Because of the presence of the black in those areas of major economic and demographic intensity, it was inevitable that he should make a more positive contribution than the Amerindian to the evolving culture and society of colonial Brazil. In demographic terms his presence could not be ignored. Annual or total figures on the number of slaves imported are elusive; census returns are only available for the later colonial period and are, at best, fragmentary. The trade was at the mercy of events within Brazil and Africa, as well as highly vulnerable to political developments in Europe. Scholars have failed to agree on the exact numbers of slaves imported into Brazil during the colonial period, but a conservative estimate places the number at five million before 1800. The dearth of white women and daily interaction and proximity between whites and blacks resulted in sexual unions. Miscegenation became a characteristic in the evolution of Brazilian society. The mulatto offspring of such unions gained in numbers and in visibility to the point of being considered (and even considering themselves) not as a bridge between ethnic poles but rather as an independent ethnic and social class. Thus it is all the more remarkable that at no time did the Portuguese crown officially recognize the peculiar problems presented by a multiracial society and formulate a social policy for Brazil. In fact, with rare exceptions the crown (like the colonists) failed to distinguish between colored freedmen and slaves. Any paternalism which may have been present in its Amerindian policy was totally absent in the official attitudes toward blacks and mulattos. Slaves and freedmen were objects of discrimination and even prejudice. Ethnic criteria based on "purity of blood" excluded them from posts in government, the Church, the judiciary, religious orders, town councils, and ranking military positions. Such exceptions as there may have been merely proved the rule.

Increasing manumissions in the late seventeenth and eighteenth centuries gave rise to a free colored sector. This development was virtually ignored by the crown and was viewed with apprehension by governors and local authorities. But it is well to bear in mind that, with the exception of the demographic increase in the free colored population, especially mulattos, in all other respects—legal, economic, and social— the position of the free colored person continued to be static, with no general upward progress or amelioration. Whatever vertical mobility there may have been always remained circumscribed within certain limits. At no time did the mulatto, no matter how light-skinned, cast off his ethnic origins and become fully integrated into the white ruling class. All but a few free blacks and free mulattos in colonial Brazil were born, lived, and died in a social, economic, and ethnic penumbra.

The refusal by the Portuguese crown to formulate a social policy for Brazil was symptomatic of the royal attitude toward the colonial pact. Brazil had failed to awaken the interest of Dom Manuel, and no branch of government had been created to deal with its affairs. Instead, responsibility for Brazil had been delegated to the already overburdened Casa da India and other royal councils, whose administrative charges included a loosely connected but farflung maritime empire extending from the Moluccas to the Americas. Even with the decline of Portuguese interests in the East, a gradual appreciation of the extent of the land mass comprising Portuguese America, and the justifiable designation of Brazil as "the most precious jewel in the crown of Portugal" in the seventeenth century, no special administrative entity was established for a colony on which Portugal had become increasingly dependent for her own economic survival. Pombaline administrative reforms in the mid-eighteenth century did little to remedy this situation.

Throughout the three centuries of Brazil's existence as a Portuguese colony all administrative, economic, political, and social developments in Brazil were dutifully referred to Lisbon, and it was in Lisbon that all decisions concerning the colony were taken. Furthermore, the crown maintained firm control over all appointments made in the colony, be they administrative, military, judicial, or ecclesiastical. Its arguments that the establishment of a separate administrative entity in Brazil would be prohibitively expensive were true, but cost per se was not the overriding factor. The truth of the matter was that the Portuguese crown resisted every effort on the part of the colonists to give cohesion to a vast geographical area for fear that such an action would constitute a challenge to its dominance over every aspect of the colony's existence and might fuel autonomous (but not necessarily separatist) sentiment. In Brazil for much of the colonial period there was only one high court. Only in 1676 was an archbishopric created in Salvador and at the end of the colonial period there were only half a dozen bishoprics. There was no standing army. The Inquisition was never established but was limited to "visitations." Requests by the colonists that a university be established were rejected. Industry was forbidden. No printing press was permitted, and the two which were founded led a precarious, clandestine, and short-lived existence. All organs of government established, e.g., the royal Treasury, remained subordinate to Lisbon. The authority delegated to viceroys and governors was, in practice, restricted and subject to metropolitan approval. At all times the Portuguese seaborne empire was highly centralized in its form of government. Even purely local institutions, such as the municipal councils (Câmara Municipal) and the charitable brotherhood of The Holy House of Mercy (Santa Casa da Misericórdia), were modeled on their counterparts in continental Portugal and merely exemplify the essentially conservative policy adopted by the Portuguese crown toward its American colony.

The Eighteenth Century: Age of Regalism and Nationalism

The eighteenth century witnessed internal disruption and drastic transformations in the social, intellectual, economic, and administrative life of Portuguese America. Rapidly changing crown policies and attitudes towards Brazil affected all sectors of colonial society. Moreover, Portugal itself was facing a critical period of development, or lack of it. In addition, throughout the eighteenth century the major European powers exhibited increasing interest in the Luso-Brazilian world, an interest which reached its highest point in the early decades of the nineteenth century. A flurry of international diplomatic activity and the changing of alliances involved Portugal, and therefore Brazil, more deeply in the political vicissitudes of Europe. Changes within Brazil, changes within Portugal, changes in the nature of the colonial pact, and international pressures and involvement all contributed in varying degrees, but none the less decisively, to Brazilian independence. It must be emphasized that these were long-term underlying factors which, although of minor importance if taken individually, exerted a cumulative effect over a period of time. In contrast to such preconditions, the number of actual precipitants, or events with immediate causal impact, were few. The opening of the ports of Brazil to international trade in 1808 and, to an even greater extent in this context, the attitude adopted toward Brazil by the Portuguese Côrtes in the year 1820–1821 were such events. The colonial pact could have survived the opening of the ports. Brazil, albeit in a position of colonial subordination, but a colony with its own organs of government independent of Lisbon, could have survived the decree of 1808. But the intransigent attitude of the Portuguese Côrtes and its evident intention to recolonize Brazil spurred Dom Pedro to his famous declaration of "I shall remain" and made inevitable his proclamation of independence.

One single event heralded the new age for Brazil. This was the discovery of gold in Minas Gerais, Mato Grosso, Goiás, and Bahia. The alluvial deposits of Minas Gerais were to be the most durable and most rewarding. The turmoil into which this discovery cast the economy and society of

Brazil was intensified by the discovery of diamonds in the same captaincy in the 1720s. These two events disrupted the colony's economy, severely affected future patterns of colonization, dislodged the center of political power from the littoral zones of the northeast, still further undermined the rickety price structure of the Portuguese empire, aroused the cupidity of the European powers, and radically altered the nature of the colonial pact. No sooner had news of the first strikes reached the coast, the Atlantic islands, and Portugal than Brazil became immersed in gold rush mania. Whites, mulattos, blacks, slaves and freedmen, ecclesiastics and laymen, deserters from the coastal garrisons, and renegade friars from as far afield as the Maranhão invaded the "General Mines." Violence, moral laxity, chronic instability, financial opportunism, inadequate supplies of food, and a total absence of law and order characterized the early years of the mining encampments. National, ethnic, and economic differences were exacerbated. International interest was aroused.

Having waited so long for the realization of dreams of a Portuguese Potosí, the Portuguese crown was overcome by an almost paranoid fear that Brazil would be invaded by foreign nations. The Dutch invasion and occupation of the northeast of Brazil (1630 to 1654), inspired by the prosperity of sugar production in that area, had not been forgotten. Nevertheless, the crown reacted sluggishly to the new discoveries. Half-hearted attempts by the king and the governor in Rio de Janeiro, in whose jurisdiction lay the mining areas, at imposing judicial, fiscal, adminis-trative, or ecclesiastical control were ineffectual. Dom Pedro II (1683–1706) hesitated, heeding the complaints of the municipal councils of cities in the northeast that labor shortages caused by the movement of slaves to the mines would devastate the sugar economy, and the result was that the crown lost its chance to assert royal control over the unruly miners, who ignored royal and gubernatorial decrees limiting the traffic of slaves to Minas Gerais, restricting the importation of merchandise, and imposing taxes on gold production. The smuggling of gold dust and the evasion of payment of a tax of one fifth of the gold extracted (*os quintos*) characterized the decade following the first discoveries. Of greater im-portance for our purpose is that the strikes of alluvial gold in the valleys of the Rio das Velhas, Rio das Mortes, and the Rio Doce catalyzed attitudes on the part of the colonists and the Portuguese crown which might otherwise have lain dormant. Moreover, these discoveries opened up for Brazil new perspectives, new options, and new hopes which not even the most farsighted visionary could have countenanced at the time. It is to such attitudes that we must turn to appreciate those factors whose evolving presence and roles, now as stimuli and now as responses, now as constants and now as variables, the vehicles for and sometimes the victims of changing emphases and nuances, gave an essentially Brazilian tone to the transition from colony to independent nation in Portuguese America.

It was by one of those coincidences of history that the half century following the initial gold strikes should see at the helm of the Portuguese ship of state a king, Dom João V, whose ambition it was to emulate Louis XIV and inaugurate a golden age of royal absolutism in Portugal. During his reign, the longest in Portuguese history (1706–50), steps were taken to establish and strengthen crown authority in the mining areas in particular and in Brazil in general. Fiscal and economic measures predominated. The economic stagnation of continental Portugal in the late seventeenth and eighteenth centuries had made it increasingly dependent on Brazil and Angola for its very survival. No longer were the colonies viewed solely as producers of raw materials for the home market and for re-export from Lisbon to Western Europe. Instead, revenues derived from the colonies had become an essential part of the royal budget. Numerous appeals for financial "donations" by the crown to the colonies in the course of the eighteenth century went so far as to imply that the colonists were morally bound to help offset expenditures made by the crown within Portugal for domestic purposes which were of no conceivable relevance or benefit to the colonies. During the reign of Dom João V new directives and regulations flowed incessantly from Lisbon, and they continued during the reign of Dom José (1750–77). Such measures drastically altered the concept and balance of responsibility of the colonial pact. It was a bitter irony that the absolutist and centralizing policies of the brilliant minister of Dom José, the marquis of Pombal (so zealous in his efforts to preserve Luso-Brazilian commercial ties), unwittingly sowed the seeds of the future independence movement in Brazil.

Laws for the mining areas were formulated in 1700, and appointments were made at the regional level for their enactment. These proved ineffectual. Regulations could be enforced neither by a king across the water in Lisbon nor by a governor across the mountains in Rio de Janeiro with blanket authority over a vast expanse of the interior but without the means of communication or "muscle" to make his presence felt. In 1709 António de Albuquerque traveled to the "General Mines" and in 1710 was sworn in as governor of the new administrative entity of "São Paulo and the mines of gold." His policy was one of encouragement tempered with restraint. While offering incentives for further exploration, he took strong measures to curtail the smuggling of gold dust and to enforce laws concerning collection and payment of the royal "fifths" on gold extracted. Albuquerque gave a degree of stability to the mining areas by creating townships, establishing a bureaucratic machinery for firmer fiscal control, setting up militia companies for policing the mining areas, and appointing crown judicial officials. The problems which confronted

Albuquerque were to bedevil all future governors of Minas Gerais. Their effectiveness in meeting the challenge was the subject of numerous legal enquiries at the end of each of their terms of office.

In all matters concerning the mining areas the Portuguese crown pursued a policy of vigorous intervention and tight control. Whatever freedom of action may have been enjoyed by governors by virtue of their comparative isolation was more than offset by the intensive royal interest in every development. This is not the place to discuss the implications of such a policy, and a brief description will suffice to illustrate the form taken by the royal "tightening of the screw." In 1719 two companies of dragoons were dispatched to Minas Gerais for patrol and escort duties. In 1721 Dom João V ruled that the captaincy of Minas Gerais should be separated from that of São Paulo and be given its own governor and bureaucracy. Quotas were imposed on the numbers of slaves entering Minas Gerais. Merchandise and meat on the hoof were subject to import taxes on entering the mining area. Registers were established on routes to Minas Gerais to enforce these restrictions, collect dues, and ensure that no gold left the mining areas without payment of the "fifths." The opening of new roads to Minas Gerais was forbidden by law. Foundry houses for smelting gold dust and collecting the "fifths" were established in Vila Rica in 1725 and in Sabará and São João d'El Rei in 1734. A mint was created at Vila Rica for producing provincial coinage in 1725. Restrictions were imposed on the circulation of currency beyond the captaincy. Methods for collecting the "fifths" were as complex as they were bewildering, ranging from "head' taxes to payment in the smelteries. An inadequately staffed crown bureaucracy succeeded in curtailing but never in abolishing contraband. These administrative measures were later extended to the new mining discoveries in Mato Grosso and Goiás. In a modified form, but with draconic harshness, they were also applied to the Diamond District. In 1753 the crown assumed control of the diamond contract. In 1771 Dom José I culminated half a century of progressive royal dominance over the extractive industries in Brazil by abolishing the diamond mining contract and making diamond-mining operations in Brazil a crown monopoly, a state of affairs which survived, albeit in an attenuated form, the declaration of Brazilian independence.

Heightened crown dominance over colonial affairs was not limited to the mining areas and extractive industries but affected all aspects of Brazilian life. The major impact was felt in economic and fiscal matters. The absolutist aspirations of Don João V were matched by the regalist policies forced on Dom José I by the ardently nationalist marquis of Pombal. The accession to the throne of Queen Dona Maria I in 1777 did not change Pombal's traditional colonial policies. Brazil continued to be regarded as the "milch cow" of Portugal. All recognized that Portugal's chances for economic survival lay in the colonies and the vicissitudes of the South Atlantic trade. Pombal directed his efforts at nationalizing the Luso-Brazilian economy and ensuring that profits derived from the Portugese colonies of Brazil and Angola would remain in Portugal rather than being diverted to England and northern Europe. Monopolistic chartered trading companies were created for Grão Pará and the Maranhão in 1755 and for Pernambuco in 1759. In 1755 a Board of Trade was established in Lisbon under strict crown control. In 1751 Boards of Inspection were created in Brazil in the major ports to oversee the production and sale of sugar and tobacco. Although local merchant communities were represented on these boards, crown appointees ensured adherence to royal policies. The boards were highly successful: the northeast revived economically and the Maranhão developed as an area for the production of export crops such as cacao, rice, indigo, and cotton. These measures strengthened Portugal's control over all aspects of commodity buying and selling (including slaves) in the South Atlantic trade and over agricultural production in Brazil.

The eighteenth century witnessed a taxation system in Brazil which grew increasingly oppressive. A prime source of contention was the crown policy of establishing an increasingly comprehensive monopolistic contract system. It had been intended to eliminate the need for crown expenditures on salaries and new administrative entities and to provide a guaranteed annual income for the Exchequer. At different times the supply of tobacco, salt, olive oil, wine, and sugar-cane brandy (*cachaça*) was governed by such contracts. The unsavory practices of high-handed and self-interested contractors made the colonists the victims of high prices and irregular and sporadic supplies of these commodities. An even greater source of hardship were the contracts farmed out by the crown for the collection of dues and taxes, ranging from contracts on river passages, bridges, and the opening of roads to the collection of tithes and dues on slaves, cattle, and merchandise entering the mining areas. Great resentment was felt because many essentially regional contracts were leased in Lisbon, and local bidders were ignored. Rather than enhancing the efficiency of collecting such dues, the excessive demands made by the contractors provoked a high incidence of concealment and smuggling. Moreover, if a contractor feared that his returns would not cover his capital investment, he was perfectly capable of exceeding the terms of his contract and resorting to extortion and even violence. In addition to such everyday fiscal demands (to which might be added the payment of the royal "fifths" and tithes), the colonist had to contend with crown demands for extraordinary "voluntary" donations for royal weddings, the rebuilding of Lisbon after the earthquake, or the construction of the royal palace at Mafra. Furthermore it was the colonists, as consumers, who were the ultimate victims of the heavy duties imposed by the customs at Lisbon on goods exported or re-exported to Brazil.

The repercussions of crown intervention were felt at all levels of colonial government. A backlog of paperwork had led Dom João V in 1713 to give a larger role in the decisionmaking process to royal councils, but the king maintained firm personal control over the formulation and implementation of policy and appointments for Brazil. The opening up of the interior and territorial gains in the Maranhão and Pará demanded closer administrative supervision than had previously been the case. Recent research has shown that the crown played a more important role than had been thought in accomplishing a well-orchestrated and planned policy of westerly expansion in Mato Grosso in the years 1737 to 1752 in collaboration with frontiersmen, missionaries, and free lances. Cartographic expeditions were dispatched to chart boundaries between the captaincies and to establish lines of demarcation between Spanish and Portuguese America. The treaty of Madrid of 1750 and the treaty of San Ildefonso of 1777 gave Brazil a territory not notably different from that of the present day. New captaincies were created for Mato Grosso and Goiás. Communities and encampments were granted township (vila) status in an attempt to give them stability and to endow colonists far from the littoral centers of government with a sense of participation in empire and an appreciation of crown interest. The crown tried to enforce law and order by dividing vast captaincies into smaller judicial units headed by royal appointees with a legal training. Attempts were made to improve the collecting of taxes by creating regional branches of the royal Treasury. Such crown intervention was not limited to the secular bureaucracy: the privileges and prerogatives of the Catholic Church were abrogated by the king, and the jurisdiction of the ecclesiastical authorities was severely curtailed.

Throughout the colonial period the viceroy of Brazil was less important than his counterparts in Mexico and Peru, but it was only in the eighteenth century that his jurisdiction came under serious challenge. Although repeated complaints by viceroys had led the king to order all governors of captaincies to inform the viceroy of developments in their areas, the admonition was largely ignored. Petulance and rancor characterized the relations between the viceroy and the governors throughout the eighteenth century. The effective authority of the viceroy was diminished, in part because of increased regalism but even more because of the enhanced authority granted to governors of the newly created captaincies. From being *primus inter pares,* the viceroy was now placed on almost equal footing with the governors of the captaincies. This shift was accelerated by the change in the economic epicenter from the

northeast to the central-southern area, coupled with the need to have a
seat of authority to oversee diplomatic negotiations and military supplies
for the Luso-Spanish war in the Platine area. In fact, since 1748 the
jurisdiction of the brilliant Gomes Freire de Andrada (governor of Rio
de Janeiro from 1733 to 1763) had embraced the entire central and
southern regions of the colony, giving him greater importance than the
viceroy in Salvador. The transfer of the capital from Salvador to Rio de
Janeiro in 1763 was indicative of this change of emphasis and was to be
decisive in the future fortunes of Brazil.

At the local level of government, there was increased intervention
in municipal affairs by viceroys, governors, and officers of the fisc and
judiciary. The king sought to curb the excesses of self-opinionated and
dynamic town councilors by appointing a trained lawyer (*juiz de fora*)
to preside over the meetings of Câmaras municipais in regions of critical
economic or political importance. Local crown judges (*ouvidores*) exercised increasing vigilance over municipal elections and caused frequent
complaints of infringement of municipal autonomy. On more than one
occasion the governor of Minas Gerais declared elections null and void
because of dishonesty, influence-peddling, and conflicts of interest on the
part of councilors. Although the town councils of Portuguese America
were more representative of local interests and had more "muscle" than
their counterparts in Spanish America, in the eighteenth century there
was a concerted attempt by the crown to whittle away at their jealously
guarded autonomy and a growing tendency to reject the plethora of
petitions for the granting of prerogatives and privileges to municipal
councils in Brazil.

The composition of society and the evolution of culture in colonial
Brazil did not escape the attention of the crown, although here royal
policies had less far-reaching consequences and aroused less open hostility on the part of the populace. The crown-sponsored migrations of
married couples from the Atlantic islands, mentioned above, contributed
to the settlement and colonization of the southern captaincies in the late
seventeenth and eighteenth centuries. In contrast, the racial composition
of the north of Brazil, previously associated with an Amerindian and
mameluke population, was dramatically altered by the importation of
large numbers of slaves from West Africa under the auspices of the
Maranhão-Pará company. Legislation promulgated during the reign of
Dom José I was to have a profound influence on human relationships.
The marquis of Pombal decreed not only that Amerindians who had
become Catholics should be on an equal footing with white settlers in
the eyes of the law and be eligible for administrative posts but also that
special benefits should be granted to white settlers marrying Amerindians.
The pejorative term *caboclo* was outlawed. Pombal's measure abolishing

the distinction between "Old Christians" and "New Christians" and his harsh laws against anti-semitism represented liberation from a value system which had divided Portuguese society since 1497. It is worth noting, however, that if "purity of blood" (a changing concept susceptible to regional variations) was no longer demanded of crypto-Jews and Amerindians, it continued to apply to blacks and mulattos; Pombaline measures abolishing slavery in Portugal (1761–73) were not extended to the slavocratic society and economy of Brazil.

The most serious casualty of the Pombaline brand of regalism was the Society of Jesus. The expulsion of the Society from Portugal and her dominions in 1759 resulted in the secularization of the missionary *aldeias* and destroyed overnight the educational programs of the Jesuit colleges throughout Brazil, which had become centers of intellectual and cultural activity. The intellectual life of the colony was further stultified throughout the colonial period by repeated royal rejections of petitions for the establishment of an university on Brazilian soil. An increasing number of Brazilian families sent their sons to the universities of Montpelier, Coimbra, Edinburgh, and Paris, and it was this generation of graduates who imported into the colony the ideas of the Enlightenment in eighteenth-century Europe and publications prohibited by crown censorship. These found fertile soil in the academies and groups of scholars which flourished in Brazil during the eighteenth century. There can be little doubt that the philosophy of the Enlightenment, disseminated by the printed word and by word of mouth, played a vital role in the *inconfidências* of the second half of the eighteenth century and contributed to that intellectual ambience in which ideas of independence fermented and finally crystallized in the early nineteenth century.

It should not be forgotten that, in part at least, the adoption of regalistic and nationalistic policies by the Portuguese crown was the outcome of international political developments and shifting alliances in Europe. These reduced the number of options available to the sovereigns of Portugal and dictated, to some extent, the course of national policy in the seventeenth and eighteenth centuries. Metropolitan attitudes toward the colonies changed. The nature and objectives of the colonial pact were scrutinized and reappraised. The commercial development of Portugal's South Atlantic empire was affected. No longer could Brazil remain untouched by events in Europe. The result of protracted disputes with the United Provinces for over half a century (1600–1663) on three continents was the reduction of the Portuguese seaborne empire in the Far East, Dutch occupation of the northeast of Brazil (1630–54), and Dutch domination of the slave trade on the Gold Coast from the fortress at El-Mina (São Jorge da Mina). In the thirty years following the restoration of the monarchy in Portugal in 1640 Portugal's limited human and financial reserves were further depleted in the struggles with Spain. During the last three decades of the seventeenth century Portugal's already tottering economy came under renewed attack because of a decline in European market prices of agricultural export commodities from the colonies and a corresponding rise in the prices of essential manufactured imports from northern Europe into Portugal and thence to its colonies.

Dom Pedro's final commitment to the Grand Alliance in 1703 and the Methuen treaty later the same year were disastrous for mother country and colony. The countries of northern Europe, and England in particular, were the major beneficiaries of mineral discoveries in Brazil. Much of the proceeds from the Brazilian gold and diamonds entering the royal coffers had to be disbursed immediately in payment for imports of woolens and other manufactured goods from England and Holland. Hopes that the fabulous discoveries in Minas Gerais, Mato Grosso, and Goiás would provide a much needed stimulus to the Portuguese economy were largely unrealized. Furthermore, a well-organized contraband system ensured that vast quantities of Brazilian gold arriving in the Tagus were snatched away from under the very noses of Portuguese maritime and customs officials by commanders of the Royal Navy and captains and personnel of the Falmouth packet, who were exempt from search. In the first decade of the eighteenth century parts of Portugal were devastated by Franco-Spanish forces; the Colônia do Sacramento (founded 1680) on the river Plata was abandoned to a Spanish force; and the French raided Príncipe, São Tomé, and the Cape Verdes and penetrated into some districts of Rio de Janeiro for short periods on two occasions in 1710 and 1711. During the next half-century Portuguese and Spanish diplomats, emissaries, soldiers, missionaries, and frontiersmen disputed territories in the Amazon basin, on the river Plata, in the far western Maranhão-Pará-Mato Grosso frontier, and in Rio Grande do Sul. A series of treaties between Spain and Portugal (Madrid, 1750; Pardo, 1761; San Ildefonso, 1777) resulted in the confirmation of Portuguese territorial gains in Amazonia and in the west and retention of Rio Grande do Sul by Portugal in return for renouncing claims to Sacramento and the area of the Jesuit mission stations ("Seven Peoples") on the left bank of the river Uruguay. If, by the third quarter of the eighteenth century, Brazil had achieved those boundaries which have been preserved to the present day, the retention and confirmation of such gains by Portugal had only been gained by draining the metropolitan economy and by straining the colonial pact to the utmost.

The Colonial Response

The Brazilian reaction to increased crown control over colonial affairs ranged from grumblings and mutterings by disaffected groups to passive resistance and actual dissent. Frequently, it is difficult to ascertain whether insurrections were really worthy of the designation "revolts" or were no more than urban *jacqueries*. Nevertheless, they were symptomatic of an increased tendency to question the relevance of crown authority to the colony. Orders emanating from Lisbon were scrutinized; their applicability to the Brazilian situation was assessed; outrage was expressed at the crown's preference for Portuguese-born officials for senior posts within and outside the government. In short, there was greater demand for more colonial consultation and even participation in the determining of policies dealing specifically with the oceanic commerce of Brazil as well as with domestic issues.

Discussion of the origins, content, and nature of the colonists' resistance to the increasing imposition of metropolitan authority during the eighteenth century must be prefaced by brief consideration of two important factors. The first is regionalism, which prevailed (and still prevails, in large part) throughout the colonial period. The second is the very nature of the infrastructure of Brazilian society. Neither was a direct precipitant of the independence movement, but both were constant factors in the historical background against which individual incidents were enacted. The two were interrelated and together bore on the economic progress of the colony. As such they were to be affected by crown attitudes and policies.

By the mid-eighteenth century Portuguese America comprised a land mass of some 8.5 million square kilometers, largely unexplored and with great diversity of climate, vegetation, temperature, soil fertility, and geology. Settlement was concentrated in those parts of the narrow coastal strip with the richest soil and regular rainfall. Only in the late seventeenth and eighteenth centuries were significant inroads made into the *agreste,* the *sertão,* and the highlands of the central-southern area. Even along the coast, settlement was not uniform but was characterized by isolated urban clusters, e.g., the Recôncavo of Bahia and the Várzea of Pernambuco. There were no roads along the coast, and communications between Belém, Recife, Salvador, Rio de Janeiro, and Santos were by boat. There was no policy for the building of roads to the interior; such trails as did exist were often flooded in the rainy season. The importance of the River São Francisco in the development of the interior was less as a fluvial passage than as a valley where crops could be cultivated and cattle grazed. Goiás and Mato Grosso depended on rivers and annual expeditions (*monsões*) for supplies and contact with the outside world. Ironically, the difficulty of land communications in the more settled parts of Brazil contrasted with the ease of transportation between settlements in the underpopulated Amazonia because of the fluvial network provided by the Amazon and its tributaries. These geographic factors alone produced a chronic demographic imbalance not only between the littoral and the hinterland but even among different areas of the coastal region itself. Furthermore, crown policy failed to encourage the opening of roads and actively discouraged commerce between the different regions. It is small wonder that for many a Brazilian student attendance at Coimbra University not only introduced him to Europe but enabled him for the first time, through contact with students from other parts of Brazil, to appreciate the vastness and diversity of his own country. It was this understanding which contributed so decisively to the ideology behind the movement toward independence in Brazil.

Regionalism was only one of the profound structural weaknesses pervading the society of colonial Brazil. Homogeneity and commonality of purpose were totally absent in a highly stratified and privilege-oriented society. Status was all-important. But there were inconsistencies in the ascribed positions of certain groups, and factors determining the standing of an individual within society could change. Slavocratic societies are frequently depicted either in terms of a master-slave dichotomy or in terms of a pyramid, with a white landowning aristocracy at the top and black dispossessed slaves at the bottom. Neither model is applicable to colonial Brazil, where status was determined by a variety of factors, each of importance in its own right and in its interaction with others. For a white person these were: color of skin, place of birth, religion, financial position, parentage, professional training, and social position of spouse. These factors also applied to coloreds, with the addition of civil status, *viz.*, slave or free. The importance of any one factor varied depending on regional and chronological differences, and their relationship to each other also varied accordingly. The particular strength of one, e.g., financial position, in an individual could offset a weakness, e.g., "defect of blood," but no single positive factor could eradicate a combination of negative attributes. In the eighteenth century greater social mobility resulted in the reassessment of many traditional criteria for determining social standing, and this provoked resentment and even animosity among different social groups.

If the sugar planters and cattle ranchers were considered (and considered themselves) as comprising a landed aristocracy, by the early eighteenth century the emergence of an urban mercantile class was making itself felt precisely in those areas which had been dominated by the rural aristocracy. The transition was not effected without strife, as demonstrated by the so-called War of the Peddlers (*Guerra dos Mascates*) in Pernambuco in 1711, which found echoes elsewhere. This episode also casts light on another stress point in Brazilian colonial society: the animosity felt by Brazilian-born Portuguese subjects (white or black) for those other "loyal subjects of the king of Portugal" born in Portugal or coming from West Africa. This aversion was critical in the course taken in the evolution of Brazilian society and, in a more refined form, was to contribute decisively to the current of opinion which spurred Brazil toward independence. Also, it should not be forgotten that for much of the colonial period Brazilian society was divided between "Old Christians" and "New Christians." If the Pombaline decrees effectively outlawed this distinction, they failed to eradicate from the popular mind the requirement of "purity of blood" demanded of their appointees for two and a half centuries by church and state.

It cannot be overemphasized that internal dissent and division was not limited to the white community. Among coloreds antagonism and tensions existed between freemen and slaves, between mulattos and blacks, and between Brazilian-born free blacks and mulattos and African-born slaves who had earned their freedom; cultural and tribal distinctions and language barriers also carried over into the New World and effectively destroyed any cohesion among coloreds in Brazil.

Regionalism and the stresses and strains in Brazilian society were exacerbated in the course of the eighteenth century as the result of unforeseen (and unforeseeable) developments in the economy and the indifference shown by the Portuguese crown toward their social repercussions. The discoveries in Minas Gerais threw into sharp focus tensions and differences which might otherwise have smouldered below the surface for decades had it not been for the violent dislocation of the economic epicenter of Brazil from the northeast and the no less dramatic relocation of people. The economy of the northeast had been based on agriculture. The financial return was good but not spectacular. The fortunes of men, be they plantation owners, overseers, or slaves, were tied to the land. A large initial capital investment guaranteed a stable, patriarchal society based on black labor. Salvador and Recife were governed from country estates, whose owners rode into the city to attend council meetings and functions of the more prestigious brotherhoods. This security was destroyed by the discovery of gold. Sugar plantations were deserted; slaves were beyond the means of debt-crippled planters; the pool of free and slave labor moved inland; currency was in short supply. Salvador ceased to be the capital of Brazil. The society of Minas Gerais, radically different from that of the coast, was characterized by mobility, by insecurity both physical and financial, by opportunism, and by the almost complete absence of patriarchalism. In some respects its great wealth enabled it to be cosmopolitan as Salvador or Recife had never been, but its inhabitants could never shake off the psychological barrier of being beyond the mountains.

The avowedly mercantilist policy of the Portuguese crown was to view with apparent equanimity the decline of agriculture in the northeast; it did not hesitate to throw its support behind the mining industries because of the quicker returns to be derived from gold and diamonds. Repeated petitions of an admittedly hysterical nature from the city councils of Recife and Salvador that the king stop the exodus of slaves from the littoral or even close down the mines altogether were largely ignored by Lisbon. Moreover, the influx of "outsiders" in search of fortune was resented by those who had come to Brazil as colonists and felt with some justification that the fruits of the sudden windfall should be theirs. The Portuguese crown showed little interest in attempting to effect a reconciliation between the *reinóis* and the Brazilians so long as the antagonism between the two did not erupt into open hostility which could affect production adversely. Nor did it formulate a policy to correct the chronic economic and demographic imbalance between the agricultural littoral and the mining highlands.

Regional tensions were to become increasingly apparent in the years immediately preceding independence. It was no coincidence that it was in the northeast that Dom Pedro found it difficult to establish a constituency. This opposition was not directed against the prince personally, nor did it represent disapproval of the perpetuation of a monarchical form of government rather than the establishment of outright republicanism. Rather, it expressed the *nordestinos'* resentment of the attitudes of the court in Rio de Janeiro toward the region.

The crown contributed to the tensions within Brazilian society because of two aspects of royal policy: the king's attitude toward native-born Brazilians, and the concession of privileges. The king's correspondence with viceroys and governors alike is liberally peppered with pejorative epithets about native-born Brazilians, who are portrayed as lazy, immoral, and spendthrift. These characterizations are frequently coupled with an insistence on the "purity of blood" of crown appointees. To be Brazilian-born was to be suspect. Thus the crown persistently preferred Portuguese-born subjects over native applicants for posts in Brazil, causing intense rivalry between the *reinóis* and the Brazilians. The crown policy of bestowing benefices and granting privileges to individuals and corporate groups further divided Brazilian colonial society. Briefly these special favors may be categorized as follows: those granted to individuals in return for particular services, e.g., mining discoveries; those granted to the members of a guild, society, or brotherhood, e.g., goldsmiths or the Santa Casa da Misericórdia; those granted to people in certain professions or occupations, e.g., soldiers of the garrison, students, or employees of the royal mints; corporate privileges, e.g., those given to a town or city. At the individual level such concessions effectively restricted interpersonal relations, imposing further artificial divisions on an already highly stratified society. Corporate privileges inspired rivalries and competition in a nation whose development demanded collective efforts and cooperation. Whether or not the intention was to unify the population of Brazil or whether this was another instance of regalism by the assertion of royal control through privileges is debatable, but the result was the division and not the coalescence of Brazilian society.

A casual reader of Brazilian history might gain the impression that the eighteenth century was characterized by wars and revolts. Nationalist fervor on the part of Brazilian writers and loose translations by English-speaking scholars have furthered this erroneous impression: we hear of the "war" of the *emboabas*, the "war" of the *mascates*, the "revolt" of Vila Rica (1720), the Minas "conspiracy" (1789), the "social revolution" in Salvador (1798), to name but a few. Three points must be made to place such events in perspective. First, in no case did such a cause gain overall support from all sectors of society; second, in all cases the impact of the struggle remained localized, and there were no repercussions beyond the immediate region; third, despite loose talk of separatism in Pernambuco in 1710 and 1711, in no case did there exist any planned strategy to cast off royal control and establish a republic. Antipathy towards metropolitan authority, and more particularly towards crown appointees, was strong, but in no instance was it directed against the sovereign personally or against the institution of monarchy. In fact, invariably the cause of such "revolts" or disturbances is to be found in a change or a challenge to the accepted social and economic status quo.

The "war" of the *emboabas* in Minas Gerais in 1708–9 exemplifies the fusion of social and economic interests which culminated in hostility. This "war" was no more than the explosion of tension which had been building up between the "sons of the soil" (in this case the *Paulistas*) and "outsiders" or *forasteiros* (which term included anybody not a *Paulista*, albeit Brazilian-born) who had "jumped" mining claims and had gained the reward for gold discoveries which the *Paulistas* deemed their own. Crown support for the "outsiders" exacerbated this tension. *Paulista* antagonism was thus not leveled at the king but against the outsiders who had invaded the *Paulista* stamping grounds and with whom the Tupí-speaking, nomadic, mixed-blood *Paulistas* had nothing in common. The "war" of the peddlers in Pernambuco bears many of the same characteristics of hostility between "sons of the soil" and "outsiders," but here there was a more complex melding of economic and social pressures. The position of the merchant in the Portuguese empire had always been ambiguous, and few succeeded in shaking off the "New Christian" stigma attached to the occupation. In few places was there such social cohesion and identity of interests as among the landed, Catholic, patriarchal, plantation aristocracy of Pernambuco, centered on Olinda. It was inevitable that the emergence in Recife of a powerful mercantile class, whom the planters despised socially but on whom they depended for financial support, should culminate in the virulent antipathy and violence of 1710 and 1711. If such "wars" did possess any nationalist content, it was of limited importance. Their interest is rather as indices of the unrest and tensions which pervaded eighteenth-century Brazil and which created an ambience sympathetic to the ideas of the Enlightenment for those who saw the American and French revolutions as signposts to self-determination and independence.

Despite the undeniably dramatic content of such "wars," the tenor of colonial reaction to metropolitan pressures can best be gauged from a series of disconnected social, political, and economic episodes which occurred in different areas of Portuguese America during the eighteenth century. Only on rare occasions did these constitute outright rejection of royal directives. For the most part, the colonists adopted the strategy of interpreting rather than blindly executing orders from Lisbon; if this tack failed, they tried to dissipate the impact of an unpopular order by resisting its implementation to a greater or lesser degree. When all else failed, they attempted to force the crown to adopt a compromise solution or to rescind the order entirely.

The colonists' strongest reaction was against economic measures intended to strengthen crown control of the extractive industries and commerce. In the mining districts, differing methods for collection of the royal "fifth" engendered resentment, evasion, and outright resistance. Frequently the governor of Minas Gerais found himself the object of both the colonists' resentment and crown disapproval. Albuquerque's imposition in 1710 of a collection method based on the number of *bateias* (pans used for washing gold) in use caused hardship to miners who had not been lucky but who were assessed at the same level as their more fortunate colleagues. His successor opted for payment of an annual fixed sum guaranteed by the town councils, but this proposal failed to gain crown approval. Dom João V insisted on a return to the *bateia* method, but popular opposition and public disturbances forced the king to back down. Dom João V tried a new approach, in the hope of increasing income from the "fifths." In 1719 he ordered the building of smelting houses in Minas Gerais. This proposal was greeted by public demonstrations throughout the mining area and culminated in the famous insurrection in Vila Rica, which smouldered from June 28 to July 14, 1720, until it was suppressed by Dom Pedro de Almeida at the head of an armed column. The leader was garrotted, the ringleaders deported, their houses burned and possessions confiscated, but the crown temporarily shelved its plans for the establishment of the smelting houses. Only with a change of governor (Dom Lourenço de Almeida, 1721–32) did Dom João V succeed in establishing foundry houses in Minas Gerais. From

1735 to 1750 the crown reverted to collection of the "fifths" by a capitation tax, later resorting to the smelting houses again. This final method, which was in force throughout the remaining colonial years, was reinforced by the levying of a per capita tax known as the *derrama* to guarantee the annual quota demanded by the crown. Both methods, and especially the *derrama*, were unpopular, and pockets of discontent erupted in the villages and townships of the mining areas, but never with the intensity and far-reaching effect of the disturbance in Vila Rica in 1720.

In the Diamond District also the implementation of repressive crown measures was delayed as the result of local protest. The enforcement of the draconic royal edict of March 16, 1731, delineating the mining area, controlling mining practices, and severely prejudicing the social and economic well-being of the local populace provoked so many complaints from individuals and from the town council of Vila do Príncipe that the governor moderated the system. Crown displeasure and a change of governor saw the royal will imposed despite ineffectual local protests alleging hardship. The luckless inhabitants gained no relief from the introduction of a contract system which remained in effect from 1740 to 1771. In fact, the contractors and their appointees proved as despotic and inhumane as were the crown authorities before the system began and after its abolition, when the industry became a crown monopoly. The Diamond District proved a classic instance of the subordination of local colonial interests to those of the metropolis. Unrest there was, but ruthless crown suppression of dissent destroyed any possibility of organized resistance.

Colonial reaction was by no means limited to the mining areas. Crown attempts to gain control of oceanic commerce caused resentment, as did crown support for merchants in Lisbon who were trying to get more of the triangular trade than was their due or to capture a share of the direct trade between Brazil and the west coast of Africa. In the early eighteenth century Dom João V wished to abolish the trade between Salvador and the gulf of Benin altogether, on the grounds that it was financed in part with contraband gold and that it provided opportunities for the illicit purchase of Dutch and English manufactured goods. The merchants of Salvador found an ally in the viceroy, the count of Sabugosa, who told the crown in no uncertain terms that the implementation of such a policy would plunge Salvador and the northeast into severe economic depression. Dom João V heeded his viceroy and shelved his proposals.

The strongest reaction by the colonists was against the Pombaline policy of nationalizing the Luso-Brazilian trade. All too often it was the Brazilian merchant who felt that his interests were being sacrificed to those of the crown and the metropolitan merchant as was the case with Pombal's policy of establishing monopolistic chartered companies for Brazil. That the English merchants of Lisbon should be dismayed at this development was understandable but foreseeable. However, insufficient thought had been given to the impact of this policy on small traders in Portugal and Brazil, who saw their livelihood threatened by such companies and were vociferous in denouncing them. They formed common cause with the Jesuits in the Mesa do Bem Comum, whose deputies harangued the crown and Pombal from streetcorner and pulpit. The authorities took a strong stand, viewing such resistance as subversion of royal authority. The Mesa was suppressed in 1755. Furthermore, some policies intended for the good of Brazil engendered resistance rather than cooperation. This was the reaction by the colonials of Salvador, Recife, Rio de Janeiro, and São Luís to the Pombal-inspired Boards of Inspection intended to protect, stimulate, and fiscalize the production of major export crops, especially sugar and tobacco. In reality, Brazilian producers saw the boards as threatening their commercial interests while furthering state intervention in their enterprises.

Many crown measures viewed by the king and his counsellors as being purely economic in content and applicability had unforeseen repercussions in different sectors of Brazilian society. Colonial resistance was often aroused more by the social implications of a measure than by its openly economic and fiscal purpose. Royal attempts in 1695, 1697, and 1699 to enforce legislation restricting the size of *sesmarias,* or land grants, and providing for the expropriation of uncultivated lands would have struck a severe blow against the political and commercial power of the *poderosos do sertão* ("lords of the backlands"). In fact, the legislation was largely ineffectual, but families such as the Guedes de Brito of the house of Ponte or the Dias d'Avila of the house of Tôrre, in whose hands lay the reins of power in the northeast, were harassed with lawsuits and boundary disputes by zealous crown officials and were forced to bargain with the crown and compromise over the extent of their estates. No family went so far as did the charismatic Manuel Nunes Viana, the pet aversion of viceroys in Salvador and governors in Minas Gerais in the early decades of the eighteenth century. He was accused of lese majesty, preventing meat supplies from entering Minas Gerais, fomenting revolt, nonpayment of the "fifths," and worse. His very survival for so long and the fact that Dom João chose to adopt a compromise rather than outright punishment shows the possibility of resistance and the awareness of the crown that further unrest would shake the very foundations of the social structure. The strength and cohesion of such families is well illustrated by their legacy of *coronelismo,* or "bossism," so prevalent in the interior and northeast today.

The crown attempted to forestall colonial opposition to economic measures by inducing influential Brazilians to participate in the implementation of legislation. All such attempts were doomed because of the failure on the part of the authorities to understand the "system." Hallowed by tradition, it was based on a series of tacit understandings governing social intercourse and colonial trade. The institution of the Boards of Inspection affords a classic instance of lack of appreciation in the metropolis for this delicate mesh of power, patronage, and profit. The boards awoke indignation in widely differing groups: city councils resented the usurpation of their traditional privileges to fix prices; planters resented being institutionalized and compelled to abide by the rules of the boards, which they believed favored the interests of the merchants; and finally there was the touchy issue of local participation in the state bureaucracy. Dom João V and his successors adopted the policy of reserving some positions on boards such as the Boards of Inspection for agriculture and of giving the largely honorary post of treasurer of the mints and smelting houses to local nominees. In fact, appointees to such posts invariably already formed part of a privileged minority who dominated the town councils and the Santa Casa da Misericórdia and other brotherhoods and held colonelcies in the local militia regiments. In short, such local participation was no more than a sop to Cerberus and an illusion of democratic decision-making in government; in the final analysis it only intensified existing conflicts in Brazilian society.

It has been suggested that, wittingly or unwittingly, the crown created antagonism by its policy of granting such privileges to individuals and groups. At the individual level, such resentment rarely surfaced to the extent of being recorded in official correspondence. No such silence surrounds corporate privileges. Throughout the eighteenth century black and mulatto brotherhoods and soldiers struggled for the privileges and prerogatives granted to their white counterparts. Many achieved their aim, but only after protracted correspondence and heated struggles, which on occasion culminated in violence. Such petitions were in part byproducts of the growth of towns and cities in the eighteenth century and of a heightened urban consciousness, which set off a wave of demands for the concession by the crown of more privileges to municipalities. Such requests ranged from elevation of a township to the status of a city to exemptions from billeting and from appropriation of possessions at times of crisis to immunity from torture for aldermen and municipal councilors. It was doubly unfortunate that this urban growth should coincide with increasing regalism on the part of the crown, revealed in a concerted attempt to place restraints on the power enjoyed by certain groups in colonial society and even to strip the councils of traditional privileges and prerogatives. The reaction was a plethora of colonial petitions, which were rejected or ignored by the crown. Even when popular requests were wholly justified and had the support of town councils, such as the oft-repeated petition by the populace of Minas Gerais for the establishment of a second High Court in Rio de Janeiro, they were refused out of hand and without explanation. Some crown magistrates, incorporated into colonial society by virtue of kinship and commercial ties, served as intermediaries between crown directives and local interests. But by and large, the resentment engendered by such refusals was translated into an unwillingness to cooperate with crown appointees and jealous vigilance over privileges already gained even if such vigilance required personal sacrifice and was detrimental to the community.

Reaction against crown authority also took on more subtle forms: evasion, clandestine dealings, and subterfuge were inescapable facts of colonial life. Attempts by the crown to subject ships in the Brazil trade to a fleet system with a regular schedule failed because captains preferred to sail at their own convenience. Tighter enforcement of the *sesmaria* laws proved unworkable because of distance and the power exerted by the *poderosos,* who bought off magistrates and clerks with money or threats. The crown rang the changes on many different methods of collecting the "fifths" on gold, described above, in the forlorn hope of reducing the rampant contraband trade in gold and gold dust. Evasion of payment of taxes, tithes, and donations was endemic. Clandestine shops and taverns multiplied. Masters failed to register their slaves. There were reports of illegal mints making counterfeit coins and bars. At least two illegal printing presses came into existence for a short time despite official bans, and an illicit book trade developed in Minas Gerais. Such methods undermined the effectiveness of crown authority, especially during the eighteenth century. Brazilians were brought to the position of embracing an ideology of evasion whose legacy has survived to the present day in the *jeito.*

In an age of regalism, increased metropolitan domination of the colonial pact, and greater nationalization of the economy, a curious paradox was born in Portuguese America. On the one hand, there developed a very real consciousness of and pride in being Brazilian-born and an American. On the other hand Brazilians became more aware of the changes taking place in eighteenth-century Europe and more cosmopolitan in their social mores and ideological development. Whether or not such heightened consciousness and awareness may justifiably be seen as symptomatic of nationalism is debatable and, in my view, doubtful. The defense of northeast Brazil in the War of Divine Liberty of 1645–54 against the Dutch, which crossed boundaries of race and class, the struggles of "sons of the soil" in Pernambuco and Minas Gerais against the "outsiders," the *mineiros'* rallying to Albuquerque's support regardless of personal cost when he issued a call to expel the French from Rio de Janeiro in 1711—all have been seen as examples of emerging nationalism. A less sensational example, but of equal importance as an indication of the depth of the pride in being Brazilian, is afforded by the group of Brazilian students at Coimbra University in the 1690s. From the correspondence of one student to his father in Salvador emerges the picture of a true esprit de corps among the Brazilian students, who saw the success of one of their number as a feather in the cap for Brazil. The student wrote defiantly that "if in matters of intellect the sons of Brazil do not exceed those of Portugal, at least they are their equals." These students and their successors in European universities played a vital role in thwarting the efforts of the Portuguese crown to curb the introduction into Brazil and dissemination of the ideas and writings of the Enlightenment taking place in France and England. English ideas and "abominable French principles" found fertile soil in Brazil. Their direct impact was frequently limited to the upper classes and intellectuals, and they stimulated a flurry of revolutionary activities among the upper classes of Brazilian society in the late eighteenth and early nineteenth centuries, either openly or under the protective shield of the Masonic lodges which flourished as centers of debate and discussion.

One may fairly ask to what degree the true nature of liberalism and the implications of constitutionalist principles were understood in Brazil. The prism through which the Brazilian viewed such currents of opinion differed markedly from that of his European counterpart. The infrastructure, the needs, and the aspirations of Brazilian society had little in common with English and French society of the period. Appreciation of the very nature and aims of the Enlightenment was difficult for a Brazilian. The transfer of its implications to the Brazilian milieu was all but impossible. Despite these caveats, however, there can be no doubt that such ideological innovations and nationalist spirit were factors in the abortive Inconfidência Mineira of 1789 and the Inconfidência Bahiana of 1798. For those not versed in the literature of the Enlightenment the dramatic precedents of the American war of independence and the French Revolution carried an unambiguous message. Both *inconfidências* saw the active involvement of intellectuals, soldiers, royal appointees, servants of the crown, and coloreds. For each group the significance and implications of the *inconfidências* were different, satisfying the hopes and aspirations of an individual or one sector of the community. A great deal of ink has been expended on these two insurrections, and the participants in the outbreak in Minas Gerais have been glorified as martyrs in the national pantheon of heroes (ironically enough, the colored leaders of the Bahian conspiracy were not so honored). But it is well to bear in mind that in both cases the immediate precipitants were of an economic and social nature. The increasing cost of food stuffs and a decline in mining production caused hardship in Minas Gerais. The imposition of the *derrama* by the count of Barbacena was the proverbial final straw. In Bahia there was dissatisfaction with inequality in pay and privileges between colored and white soldiers of the garrison and with the closing of certain ranks to coloreds. In both cases there was an intellectual undercurrent, slogans of liberty and equality were flaunted, and rumors of the establishment of a republic and self-rule were common. But in reality the cause was espoused by certain classes only, its repercussions were local, the outbreaks were badly organized, and the revolts were easily suppressed. In fact, the only revolt in colonial Brazil worthy of the name occurred in Pernambuco in 1817. With openly republican intentions from the outset, the dissidents in Recife found supporters among clerics, laymen, administrators, planters, and soldiers in the surrounding region. The revolt gained rapid momentum, faltered, and was finally suppressed after two months. The severity of the reprisals failed to quench the republican spirit and merely succeeded in fueling the animosity between Brazilians and the Portuguese soldiers of the garrison. It was not surprising that this region was to be at best lukewarm in its support of Dom Pedro and was the stage for further disturbances later in the century.

The Move toward Independence

The transfer of the royal court from the mother country to her richest colony was full of dramatic and emotional content and affected the development of Luso-Brazilian relations. In fact, the idea had first been proposed in 1580 and reappeared in different forms in the reigns of Dom Afonso VI (1656–67; deposed) and Dom João V. The arrival in Brazil of the future Dom João VI and the establishment of a royal court in Rio de Janeiro in 1808 signified to the Brazilian people that there would be a change in emphasis and balance of power in the colonial relationship. The psychological and economic benefits accruing to the colony from the presence of the court cannot be overemphasized. From the time of his first landfall Dom João went out of his way to grant privileges and favors to individuals and groups and to encourage trading interests. But the mere arrival of a monarch with his court could not dispel the problems confronting the colony. Colonial society was still in a state of evolution rather than consolidation. Regional tensions and antagonisms between different groups were as strong as ever. There was chronic maldistribution of wealth, and rates of economic growth varied enormously from region to region. The only constant was the presence of slavery as a basic ingredient of colonial life, and attitudes toward the role of the slave remained immutable and impervious to outside influences.

By a decree of January 28, 1808, Dom João opened the ports of Brazil to foreign trade. This was an event of momentous importance, transcending the arrival of the royal court and even the declaration of independence. At one stroke of the pen Dom João reversed the Pombaline policies for the nationalization of the Luso-Brazilian trade; swept away three centuries of crown suspicion, distrust, and paranoia toward foreign merchants and traders in Brazilian waters; and permitted Brazilians to trade legally beyond the narrow commercial network of the Portuguese empire. It was ironic that the transfer of the court and the resulting euphoria which swept Brazil would not have been possible without British naval dominance of the South Atlantic. The opening of the ports freed Brazilian commerce from the fetters of Portugal only for it to fall victim to the economic imperialism of the United Kingdom.

As had been the case so often before, the destiny of Brazil was determined by events beyond its shores as much as by internal developments. In fact it is doubtful whether, had it not been for such external pressures, there would have been any factor in Brazil of sufficient force and overall appeal to bring about a unilateral declaration of independence. Obviously, the French invasion of Portugal in 1807 directly motivated the flight of the court to Brazil, and the new range of possibilities and options which this presence on Brazilian soil afforded brought to a head many of the tensions within the country. Some historians point to the constitutionalist liberal revolution in Oporto in 1820 as a precipitant of Brazilian independence. But this uprising was an expression of internal dissent in Portugal and did not radically affect the chain of events already set in motion in Brazil. Although more distant in space, events in North America and northern Europe were what provided the ambience for and made possible the declaration of independence in Brazil. The declaration of independence by the English colonies in North America had a profound psychological effect throughout the continent and served as an example for Latin neighbors. The maturing of industrial capitalism in England and the advocacy of mercantilist policies and economic liberalism had far-reaching effects on trading patterns and customs in the nineteenth century. Furthermore, the discord prevailing in Europe in the early nineteenth century lessened the likelihood of European military intervention in the Americas, a situation well appreciated in the United States, which was encouraged to recognize new revolutionary governments in certain areas of Latin America.

The return of Dom João VI to Portugal in 1821, leaving Dom Pedro in Rio de Janeiro, did nothing to calm the tensions existing between colony and mother country. The decision to transfer the court to Brazil had been ill-received in Lisbon, although it was an inevitable expedient. Once the immediate threat of French occupation of Portugal had diminished, the continued presence of the king in Brazil merely fueled the resentment already felt towards the colony by members of the Côrtes in Lisbon. Recognition that the roles of colony and metropolis had been neatly reversed was bitter but unavoidable. The decree of December 16, 1815, whereby Brazil was raised to the status of a kingdom on a level with Portugal, did nothing to smooth the already ruffled feathers of the deputies in the Côrtes. Thus the reception accorded to the Brazilian deputies to the constituent Côrtes was not calculated to be friendly, nor was their brief likely to inspire any rapprochement with their Portuguese counterparts: political and economic equality between the two countries, the establishment of parallel organs of government in Portugal and Brazil, and alternation of the seat of government between Lisbon and Rio de Janeiro. The rejection of these proposals out of hand by the Portuguese deputies demonstrated their political myopia. Their ridicule, contempt, scorn, and open antagonism were widely reported in the colony and contributed to a common feeling of insult and outrage which brought together otherwise disassociated factions.

In Brazil it is doubtful whether at any time there had been any intention of definitive separation from Portugal or any large support for a republican cause. Although in the eighteenth and early nineteenth centuries factions in Minas Gerais and in the northeast espoused republicanism, their influence and following were limited. For the most part Brazilians were content to accept the continuation of a monarchical form of government. The struggles between republicans and royalists which took place in Spanish America were absent in Brazil. In fact the social tensions, regionalisms, economic disparities, and presence of a hard-core colonial administration prevented the independence movement in Brazil from being truly nationalist in spirit or revolutionary in execution. But there was a general determination to be Brazilians and to be recognized as such, coupled with the demand for recognition of the very quintessence of Brazilian civilization, as something sui generis, imbued with *Brésilianité*. Finally, the Brazilians wanted recognition of the special nature of Brazilian society and the particular interests of the Brazilian economy, but few saw it as a prelude to independence, or failure to gain it as a prerequisite for a separatist movement. In fact, Brazilian deputies constantly emphasized Brazilian loyalty to the crown of Portugal, union of the kingdoms of Portugal and Brazil, and a willingness to negotiate and to reach an accommodation.

Any hopes of such an accommodation were dimmed by the attitude of the Portuguese Côrtes towards Brazil in 1821 and 1822. Brazilian fears that Portugal intended to reduce Brazil to its former colonial status were obviously well founded. Any doubts as to the intention of the Côrtes to re-establish unilateral control, by force if necessary, were dispelled. Fear of "enslavement" to Portuguese interests brought together sectors of society previously divided or undecided. Many of the most influential figures in Brazilian society publicly supported union with Portugal; others of no less prominence and distinction favored the total independence of Brazil; still others remained undecided and, in some cases, resigned to the outcome. In the end, the more extreme groups were willing to compromise, and polarization was replaced by accommodation. There can be little doubt that, had it not been for the intransigent and highhanded attitude adopted by the Côrtes, compromise and negotiation would have been possible even on the eve of independence.

Three factors contributed to Brazilian acceptance, albeit reluctant, of the fact that no viable alternative to independence from Portugal existed: first, the inability of Dom João to provide decisive leadership, coupled with the accession issue; second, British pressure; third, the administrative and militaristic policy of the Côrtes. Rather than firmly supporting either free trade or mercantilism, Dom João attempted to free the Brazilian economy while continuing to protect Portuguese interests. The result was a series of conflicting and contradictory measures which failed to win the approval of either Portuguese or Brazilian merchants. British pressure on the king to loosen economic restrictions was strong. In the wake of the establishment of a representative government in Portugal, England was particularly insistent on the return of Dom João to Portugal. Finally, the changing administrative and economic policies of the Côrtes after 1821 made reconciliation impossible. Measures intended to harass foreign merchants were passed; an attempt was made to make the provincial governors in Brazil subordinate to the Côrtes in Lisbon and not to Rio de Janeiro; other administrative reforms were aimed at enhancing the authority of the metropolis. The final blow was the ill-advised decision to dispatch Portuguese troops to Rio de Janeiro and Pernambuco. The question of the nature of independence had been reduced to one of direct confrontation, with the Côrtes on the one hand and Brazil, striving to preserve its few existing concessions and liberties, on the other. For political, economic, social, and emotional reasons, independence had become a necessity for Portuguese America.

Dom Pedro's somewhat melodramatic cry of "Independence or death" did not resolve the issue. It was not based on any foundation of solid support from any sector of society, nor did it spark any wave of popular enthusiasm and solidarity. In fact, in Bahia and the north it roused the Portuguese garrisons to open resistance, which was only suppressed by foreign troops. In Bahia the garrison was finally subdued by the

French general Labatut; in Pará and the Maranhão loyalist forces put up a spirited resistance until confronted by a detachment under Thomas Cochrane. Nor was the path of independence any smoother in the political sphere. The prime architect of Brazilian independence, José Bonifácio de Andrada, was forced to resign on July 12, 1823. The much heralded Constituent Assembly was dissolved after a life of only six months, the victim of inexperience, self-interest, and factionalism. It is conceivable that even at this juncture the consolidation of Brazilian independence might have hung in the balance but for the obduracy of the Côrtes, mounting pressures within Brazil itself, and the successful diplomatic overtures of the representatives of Dom Pedro.

Dom Pedro may be faulted on many matters, but his choice of emissaries to advance Brazil's cause in the more influential courts of Europe and in Washington was wise and prescient. In London Caldeira Brant rapidly gained the confidence of Foreign Minister Canning. In Vienna Silva Caminha found Francis I and Metternich well disposed toward Brazil. Brazilian fears of unfavorable repercussions from Britain's long-standing treaties with Portugal or of opposition by the Holy Alliance proved unfounded. In Washington the reaction was no less positive. In the negotiations between Portugal and Brazil, England rapidly assumed a major role as mediator while ensuring that Portugal was left in no doubt as to British support for Brazilian aspirations. By adopting such a policy Canning hoped for British access to the valuable markets of South America and for the conclusion of a treaty abolishing the slave trade to Brazil. Changes in the balance of political power in Portugal furthered Brazil's move toward autonomy. By June of 1823 the Côrtes had succumbed to mounting pressures and ceased to exist. But any hopes that, with the removal of the prime irritant, a compromise might be negotiated between Portugal and Brazil were dashed. A peace overture on the part of the Portuguese was brusquely rejected by Dom Pedro. The issue of the successor to Dom João, the settling of financial commitments between the two countries, and the question of reciprocal citizenship remained obstacles to agreement.

The final stages of the negotiations were characterized by diplomatic initiatives on the part of England, whereas Austria took a more conciliatory but no less important stand. To Metternich must go the credit for navigating a tricky course between Austrian commitment to the Holy Alliance and the ties of kinship existing between Francis I and Dom Pedro. In London, Foreign Minister Canning played the role of intermediary between Portugal and Brazil. All such efforts proved fruitless, and negotiations reached a stalemate. It was largely the result of an extraordinary diplomatic initiative on the part of the British, whereby the Portuguese were induced to accept Sir Charles Stuart as an official negotiator on behalf of Portugal, that Brazil finally gained recognition of her independent status by Portugal. The treaty of 1825 represented a major success for Brazilian diplomacy.

De facto independence and international recognition did not herald a "golden age" for Brazil. Independence offered prospects which were at best uncertain and at worst illusory. Nor could it achieve the well-nigh impossible miracle of unifying the many Brazils which comprised the heterogeneous human and physical resources of Portuguese-speaking America. Not even the most fanatical Brazilian patriot could fail to realize that the achievement of independence was no panacea for the country's ills. Class solidarity on a national level was clearly impossible. Divisions within society were too deep to be healed by a mere treaty. Any unity born of common opposition to the arbitrary demands of the Portuguese Côrtes was short-lived. For many, pre-independence resolution gave way to post-independence resignation. For those few who had remained loyal to Portugal, integration into their adopted country was clearly impossible, as was their acceptance by people whose aspirations they had attempted to thwart. For others, disenchantment with the colonial pact was replaced by a no less bitter disillusion with the form of centralized government advocated by Rio de Janeiro, a disillusion which culminated in revolts, disturbances, and further schisms within Brazilian society in the course of the nineteenth century. In a society still in a state of evolution, the presence of the royal court provided yet another source of tension and antagonism. In this evolving human polygon, the institution of slavery alone remained constant. It may be questioned whether social mobility was possible in a society in which one component remained the focus for polarized political, ideological, and emotional attitudes. The very size of Brazil precluded the possibility of any sector, let alone the population as a whole, taking any position as a matter of conscience and enforcing adherence to a single policy or ideology. A heterogeneous population and geographical vastness contributed inevitably to separatism in the political arena, imbalance in economic productivity, and the impossibility of finding a common solution to human problems.

Once the fanfares, eulogies, bombast, and emotionalism which accompanied independence died away, it was clear that in many sectors of private and public life there had been no substantial change in the political and economic structure of the colonial period. To be sure, in some areas of government there was greater administrative authority at the regional level, but for the most part the court in Rio de Janeiro was as impervious to requests and petitions, especially from the northeast, as the Overseas Council in Lisbon had been. No common political ideology emerged in the years immediately following independence. Regional factionalism persisted. In the economic sphere, throughout the northeast and in the Maranhão and Pará the colonial structure of production dependent on slavery persisted. At the international level, an independent Brazil discovered that the mantle of Portuguese domination had been cast off only for the economic tutelage of Great Britian.

The history of Brazil is traditionally broken into the periods of colony, empire, and republic. However such periodization suggests cleavages which never existed. Many colonial traditions persisted after independence, and the solution chosen by Brazilians after independence was monarchical. Although Brazil was not unique in choosing this course, she was the only nation in the Americas to preserve a monarchical tradition for so long after independence. Those historians who have been wont to see colonies undergoing an apprenticeship or age of puberty prior to achieving the status of master or adulthood as represented by independence must reckon with the Brazilian example.

There were sharp differences between the Portuguese development and the development in the American colonies of Great Britain and Spain. In the English colonies in North America the transition from colonial to independent status was remarkably swift, the result of a rush of events which culminated in the Declaration of Independence. Feelings of certainty, self-confidence, decisiveness, resolution, and public support survived the war and were only strengthened by opposition. The Declaration was a logical climax to a concurrence of events. The movement toward independence in Spanish America was different. Many factors—economic disparity, opposition to metropolitan influence, opposition to monopolies, rising resentment at exploitation and excessive taxation, status inconsistencies, and divisions within society—were common to independence movements elsewhere in the Americas. It was the blending of the mixture which was different: the degree and effectiveness of crown authority diffused over greater or lesser areas, the division of territories into semi-autonomous units, and colonial participation in the whole process of hispanification. The strengths and weaknesses of these respective factors gave rise to struggles and reverses and the final division of Spanish America into a series of republics.

For Brazil, the recognition of independence in 1825 by Portugal did not solve the nation's ills. In many instances there was the perpetuation of colonial administration, life styles, human relations, and social divisions, and even of a colonial economy. There was no sudden breakthrough of a new political order, nor was there a surge of innovative concepts of social and political order. Independence had not been achieved with popular support. It had not been a collective movement against the metropolis, or against an outmoded form of government, or against a system no longer of relevance for an emerging nation. In fact, not before the middle of the nineteenth century was there to be even a partial achievement of national unity. The colonial heritage survived the formal declaration of independence and to some extent persists in the modern era. For Brazil, as for few other countries, a knowledge of colonial antecedents is essential for any understanding of its present and future role in the world.

Political Aspects

EMÍLIA VIOTTI DA COSTA

The Political Emancipation of Brazil

Traditional Historiography

Brazilian historians have spent more time and energy in the study of independence than in any other phase of Brazilian history. Still, it remains ill-understood, stubbornly resistant to interpretations and analysis. Until the 1930s the long shadow of three early historians lay over the subject: Francisco Adolfo de Varnhagen, Oliveira Lima, and Tobias Monteiro.[1] Their facts and their interpretations were repeated over and over in new histories and textbooks. A new incident or a new document might occasionally make its unobtrusive appearance, but in broad outlines a traditional semi-official picture of independence remained intact.

Traditional historians relying only on eyewitness documents produced minutely detailed accounts of political events. Given the nature of their sources, their histories were unable to escape the limited points of view of the actual participants in the independence movement. Historians identified themselves with participants relating events they had indirectly "witnessed." They overestimated the importance of particular individuals and the significance of circumstantial episodes. In this tumble of facts, independence was reduced to an anarchic play of individual wills, clashes of personal interest, petty emotions, and inexplicable dreamings of liberty.[2]

Most of what was presented under the color of erudition and scientific scholarship was actually no more than a set of legends and myths—forged

This chapter was translated by the editor and revised by the author from "Introdução ao estudo da emancipação política do Brasil," in *Brasil em perspectiva* (São Paulo: Difusão Européia do Livro, 1968).

[1] Francisco Adolfo de Varnhagen, *História da independência do Brasil até o reconhecimento pela antiga Metrópole, compreendendo separadamente a dos sucessos ocorridos em algumas províncias até essa data* (São Paulo, 1957); Manoel de Oliveira Lima, *O movimento da independência (1821–1822)*, (São Paulo, 1922), and *Dom João VI no Brasil*, 2d ed., 3 vols. (Rio de Janeiro, 1945); Tobias do Rêgo Monteiro, *História do Império. A elaboração da independência* (Rio de Janeiro, 1927).

[2] Otávio Tarquínio de Souza, *Introdução à história dos fundadores do Império do Brasil*, Ministério de Educação e Cultura, Serviço de Documentação (Rio de Janeiro, 1957).

by the leaders of the independence movement themselves. Facts sanctified by propaganda and clothed in the passion of participants were confused with objective reality. Most of the documents that traditional historians relied on so heavily merely reflected the state of mind of active partisans, each with his own point of view and interest. Whenever their documents were at odds with each other, or were obviously partial, historians could only leave contradictions unsolved or adopt one partisan interpretation or another. All in all, the documents controlled the historians, who lacked any theoretical means of controlling the documents.

New Historiography

More than thirty years ago new guidelines were established for the study of independence. Caio Prado Júnior suggested a new course to be followed in *The Political Evolution of Brazil* (1933) and later in his preface to the facsimile edition of *The Tamoio* (1944).[3] In these essays he found explanations for the independence movement in the internal contradictions of the Brazilian historical process.[4] In his *Economic History of Brazil,* Caio Prado showed how the development of industrial capitalism in Europe and the internal development of the colony combined to destroy the colonial pact, forcing the breach of those restraints created by the colonial system. Without resources and outside the main trends of capitalist development, Portugal was incapable of controlling the colony or fulfilling the role as intermediary which she so jealously guarded.[5]

From a similar standpoint, Nelson Werneck Sodré studied the political emancipation of Brazil within a broader context which embraced the changes stemming from the Industrial Revolution and from ideologies connected to the bourgeois revolution in Europe. He studied the independence movement in Brazil in relation to similar movements elsewhere in the Americas, and adopted as his starting point the contradictions which appeared among different strata of society and between Brazil and Portugal. Werneck Sodré saw the movement as resulting from the action of the ruling class, which became the mouthpiece for national aspirations and emerged as the only class capable, at that time, of bringing the movement to a successful outcome.[6]

Since these interpretations, little progress has been made in this field. The new method and perspectives proposed by Caio Prado Júnior and

[3] Caio Prado Júnior, *Evolução política do Brasil* (São Paulo, 1933), and *O Tamoio* (São Paulo, 1944), facs. ed. with preface by Caio Prado Júnior.

[4] Caio Prado Júnior, *The Colonial Background of Modern Brazil,* trans. Suzette Macedo (Berkeley, 1967).

[5] Caio Prado Júnior, *História econômica do Brasil* (São Paulo, 1949) , p. 131 et seq.

[6] Nelson Werneck Sodré, *Formação histórica do Brasil* (São Paulo, 1942), and *As razões da independência* (Rio de Janeiro, 1965).

Werneck Sodré require research into documentary sources still scarcely touched by historians. They also demand a reassessment of facts considered relevant or irrelevant by traditional historians which may take on new dimensions when considered from new points of view.

Studies published so far have established basic directives which should guide analysis of independence. First, this event should be studied as part of a broader historical process, related on the one hand to the crisis in the traditional colonial system and absolutist forms of government and, on the other, to struggles for freedom and nationalism taking place in Europe and the Americas since the end of the eighteenth century. Second, it is essential to study the internal contradictions in Brazilian society. How was the crisis in the colonial system reflected in Brazil? To what extent did the development of the colony create conditions conducive to the rupture of the colonial pact? How did the different social groups become aware of the disadvantages of the colonial situation? How did they react to libertarian ideologies? Which social classes provided the most revolutionaries? What was their degree of involvement and their potential for action? To what extent and why did the ruling classes, traditionally allied with colonial policy, dissociate themselves from it and what were their motives? Finally, what repercussions did political events in Europe have in the Americas? Statements of individuals and the opinions of contemporaries must all be viewed from the broader perspectives which give them meaning.

The Crisis of the Colonial System

Since the "age of discoveries" relations between mother country and colony had been established to further the interests of the mercantile bourgeoisie and to meet the requirements of the modern state. The weakness of incipient capitalism and of governmental institutions which failed to adjust rapidly to new forms of supply and demand led to the alliance between merchants and the crown. In order to secure profit, a system of monopolies and privileges was institutionalized, binding the merchants to the state.

Of consuming interest to the mercantile bourgeoisie was the establishment of a state with sufficient strength to "protect the commercial interests and break those medieval barriers thwarting the expansion of trade." [7] The system of controls, privileges, and monopolies that guarantees markets for the merchants also benefits the state.

Mercantilism was the theoretical expression of this alliance between commercial capitalism and the state. The merchants identified the wealth of a nation with the amount of gold and silver in its possession. This

[7] Eric Roll, *A History of Economic Thought,* rev. ed. (London, 1954).

explains the eagerness of the colonists to discover mineral deposits in the Americas. When capital is identified with money, profit is seen as the difference between the purchase price and the sale price of commodities. The main object of production is to obtain an exportable surplus. Imports should be limited in order to create a favorable balance of payments. In the view of the merchant, it is the duty of the state to protect commercial interests, since profit made by the individual merchant is a factor contributing to the greatness of the state.[8] Initially, colonial policy was organized on the basis of such premises. Colonies were looked upon as sources of mineral and agricultural wealth. They should concentrate on the production of those commodities difficult to obtain in the European market. At the same time restrictions were placed on other colonial activities. The colonies were compelled to obtain needed supplies in the mother country or via the mother country. The organization of the colonial economy was a function of the international market. Production and commerce were strictly controlled by the mother country. A series of regulations and laws, which became increasingly restrictive, enmeshed the colony in a web of monopolies, privileges, and dues which led to its total subordination to the metropolis.

The colonial system as it was organized under commercial capitalism was threatened when industrial capital became predominant and the absolutist state was challenged by the aspirations of the new bourgeoisie, eager to gain power through representative forms of government. From that moment on, the system of monopolies and privileges governing relations between mother country and colony began to erode. Economic theory was reformulated. Mercantilism gave way to free trade. A new concept of the colony evolved, which required a new colonial policy. There was a clash between a capitalism directed towards fiscal and colonial opportunities and the state monopolies and a capitalism directed towards the automatic opportunities provided by the market.[9] Extraordinary increases in productivity made possible by machinery were incompatible with the continuation of closed markets and the restrictions of trade imposed by the system of monopolies and privileges.

[8] Few texts better express the ideology of the mercantile bourgeoisie in the Iberian Peninsula than *Discursos sobre los comercios de las dos Indias* of Duarte Gomez Solis. He faithfully adheres to the thesis of the importance of metals, the theory of commercial balance, and protectionist solutions. He attributes considerable importance to currency circulation and holds in high esteem the occupation of merchant while scorning social occupations he considers idle—men of letters, friars, and courtiers. His anticlericalism, toleration for Jews (an unusual attitude in the Iberian Peninsula), concern with replacing traditional teaching by education with greater relevance to everyday life, and desire to convert the state into an instrument of commercial interests were typical of the aspirations of the mercantile bourgeoisie which inspired colonial policies initially.

[9] Max Weber, *General Economic History*, trans. F. H. Knight (London, 1927).

In 1776, Adam Smith criticized mercantile policy and condemned restrictions, monopolies, and slave labor. He proposed the practice of free trade and asserted the superiority of free labor over slave labor.[10] His successors were to go further. In his *Treatise on Economic Policy* of 1803, Jean Baptiste Say observed that colonies are a financial burden to the mother country, requiring expenditures for a standing army, a civilian administration, the judiciary, public buildings, and fortifications. He maintained that commercial privileges binding the mother country to the colony and allegedly favoring colonial products were illusory. France was paying fifty francs for sugar in Guadeloupe when it was obtainable in Havana for thirty-five. He concluded that "the true colonies of a commercial nation are the independent nations of the world." Thus he believed that every commercial nation should desire the independence of all nations. The more numerous and more productive such nations were, the more advantages and opportunities there would be for trade. Say's criticism struck at monopolies, privileges, and slavery. It was the traditional concept of colony which he condemned.[11]

This criticism of the colonial system corresponded to changes in political and commercial relations between mother country and colony. However, it did not imply changes in the basic structure of colonial production, which industrial capitalists desired to preserve intact. The new concept of colony expressed the aspirations of groups allied to industrial capitalism, who succeeded in having their views reflected in foreign policy. The transition from commercial capitalism to industrial capitalism first took place in England. As soon as her most important colony gained its freedom, England drew up new guidelines for colonial policy toward the Americas. From that moment, the Ibero-American colonies enjoyed more favorable conditions in their struggle for political independence because they could count on the sympathy and support of England.

The Marginal Position of Portugal and the Traditional Colonial System

Whereas England was on the way to industrialization and had progressed to the stage of initiating new types of colonial relations, Portugal and Spain remained bound to the traditional forms of production and found themselves in the dubious position of defending the traditional colonial system. Jorge de Macedo has demonstrated how, in the middle of the eighteenth century, the marquis of Pombal was striving to

---

[10] Adam Smith, *An Enquiry into the Nature and Causes of the Wealth of Nations* (New York, 1927), bk. 4, ch. 7, secs. 2–3.

[11] Jean Baptiste Say, *A Treatise on Political Economy*, trans. from 4th French ed. by C. R. Prinsep, 2 vols. (London, 1821).

strengthen colonial ties and to rationalize the traditional system. This was a difficult task at that time but one which he was constrained to undertake because of the general trends of Portugal's economy.[12] Only at a much later date was the new ideology of free trade to find acceptance in Portugal, and even then with many reservations.

The Portuguese point of view has been admirably expressed in an eighteenth-century document, "Log Book of a Journey from the Maranhão to Goiás," cited by Caio Prado Júnior in his *Colonial Background of Modern Brazil*.[13] The author tried to demonstrate that colonies were established for the exclusive benefit of the mother country. This benefit derived from the production and export of commodities which the mother country needed, not only for her own requirements, but also for trade with other countries. The colonies should be organized to further these objectives. Settlers in the colonies should not engage in activities which were not beneficial to the commerce of the mother country. The only exception to this general rule was the production of foodstuffs essential for the subsistence of the colonial population which it would be impractical to import. However, despite Portugal's efforts to maintain the traditional colonial system, the general crisis of the system was in the long run to disrupt her relationship with the colony.

The Crisis in the Colony

Monopolies were the targets of much criticism during the colonial period. At the international level, the monopolistic system gave rise to constant friction between nations preserving monopolies and nations unable to participate in the trade. Occupations of part of Brazil by the Dutch and French, together with acts of piracy and smuggling—committed with increasing frequency by the English, the French, the Dutch, and other nationalities along the Brazilian coast—were all expressions of the international struggle against monopolies and privileges. Contraband increased with the development of manufactures in England, whose products found a larger market in Brazil because of the demographic increase and greater prosperity of the colonists. In the colony itself there existed an atmosphere of unrelieved tension between producers and distributors and between those who vied for privileges. Several conflicts, still scarcely studied, resulted from these tensions: for example, the War of the Peddlers (*Guerra dos Mascates*) in Pernambuco, the Beckmann revolt in the Maranhão, and uprisings in Minas Gerais during the gold-mining era, especially the Felício dos Santos revolt.

[12] Jorge de Macedo, "Portugal e a Economia Pombalina," *Revista de história* 19 (1954): 81 et seq.
[13] Caio Prado, *The Colonial Background*, p. 142.

By the end of the eighteenth century the monopolistic system was deteriorating rapidly. The impossibility of eliminating foreign competition and the involvement of the colonists in contraband made the monopolies inoperative for the crown. This topic has not been studied in depth. Only two studies of the crisis of monopolies have been published, both by Myriam Ellis, one on the crown monopolies on salt and the other on whaling.[14]

The increasing size and wealth of the Brazilian population, especially after the discovery of gold, led to greater demands for trade. The growth of the international market increased the demand for colonial products. These combined factors made monopolies and restrictions on trade appear harmful, generating in the colony hostility toward the mother country and receptivity to revolutionary ideas. The interests of the colonial producer, the merchant, and the crown no longer coincided. The colonial pact ceased to be a pact between brothers and became a unilateral contract. As such, many colonists believed that it should be annulled.

However, the lack of viability of the system as such was only gradually perceived by contemporaries. Each side was aware of those contradictions which affected its immediate interests. The Portuguese crown and its representatives were keenly aware of the contraband in gold, of losses resulting from smuggling, and of the decline in proceeds from taxation. For their part, the colonists rebelled against certain restraints imposed by the crown, excessive taxation, and the abuses of royal administrators. Conflicts of interest, uprisings, and violent repression made the colonists conscious of fundamental contradictions. They gradually realized that the colonial system was not viable. Colonists who had looked on themselves as "the Portuguese of Brazil," believing that only their geographical location distinguished the inhabitants of one part of the Portuguese empire from the other, began to see that their interests were incompatible. The struggle, which had begun as a conflict between subjects and king, changed in meaning and became a struggle of colonists against mother country.

Enlightenment criticism of absolutism in Brazil became, in essence, criticism of the colonial regime. Criticism of the crown and of the absolute authority of the king was equated with the struggle for the dissolution of ties between the colony and the mother country. Initially, the crown had been perceived as the mediator in the conflicts between its subjects: producers in Brazil, merchants in Portugal, Jesuits, civil servants, etc. The colonial pact was thought to be a mutually beneficial agreement between Portuguese in Brazil and Portuguese in Portugal.

---

[14] Myriam Ellis, *O monopólio do sal no Estado do Brasil (1631–1801)* (São Paulo, 1955), and *As feitorias baleeiras meridionais do Brasil colonial* (São Paulo, 1966).

Once monopolies and privileges became obstructive and the colonial pact harmful to the Brazilian producer, the crown became the target of colonial criticism and the colonists recognized the gulf separating their interests from those of the mother country. In the eyes of the colonists, crown interests were identified with those of Portugal. Thus for Brazilians, anticolonialism implied criticism of the absolute power of the king and affirmation of the principles of the sovereignty of the people and their right to develop freely, in accordance with their own wishes.

As privileges and monopolies became inoperative, criticism in Portugal began also to undermine the theoretical foundations of the colonial system. Azeredo Coutinho (1745–1821) extolled the abolition of monoplies and privileges, which, in his opinion, hindered the development of agriculture, industry, and commerce.[15] Criticism in Portugal, however, was not as radical as that in England and France, to which the Portuguese looked for inspiration. Azeredo Coutinho wavered between mercantilism, physiocracy, and the new liberal ideas. While recommending the revision of Portuguese colonial policy to reconcile the economic interests of metropolis and colony and the abolition of monopolies such as that on salt, he still considered it essential to maintain colonial ties and keep certain restrictions, for example, the prohibition on manufacturing in Brazil. He believed that the colony should restrict itself to supplying raw materials to Portugal, from which it would continue to receive manufactured goods. The contradictions in his thought indicate the difficulty of adapting the tenets of liberalism—bourgeois ideology—to Portugal and Brazil, where Azeredo Coutinho was interpreting the interests of an "aristocracy" of great rural landowners.[16]

In Portugal the harshest critic of the colonial system was José da Silva Lisboa (1756–1835), who guided the economic policy of Dom João VI in Brazil and who was one of the strongest supporters of the opening of the Brazilian ports in 1808. Upholding liberal principles, he spread the ideas of Adam Smith in numerous works.[17] Although he was a leading proponent of liberalism in Brazil, his advice on economic policy was not free from contradictions. In 1823 in the Brazilian Constitutional Assembly he was to defend the preservation of guilds of artisans in the belief that restrictions imposed by such guilds could be reconciled with the principle of freedom of industry.[18]

---

[15] *Obras econômicas de J. J. da Cunha Azeredo Coutinho,* intro. Sérgio Buarque de Holanda (São Paulo, 1966) .

[16] *Ibid.,* p. 30.

[17] On economic thought in Portugal, of special interest is Moses Bensabat Amzalak, *Do estudo e da evolução das doutrinas econômicas em Portugal* (Lisbon, 1928).

[18] Sérgio Buarque de Holanda, "A herança colonial—sua desagregação," in *História geral da civilização brasileira,* ed. Sérgio Buarque de Holanda (São Paulo, 1960–64), 2 (1): 27.

The new principles of liberalism were welcomed by the majority of people in Brazil but aroused the outright opposition of monopolists, for the most part Portuguese merchants and producers who, in the final analysis, thwarted the interests of the crown. Despite the fact that the colonial system had stood condemned since the late eighteenth century and that Portugal and Spain were not in a position to resist, in the long run, the pressure of nations undergoing industrialization, both attempted to keep their colonies in their former state of dependency and to preserve the colonial pact.

An unexpected event precipitated the breakdown of the system, which otherwise would probably have survived longer. This was the French invasion of the Iberian Peninsula and the transfer of the Portuguese court to Brazil with the full support of the British government, which decisively altered the relationship between mother country and colony.

The "Liberal" Policy of Dom João VI

After his arrival in Brazil, the first step taken by Dom João VI was to open the Brazilian ports, "as a temporary measure," to foreign trade (royal order of January 28, 1808), with the exception of a few products still under royal *estanco*. Subsequent measures revoked any prohibitions on production and commerce in the colony which would be inconsistent with Brazil's new position as the seat of the monarchy.[19] The decree of April 1, 1808, freely permitted the establishment of factories and manufacturing concerns and revoked all previous restrictions. On March 27, 1810, the king revoked orders of 1749 and 1751 and allowed all subjects to sell any merchandise on the streets and from door to door, provided the relevant dues had been paid. The decree of September 28, 1811, continued the policy of liberalizing the economy by revoking the decree of December 6, 1755, and permitting all subjects to trade in any commodity except those forbidden by law. On January 11, Dom João revoked previous decrees and authorized the Treasury (Conselho das Fazendas) to grant licenses for cutting Brazilwood. The decree of July 18, 1814, permitted vessels of any nation to enter any port in the Portuguese empire and also allowed Portuguese vessels to sail for foreign ports. Prohibitions established by the royal order of July 30, 1766, were abolished by the decree of August 11, 1815, which permitted goldsmiths to manufacture and trade in gold and silver objects. The whole series of liberalizing measures culminated in the law of December 16, 1815, which raised the state of Brazil to the status and position of a kingdom.

[19] All references to legislation by Dom João VI and during the regency of Dom Pedro are based on the relevant volumes of the *Leis do Brasil e decisões* for the years 1808–22 inclusive.

The justification presented at the promulgation of the decree of March 27, 1810, authorizing the open sale of any commodity in the streets and from door to door, reveals the principles that governed the new economic policy. It stated that strict enforcement of restrictive measures, "totally at variance with all principles of economic policy," had always been impossible. Moreover, it was in the general interest that all subjects be free to seek "a means of subsistence in the useful division of labor, according to the choice of each and every individual." The document plainly revealed the official policy of enlarging the market and stimulating both industry and commerce, "whose growth should be encouraged but whose balance should be maintained by competition." Finally, the document stated that corporate private interests should not be placed before the public good. It expressed the principles of liberty and free competition and the intention of abolishing monopolies and privileges which had inspired the new policy of the crown. The principle of free trade, described as "far superior to the mercantile system," was also upheld in the manifesto in which Dom João VI sought to justify the treaties signed with Great Britain.[20] One by one, laws which had ensured the operation of the colonial pact were revoked.

It would be wrong, however, to think that the entire system was modified. Despite liberal measures, numerous privileges and restrictions were maintained, and some of these were only to be abolished after independence. The preoccupation with guaranteeing the interests of the Portuguese and the crown, which were often interchangeable, inevitably limited the liberalism of these measures. The decree opening the ports stressed the provisional nature of the measure and excepted Brazilwood and other products governed by royal *estanco*. Subsequently, various decrees were issued with the object of protecting Portuguese trade, especially when the treaty of 1810 created discontent among Portuguese producers and merchants by favoring English interests.

A law of October 11, 1808, exempted textiles made in factories in Portugal from payment of customs dues on entering Brazil. The decree of May 13, 1810, similarly exempted merchandise from China, provided that it was imported directly and was the property of Portuguese subjects. This was one way of eliminating English competition. The decree of October 18, 1810, ordered that all commodities and merchandise imported from England "on behalf of Portuguese subjects" should be subject to a tariff of 15 percent of dues leviable. This measure was intended to place Portuguese merchants on equal terms with their English counterparts. The decree of June 20, 1811, laid down prerequisites and conditions for the admission to Portuguese and Brazilian

20 Roberto Simonsen, *História econômica do Brasil, 1500–1820*, 3d ed. (São Paulo. 1957), p. 403.

ports of ships originating from foreign ports. The decree of July 13, 1811, was an attempt to favor Portuguese-manufactured goods imported into Brazil. The decree of January 21, 1813, declared that all merchandise and manufactured goods from Portugal should be exempt from all import dues.

Similar resolutions were taken in the following years with the primary object of protecting the interests of Portuguese producers and merchants. Concessions favoring foreign trade made by Dom João were counterbalanced by protectionist measures favoring the Portuguese. The decree of September 28, 1811, permitted freedom of trade in all commodities except those restricted by law. However, a further decree of November 19 ruled that unless a ship was owned by a Portuguese subject residing in the territories of the Portuguese empire and manned by a Portuguese master and by a crew of at least three-quarters Portuguese subjects, it would not be allowed to unload, at any port in Portugal, Brazil, the Azores, Madeira, Cape Verdes, or islands subject to the Portuguese crown on the West African coast, any article produced or manufactured in Asia, China, or any port or island beyond the Cape of Good Hope and the South Seas. The law of November 15, 1814, prohibited foreigners from coastal trading. Another law explained that this prohibition applied to both foreign and national commodities. In justifying such a step, the king alleged that he feared foreigners might monopolize trade "because of their greater financial resources." Two years later, probably under pressure from foreign interests, Dom João declared that foreigners could export their agricultural products to any port of the Portuguese empire but insisted that this was on condition that "such exports be carried in Portuguese vessels."

The contradictions inherent in the economic policy of Dom João are apparent in the regulations and explanations of the royal decree of April 25, 1818, which stated that it was essential to increase proceeds derived from the collection of taxes. To achieve this, the decree began by suspending, for a period of twenty years, all concessions and exemptions from taxation. Furthermore, it imposed a tax of 2 percent on all Brazilian products which were exported and which so far had been exempt from dues. It lifted the ban (imposed by the decree of September 20, 1770) on the entry of foreign wines into Brazil but at the same time established tariffs extremely favorable to Portuguese products. It was alleged first, that it was no longer feasible to prohibit completely the import of foreign wines, and second, that it was not fair that such imports should be detrimental to trade in Portuguese wines, which "should be preferred not only because they are national but because of their superior quality." Thus dues of 9 to 12 milréis were levied per barrel of Portuguese wine and 20 milréis per barrel of Portuguese brandy, but foreign wines and brandies were taxed at 36 and 50 milréis per barrel, respectively. This decree clearly illustrated the efforts of Dom João to please his subjects. In an attempt to favor Portuguese wares, he lowered the import dues from 16 to 15 percent and in some instances made even greater reductions. At the same time he ordered that dues on salt, which until then had been different for foreigners and for Portuguese, should be made the same for all. To protect Portuguese shipping interests, he lowered dues on foreign goods carried in Portuguese ships with a Portuguese captain or crew. He further stipulated that foreign ships at any port of Portugal or Brazil should be subject to the same dues—based on tonnage and pilotage, anchorage, and port fees, etc.—which Portuguese ships had to pay at their various ports of departure.

It is easy to see that by taking measures intended to conciliate foreign producers and merchants, Portuguese and Brazilian producers and merchants, and the interest of the crown itself, Dom João succeeded in pleasing no one. Throughout 1820 more decrees were issued favoring Portuguese interests. News of the Spanish revolution in January of that year created uneasiness at the court in Rio de Janeiro. The king's advisors feared that the Portuguese, unhappy because of their relegation to a secondary position in the empire, would also revolt. Acting on the advice of his ministers, especially Tomás António de Vila Nova Portugal, Dom João issued new decrees favoring Portuguese products and their importation into Brazil. An official notice of May 30, 1820, sought to create better conditions for the wine and olive oil industries by suspending privileges previously granted to foreign products and by imposing a surtax on foreign wines. Furthermore, the notice ordered that wheat, maize, barley, rye, and flour from abroad should pay an entry tax of one-tenth in kind. Import taxes on salt produced in Portugal or the Algarve were cut by half, and salt from other parts of the Portuguese empire paid 80 réis per *alqueire*. In contrast, the import tax on foreign salt was doubled. Furthermore, tuna, herring, and other fish from Portugal or the Algarve were exempted from entry dues in any port of Brazil and elsewhere in the Portuguese empire. This exemption also applied to some textiles made in Portugal. In an attempt to compensate the Exchequer for losses resulting from such tax exemptions, a tax was imposed on "brandy for consumption in the cities, towns, and villages of Brazil."

Measures intended to regain the support of Portuguese producers and merchants were sources of annoyance not only for Brazilians but for foreign merchants, especially the English, who resented the progressive abrogation of privileges granted to them by the treaty of 1810. Nor were such measures adequate to prevent the liberal revolution from extending to Portugal. On August 24, 1820, it broke out in Oporto.

Reactions to Dom João's Economic Policy

Since 1808 Dom João had wavered between his wish to free the economy and his wish to protect Portuguese interests. The former, consonant with contemporary tendencies and British demands, led him to accept the principles of free trade. The latter led him to take measures of a markedly mercantilist nature. Total adherence to the principles of economic liberalism would have destroyed the bases of the crown's support. However, the preservation of the colonial system was no longer possible, hence the contradictions in the crown's economic policy. The resulting conflicts made both colonists and agents of the mother country aware of their divergent interests. The colonists saw the advantages to be derived from increasing their freedom of action; the Portuguese were convinced of the need to limit this freedom. Opposition between the two factions came into the open when Brazilian and Portuguese deputies confronted each other in 1821 in the Portuguese Côrtes. The policies of Dom João had made it clear that the interests of colony and of mother country were irreconcilable. The rupture of relations between Portugal and Brazil was now inevitable.

In 1808, when the ports were opened, and in 1810, when the commercial treaty with England was signed, the Portuguese government felt compelled to justify its decisions to its subjects. These arguments and those presented against these decisions by the crown revealed the conflicts of interest which threatened the unity of the Portuguese empire. The government sought to assuage the well-justified fears of its subjects by giving assurances that Portuguese manufactures would not be harmed by the treaty. The government spokesman, the viscount of Cairú, tried to justify the policy of opening the ports. In his *Observations on the Free Trade of Brazil,* he noted that the government would derive increased revenue from trade as a result of this measure.[21] In his opinion, the resulting competition would rouse Portuguese industries from the lethargy into which they had fallen. The "energy of the individual, once left to develop its inherent flexibility to its full potential," could only be beneficial. He subscribed to liberalism as an act of faith and asserted that "where there is commercial competition the spirit of speculation is always more active in seeking out better ways to use capital." Finally, he insisted on the benefits which Portugal would derive from welcoming "with enthusiasm advances of capital as long-term loans on favorable conditions in order to undertake new commercial ventures." The viscount further argued that no industries should receive special favor except those like iron, which were indispensible to the security and defense of

21 Visconde de Cairú, *Observações sôbre o comércio franco do Brasil pelo autor dos Princípios do Direito Mercantil* (Rio de Janeiro, 1808).

the state. He believed that protection for local industry would only create inertia and diminish "the feelings of noble emulation." In an appendix to the book, published in 1808, someone signing himself as a friend of José da Silva Lisboa agreed enthusiastically with the author's ideas and went on to say: "In countries where the population is not in proportion to the area of land which should be put to cultivation, the high costs of labor and materials made the promotion of agriculture infinitely more important than the encouragement of industry. At no time will their manufactures be able to compete with those of countries where the opposite set of circumstances prevails." The anonymous writer concluded by citing the example of the United States. The Portuguese government was thus advocating the principle of free enterprise and welcomed the influx of foreign capital while affirming its belief that agriculture was the basis for the future economic prosperity of Brazil. After independence the political predominance of rural groups and merchants linked to the export economy and foreign capital was responsible for the survival of these principles of economic planning.[22]

The new direction of Portuguese economic policy toward Brazil, as defined by José da Silva Lisboa, provoked violent discussions. The opening of the ports aroused the displeasure of those who had benefited most from the commercial monopoly until that date, i.e., Portuguese merchants and producers. The latter argued that foreigners would carry off all currency and precious metals. They would rival Portuguese merchants and eventually, because of their superiority, monopolize all trade. Portuguese shipping and industry would be destroyed, damaging both the mother country and the colony. Both in Portugal and in Brazil factories would be ruined and the populace thrown into poverty. Industrial arguments were to be invoked at a later date, when the Portuguese Côrtes abolished concessions made by Dom João to Brazil.

Conflicts of interest were not limited to the area of foreign trade. In the internal sector clashes between the old holders of privileges and those working to abolish them increased daily. The retail merchants of Rio de Janeiro saw a threat to their interests in the lifting of prohibitions on the sale of merchandise. They addressed an appeal to the Royal Council for Commerce, Agriculture, Factories and Navigation, asking that earlier measures (decrees of May 24, 1774, and April, 1755) be observed because otherwise they would be made virtually meaningless by the "new and liberal system." The Council, however, ruled against the merchants. In another case related to the same decrees, the government took a different tack and, instead of following liberal precepts, favored the maintenance of privileges. A decision of April 2, 1813, forbad the sale of

---

[22] On British imperialism in Brazil, see A. K. Manchester, *British Preeminence in Brazil—Its Rise and Decline. A Study in European Expansion* (London, 1933).

locally manufactured shoes on the streets of Rio de Janeiro, on the basis that the making of shoes was the exclusive privilege of members of the appropriate guild, which was governed by statutes and subject to municipal regulations. The government also opted for preserving monopolies on wines: in a ruling of June 6, 1820, Dom João rejected a request by some merchants that they be allowed to dispatch wines from the region of the Alto Douro in Portugal without first obtaining the permission of the Company of the Alto Douro. The king alleged that the free importation of such wines was impossible because the privileges enjoyed by the Company had not been revoked. Thus the Company held the exclusive monopoly of that trade.

In summary, though the laws passed by Dom João did contribute to undermining the colonial system, they were not sufficiently broad to restructure it completely, nor was this their purpose. Privileges and monopolies continued to exist. The burdensome and irrational fiscal system remained intact, as did the decrepit administrative machine and the innumerable prohibitions—of freedom of movement or the right to open new roads—to say nothing of the discriminatory legislation and privileges which separated Portuguese from Brazilians and created animosity between them. It is essential to recognize that the liberal economic policy of Dom João contained mercantilist and colonial features totally opposed to liberalism. Their importance must be recognized in any appreciation of the independence movement in Brazil.

A document which appeared at the time of the revolution of 1817 revealed one of the reasons for discontent, the persistence of colonial directives in the administration and economy of Brazil. A case in point was the monopoly on trade in cotton held by certain merchants known as *prensários* (literally, "squeezers"). The entire cotton production of the captaincy of Pernambuco, estimated between sixty and seventy thousand sacks and with an annual return of from five to six million cruzados, passed through the "sly and crooked hands" of eight men who had the monopoly on the trade. Such a situation created great discontent among plantation owners and buyers. Not a day passed without disputes between the different parties.[23] A more careful study will probably show that the continuation of the system of monopolies and privileges in different sectors of the economy was an ever-present source of discord and conflict contributing to the development of revolutionary attitudes. Farmers and merchants became more sympathetic to any revolutionary movement which promised greater freedom of trade and the abolition of privileges.

Once the Brazilian ports had been opened to international trade, the

---

[23] *Documentos históricosp da Bibliotheca Nacional do Rio de Janeiro*, 120 vols. (Rio de Janeiro, 1928–) (hereafter cited as *DHBNRJ*). Vols. 101–8 deal with the revolution of 1817 in Pernambuco; see 107:261.

growing demand for tropical products on the world market made the continuation of colonial restrictions on production impossible. Hipólito da
Costa wrote in the *Correio braziliense* (no. 18) of 1817 that it was
"morally" impossible for a country such as Brazil, whose demographic
growth and cultural and social development had established it as a great
nation, to continue to tolerate the system of military government and
colonial institutions established when Brazilian settlements were no more
than garrison posts or cotton plantations. Years later Baron von Weech,
who traveled through Brazil and the Platine provinces from 1823 to 1827,
was to observe that the reign of Dom João could be characterized as
follows: lack of innovation in business practices, "the auctioning off of
favor and graces," and "exploitation of the people by contract monopolies
and by the absurd obstacles placed by customs tariffs on international
trade." [24]

Contradictions in the policy of Dom João created an atmosphere favorable to the development of liberal ideas in Portugal and in Brazil and
contributed to increased pressure for the introduction of representative
government. The meaning of liberalism, however, was different at home
and abroad; the colonists' advocacy of liberalism implied their support for
the concept of free trade; the liberal Portuguese of the mother country
wished to limit the arbitrary nature of the authority of the king, who was
harming Portuguese interests by his liberal policies.

Ideological Assumptions of the Independence Movement

The history of liberal ideas in Brazil goes back to the end of the
eighteenth century, when tensions created by the crisis within the
colonial system spawned a series of revolutionary movements and plots
against the crown: the Inconfidência Mineira of 1789, the plot in Rio de
Janeiro of 1794, the Revolt of the Tailors in Bahia of 1798, and the
conspiracy of the Suassuna brothers of 1801. They culminated in the
revolution in Pernambuco in 1817, the most important of all such movements.

All these revolts found their source of inspiration in the ideology of the
Enlightenment in Europe. The influence of the "abominable French
principles" is clear. The record of the trial of the Inconfidência Mineira
reveals the existence of a "French faction" in Minas Gerais. Major
authors of the Enlightenment figured among books seized by the authorities. Books confiscated from the library of Canon Luiz Vieira da Silva
included works by Montesquieu, d'Alembert, Mably, Turgot, Raynal, and

---

[24] J. Friedrich von Weech, *Reise über England und Portugal nach Brasilien und den
vereinigten Staaten des La-Plata-Stromes während den Jahren 1823 bis 1827* (Munich,
1831), cited in Manoel de Oliveira Lima, *O movimento*, p. 36.

Bierfil and Diderot's *Encyclopédie*. The *Recueil des lois constitutives de l'État d'Amérique*, a textbook of considerable importance for the revolutionaries, was also seized. Various witnesses testified that Tiradentes had tried to find a translator for one chapter of this book and had visited Rio de Janeiro in search of other "English" works. The works of Thomas Paine were also a source of inspiration. The independence of the United States became an essential point of reference for Latin American revolutionaries.[25] The *inconfidentes* constantly cited the example of the "English Americans," who "had waged such a great war, on wave-swept shores with little more than some dried fish, wheat, and few other resources." [26] With fewer arms than those available to their Brazilian counterparts the North Americans had held out until they gained their liberty.[27] Guided by the North American example, the *inconfidentes* dreamed of creating in Brazil a "republic as free and prosperous as English America." [28] Their ever-present hope was that help would be forthcoming from the newly emancipated North American nation. José Joaquim de Maia was not alone in seeking support from the government of the United States for the cause of liberty and emancipation. However, nothing positive emerged from such approaches. The revolutionaries of 1817 were to be equally disillusioned.

The French Revolution gave new relevance to the thinking of the philosophers of the Enlightenment. The "French faction" gained more followers, and the prestige of French books increased. In 1794, the viceroy, the count of Resende, ordered a legal inquiry in Rio de Janeiro to identify those people who dared to speak of matters offensive to religion and of public events in Europe.[29] The inquiry revealed that the accused were admirers of the French Revolution and espoused anticlerical and nativist ideas. They were accused of reading "subversive" books, of wishing to extend the "French system" to Brazil, and of stating that kings are no longer necessary and that men are free and can, at any time, reclaim their liberty. They criticized religion and contested the authenticity of miracles, and one of them went so far as to assert that according to Scripture authority is granted not only to kings to punish their subjects but also to subjects to punish their kings. According to reports, another of the accused had said that the revolutionaries of the Inconfidência had been treated as rebels because they had failed but that if their efforts had succeeded they would have been heroes. Among the

---

[25] *Autos da devassa da inconfidência*, 7 vols., Ministério da Educação, Biblioteca Nacional (Rio de Janeiro, 1936), 1:143, 161, 108, 102, 110, 137.

[26] *Ibid.*, p. 170.

[27] *Ibid.*, p. 159.

[28] *Ibid.*, p. 108.

[29] *Anais da Biblioteca Nacional do Rio de Janeiro* (hereafter cited as *ABNRJ*) 61 (1939).

many volumes confiscated during the inquiry were the works of Mably, Rousseau, and Raynal and numbers of *Le Mercure*.

Three years later, in 1797, another conspiracy was discovered in Bahia. The conspirators proclaimed the principles of liberty, equality, and free trade. They based their ideology on "French principles" and proposed to establish a republic which would encompass all of Brazil.[30] Apparently discussions among members of the Areopago of Itambé were of a similar nature. The Areopago was a secret society, probably affiliated with Masonry, which was established in Pernambuco by the priest Manuel Arruda Câmara to disseminate liberal ideas. The Suassuna brothers, members of the Areopago, were accused in 1801 of plotting against the government.

Cries of "long live our country," "long live liberty," and "death to the sailors" (the last a pejorative reference to the Portuguese) were heard among revolutionaries of 1817. Terms of address such as "patriot" and "ye" replaced the more customary "your grace" in correspondence dated "Year I of Independence."[31] On the walls of the house of Cruz Cabugá, a leader of the movement, hung portraits of French and English revolutionaries. Once the success of the revolution was assured, the members of the provisional government met to draft a constitution, modeled on the French constitutions of 1791, 1793, and 1795. In his criticism of the ideological orientation of the 1817 revolutionaries, Tollenare, a French merchant residing in Pernambuco, observed that they followed "the philosophy of the eighteenth century which has now been discredited in France."[32] Ideas of liberty and nationality constituted the credo of the revolutionaries; they sought to express these principles even in the most insignificant acts. A story goes that in a display of nationalism the conspirators of 1817 refused to serve European bread and wine at their tables, ostentatiously preferring manioc cakes and Brazilian brandy, with which they drank toasts to independence and denounced royal tyranny and Portuguese born in Europe.[33]

Despite the evident influence of French ideas, English publications were considered even more dangerous. This is understandable if we remember that England was the country with the greatest interest in the independence of Brazil. In a memorandum on the revolution of 1817, an anonymous writer advised that pamphlets published in England should be

[30] "A inconfidência da Bahia em 1798—devassa e sequestros," *ABNRJ* 43–44 (1921): 87.

[31] *DHBNRJ* 102:6–7.

[32] L. F. de Tollenare, *Notas dominicais tomadas durante uma residência em Portugal e no Brasil nos anos de 1816, 1817, 1818*. The part referring to Pernambuco was translated from the unedited French manuscript by Alfredo de Carvalho and was published in Recife in 1905 with a preface by Manoel de Oliveira Lima, see pp. 120–86.

[33] *Ibid.*, p. 176.

burnt and "rigorously prohibited because they are more incendiary than instructive." In his opinion, subscribers or those having such pamphlets in their possession at the first offense should be liable to a fine equivalent to a quarter of the total value of their possessions. Further offenses would be punishable by the confiscation of all their possessions and by exile.[34]

Attempts to restrict the entry of books and revolutionary ideas into Brazil had always met with failure. Even during the colonial period, when the import of foreign books was banned, it was impossible to prevent their entering the country either as contraband or in the luggage of students returning from studies in Europe. Since the opening of the ports in 1808, books could enter freely. However, censors remained active in confiscating books which might threaten the public order. For example, a pamphlet entitled *The Black and the Jungle Monkey (O prêto e o bugio de mato)* was banned on November 14, 1816, on the grounds that its contents "were totally unsuitable for dissemination in Brazil," where there were many slaves.[35] Closer ties with Europe and the increasing numbers of foreigners entering Brazil after 1808 encouraged the spread of liberal and nationalist ideas, which found fertile ground in the secret societies that were springing up.

Secret Societies and Revolutionary Movements

The Masonic lodges were the focal points for most of the revolutionary movements.[36] There can be no doubt that in Rio de Janeiro and Bahia and in the 1817 revolution in Pernambuco, secret societies cultivated the "abominable French principles" and planned revolutionary uprisings. This was also the case in Europe. The Bahian conspiracy coincided with the establishment (July 14, 1797) in Salvador of the Masonic lodge Knights of Light (Os Cavaleiros da Luz). In Pernambuco the Areopago gave rise to two academies, Paradise and Suassuna. Paradise had its seat in Recife and was presided over by the Reverend João Ribeiro, one of the most forceful revolutionaries of 1817. Suassuna was established on the plantation of the Suassuna brothers and was presided over by Francisco de Paula Cavalcante de Albuquerque, also implicated in the 1817 revolution. It appears that another participant in the revolution of 1817, António Carlos Ribeiro de Andrada, was the founder of the lodge Democratic University (Universidade Democrática), with which were affiliated the lodges known as the Orient of Pernambuco (Pernambuco do Oriente) and

[34] *DHBNRJ* 107:238.

[35] *Coleção de Leis do Império de Brasil*, November 14, 1816.

[36] Secret societies are discussed in Carlos Rizzini, *O livro o jornal e a tipografia no Brasil* (São Paulo, 1945); Mario Behring, *Introdução, ABNRJ* 43–44 (1921); Célia de Barros, "A ação das sociedades secretas," in *História geral da civilização brasileira* 2 (1):191–206.

the Occident of Pernambuco (Pernambuco do Ocidente). These were established in the homes of António Gonçalves da Cruz Cabugá and Domingos José Martins, respectively, both of whom were leaders in the revolution of 1817. The revolution was plotted within the walls of the lodges, and the revolutionaries had contacts with lodges abroad, if we are to believe a letter sent by Carlos Alvear to Matias Irigoyen and quoted by Manoel de Oliveira Lima.[37]

Following the pattern established in the northeast, several Masonic lodges were founded in Rio de Janeiro. The count of Arcos rigorously persecuted them, forcing the closing of the Constancy and Philanthropic lodges in 1806. Despite official harassment, however, lodges continued to function. After the revolution of 1817 Dom João decided to put an end to Masonic activities and on March 30, 1818, ordered the closing of all lodges. However, after reorganizing, they were functioning again by 1821. Disturbances in the Praça do Comércio at the beginning of that year have been attributed to Freemasons.

Freemasonry recruited its members from the upper classes of colonial society: teachers, public servants, merchants, plantation owners, and even numerous priests (despite the anticlerical nature of Freemasonry in Europe). It was responsible for the majority of revolutionary movements of this period and gave them an elitist character. The ringleaders of the so-called Suassuna conspiracy, as noted above, were leading plantation owners, the Cavalcante de Albuquerque family. Among those brought together by the revolution of 1817 were Crown Judge António Carlos, whose father was one of the richest men of Santos; Domingos José Martins, a wealthy merchant; Cruz Cabugá, a man of means of Pernambuco; and others descended from "the best nobility" and prominent in colonial society. At the inquiry held after the revolution to establish responsibility, most of the accused cited as proof of innocence their positions as members of the nobility of Pernambuco. They portrayed themselves as having been raised to believe in the natural order of society, which was made up of people from different classes and different ranks.[38]

The presence of prominent Brazilians in Masonic lodges was evident on other occasions. In 1821, when there were disturbances in Rio de Janeiro shortly before the departure of Dom João VI for Portugal, palace gossip had it that powerful senior civil servants, ecclesiastics, businessmen, and plantation owners—all prosperous members of the conservative classes—were Freemasons, *"carbonarios,"* *"comuneros,"* and radicals, as António Teles da Silva, later marquis of Resende, was to describe them in his testimony to José Bonifácio. Such people swore in

---

[37] Francisco Muniz Tavares, *História da revolução de Pernambuco em 1817*, 3d ed. (Recife, 1917), commemorating the first centenary, revised and annotated by Manoel de Oliveira Lima.

[38] *DHBNRJ* 107; 7, 11 (preface by José Honório Rodrigues).

the lodges to defend liberal and constitutionalist principles, in accordance with the precepts of Freemasonry in Europe.

The Limits of Liberalism in Brazil

Although there can be no doubt of the influence of European revolutionary ideas on movements in Brazil, its importance should not be overestimated. The revolutionaries turned to European books for inspiration, but first-hand knowledge of their contents was limited to a small group of men of letters—civil servants, landowners, merchants, doctors, and lawyers—many of whom read with enthusiasm rather than critical judgment. The vast body of the population, illiterate and backward, had no means of learning about the new doctrines.

Whatever the material barriers to the diffusion of Enlightenment ideas, such as illiteracy and inadequate communications, the greatest obstacle was the nature of the Enlightenment itself, which was in many respects totally incompatible with the reality of life in Brazil. In Europe, liberalism and nationalism expressed the aspirations of a bourgeoisie intent on reorganizing society, re-examining traditional values, attacking the privileges of the nobility and the clergy, and challenging the absolute power of the sovereign. It strove to reorganize the state in such a way as to be able to exercise direct control and to eliminate the obstacles to the development of an integrated national economy. Thus the bourgeoisie substituted loyalty to the nation for loyalty to the king. Their commitment to the rights of man—the right of ownership, the right to liberty and equality before the law, the right to representation, the right to participate in basic governmental decisions—was instrumental to their purposes. Here, too, was the explanation for the anticlericalism which was so typical of bourgeois attitudes of that period. Because the Church was associated with the status quo and the monarchy, any struggle against the absolute power of the king was also a struggle against the Church. For the bourgeoisie in Europe the organization of a liberal, national, and secular state was essential.

In Europe, then, the ideas of the Enlightenment served a forceful bourgeoisie, committed to the development of manufacturing interests and industry, in its struggle against an aristocracy in crisis. In Brazil such ideas were taken up by the "rural aristocracy" and by a weak and inarticulate bourgeoisie which was almost totally dependent on the state and on the "rural elite." The development of a bourgeoisie on the European model was out of the question in a fundamentally agrarian and slavocratic economy. Except for a few cities whose prosperity was based on exports, such as Recife, Salvador, and Rio de Janeiro along the coast and Vila Rica in the mining area, urban centers were of little significance.

The ardent advocates of liberal and revolutionary ideas were for the most part recruited from the urban population. However, although some of the leaders of the conspiracies in Rio de Janeiro and Bahia and of the Inconfidência Mineira could be classified as "urban," there were several landowners among them.[39] In Pernambuco in 1817 numerous landowners, cotton and sugar planters, and cattle ranchers worked for the revolutionary cause alongside merchants, civil servants, soldiers, and clerics. A brief examination of the distribution of wealth in Recife at that period reveals that the richest people often invested money in both urban and rural sectors of the economy.[40] Men of letters usually had family connections with, or depended on, the propertied elite.

The dominant sector of the bourgeoisie was composed of merchants, the majority of whom were Portuguese, and civil servants of the crown. Most of them were interested in the preservation of the colonial system and the usufruct of privileges and were unreceptive to liberal reforms and ideas of emancipation. In 1817 the leading merchants of Recife joined together and offered to pay five hundred thousand francs to members of the provisional government if they gave up the revolution.[41] Government informers unanimously agreed that merchants were a peaceloving and orderly class loyal to the crown. As we have seen, this loyalty was relative: in Oporto the merchant bourgeoisie gladly supported the constitutional revolution. However, they did so in the hope that the revolutionaries would abolish those liberal measures adopted by the king which favored Brazil.

For their part the landed aristocrats gave themselves the airs and graces of nobility and gratefully accepted the titles which Dom João VI and later Dom Pedro distributed so freely. They were devoted to preserving the freedom of trade recently gained and to freeing themselves from the control of the Portuguese administration. But they were not prepared to renounce their slave holdings. Slavery was a barrier which liberalism in Brazil could not overcome. Property rights were invoked to preserve this institution. In 1817 the revolutionary government of Pernambuco, in a proclamation intended to assuage fears that the "liberal" revolution intended to bring about "the indiscriminate emancipation of coloreds and slaves," addressed itself to slaveowners in these words: "Patriots, your property rights are sacred, no matter how repugnant this may be to the ideal of justice." [42] Given the alternative of defending the right of slaves to be free or the property rights of their owners, the revolutionaries opted for the latter.

[39] Augusto de Lima Júnior, *Pequena história da inconfidência de Minas Gerais*, 3d ed. (Belo Horizonte, 1968).

[40] *DHBNRJ* 105:241.

[41] Tollenare, *Notas dominicais*, p. 214.

[42] *DHBNRJ* 103:vi; reproduced from the *Correio braziliense* 18(1817):618–19, cited by José Honório Rodrigues.

Another characteristic of Brazilian liberalism in this period was its real or apparent ability to compromise with the Church. Tollenare maintained that it was only apparent. He said that the revolutionaries were interested in gaining the support of the pious Catholic masses and did not dare to voice open criticism of religion, despite their disagreement with its tenets. This does not seem to be the correct explanation. The fact that many ecclesiastics joined revolutionary movements would appear to indicate that in Brazil a high degree of conciliation between liberalism and the Church had been achieved. The manifestos of 1817 proclaimed: "Long live the country, long live our Catholic religion, long live the Virgin Mary, and death to the aristocrats." [43]

Whereas in Europe bourgeois ideology was permeated with anticlericalism, in Brazil the clergy, feeling wronged by the crown (which directly interfered in the life of the Church by virtue of the right of Royal Patronage [*Padroado Real*]), openly espoused the revolutionary cause. In fact, so many clerics took part in the revolutionary movement of 1817 that it was described as a "revolution of priests." At the legal inquiry several priests were accused of complicity in the revolution. It was alleged that some had frequented "the clubs" (Masonic lodges) and that others had defended from their pulpits the ideals of nation and liberty against the concept of monarchy. Some were accused of having misled the young in the classroom, others, such as Father José Martiniano de Alencar, of having actively collaborated with the revolutionary government, serving as emissaries to the interior of the country. Finally, some, like Father Caneca, later involved in a new conspiracy in 1824, were accused of being "guerrillas." [44] There was a story that in 1817, Dean Manuel Vieira de Lemos Sampaio, responsible for the administration of the diocese of Pernambuco, published a pastoral declaring that revolution was not contrary to the Gospel, that authority and privilege had been granted to the house of Braganza by bilateral agreement, and that when a dynasty failed to meet its obligations, the people were freed from their oath of loyalty. [45]

The limited importance of the bourgeoisie, made up primarily of Portuguese merchants, the predominance of agrarian groups interested in the retention of slave labor, and the revolutionary tendencies of the clergy all imbued liberal and nationalist movements in Brazil with a flavor of their own. At this period liberalism meant the liquidation of

[43] Tollenare, *Notas dominicais*, p. 197.

[44] *DHBNRJ* 106:154, 150, 187, 190, 206, 216, 219.

[45] On clerical participation, see Maria Graham, *Journal of a Voyage to Brazil and Residence There during the Years 1821–1823* (London, 1824), trans. into Portuguese as *Diário de uma viagem ao Brasil* . . . (São Paulo, 1956), p. 121; John Armitage, *The History of Brazil*, 2 vols. (London, 1836), trans. into Portuguese as *História do Brasil* (Rio de Janeiro, 1943), p. 25; Muniz Tavares, *A revolução*, p. 41.

colonial ties. There was no intention of reforming the colonial structure of production, no attempt to change the structure of society. In fact, all the revolutionary movements made a point of guaranteeing the right to own slaves. The chief goal was to liberate the country from colonial restrictions and from obstacles to free trade.

Because such movements were anticolonial rather than antimonarchical and because their opposition to Portugal found stronger expression than their defense of nationalism, the idea of total independence took clear shape only when it became evident that it was impossible for Brazil to continue as a United Kingdom with Portugal and still retain the freedom of trade and the relative autonomy which had been gained already. For the same reason a monarchical regime was relatively easy to accept. In Brazil, the struggle for liberty took the form of a struggle against the monopolies and privileges guaranteed by the Portuguese crown. Furthermore, nationalism did not find fertile soil in a country in which an industrial bourgeoisie was yet to be formed and whose economy relied on overseas markets. The Brazilian provinces had stronger economic ties with Europe than with each other, there were no motives for national integration, and nationalist ideas would have sounded artificial at this time. This situation explains José Bonifácio's fears that Brazil would be partitioned into different provinces.

All the revolutionary activities in Brazil preceding the independence movement itself had been more or less local, although at the time of the Inconfidência Mineira there were vague rumors of possible support in Rio de Janeiro and São Paulo. Even the 1817 revolution—the most far-reaching and important of all during the colonial period—was able to count on the support of only a few provinces in the northeast: Paraíba, Pernambuco, Ceará, and Rio Grande do Norte. At this time, it was difficult to promote a revolutionary movement which would rouse the whole country. In the Portuguese Côrtes the Brazilian deputies did not regard themselves as deputies for Brazil but for their respective provinces. Feijó, in a speech to the Côrtes in 1822 said: "We are not deputies for Brazil . . . because nowadays each province is governed independently." [46] Territorial unity was maintained not by any strongly nationalist ideal but by recognition of the need to preserve the unity of the national territory in order to guarantee independence. After the proclamation of independence all plans for recolonization were aimed at exploiting the well-known lack of unity among the different provinces. The unity of the provinces thus became essential to Brazilian autonomy.

The limitations of liberal and nationalist ideology in Brazil corresponded to limitations of revolutionary practices. Besides the vast geographical distances, disunity among the provinces, and inadequate

[46] Buarque de Holanda, "A herança colonial," p. 16.

means of communication and transportation, there were also the enormous social disparities separating the small elite of educated people from the illiterate mass of slaves, free or manumitted blacks and mulattos, and poor whites. The elite distrust of the masses, whom they expected to revolt against them, is apparent in any document of the period.

At the time of the Inconfidência Mineira some thought had been given to the difficulties of fomenting a revolution in a country where the free whites were heavily outnumbered by blacks and slaves. There was the risk of general revolt. Alvarenga's suggestion that the slaves should be given their freedom was not well received by those who believed that mining and agriculture would be impossible without slave labor. Given the revolutionaries' intention to maintain slavery, manifestos in favor of representative forms of government, speeches affirming popular sovereignty, or sermons preaching liberty and equality as inalienable human rights could not be anything but false or meaningless for a great part of the population. It was estimated that slaves comprised more than 60 percent of the population in the Maranhão. The percentage varied between 30 percent and 40 percent in the remaining provinces, and exceeded 70 percent in some rural areas. The major weakness of revolutionary movements before independence was the leaders' deep-rooted fear of the masses. Tollenare, a contemporary of the 1817 revolution in Pernambuco, noted that the revolutionaries would only discuss the doctrine of the rights of man with initiates and appeared to fear that its tenets might be misunderstood by the canaille, or mob.[47] It would be more accurate to say that what the revolutionaries feared was that the doctrine *would* be understood by the masses.

The democratic intentions of the common people scandalized the upper classes, who referred to them as "explosions of insulting equality." In a letter of June 15, 1817, João Lopes Cardoso commented on the situation in Recife during the revolution, noting that "the half-castes, mulattos, and creoles were so overwhelmingly arrogant that they said that all men were equal and that they themselves would only marry white women of the best stock." Pharmacists, surgeons, and bloodletters gave themselves airs of importance. Even barbers refused to shave Cardoso and claimed that they were "employed in the service of the country." To his horror Cardoso was forced to shave himself. Even worse, he found the manner of the "half-castes" (*cabras*) somewhat too familiar and lacking in respect. He wrote to his friend: "Your Grace would not permit that a half-caste should come up to you, hat on head, and clapping you on the shoulder should address you: 'Well met, patriot, how are you? How about giving me a smoke, or take some of mine,' for such was the offer by one of Brederodes' slaves to Crown Judge Afonso!" Fortunately, Cardoso con-

---

[47] Tollenare, *Notas dominicais*, p. 184.

cluded with evident satisfaction, the half-caste received his well-deserved punishment: "He has already been regaled with five hundred lashes." [48] Cardoso was horrified to see Domingos José Martins, a leader of the movement, walking arm in arm with lower-class people who sported blunderbusses, pistols, and unsheathed swords.

This distrust of the masses frequently manifested itself as fear of a clash between whites and blacks or half-castes. Blacks and half-castes comprised the poorest class of society. While it was undeniable that among the most important families there were "whites" who could not really be classified as such, for the most part such families were white. During the colonial period these enjoyed special privileges. Legal acts forbade the appointment of blacks and mulattos to any position of importance in the administration. Where mulattos succeeded (because of special circumstances) in advancing socially, they were looked on as whites. The English traveler Henry Koster, who was in the northeast of Brazil from 1809 to 1814, told a story which, even if apocryphal, gives a good picture of the situation. In conversation with a "man of color" in his service, Koster asked him if Capitão-Mor so-and-so was not a mulatto. The man replied "he was, but is not now." Seeing Koster's perplexity, the man explained by posing the question: "Can a Capitão-Mor be a mulatto man?" Comparing the interracial situation in Brazil with that of the English, French, and Dutch colonies, Koster noted "how little difference is made between a white man, a mulatto, a negro, if all are equally poor and if all have been born free." However, the upper classes were reluctant to establish ties with mixed bloods, and blacks were not seen among them. For the most part free blacks never became more than artisans, and those few who succeeded in being ordained in the ministry merely proved the rule. Koster went on to observe:

Marriages between white men and women of color are by no means rare, though they are sufficiently so to cause the circumstance to be mentioned when speaking of an individual who has connected himself in this manner; but this is not said with the intent of lowering him in the estimation of others. Indeed the remark is only made if the person is a planter of any importance, and the woman is decidedly of dark color, for even a considerable tinge will pass for white; if the white man belongs to the lower orders, the woman is not accounted unequal to him in rank, unless she is nearly black. [49]

The conflict which was perceived as racial was rather a conflict between the poor and the rich, the ruling classes and the mass of the people.

One of the revolutionary leaders in the Bahian conspiracy, João de

[48] *DHBNRJ* 102:12.
[49] Henry Koster, *Travels in Brazil* (London, 1816), pp. 391, 317, 397, 393.

Deus, "a colored man (*pardo*) with a tailor's shop," tried to drum up popular support for the movement by convincing the people of the advantages they would derive from becoming "French" (adopting the revolutionary ideas). He promised them that they would be able to live "in equality and abundance"; riches would be theirs, and they would be "freed from the hardships of everyday life. Differences of white, black, and brown would be abolished and everybody, without discrimination, would be eligible for posts in ministries and in the civil service." The desire of the masses for unlimited access to governmental posts can be more readily understood if we remember that certain positions were closed to manual workers and people of color. When Alvarenga Peixoto applied for the chair of law at the University of Coimbra he had to prove that his ancestors were of "clean blood," i.e., that they were not Jews or blacks and had not followed any manual trade. Faced with the accusation that a grandfather had made religious statues, Alvarenga had to prove that this had been merely a hobby and not a permanent job. Equality before the law was thus an ideal close to the hearts of people involved in manual labor.[50]

For the mass of the people, largely blacks and mixed bloods, the revolution for independence was essentially a struggle against the whites and their privileges. One of the coloreds indicted in the Inconfidência said: "We will soon throw out of Brazil those whites from Portugal who wish to take over our country." [51] It is not surprising that the "whites" should have been terrified by the prospect of rebellion and should hesitate to have contact with the people, often characterized as "this mob of mulattos and blacks." [52] For the dispossessed the revolution meant, above all, the subversion of civil order, which the privileged minority intended to maintain. In 1821, less than a year before independence, Carneiro de Campos, who soon became part of the group of José Bonifácio who conspired for independence in the Apostolado lodge in Rio—a high officeholder in the administration, a councilor, and subsequently deputy, senator, and minister—confessed in a letter to a friend that he feared the heterogeneity of the population, composed largely of slaves. Carneiro de Campos was of the opinion that "they, together with free coloreds, were congenital enemies, and justifiably so, of the white man." If there were to be a revolution, blacks and mulattos, having the prospect of liberty, would join forces. The horrors of Saint Domingue, where the blacks had revolted and massacred the white population, would be repeated in

50 "A inconfidência da Bahia," *ABNRJ* 43–44 (1921):87; Augusto de Lima Júnior, *Pequena história da inconfidência* 1:64.

51 "Autos da devassa da inconfidência," *DHBNRJ* 107:181.

52 *DHBNRJ* 107:247.

Brazil.[53] Even in 1823, at the time of the uprisings in Pernambuco, such verses as this were being sung:

> Portuguese and White men
> are all destined to meet their doom,
> because only *pardos* and blacks
> will inhabit the country.[54]

Upper-class fears of a mass rebellion explain why the idea of achieving independence with the support of the prince was so attractive: the nation would be freed from the yoke of Portugal without having to resort to mass mobilization.

Facets of the Revolution

The absence of a real revolutionary class and the intention of movement leaders to continue the traditional system of production limited the revolution both in theory and practice. On the other hand, from the point of view of different social groups revolution took different and at times contradictory forms. For the slave it appeared to offer a promise of emancipation, a promise that slaveowners had no intention of making. For poor people in urban areas, most of whom were blacks and mulattos— those people who had united under the leadership of João de Deus in the Bahian conspiracy of 1798 and who later (in 1817) in Recife were fired with prospects of freedom—the goal was to abolish color barriers and achieve economic and social equality. But wealthy and influential whites had no intention of making important concessions to the poor or to the colored population.

In the cities the masses, made up of pharmacists, tailors, "barbers," soldiers, artisans, and small retailers, were easily fired by revolutionary ideas, but in the rural areas most people were not influenced by revolutionary principles and passively followed the lead of their local "chiefs." On the eve of independence the French naturalist Saint-Hilaire, who was passing through São Paulo, was surprised by the *Paulistas'* lack of interest in events taking place in Rio de Janeiro and in Portugal.[55] The populace remained indifferent to the ouster of the governor-general and his replacement by a governing junta. Saint-Hilaire commented that the only thing the *Paulistas* understood was "that they would be harmed by the re-establishment of the colonial system because if the Portuguese were

---

[53] *Documentos para história da independência,* Oficinas gráficas da Biblioteca Nacional, (Lisbon, 1923) 1:362.

[54] José Honório Rodrigues, *Conciliação e reforma no Brasil-um desafio histórico-cultural* (Rio de Janeiro, 1965), p. 38.

[55] A. Prouvensal de Saint-Hilaire, *Segunda viagem a São Paulo e quadro histórico da Província de São Paulo* (São Paulo, 1953), p. 100.

the sole purchasers of their sugar and coffee they [the *Paulistas*] would no longer be able to sell these commodities for the high prices they charge at present."

There was nothing to suggest that liberal or republican ideas had found adherents among the *Paulistas*. The people continued to show the customary respect for authority and still regarded the king as the supreme arbiter of their existence. Wherever he went, Saint-Hilaire found the rural population uninformed about and uninterested in important events occurring in Rio de Janeiro. In the opinion of people in the country the uprisings in January (*O Fico*) had been contrived by Europeans; revolts in the provinces were the work of a few rich and powerful families. The mass of the people seemed to ask, like the donkey in the story, "Won't I have to carry the packsaddle all my life?" Saint-Hilaire stated that Brazilians in general had no coherent political views and no knowledge of the governmental process. Conflicts between people in the various provinces were attributable not to differences in ideology but to intercity rivalries, family feuds, individual whims, or "such petty motives as these." [56] In fact, what seemed to be important in the backlands was the attitude of the local "chief" and not political ideas. The political ignorance of the backland population is illustrated in an event described by João Brígido, which took place in Ceará less than eighteen months before independence. Town councils were ordered to swear an oath of allegiance to the Portuguese constitution. The very word "constitution" provoked a wide variety of responses, reflecting the ignorance of the majority of the population. João Brígido described the reaction, in an area which had played an active part in the revolution of 1817, made in the name of liberalism and constitutionalism:

Some maintained that "constitution" was a new form of government and was damaging to the sovereign. Hence it was an impiety and an attack on religion, according to the affinities which they believed to exist between God and the king. Those who looked on any decree as a plot against the poor held the view that "constitution" was an attempt to curtail the freedom of the masses and alleged there was a scheme afoot to throw the poor into captivity. Others believed that "constitution" was a palpable entity and attributed to it a terrifying perversity.[57]

In Crato no oath of allegiance was taken to the constitution because the local political leader, Capitão-Mor José Pereira Filgueiras, refused to allow it. However, in the nearby township of Jardim, the vicar António

---

[56] *Ibid.*, pp. 103, 106.

[57] João Brígido, *Apontamentos para a história do Cariri*, pp. 80–81, cited by Maria Isaura Pereira de Queiroz, "O mandonismo local na vida política brasileira (da colônia à primeira república)," *Estudos de sociologia e história* (São Paulo, 1957), p. 216.

Manuel supported the constitution and the oath was taken without the slightest hesitation.

Most of the sugar mill owners supported the revolution of 1817 in Pernambuco not out of any liberal convictions but because they were dissatisfied with the administration. Liberal and nationalist ideas, as noted earlier, only had meaning for the enlightened minority. For most of the Brazilian upper class the concept of independence did not imply subversion of civil order. It merely meant freedom from the restrictions created by their subordination to Portugal.

The Idea of Independence

Texts published in 1822 show that the word "independence" was not always associated with the idea of total separation from Portugal. Often it merely meant administrative independence. With the exception of a radical minority, people nearest to Dom Pedro hoped for a dual monarchy till the very end. The idea of complete and irreversible independence only occurred to the elite at the last moment, as a direct response to decrees passed in the Portuguese Côrtes which aimed at recolonization.

Some months before independence a deputy from the province of Paraíba do Norte advocated the "just cause of political independence and the integrity and centralization of the kingdom of Brazil, preserving, however, the union with the fraternal kingdom of Portugal and the Algarves, and continued obedience and recognition of Dom João VI, our constitutional monarch, as supreme executive throughout the monarchy." The deputy spoke "in the name of the people" and explained his point of view as follows:

Through me as its legitimate representative, the people of Brazil unanimously endow your royal highness with the authority to govern and to grant their petitions without their having to resort to the Old World across thousands of leagues of ocean. The people want political representation which is the right of a free people; the people want to enjoy those privileges and perquisites which are inherent to a free people. The people are subjects of Dom João VI, constitutional king of the united kingdom of Portugal, Brazil, and the Algarves, to whose generosity the people of Brazil owe their independence.[58]

The deputy wanted the crowns to remain united, and a center of authority created in Brazil from whence would emanate concessions and favors. Finally, he expressed the hope that the Côrtes in Lisbon would not be so shortsighted and stubborn as to prefer the horrors of a fratricidal civil war to a "well-established union based on equality and reciprocal interests and benefits."

[58] ANRJ, codex 896. At this time José Bonifácio de Andrada e Silva was deputy for Paraíba.

The majority of those pressuring the prince to stay in Brazil hoped for a close alliance between the kingdoms of Portugal and Brazil based on "reciprocity and equality of rights and interests." [59] In his speech on the occasion of *O Fico*, Clemente Pereira stressed that it was enough to have in Brazil a unifying and centralized center of activity, a legislative body, and a branch of the executive with strong, liberal, and far-reaching authority. These should be organized to comprise a single legislative and a single executive authority, one Côrtes under one king. "May Portugal and Brazil," he said, "always be a single family, a single people, a single nation." He went on to recall similar European examples, citing in particular the case of Ireland and England. Clemente Pereira was convinced that this solution would neutralize those factions which were striving for total separation from Portugal.

The minutes of the municipal council in Rio de Janeiro for January 9, 1822 (*O Fico*), show that the meeting concluded with the council president cheering from the palace windows: "long live religion"; "long live the constitution"; "long live the Côrtes"; "long live the constitutional king"; "long live the constitutional prince"; "long live the union of Portugal and Brazil." He was joined by an immense crowd which had gathered below. Thus, at the very meeting at which a decision had been taken to disobey decrees of the Côrtes—ordering the return of Dom Pedro to Portugal and the subordination of the administrative juntas to the authority of the Côrtes—there were resounding cheers for the Côrtes and a publicly expressed intention of preserving the union of the two kingdoms.[60] The Portuguese foreign minister, Silvestre Pinheiro Ferreira, correctly assessed the situation. Informed of events in Brazil, he asserted in 1822 that the provinces only desired that "measures concerning the internal affairs be initiated, and be decided, within the respective province. They should be discussed, evaluated, and voted on by residents of the province elected by the people of that province." Thus the majority of the conservative faction sought administrative autonomy, not total independence.[61]

On May 23, 1822, less than four months before independence, the city council of Rio de Janeiro called for a general assembly of representatives from the provinces of Brazil to discuss the just conditions for the continued union of Brazil and Portugal. Furthermore, such an assembly was to study the applicability to Brazil of the constitution written in the

[59] Letter from Caetano Pinto Miranda Montenegro to the prince regent, *Documentos para história da independência* 1:374.

[60] "Termo de vereação," ANRJ, box 740, envelope 1 (pamphlet).

[61] "Informação verbal do Ministro dos Negócios Estrangeiros e atos das conferências de 15 de março da comissão das Côrtes sobre os negócios do Brasil," cited by Councilor Silvestre Pinheiro Ferreira in "Cartas sobre a revolução do Brasil," *RIHGB* 61 (1888): 369 et seq.

Côrtes Gerais of Lisbon. Finally, the assembly was to draw up a list of amendments which would be necessary if the constitution were to be adopted in Brazil. The motion of the council stated that the assembly would make every effort to maintain written contact with the Côrtes in Lisbon in order to preserve that union with Portugal which Brazil wished to maintain.[62] On June 17, at a session of the Portuguese Côrtes the commission charged with drawing up amendments to the constitution for Brazil suggested the creation in Brazil of a dual monarchy, two congresses, a regent, and tribunals. The minutes of the Council of State show that on the very eve of independence this was still the intention of the councilors, including José Bonifácio de Andrada e Silva, Gonçalves Lêdo, José Mariano de Azeredo Coutinho, Lucas José Obes, José de Oliveira Pinto Botelho Mosqueira, and Estevão de Resende. At a meeting on June 3 the Council drew up a memorandum asking Dom Pedro to convoke a general assembly of the representatives of the provinces of Brazil. The memorandum read:

In no way does Brazil wish to challenge Portuguese rights, but it strongly opposes any attempt by Portugal to challenge the rights of Brazil. . . . Brazil wants to have the same king as Portugal but does not wish to be governed by deputies in the Congress of Lisbon. . . . Brazil seeks independence but on the understanding that this should not weaken its ties to Portugal. This union should be of two great families, each governed by its own laws, but with common interests and common loyalty to the same king.[63]

Hopes that Portugal and Brazil could remain united, each as an administrative entity and with Brazil independent of the Côrtes, would have been tantamount to acceptance of its economic independence and the continuation of free trade, which had been instituted in 1808 merely as a "provisional measure." Such recognition would have been diametrically opposed to the intentions of the majority of Portuguese deputies in the Côrtes in Lisbon.

"Portuguese" vs. "Brazilian" Points of View

Until the arrival of the court in Brazil, Portugal had conducted the bulk of her international trade with Brazilian products. By virtue of the colonial pact Portugal was not only a consumer but the distributer for all Brazilian commodities overseas. Portuguese ships profited from maritime freight, the customs at Lisbon profited from dues on Brazilian imports, Portuguese agents profited from the resale of Brazilian commodities; furthermore, the Portuguese customs collected the duties on imports of

[62] *Documentos para história da independência* 1:378.
[63] MSS, ANRJ, box 295.

manufactured items for use in Portugal and Brazil. Customs duties comprised the largest single source of income to the Portuguese government. Income from Portuguese capital invested in Brazil afforded a further opportunity for taxation.[64]

The whole system collapsed with the opening of the ports in 1808 and the treaty of 1810, by which England obtained a preferential tariff of 15 percent, lower than that granted to Portugal, which paid 16 percent, and other countries, which paid 24 percent. This state of affairs was only remedied in 1816. Measures taken by Dom João to improve the lot of Portuguese producers and merchants failed to satisfy them. Their only desire was the re-establishment of privileges, the annulment of concessions made to foreigners, and the abolition of free trade—in other words, the recolonization of Brazil. This intention was manifestly apparent in 1820. The revolution of Oporto was to reveal the conflict of interests between Portugal and Brazil which culminated, in less than two years, in complete separation.

The Portuguese blamed the impending depression on royal policy. They regarded the liberal measures taken by Dom João as exclusively responsible for the crisis. They remained blind to the more deep-rooted cause, the weakness of the Portuguese economy and its traditional subordination to Great Britain, a problem which had been exacerbated by the development of British industry. Better conditions of production in England made it impossible for Portuguese products (with some few exceptions) to compete with English products at the internal or international level. The Portuguese merchant navy could not compete with that of Britian. Duties on British products failed to prevent their entering Portuguese and Brazilian markets, to the detriment of the Portuguese economy.

This situation was well exemplified by the market in grains. The government imposed a tax of 80 réis per *alqueire* on foreign grain imports. However, this measure failed to eliminate them from the market. Each *alqueire* produced by Portuguese farmers could not be sold for less than 500 to 600 réis without loss; an *alqueire* of imported grain, despite duties, was selling for 400 réis and sometimes less. Given this situation, the decline of Portuguese agriculture was inevitable. The few existing factories in Portugal found it impossible to compete with British factories: silk factories in Chacim and cotton factories in Tomar were in a pitiable state; cloth factories in Pôrto Alegre had to close; factories in Redondo, Covilhã, Leiria, and elsewhere pleaded for government aid. Commerce was upset by this situation.[65]

[64] Simonsen, *História econômica*, pp. 389, 390.

[65] José António de Miranda, *Memória constitucional e política sôbre o estado presente de Portugal e do Brasil, dirigida a El Rey Senhor D. João VI e oferecida a Sua Alteza o Príncipe Real do Reino Unido de Portugal, Brasil e Algarve e Regente do Brasil* (Rio de Janeiro, 1821).

Abolition of free trade, abrogation of the treaty of 1810, and a return of Brazil to its former status as a colony were basic steps advocated by the Portuguese, who saw all their economic ills as resulting from the disruption of the colonial pact. Portuguese attempts in this direction were opposed not only by Brazilians but also by foreigners settled in Brazil, who sided with the Brazilians in their struggle for independence. The Portuguese viewpoint is well illustrated by publications which began to appear in the months immediately following the revolution of Oporto, when a major topic for discussion was the issue of Dom João's return to Portugal. The author of a pamphlet entitled *A Critical and Analytical Examination of the Solution to the Question: In the Present Circumstances Should the King and the Royal Family of the House of Braganza Return to Portugal or Stay in Brazil?* sought to refute the opinion that in view of Portugal's economic dependence on Brazil, it was advisable that Dom João should remain in Brazil, the economic center of the Portuguese empire, if he did not wish to lose it.[66] The author alleged that if the Brazilians broke with Portugal Brazilian trade would fall under foreign control and the Brazilian people would be no better than slaves. In the author's opinion it was preferable for both countries that they continue to be united in a single kingdom.[67] In another pamphlet published in 1822 the author tried to show the advantages of preserving the empire, albeit with considerable autonomy for Brazil in administrative matters. He even suggested the possibility that the Portuguese court might establish itself permanently in Brazil. In such an eventuality a regency would be created for Portugal. The author believed that freedom of trade had proved so harmful that it should be abolished.[68]

In Brazil the colonists saw the benefits to be derived from freedom of trade and totally opposed such opinions. They could accept union with Portugal so long as those privileges they had gained continued to be respected. They believed that Brazil should lead Portugal "as a grateful son leads his decrepit father by the hand," in the words of a publication which appeared in 1822 dedicated to Dom Pedro.[69] After showing the

[66] "Le Roi et la famille royale de Bragance doivent-ils, dans les circonstances présentes, retourner en Portugal, ou bien rester au Brésil?" *Documentos para história da independência* 1:201 et seq.

[67] *Exame analítico-crítico da solução da questão: O rei e a família real de Bragança devem, nas circunstâncias presentes, voltar a Portugal ou ficar no Brasil?, ibid.,* p. 208 et seq.

[68] José Vicente Gomes de Moura, *Reflexões sôbre a necessidade de promover a união dos estados de que consta o reino unido de Portugal, Brasil e Algarve nas quatro partes do mundo* (Lisbon, 1822). Francisco Sierra y Mariscal was fired by the same spirit in his criticism of freedom of trade and the treaty of 1810 in "Idéias gerais sobre a revolução do Brasil e suas consequências," *ABNRJ* 43–45 (1931).

[69] *Memória sôbre as principais causas por que deve o Brasil reassumir os seus direitos e reunir as suas províncias oferecida ao príncipe real por R. J. G.* (Rio de Janeiro, 1822).

conflict between Portugal's need to recolonize Brazil and Brazil's need for independence, the author proposed the establishment of a constitutional government which would be headed by Dom Pedro. The "fraternal relationship" with Portugal would be preserved. The idea of being led like a "decrepit father" could not have been pleasing to the Portuguese.

The Policy of the Côrtes and the Rupture of the Colonial Pact

Debates in the Côrtes between Brazilian and Portuguese deputies were soon to show the impossibility of any conciliation. Those in Portugal and Brazil who dreamed of a dual monarchy soon recognized its impracticality. Positions began to polarize: in Portugal the more reactionary wing assumed control and took drastic steps, including the issuance of a decree ordering the return of the prince to Portugal; in Brazil even the more conservative factions looked on total independence as the only possible solution. The regent, who had resolved at the outset to obey the decisions of the Côrtes, found himself compelled by the developing situation to break with the Côrtes and proclaim the independence of Brazil.

In Brazil the majority of those citizens with the slightest political consciousness opposed the recolonizing aspirations of the Portuguese Côrtes, with the exception of some of the Portuguese troops, civil servants loyal to the crown, and Portuguese businessmen who identified their interests with the policy of the Côrtes. Foreign merchants, especially British merchants, whose interests were supported by their government, sided with the Brazilians. In view of the importance of Brazil to English trade, this was perfectly understandable. Figures for 1812 show that exports to Brazil made up four-fifths of all English exports to Latin America.[70] On the occasion of Brazilian independence the English government made clear to Portugal that Great Britain was more interested in preserving the benefits derived from trade with Brazil than in maintaining good relations with the Portuguese court.[71] When the count of Vila Real was sent by the Portuguese government to England to discuss the issue of Brazilian independence, Canning made it clear that any attempts on the part of European powers at collective intervention in the Americas "would be enough to induce His Majesty's Government immediately to recognize the independence of the aforesaid colonies"! [72]

With the return of Dom João to Portugal recolonization appeared

[70] Olga Pantaleão, "A presença inglesa," História geral da civilização brasileira 2 (1):92. On the role played by foreigners in Brazilian independence, see Carlos Guilherme Mota, "Europeus no Brasil na época da independência. Um estudo," Anais do Museu Paulista 19 (1965):11-27.

[71] Documentos para história da independência 1:86 et seq.

[72] Ibid., p. 141. Cf. the commentaries made by José da Silva Lisboa, História dos principais sucessos políticos do Império do Brasil, 4 vols. (Rio de Janeiro, 1830), p. 154.

imminent. Those Brazilians who, on receiving news of the constitutionalist revolution in Oporto, enthusiastically supported the idea of the convocation of the Côrtes, took the oath to the constitution, and elected their
representatives could appreciate, by the end of 1821, the extent of the
differences separating Brazil from Portugal. The series of measures taken
by the Côrtes after July 1821 showed a change in economic and administrative policy toward Brazil and revealed the true intentions of the Côrtes.
Some measures attempted to annul privileges conceded to English merchants by the treaty of 1810 as well as later decrees. The decree of July 16,
1821, was phrased as follows:

In view of the very serious harm to the national budget and national industry
caused by the Resolution of May 5, 1814, by which import dues on British
woolen cloth were reduced to 15 percent, which contravened the memorandum
of the Treasury Council of September 28, 1813, and article 26 of the commercial
agreement of February 1, 1810, the Portuguese Côrtes do hereby revoke the
resolution of 1814 and rule that henceforth woolen cloth and other woolen
products from Great Britain which are imported into the kingdom of Portugal
shall pay dues of 30 percent as has been the practice in the past.[73]

The Côrtes considered that conditions stipulated in the decree of
February 4, 1811, were harmful to the national commerce. Whereas this
decree made it difficult for Portuguese to trade with Asia, it facilitated the
importation of articles of European manufacture into the Portuguese and
Brazilian ports by virtue of the treaty of 1810. On December 28, 1821, the
Côrtes modified the law and gave greater advantages to Portuguese
commerce. These measures heralded a complete reversal of Portuguese
governmental policy towards foreign merchants, who could not fail to be
displeased by the new legislation, nor were such measures better received
by the Brazilians. However, the decisions which were to provoke the
greatest reaction in Brazil were those concerning administrative autonomy. On April 24, 1821, the Côrtes declared that provincial government in Brazil would henceforth be independent of Rio de Janeiro and
directly subordinate to the Côrtes in Lisbon. On September 29, 1821, even
before the arrival of Brazilian deputies in Lisbon, the Côrtes debated
matters of great importance to Brazil. Decisions were taken to transfer to
Lisbon the judge presiding over the Court of Appeals, the Tribunal of
Conscience and Orders (Mesa de Consciência e Ordens), the Treasury
Council, the Commercial Junta, the Court of Appeals itself, and several
other governmental organs established by Dom João in Brazil. Subsequently, decrees of September 29 and of October 1 and 18 ordered the
return of the prince regent to Portugal and appointed a military governor
for each province who would be a delegate of the executive branch and

73 *Coleção de leis do Brasil de 1821*, pt. 1 (Rio de Janeiro, 1889), pp. 28–29.

would be independent of the juntas. Furthermore, the Côrtes sent new troops to Rio de Janeiro and Pernambuco.

These decrees were tantamount to a declaration of war and provoked disturbances and displays of displeasure. It had become evident that the Côrtes intended to reduce Brazil to colonial status again. It was also evident that the Brazilian deputies were in such a minority (out of 205, 75 were Brazilian representatives, and only 50 of these actually were in attendance) that they could do little or nothing in Lisbon, where Brazilian claims were received with hoots of derision. As the decisions of the Portuguese Côrtes with regard to Brazil left less and less room for doubt about its true intentions, an increasing number of people supported the movement for Brazilian independence. As early as October 1821 verses were posted on street corners in Rio de Janeiro suggesting to the prince that it was better to be Dom Pedro I now in Brazil than to wait to be Dom Pedro IV later in Portugal. The proclamations announced that separation from Portugal was inevitable and accused the Côrtes of attempting to reduce the country to the position of a colony by its recent measures.[74] In a letter of December 18, 1821, the prince told his father that the publication of the decrees had so profoundly shocked Brazilians and foreigners living in Brazil that people were openly commenting on the streets, "If to have a Constitution can bring us nothing but trouble, then to hell with it. We shall have to take steps to stop the prince from leaving, even if we have to assume responsibility for the loss of Brazil by Portugal." It was rumored that if Dom Pedro were not to remain in Brazil, independence would be gained, no matter how, with the help of "English Europeans" and "English Americans."[75] From then on protests grew in strength and in number. The provincial junta of São Paulo addressed a "representation" to the prince criticizing the decisions of the Côrtes and charging that the intention of having "the enormous kingdom of Brazil without an administrative center and without a representative of executive authority" was founded on profound ignorance, insanity, or foolhardiness. The Côrtes was denounced for attempting to enslave Brazil and reduce it to the position of a colony.[76]

Printed circulars began to appear urging Dom Pedro to stay in Brazil. One of them, entitled *Manifesto by the People of Rio de Janeiro on the Residence of H. R. H. in Brazil*, was directed to the city council of Rio de Janeiro in December 1821. It asked that the prince's attention be drawn to the absolute necessity of revoking decrees 124 and 125 issued by the Côrtes. On January 2, 1822, another printed document of the same

[74] *Documentos para história da independência* 1:361.

[75] *Coleção de correspondência oficial das províncias do Brasil durante a legislatura das Côrtes constituintes* (Lisbon, 1822).

[76] *Ibid.*

tenor appeared, signed by the same group of businessmen and bureaucrats from Rio de Janeiro. Still another document told the populace where they could sign the "representation" which was to be sent by the city council to Dom Pedro requesting him to stay in Brazil.[77] Such attempts were intended to activate the masses and give rear-guard support to the prince. One petition by the city council of Rio de Janeiro stated that the ship taking Dom Pedro back to Portugal would anchor in the Tagus with the flag of an independent Brazil at its masthead.[78] Clemente Pereira said that the departure of the prince would be the "fatal" decree sanctioning independence. He referred to republican disturbances in some provinces, recalled that a republican party had been in existence since 1817, and insinuated that a foreign power would protect republican interests. Finally, he remarked, that if some provinces had initially resisted orders from the government in Rio de Janeiro and had preferred to remain subordinate to Lisbon, all had now changed, and these provinces not merely accepted but supported the government of Dom Pedro "as the only possible means of salvation against factions working for independence." [79]

On January 9, 1822, Dom Pedro bowed to these demands and resolved to disobey orders from Lisbon and remain in Brazil. On February 16 a decree convoked a Council of Procurators-General of the Provinces of Brazil. Its purpose was to advise the prince and to assess the degree to which laws approved by the Côrtes were applicable to the situation in Brazil, "where unfortunately all too often it has been assumed that legislation which is suited to Portugal is equally appropriate for Brazil." A further purpose in creating the Council of Procurators was to promote, insofar as executive authority would allow, reforms and improvements which were essential to the country's future prosperity and development.[80]

A resolution of February 17, 1822, forbade the landing in Brazil of troops from Portugal. Shortly afterwards, Dom Pedro ordered the return of all Portuguese troops to Portugal despite their protests and the threatening attitude of General Avilez, commanding officer of the Portuguese forces in Rio de Janeiro. In May 1822 Dom Pedro ruled that no decree originating from the Côrtes should be enforced in Brazil without his approval. The naval squadron which had orders to escort the prince to Lisbon was forbidden to enter the harbor of Rio de Janeiro until its commander agreed to obey orders from Dom Pedro. Less than three

---

[77] ANRJ, box 740, envelope 1, "Independência do Brasil" (pamphlets), "Aconteci-mentos precursores, 1820–1822."

[78] Coleção de correspondência oficial.

[79] "Termo de vereação do Senado da Câmara do Rio de Janeiro no dia 9/1/1822," ANRJ, box 740.

[80] The justification for calling the Council of Procurators is given in the resolution of May 27, 1822, published in Coleção das decisões do govêrno do Império do Brasil de 1822, pt. 1 (Rio de Janeiro, 1887), p. 39.

weeks later, after taking on supplies, the squadron returned to Portugal, leaving behind in Brazil some six hundred men loyal to the regent's cause. On May 13, 1822, the city council of Rio de Janeiro asked the prince to assume the title of "Perpetual Defender of Brazil." On June 2 the Council of Procurators was installed. Its intention was to convoke a Brazilian constitutional assembly. On June 3 the procurators-general of the province of Rio de Janeiro and the procurator-general of the state of Cisplatina informed the prince that it was highly desirable to convoke a general assembly of representatives from all the provinces of Brazil. Joaquim Gonçalves Lêdo, José Mariano de Azeredo Coutinho, and Lucas José Obes were cosignatories of this petition.[81] The prince issued a decree convoking a "Luso-Brazilian" assembly with the objective of establishing guidelines for independence as well as for "Brazil's union with other parts of the great Portuguese family." As yet there had been no mention of irrevocable and total independence.

A representation sent by the city council of Rio de Janeiro to Dom Pedro in the name of the people was bolder and more threatening.[82] It stated that independence "is as integral a part of the process of colonization as the separation of families is of humanity." It argued that in nature no satellite was larger than the planets. Finally, anticipating the Monroe doctrine, it stated that America should belong to America and Europe to Europe. It was no accident that the "Great Architect of the Universe" had separated them by an ocean. No longer could Brazil be subject to a small and distant nation incapable of coming to its defense, let alone of conquering it. Another representation by the city council of Rio de Janeiro on May 23, 1822, protested against the policy of the Portuguese Côrtes. It referred to the "devastating project of once again making Lisbon the emporium and exclusive outlet for Brazilian commerce. This would ruin Brazilian agriculture and prevent the establishment of factories in Brazil. Such a policy would constitute a violent attack on the property of our farmers and infringe their inalienable right to sell their products in the best available market." Equally violent was the representation made by Vila Real da Praia Grande on May 26, 1822 which referred to the "absurd, unjustified, illegal and Machiavellian conduct of certain members of the Côrtes whose sole object was to reduce Brazil to slavery." [83]

Thus, while they stated their intent to keep Brazil united to Portugal, such representations stressed the differences which made the two countries totally incompatible. For some the word "independence" continued to mean no more than relative political and administrative autonomy and continued union with Portugal; for others it meant final separation.

---

[81] "Atas do Conselho de Estado, 1822–1823," ANRJ, box 295.
[82] *Coleção de correspondência oficial*, p. 25.
[83] *Documentos para história da independência* 1:378–81, 383, et seq.

Differences between radical and conservative factions were equally apparent on other issues. During the discussions before the convocation of the Constitutional Assembly, José Bonifácio presented to the Council of State a proposal for indirect election. Gonçalves Lêdo opposed it on the grounds that "he who governs with the support of the people governs with strength" and stated that the wish of the people was for direct elections. He said, "the will of the majority must be the law of all. If the majority wants direct elections, they must be sanctioned by law. Only then can it be said that the people elected their representatives. Otherwise, the representatives are merely the organs of a select minority." Gonçalves Lêdo posed the question: "what justification can we give, what right can we invoke, to justify depriving individuals of the privilege of nominating their own representatives?" The democratic tone of his arguments did not please the majority of the councilors, who favored indirect election. Their attitude was in keeping with their distrust of the masses and their desire to ensure that the people played no part in government. In the session of June 16, Gonçalves Lêdo defended the principle of freedom of the press. Shortly afterwards he was to pay dearly for his ideas, which were too radical for the conservative majority around the prince. They demanded that he be imprisoned or banished.[84] In his instructions to the legislative assembly on electoral procedure Caetano Pinto de Miranda Montenegro justified the adoption of the system of indirect election with the argument that "in a country with a homogeneous population where qualities and virtues are distributed over a broad spectrum of society, direct elections are preferable." Since this was not the case in Brazil, he considered indirect elections more appropriate.[85]

A decision of June 19 gave the ballot to any citizen, married or single, over twenty years of age who was not living at home (with his parents). Excluded were those whose income came from any type of wage, with the exception of clerks in commercial firms, retainers of the royal household not of white-chevron status, and administrators of rural plantations and factories. The vote was also withheld from members of religious orders, non-naturalized foreigners, and criminals.[86] Such measures deprived the masses of the right to vote and choose their own representatives. Access to positions of authority was reserved for a minority. Even more demanding than the qualifications for voters were those required of potential electors. In addition to fulfilling the requirements for voters, electors had to have a record of integrity and honesty and possess substantial financial resources derived from employment, industry, or property. Despite the

[84] ANRJ, box 295.
[85] Caetano Pinto de Miranda Montenegro, "Instruções para eleição," *Documentos para história da independência* 1:387.
[86] *Coleção de leis e decisões,* June 19, 1822.

stringency of these requirements, they were more democratic than those stipulated later by the constitutional charter of 1824, which required that voters, electors, and deputies should all furnish evidence of high income.

Although union with Portugal was affirmed in the convocation of the Constitutional Assembly, the movement for separation gathered momentum. Dom Pedro, in a ruling of September 5, two days before the official proclamation of independence, informed the provisional government of the province of the Maranhão—which had persistently refused to execute his orders on the grounds that they were at odds with those received from the Côrtes—that "because of the attempt by the aforesaid Côrtes to reduce this kingdom of Brazil to slavery, and to relegate it once again to the pitiable status of a colony, the people of Brazil had proclaimed independence and had nominated the prince as the Perpetual Defender of their inalienable rights and prerogatives." [87]

Following the convocation of the assembly, several acts were passed which would further independence. After June 21, 1822, confirmation of any appointment in public service was to be withheld unless the nominee swore to support the union and independence of Brazil. A ruling of August 5 recommended that provincial goverments should not employ people from Portugal. On August 1 the prince decreed that soldiers from Portugal should henceforth be regarded as enemies.

Gonçalves Lêdo's manifesto of August 1, addressed to the "peoples of Brazil," and the manifesto of August 6, drawn up by José Bonifácio and addressed to those nations friendly to Brazil, were in effect true declarations of independence. The first was accompanied by a decree containing "a virtual declaration of war with Portugal," though it asserted that the Constitutional Assembly would recognize Dom João VI as sovereign. The document then urged people to unite and support the emancipation of Brazil. José Bonifácio's manifesto proclaimed the "political independence of Brazil, but as a brother kingdom with Portugal," and the continuance of a "fit and proper union with Portugal." [88]

News of events in Rio de Janeiro provoked outrage in Portugal. Contradictory and groundless rumors began to circulate. One such alleged that the blacks had revolted against the whites, had assumed power, and were committing atrocities against the Europeans. Another maintained that the English and Austrian cabinets were behind the insubordinate conduct of the prince.[89] In the Côrtes antagonism between Portuguese and Brazilians increased. There was a flurry of spirited debate. The Côrtes took measures against the convocation of the Constitutional Assembly and

---

[87] *Ibid.*, September 5, 1822.
[88] Pedro Octávio Carneiro da Cunha, "A fundação de um império liberal," *História geral da civilização brasileira* 2 (1); Manoel de Oliveira Lima, *O movimento.*
[89] *Documentos para história da inconfidência* 1:59, 60, 64.

urged Dom Pedro to return immediately to Portugal. On September 2, 1822, while he was traveling to São Paulo to quiet the insurgent populace, a meeting of the Council of State was held in Rio, presided over by Princess Leopoldina. The councilors were informed of the most recent news from Portugal: the Côrtes intended to send troops to Brazil and had adopted an attitude which the council considered insulting to Dom Pedro. The council immediately retaliated by placing an embargo on the capital holdings of the Douro Wine Company (Companhia dos Vinhos do Douro) and voted to take whatever steps were necessary for the security and defense of Brazil.[90] Dom Pedro had only two options: to obey the Côrtes and return to Portugal in disgrace or to break with the Côrtes and proclaim Brazilian independence. On being informed of the news from Portugal, he proclaimed the independence of Brazil on September 7, 1822, in São Paulo.

As it became apparent that separation from Portugal was inevitable, the differences between the radicals under the leadership of Gonçalves Lêdo and the conservatives under José Bonifácio became more clear-cut. José Bonifácio, in charge of the Ministry of the Empire, ordered that *"comuneros,"* *"radicals,"* and *"carbonarios"* be placed under strict observation. Numerous arrests resulted. To oppose the radical group José Bonifácio established the Apostolado, a secret society, into which Dom Pedro was to be initiated on June 2, 1822, as "Arconte Rei." In the Great Orient (reorganized in May or June depending on sources consulted) José Bonifácio held the office of Grand Master but Gonçalves Lêdo, Januário da Cunha Barbosa, and Alves Branco had the whip hand. On September 14, 1822, Dom Pedro, who had been initiated in July as a Freemason with the name of Guatemozin, was made Grand Master of the Great Orient (*Grande Oriente*). Thus Freemasonry, whose traditional role in Europe had been to work for the overthrow of monarchies and to oppose the institution of royalty, in Brazil was to have the prince himself as Grand Master.

Despite his support for Freemasonry, Dom Pedro, at the request of José Bonifácio, did not hesitate to order the temporary interruption of the activities of the Great Orient. This conservative victory was a sign of the times. People considered to be radicals or republicans were arrested and expelled from Brazil. Victory went to the Apostolado, which Friar Caneca, a revolutionary in 1817 who in 1824 participated in the Confederation of Ecuador, described as a "club of servile aristocrats." [91]

The statutes of the Apostolado reveal the orientation of the society. Its members swore to "work for the integrity, independence, and happiness of Brazil as a constitutional empire and to oppose despotism

---

[90] ANRJ, box 295.
[91] "Cartas de Pitias a Damião," cited by Carlos Rizzini, *O livro*, p. 297.

which might modify it and anarchy which might destroy it." [92] The prime wish of its members, who represented the social elite of the time, was to achieve independence with the minimum possible disruption to the economy or society of Brazil. The Apostolado counted among its members people of considerable importance and prominence in Brazil. Comprising a Brazilian "nobility," they occupied major posts in the administration and in government. Some later received titles in recognition of their services to the independence movement: Manuel Jacinto Nogueira da Gama (later marquis of Baependi), Estevão de Resende (later marquis of Valença), Joaquim José Pereira de Faro (later baron of Rio Bonito), José Egídio Álvares de Almeida (a former baron in Portugal, later to be baron, viscount, and marquis of Santo Amaro), Joaquim Carneiro de Campos (made viscount and marquis of Caravelas), and Clemente Ferreira França (made viscount and marquis of Nazareth in 1824 and 1826, respectively) were among its members. Also to distinguish themselves were the future barons of São João Marcos, São Gonçalo, Itapocara, Jacutinga, and Pindamonhangaba, the viscount of Macaé, the count of Rio Pardo, and the marquises of Taubaté, Cantagalo, Quixeramobin, and Jacarepagua.[93] Not all were Brazilian by birth but all felt themselves to be Brazilians. Some had been connected with the court of Dom João VI. Most of them were over fifty years old. They were plantation owners, senior civil servants, or respected merchants and were related to each other by family connections. Many had studied in Portugal at Coimbra. After independence they constituted a true oligarchy, holding posts in the ministries, the Council of State, the Chamber of Deputies, and the Senate, and serving as presidents in the different provinces. They retained positions of leadership in Brazil until the 1850s. They were pledged to the preservation of law and order and the avoidance of anarchy and " excesses by the people." Under the leadership of José Bonifácio they easily dominated the "radical" groups led by Gonçalves Lêdo and Januário da Cunha Barbosa, who lacked popular support.[94]

The consolidation of independence demanded a tremendous effort on the part of the government in Rio de Janeiro. News of independence was ill-received by Portuguese troops and merchants. In Bahia, the

---

[92] Henri Raffard, "Apontamentos acêrca de pessoas e coisas do Brasil," *RIHGB* 41, pt. 2, p. 96, cited in *ibid.,* p. 289.

[93] *Ibid.,* p. 298.

[94] Barão de Vasconcelos e Barão Smith de Vasconcelos, *Arquivo nobiliárquico* (Lausanne, 1868). For biographical details on Manuel Jacinto Nogueira da Gama (later marquis of Baependi), Estevão de Resende (created marquis in 1845), the family of Joaquim José Pereira de Faro, Belarmino Ricardo de Siqueira (created baron de São Gonçalo in 1849), José Egídio Álvares de Almeida (later marquis of Santo Amaro), Maciel da Costa, and Joaquim Carneiro de Campos (marquis of Caravelas), see Emília Viotti da Costa, "Introdução ao estudo da emancipação política do Brasil," in *Brasil em perspectiva* (São Paulo, 1968) (preface by João Cruz Costa), pp. 132–35.

Maranhão, and Pará governmental juntas controlled by Portuguese majorities—who were more interested in maintaining ties with Portugal than in placing themselves under a government in Rio de Janeiro— resisted and were only overcome after more than a year of struggle. The government in Rio de Janeiro won out by contracting the services of British and French officers and ships. Men such as Grenfell, Cochrane, and Labatut worked for the government, which could count on the support of the British crown and independent governments elsewhere in the Americas. Nevertheless, formal British recognition of Brazilian independence was only gained after lengthy negotiations between Portugal and Brazil. Portuguese acquiescence to the independence of Brazil was only obtained after Brazil agreed to assume a debt of two million pounds sterling, part of a loan Portugal had obtained in London. Having gained her independence from Portugal, Brazil fell under the tutelage of Great Britain.

The absence of a truly revolutionary class, antagonisms separating the people from the revolutionary leaders, and the fact that the independence movement was led by the upper class associated with agriculture, business interests, and governmental bureaucracy—all these factors ensured the survival of the colonial structure of production. The political organization of the country was to reflect the interests of the social groups who dominated the movement. Their prime concern was the preservation of a system of production based on slave labor and oriented toward the export of tropical commodities for the European market. Their major objectives were to organize the state without jeopardizing their own social and economic power. To achieve their aims they chose a constitutional monarchy. Representatives to the Constitutional Assembly intended to give the emperor only the right of temporary veto over parliamentary decisions. However, the emperor refused to countenance this restriction on his authority. In the Carta issued by him after the dissolution of the Constitutional Assembly he attempted to secure more extensive powers for himself. The oligarchy controlled the government through the Chamber, the Senate, and the Council of State. Senators and councilors were appointed for life by the emperor.

The constitution of 1824 attempted to guarantee considerable freedom for the individual (article 179) and to assure economic freedom and initiative. It protected the right of property in all its aspects. It accepted the principle of free elementary education for all. Nevertheless, it denied political rights to workers and domestic servants (except head clerks of merchant companies, senior members of the imperial household, and administrators of rural plantations and factories) and to anybody whose annual net income was less than the equivalent of 100 milréis and derived from property, industry, or employment. This effectively excluded most of the population of Brazil. Popular representation was further restricted by the system of indirect elections and by creating two levels of eligibility based on increasing income. Only candidates who were Catholics (in flagrant disregard of the principle of religious liberty laid down in article 179) and who had an annual net income of at least 400 milréis for representatives and 800 milréis for senators could be elected.

Article 179 guaranteeing the freedom of the individual was inspired by the Declaration of the Rights of Man issued by the French revolutionaries in August 1789—some paragraphs of the article were direct translations from the French—but the following passages were omitted in the Brazilian version: the affirmation of the sovereignty of the nation (no body or individual can exert authority not derived from the nation); the definition of law as an expression of the will of the people, and the declaration of the right of the people to resist oppression. Such omissions are understandable when one remembers that the intention was to organize a constitutional monarchy without popular representation and to keep more than one third of the population of Brazil in bondage. Furthermore, the constitution had been granted by the king to the nation after the Constitutional Assembly had been dissolved.

With these exceptions, article 179 followed the general lines of the Declaration of the Rights of Man. It stated that no citizen could be forced to do or not to do anything except as required by law. It established the equality of all before the law, and confirmed the universal right to be appointed to civilian, political, or military positions "with no other criteria than talent." It guaranteed the right of property and provided that if after due process of law it was established that the public good demanded "the use and employ of the property of a citizen" he would receive prior compensation. It also abolished privileged courts and special tribunals for civil or criminal offenses. It guaranteed the principle of freedom of thought and expression except where abuse of this principle might result in infractions of the law. It established freedom of religion provided that the state religion, Catholicism, was respected.

The constitution established measures to protect the individual and to guarantee the inviolability of the home. It endorsed the principle that nobody could be arrested without being charged except in those instances governed by law, provided that the person had been previously notified by the relevant authorities. Similarly, nobody could be sentenced except by the relevant authority and in accordance with terms of the law. Tortures were abolished. The constitution supported the autonomy of authority of the judiciary. It guaranteed freedom of initiative. No type of work, industry, or commerce could be forbidden if it did not offend public morality nor harm the health and security of the citizenry. Guilds of artisans were abolished. Nobody could be exempted from contributing to the expenses of the state according to his financial means. Furthermore, the constitution established the principle that employees of the state should be responsible for their abuses or omissions.[95]

The legislators were not disturbed by the flagrant contradiction between such legal statutes and the reality of life in Brazil. Having drafted the constitution in accord with the precepts of liberalism, they then declaimed it in sonorous but empty rhetoric in the Chamber and the Senate. For these men, brought up in the European tradition and drawn from the upper classes, the constitutional guarantees of property, freedom, and security were real. They were not concerned with the fact that for the majority of the population of Brazil such constitutional precepts were not applied. Freedom and equality for all were guaranteed, but the majority of the population remained enslaved. Right of ownership was guaranteed, but, according to Tollenare's calculations, nineteen out of every twenty people, if they were not actually slaves, were tenants living on land they did not own and were liable to be evicted at any time. Individual safety was guaranteed, but murderers acted with impunity. Freedom of thought and expression were guaranteed, but David Pamplona and Libero Badaro were not alone in paying dearly for placing their faith in such a guarantee. The autonomy of the judiciary was guaranteed by law, but in fact the judiciary was an instrument in the hands of the big landowners. Torture was abolished, but the slave master was the supreme judge, and his decisions governed the life and death of his men. In the slave quarters, the stocks, manacles, whips, and fetters continued to be used. The intellectual elite was the mouthpiece of the ruling classes and created an ideology which hid the contradictions inherent in the system and ignored the gap between the letter of the law and reality.

The political emancipation of Brazil could not overcome the limitations inherent in the manner in which it had been achieved. Independence had been accomplished by those classes of Brazilian society whose interest was the preservation of the status quo and whose sole objective had been to destroy the colonial system insofar it restricted commercial opportunities and administrative autonomy. The economic structure was to be preserved, as was the institution of slavery and the traditional forms of social stratification. Brazil as an independent nation would continue to be subordinate to a colonial economy and would pass from control by Portugal to control by Great Britain. The facade of liberalism raised by the Europeanized elite disguised the misery and servitude of the majority of people living in Brazil. To achieve the complete emancipation of Brazil, to give meaning to the principles of the constitution—these were tasks relegated to future generations.

---

[95] António Manuel Fernandes Júnior, *Índice cronológico explicativo-remissivo da legislação brasileira* (Niterói, 1819).

MARIA ODILA SILVA DIAS

The Establishment of the Royal Court in Brazil

Before attempting to make a short appraisal of the present state of Brazilian historiography on the theme of "independence," it is essential to recall and emphasize certain landmarks already established by Brazilian historians—certain features unique to the Brazilian historical process in the first half of the nineteenth century. The principal such feature is historical continuity in the process of transition from colony to empire. Next, it must be emphasized that the mere fact of "independence," i.e., the political separation from Portugal in 1822, did not coincide with the phenomenon of consolidation of national unity (1840–50), nor was it characterized by a movement either truly nationalist or revolutionary.[1] The historian is faced with the problem of disentwining the study of the formative process of Brazilian nationality in the first decades of the nineteenth century from the traditional image of the colony struggling against the mother country. At the present stage of historical studies, there can be no doubt that such an approach would not only be wise but profitable, disclosing new fields of research.[2] In no way would it imply excluding the Brazilian process from the broader context of historical parallels with other colonial societies in search of their own identity.

The basic landmarks of current historiography of the political emancipation of Brazil were stated by the Brazilian historian Caio

This chapter was translated by the editor and revised by the author from "A Interiorização da metrópole," in *1822: Dimensões*, Coleção Debates (São Paulo: Editora Perspectiva).

[1] Tobias Monteiro, *História do império. A elaboração da independência* (Rio de Janeiro, 1927), pp. 403–5, 846–47.

[2] Caio Prado Júnior attempted to show that the independence of Brazil per se was not a topic worthy of the historian's attention and was rather "the outcome of a

Prado Júnior in his *The Formation of Contemporary Brazil,* published in 1942. Caio Prado studies the commercial object of Portuguese colonization, its organization for productive and fiscal purposes alone, the geographical factors of dispersion and fragmentation of authority, and the resulting absence of moral nexus which characterized Brazilian society at the end of the eighteenth century and the beginning of the nineteenth. He describes the contradictions and internal social conflicts which made it impossible for autonomous forces to be generated capable of creating a national conscience and a revolutionary situation suitable for the reorganization and consolidation of society into a nation.[3] The same author, in the short essay entitled "Tamoio and the Policy of the Andrades in the Independence of Brazil," analyzes the serious and deeprooted social tensions which came to the surface when the liberal revolution in Oporto stimulated the spread in Brazil of aspirations to constitutional liberalism, provoked disorders and a widespread feeling of social insecurity, and gave rise to an immediate conservative reaction, the principal characteristic of events then taking place in Brazil.[4] For men of constitutionalist ideals, continued union with Portugal was essential because the dual monarchy represented the ties which bound them to European civilization, the very source of their cosmopolitan values of renovation and progress. Separation, provoked by the revolutionary Côrtes of Lisbon, possessed at the outset the reactionary connotation of counterrevolution and the stamp of the absolutist faction.[5]

Continuity in transition from colony to empire in the planning of institutions and in the economic and social structure has also been studied by Sérgio Buarque de Holanda in his essay "The Colonial Legacy—Its Disintegration," an analysis of the interaction and compromises with the colonial structure in the formation of empire in Brazil.[6] Guidelines indicated by Caio Prado have been elaborated by Emília Viotti da Costa in her "Introduction to the Study of the Political Emancipation of Brazil," where there is also an analysis of the contradictions existing in the liberal policies of Dom João. Viotti da Costa describes the pressures exerted by Portuguese traders whose interests had been endangered by the opening of the ports and by English competition,

---

chance combination of forces, none in itself and on its own tending inevitably to such an end." *The Colonial Background of Modern Brazil,* trans. Suzette Macedo (Berkeley, 1967), p. 416.

[3] Caio Prado, *The Colonial Background,* pp. 144–47.

[4] Caio Prado Júnior, *Evolução política do Brasil e outros estudos* (São Paulo, 1963), pp. 187–97.

[5] Tobias Monteiro, *História do império,* pp. 408, 411.

[6] Sérgio Buarque de Holanda, "A herança colonial—sua desagregação," in *História geral da civilização brasileira,* ed. Sérgio Buarque de Holanda, 4 vols. (São Paulo, 1960–64), 2 (1) (*O Brasil Monárquico*): 9–39.

forcing Dom João to take measures to protect them.[7] The seeds of separation have been attributed to the conflict of interests between the agrarian classes—nativists with liberal tendencies—and Portuguese traders adhering to a protectionist policy and monopolistic privileges.

Problems inherent in the maturing of industrial capitalism in England possess a wider relevance and define the general picture of changes taking place in the Western world in this period. The struggle between a mercantile policy and economic liberalism found its most violent expression in England between 1815 and 1846 and had drastic repercussions on the free-trade policies of all colonial countries directly related to the expansion of the British empire. No area was so greatly affected as the West Indies, the subject of Eric Williams' classic *Capitalism and Slavery* (London, 1946). The situation there was the pretext for the foundation of a new Portuguese empire in Brazil and was to find echoes in economic policy and the act of separation from Portugal. The historiography of that era well defined those external pressures and the international framework from which great forces of change emanate. The manner in which such pressures affected the ruling classes in the colony and the internal mechanisms inherent in the formative process of Brazilian nationality remain to be studied. Having forfeited the role of intermediaries in Brazilian trade, the only path open to Portuguese traders was to unite their interests with those of the great rural families and of agricultural producers. The latter had not always been dissociated from commerce and transportation, as exemplified by the baron of Iguape in São Paulo.[8] English pressure for the abolition of the slave trade had tended, in its turn, to awaken the hostility of agrarian interests toward central authority. Any schematic association of the interests of agrarian classes in Brazil with those sectors of society promoting British imperialism would be to oversimplify an extremely intricate situation.

Although the basic landmarks are well established, Brazilian historiography, confronted by a process sui generis of transition from colony to empire in Brazil, has yet to discard certain errors of interpretation provoked by Europeanizing attitudes. The most evident are the Rousseauian picture of the colony breaking the chains linking it to the mother country and the notion of Brazilian identification with those brands of

[7] Reprinted in this volume as "The Political Emancipation of Brazil." In other works the same author has deepened her study of the role played by José Bonifácio, analyzing the contradictions in his ideological makeup, as a product of the European Enlightenment on the one hand and as an American on the other, and the disparity between the visions projected by statesmen and the objective reality of their respective countries. See Emília Viotti da Costa, "José Bonifácio: mito e histórias," *Anais do Museu Paulista* 21 (1967):286.

[8] Maria Thereza Schorer Petrone, "Um comerciante do ciclo do açúcar paulista: António da Silva Prado (1817–29)," *Revista de história* 36, no. 73 (1968):115–38; 37, no. 76 (1968):315–43; 39, no. 79 (1969):121–27.

liberalism and nationalism typical of the great bourgeois revolution in Europe. Viotti da Costa has severe reservations about such concepts, but the contradictions still remain to be explained.[9]

For a long time studies of the political emancipation of Brazil labored under the erroneous concept of a national conscience, to which many sought to attribute emancipation. Contemporaries were dazzled by the model of independence afforded by the United States, and, to some degree, this vision continues to tarnish the perspective of present-day historians. Buarque de Holanda has referred more objectively to the struggles for "independence" as a civil war among Portuguese, unleashed in Brazil by the revolution in Oporto and not by any autonomous process in which native Brazilians rallied together to make common demands on the mother country.[10] The very fact of separation from Portugal in 1822 was not of great importance in the evolution from colony to empire. This had been a fait accompli since 1808 with the arrival of the court, the opening of the ports, and the presence of factors totally alien to the wishes of either colony or mother country. This preoccupation, evidently justified per se, of Brazilian historians with integrating the process of political emancipation with pressures on the international front has resulted up to now in an exaggerated linkage of the events of that era to some broad, general aspects of historical reality; the result has been that historiography has remained superficial. Such an attitude contributed decisively to the survival of the myth of the colony struggling against the mother country. The internal process of adaption to those same pressures—the establishment of Portuguese interests in Brazil and, above all, the reawakening of metropolitan interests in the central-southern region of the colony—has been forgotten. The fact of the matter is that the formal consummation of political separation was provoked by internal dissent in Portugal, which found expression in the program of the liberal revolutionaries of Oporto and had no effect on the chain of events in Brazil set in motion by the arrival of the court of Dom João in 1808.

The coming of the court to Brazil and the option of establishing a new empire in the tropics had already signified per se an internal cleavage among political groups in Portugal. Conflicts born of schisms and internal partisanship existing in Portugal since the French Revolution gathered momentum as differences between Portuguese of the kingdom and Portuguese of the new court in Rio de Janeiro became more evident. In the course of time, domestic unrest tended to become more

---

[9] Emília Viotti da Costa, "The Political Emancipation of Brazil."
[10] Sérgio Buarque de Holanda, "A herança colonial," 2 (1):13.

intense.[11] It is important to see this development in the context of the set of factors and pressures existing at that period without confusing it with a nativist Brazilian struggle *in abstracto* by the colony against the mother country, which would lead us back once again to distorting myths. The history of the political emancipation of Brazil must be seen, insofar as we are referring strictly to political separation from the mother country, in the context of domestic conflicts in Portugal brought on by the impact of the French Revolution. Moreover, these events in Portugal were linked to the internal struggle between the new liberal tendencies and an archaic and still feudal structure resistant to the innovations which the new court in Rio de Janeiro was to try to impose on the mother country.

The sacrifices and hardships of the French Revolution, the violent suppression of any change born of the climate of war against Napoleon, and fear of Jacobinic agitations all contributed to the awakening of jealousies and tensions between the Portuguese of Portugal and the Portuguese of the new court in Rio de Janeiro. In Portugal, the devastation and hardship of war, aggravated by pressures exerted by the old nobility, were severely accentuated by the treaty of 1810. Not only did this agreement destroy any hope of reviving the old intermediary trade in colonial products by merchants from Portuguese ports but it also set back the growth of industrialism championed by such men as Acúrcio das Neves and by "Brazilians" such as Hipólito da Costa.[12] In addition to widespread hunger, lack of foodstuffs, and disorganization of the production of wine and olive oil, the ports, initially closed by Junot, became paralyzed, without life or movement, because of the treaty. For the Brazilian historian and patriot Pereira da Silva, who wrote on this period, the misfortunes of Portugal were in no way less than those of Spain, to which he referred suggestively as being "more a cadaver than a living nation."[13] In the face of the misery of this period of crisis and

---

[11] The Austrian consul at the court in Rio de Janeiro gave suggestive evidence about the attitude of the count of Barca, the minister of Dom João VI, on this matter in 1811:—"when the consul reminded the count on one occasion of how inappropriate it was to speak slightingly of Portugal, which could lead to separation, the consul was told by way of reply that the government was prepared for such an eventuality. The count said that he would not be surprised by such a situation, and would willingly renounce Europe and become an American." Tobias Monteiro, *História do império*, p. 223. Cf. Manoel de Oliveira Lima, *Dom João VI no Brasil, 1808–21*, 2 vols. (Rio de Janeiro, 1908), 2:1020.

[12] See the article by Hipólito da Costa on industrialization in Portugal in *Correio braziliense* for June and August 1816; J. Borges de Macedo, *Problemas da história da indústria portuguesa no século XVIII* (Lisbon, 1963); Joel Serrão, "A indústria portuensa em 1830," *Bulletin d'études historiques* (Lisbon, 1953).

[13] João Manuel Pereira da Silva, *História da fundação do império brazileiro*, 7 vols. (Paris, 1864–68), 3:274. Cf. the same author's assessment of Portugal at this period: "devastated by invasion of the interior of the country for three years; resources diminished by the loss of commerce and monopolies on the Brazil trade; loss of population resulting from wars and emigration to America; now devoid of industries,

extreme decadence, the kingdom could look forward to relative prosperity and the optimistic prospects for Brazil which were being revealed.

The Portuguese minister, Dom Rodrigo de Souza Coutinho, looked
on the new empire of Brazil as the savior of the kingdom. He believed
that he could achieve a balanced economic situation in Portugal through
a purely commercial and financial economic policy. Once the circulation of coin had been revitalized and a substantial income from customs
dues had been achieved, the kingdom would be in a position to consolidate itself because it could count on benefits accruing from the
prosperity of Brazil.[11] It would be essential, however, to revive Portuguese agriculture. To accomplish this, Dom Rodrigo recognized the
necessity of modernizing the social and economic structure of the kingdom. In this attitude he may well have been influenced by pressures from
the English; they were convinced of the lack of viability of Portugal
unless the archaic structure of the system of landed properties was reformed, for which purpose they suggested that the old Côrtes should be
convoked again. The prince regent strenuously opposed English pressure with regard to the Côrtes but fully realized the necessity to
modernize the economic and social structure of Portugal because the
new empire born in Brazil could not alone shoulder the enormous costs
such reconstruction would demand. The court did not hesitate to tax
heavily the provinces of the north of Brazil, thereby accentuating those
regional characteristics of dispersion already apparent in the two previous centuries of colonization. But, because these resources were inadequate, the prince regent preferred to introduce economic and social reforms in Portugal itself in order to avoid overburdening the new court,
which was beginning to establish itself, and to strengthen the bonds
which would link the court to the central-southern region of Brazil.

During the French occupation the government had resorted to "extraordinary taxes" and voluntary subscriptions to finance the war.[15] It had
also issued currency indiscriminately, which resulted in the devaluation
of currency in Portugal in relation to that of the new court and an
increase in the illegal export of coin to Brazil.[16] When the war was over
and expenditures on public servants and members of the new court were
already considerable, even without taking into account expenditure on

---

factories, and mercantile dealings; reduced to bankruptcy by innumerable and extraordinary taxes and acts of sacrifice which exhaust its present-day resources, and give no
reason for optimism in the future; bent under the authority of criminals who have
respect neither for the letter of the law, nor the right of the individual, nor the property of others subject to their rule; reduced to the position of a colony, and a conquered colony at that; what nation could rival Portugal in suffering?" *Ibid.*, p. 274.

[14] "Representação reservadíssima de Dom Rodrigo de Souza Coutinho ao príncipe
regente de 31 de dezembro de 1810," in Pereira da Silva, *História* 3:283; cf. 2:326 and
3:346.

[15] *Ibid.*, 3:25.

[16] *Ibid.*, p. 167.

wars in Guiana and the La Plata region, the new court did not wish to continue to depend only on the already excessive taxes collected from captaincies in the north of Brazil. The prince regent therefore drew up a regalist policy of modernization for Portugal.[17] His intentions were the following: first, to avail himself of the proceeds of sales of crown and church properties in Portugal; second, to remove the last vestiges of the system of feudal contributions and impose new regular taxes, less injustly distributed and more likely to inject life into the agrarian economy of the kingdom;[18] third, to sell crown property, the prebend of Coimbra, and the chapels, and, above all, to abolish the administrative system of *lesírias*, uncultivated lands along river banks, which would be sold. The tithes due on such lands and the transfer tax on all such sales would be collected. These reforms would contribute to an increase in the number of properties and would increase productivity, eliminating large areas of uncultivated land.[19]

The more conservative sectors in Portugal opposed the policies advocated by the prince regent. Stubbornly attached to their ancient rights, they had aggravated the difficulties already present because of the devastation wrought by war on the economic life of the country. After the end of the fighting, and in flagrant disobedience of orders received from the new court, the government in Portugal, tied by family and other interests to sectors of the agrarian nobility and to the clergy, wished to continue the system of "extraordinary taxes," whose burden would fall on merchants and bureaucrats in the cities, primarily those of Lisbon and Oporto.[20] However, the combination of English pressure and the commercial policy of the new court resulted in the court's loss of the support of the more progressive groups in Portugal, which were more interested in protectionist measures, in attempts at industrialization, or in regaining ancient commercial trade privileges with Great Britain.[21]

Internal strains inherent in the process of reconstruction and modernization of Portugal thus exacerbated and threw into sharper relief the differences of interest between the Portuguese in Portugal and the Portuguese in Brazil. The new court, dedicated to the consolidation of

---

[17] On the regalist policies of Dom João VI and relations with the Vatican, see *ibid.*, pp. 253, 256–58. Consult also Damião Peres, ed., *História de Portugal. Edição monumental comemorativa do 8° centenário da fundação da nacionalidade*, 8 vols. (Barcelos, 1928–37), vol. 6; Fortunato de Almeida, *Historia da igreja em Portugal* (Coimbra, 1922–29), vols. 5–6.

[18] Albert Silbert, *Le Portugal méditerranéen à la fin de l'ancien régime, XVIIIe–début du XIXe siècle* (Paris, 1966); Gentil da Silva, "Au Portugal: l'autoconsommation (XIVe-XXe)," *Annales*, no. 2 (March-April 1969), pp. 250–88.

[19] Pereira da Silva, *História* 3:161, 165–67, 168, 280–83, 349.

[20] *Ibid.*, 3:170.

[21] F. Piteira Santos, *Geografia e economia da revolução de 1820* (Lisbon, 1962); Sandov, Sideri, *Trade and Power (Informal Colonialism in Anglo-Portuguese Relations)* (Rotterdam, 1970).

empire in Brazil, which would serve as a fortress of absolutism, could not succeed in implementing the liberalization and reconstruction proposed for Portugal, and merely added to the tensions which were to culminate in the revolution of Oporto.

Once political separation had become a reality which they had been forced to accept, albeit unwillingly at the outset, men of the generation of independence had little reason for optimism concerning the potential of the colony to transform itself into a nation, let alone into a modern nation based on the liberal principles of the constitutionalist regime. Politicians of the period were well aware of the internal tensions of a social and racial nature and of the fragmentation and regionalism which had afforded no opportunity for the appearance of a national conscience strong enough to give impetus to a revolutionary movement capable of reconstructing society. There was no lack of lofty displays of nativism and of well-defined pressures by local interests. Nevertheless, a truly "national" conscience could only be born out of the integration of the different provinces, and this would be achieved gradually and at heavy cost through the ideological "will to be Brazilians" of the new court in Rio de Janeiro and through its struggle for centralization of authority (1840–50).[22] This movement toward centralization was perhaps one of the prime moulding forces in politics during the empire—the will to achieve consolidation and to survive as a civilized European nation in the tropics despite the slavocratic and racially mixed society of the colony. It was demonstrated by those Portuguese settled in the central-southern region, who assumed the mission of organizing a new Portuguese empire.[23] The dispersion and fragmentation of authority, allied to the weakness and instability of the ruling classes, called for the image of a strong state which the new court appeared to offer.[24]

[22] António Candido de Mello e Souza, Formação da literatura brasileira (momentos decisivos) (São Paulo, 1964).

[23] Although the count of Palmela was merely a bird of passage in Rio de Janeiro, he defined with extraordinary precision the point of view of those Portuguese who had settled in Brazil. This coincided with the outlook of those Brazilians whose readings in the literature of the Enlightenment had made them no less European. Palmela commented in a letter to his wife: "White people, luxury, and good roads are lacking. Moreover, there is an absence of many things which will only come with time. But there is no shortage, as is the case in Lisbon and its environs, of water and greenery. Even at this season of the year, the worst, everything here is as green as in England." Maria Amalia Vaz de Carvalho, Vida do duque de Palmella, 3 vols. (Lisbon, 1891–1903), 1:371–72. This passage could not be bettered for its description of the vision of those men who consolidated Brazilian nationality.

[24] See Paulo Pereira Castro, "A 'experiência republicana,' 1831–40," in História geral da civilização brasileira 2:31.

When all is said and done, the conditions offered by the colonial society were not such as to foment movements of liberation of a markedly nationalist stamp in the nineteenth-century bourgeois sense. Since the arrival in Rio de Janeiro of Dom João VI, Portuguese, Europeans, and Europeanized natives had combined forces in mutual support, had armed themselves, and had expended considerable sums upon police and military equipment. The pretext had been the danger of infiltration of Jacobinic ideas by way of Spanish America or by European refugees insecure of their status as civilized men in the midst of the barbarism and primitivism of colonial society. The colonists had sought every possible means to protect themselves against the forces of internal instability. The society formed over three hundred years of colonization had no alternative, at the end of the eighteenth century, but to transform itself into a metropolis in order to maintain the continuity of its political, administrative, economic, and social structure. This transformation became possible because of events in Europe, English pressure, and the arrival of the court in Rio de Janeiro.[25]

The pressure of the court and the consolidation of the Portuguese state in the central-southern region was to hasten the metropolitanization of the colony. It was the only solution acceptable to the ruling classes in the face of the insecurity engendered by the contradictions of colonial society and aggravated by the agitations of Portuguese constitutionalism and the more generalized fermentation throughout the Western world, which neither the Holy Alliance nor the ideology of counter-revolution in Europe had succeeded in overcoming. This process, originating in Rio de Janeiro and the central-southern region, was only fully realized with the political centralization achieved by men of the caliber of the duke of Caxias, Bernardo de Vasconcelos, and the viscount of Uruguay, and came to political fruition with the marquis of Paraná and the Ministry of Conciliation (1853–56). It has yet to be studied in detail: principal factors were the organization of trade in provisions to Rio de Janeiro and the resulting integration of the central-southern region; contributory factors were the interrelations of commercial and agrarian interests, marriages with local families, and financial investment in public works and land or in the commerce of pack animals and mules from the south and in trade in jerked beef (*charque*). This whole process was watched over and participated in by bureaucrats at court; administrative privileges and the nepotism of the monarch also played their part.[26]

25 Pereira da Silva, *História* 2:40, 3:36, 52, 157.

26 See the 1821 manuscript by the viscount of Rio Seco, entitled "Exposição analítica e justificativa da conduta e vida pública do visconde do Rio Seco," Arquivo do Museu Imperial, Rio de Janeiro. The same tradition of dependence on the royal authority in Portugal is described by Jacome Ratton, *Recordacoens* (London, 1813).

The letters of Luiz dos Santos Marrocos constantly attribute the continual postponement of the return of the court to Portugal to pressure by private interests eager for privileges and concessions regarding public works. He despondently records enormous investments made locally by the leading businessmen at court, which clearly indicate their intention of remaining in Brazil. In letters of March and May of 1814 he attributes the delay in the return of the court to Portugal to the construction of the Ajuda Palace in Lisbon. He refers to the "lethargy and silence" which shrouds private interests. The return would not take place in the near future, and he wrote: "It is not because of any increase here of works of better accommodation in the future, but there are private interests and, for all I know, there may be official statements which inspire fear of a very prolonged sojourn in that climate. This feeling is apparent in ecclesiastical, civilian, and military bureaus." [27] Construction continued ceaselessly: Marrocos refers to renovation of the naval arsenal; to the building of a palace in Andarati as a residence for Dona Carlota; to additions to the summer palace of St. Christopher for the royal family (April 1815); to the palace of Sta Cruz built for short visits in February, July, and November; to a new palace at Ponte do Cajú built at an estimated cost of 77 million cruzados; to a new riding arena costing 50 million cruzados (February 1816); and to a new jail built with "money collected on the benefice day of the court theater." [28] Lotteries and voluntary subscriptions bore witness to the interest of the court in remaining. "There are many, many works, but they are those used by the pseudo-Brazilians, popularly known as *janeiristas,* to foster the rumor of our remaining here eternally," Marrocos wrote in December 1814.[29] Also of interest are his references to private investment by the wealthiest members of the court. In November 1812 he described the magnificent palace in the Lago dos Siganos under construction by José Joaquim de Azevedo, later baron of Rio Seco. In August 1813 the same "capitalist" built a second palace, equally ostentatious, in Mataporcos. Marrocos refers to Fernando Carneiro Leão's financial interests in the royal lottery for the São João theater, and to the sumptuous properties of certain ministers. For example, the count of Barca, Dom João VI's minister, bought two houses for 45,000 cruzados: there "he intends to make his residence," the librarian of Dom João VI, who saw no portents of a return to Portugal, added with evident displeasure.[30]

Marrocos supplies some curious clues to the manner in which Portuguese interests were consolidated in Brazil, not only in luxurious buildings

[27] *Anais da Biblioteca Nacional do Rio de Janeiro* (hereafter cited as *ABNRJ*) 56 (1934):188, 199.

[28] *Ibid.,* pp. 215, 216, 222, 232, 260.

[29] *Ibid.,* p. 220.

[30] *Ibid.,* pp. 154, 50n.

but also, and more important, in the purchase of land and the establishment of business concerns. He observes, "José Egídio Álvarez de Almeida is traveling to the Rio Grande to inspect and organize a large estate which he bought for 63,000 cruzados and to establish there a tanning factory in partnership with António de Araújo." The latter was the count of Barca.[31]

Yet to be undertaken is the more specific study of regionalisms and of relations between the court in Rio de Janeiro and the provinces of the north and northeast, where there is clear evidence of the continuation of the colonial political and administrative structure. As an established metropolis, the court in Rio de Janeiro lay down the bases for the new Portuguese empire, assuming for itself the control and exploitation of the other "colonies" of the continent, such as Bahia and the northeast.[32] Despite elevation to the title of United Kingdom, the spate of reforms characterizing the Joanine period had in view the reorganization of the metropolis in the colony. In fact, in so far as the other captaincies were concerned, they amounted to no more than a renewal of the processes of colonization practiced by the Portuguese in the previous century.[33]

A more penetrating study of the mechanism inherent in the ruling classes in colonial Brazil would represent a great advance. It would clarify in a more specific and systematic manner the relative continuation of institutions which characterizes the transition to empire. Only when a greater appreciation has been gained of the social predominance of the merchant and the close interdependence existing between rural, commercial, and administrative interests will the way be open for an under-

[31] Letter of February 1814, *ibid.*, p. 185. For an inventory of properties acquired by the count of Arcos, see Tobias Monteiro, *História do império*, p. 244n.

[32] Indicative of the nature of the relationship between Lisbon, the new court in Rio de Janeiro, and the other captaincies in Brazil was the manner in which the market in gunpowder was divided between the royal powder factory in Portugal and the new powder factory established in Rio de Janeiro (Pereira da Silva, *História* 3:151). The factory in Rio de Janeiro had exclusive marketing rights in Pernambuco, Bahia, São Paulo, Rio Grande do Sul, the ports on the west coast of Africa, and Rio de Janeiro itself. The factory in Portugal could sell only in the Azores, Madeira, Porto Santo, Cape Verde, and, on the American continent, in the Maranhão, Pará, and Ceará (letter of July 22, 1811, in *ibid.*, pp. 344–45). No less illustrative of the continuum in fiscal policy was the imposition by the court in Rio de Janeiro of new taxes on the provinces in the north of Brazil, with the object of meeting the costs of bureaucracy and public works in Brazil. Export dues were increased on the following commodities: sugar, tobacco, cotton, hides, etc. (*ibid.*, p. 55). In July 1811, faced with the necessity of raising 120,000 cruzados to finance reconstruction costs in Portugal, the new court in Rio de Janeiro did not hesitate to impose relevant taxes on the northern provinces of Brazil. Bahia was expected to contribute 60,000 cruzados yearly; Pernambuco, 40,000; the Maranhão, 20,000 (royal letter of July 26, 1811, in *ibid.*, pp. 285–87).

[33] The captaincies made no distinction between addressing themselves to Lisbon and to Rio de Janeiro. See António Luiz de Brito Aragão e Vasconcellos, "Memórias sobre o estabelecimento do império do Brasil ou novo império lusitano?" *ABNRJ* 43–44 (1920–21):43.

standing of the moderate process of Brazilian political emancipation. The chronic instability of the colonial economy created social mechanisms of accommodation. The relative "fluidity" and "mobility" of the ruling classes, which acted as neutralizing forces to stifle people who refused to conform and prevented displays of discontent which could give rise to a plethora of *inconfidências* and revolts, were such mechanisms. The very structure of society, with its abyss between a privileged minority and the rest of the population, polarized political forces, preserving the unity of interests of the ruling classes. The fear of "haitianism," i.e., a revolt by slaves and mixed bloods similar to that which occurred in Haiti in 1794, should not be underestimated; it is typical of the mentality of that era, a stereotyped reflection of conservative ideology and the European counter-revolution.[34] Events in Haiti acted as a political catalyst and played a decisive role at a time when regionalisms and divergent interests could have set the ruling classes in the colony against each other.

In this context the views and anxieties of men of the first two decades of the last century concerning the prospect of the colony consolidating itself as a nation are of interest. For some utopians and dreamers, clearly all was possible. But the majority of men given to considered deliberation and with a keen sense of the reality of their surroundings expressed doubts and pessimism, rooted in the fear inspired by the population of slaves or mixed bloods. José Bonifácio wrote to Dom Domingos de Souza Coutinho in 1813: "The alloy of metals so totally diverse as are whites, mulattos, free and slave blacks, Amerindians, etc., into a solid political entity would be difficult to accomplish."[35] Under the impact of the constitutionalist agitations of the liberal revolution, Sierra y Mariscal in 1823 estimated that within three years the "white race will come to an end at the hands of other races and the province of Bahia will disappear from the civilized world."[36]

There was great apprehension when the revolution of Oporto and the return of Dom João VI to the mother country threw into jeopardy the continuation of royal power and the new Portuguese state in the center-southern region, which established interests around the court wished to preserve. Moreover, throughout the colony the ruling classes viewed with alarm the exaggerated disproportion between a landowning white minority and the majority of unemployed, poor, and mixed bloods who appeared to cause greater worry than did the slave population. To these insecurities were added problems arising from the ethnic diversity of which Portuguese and established natives were very conscious. Sierra

[34] On negro revolts in Bahia, see the letter of the count of Arcos in Francisco José Rocha Martins, *O último vice-rei do Brasil* (Lisbon, 1934), pp. 35–36.

[35] *Revista de história* 27, no. 55:226.

[36] Sierra y Mariscal, "Idéias gerais sobre a revolução do Brasil e suas consequências," *ABNRJ* 43–44:65.

y Mariscal wrote, "in Portugal and Brazil men of common sense recognize that with the move of royal power Brazil will be lost to the civilized world and Portugal will lose its independence." [37] It is true that Sierra y Mariscal had allied himself to a status quo which the infiltration of English contraband into the colony and the decrease in the political and economic importance of Portugal in the course of the eighteenth century had already gainsayed.[38] Nevertheless, the court and the Portuguese administration, the monarchy, the royal power, and the myth of central authority would always appear as anchors of salvation and security. He wrote: "for these reasons the government here must have springs more capable of absorbing shocks than anywhere else. Upbringing, climate, and slavery in particular are the causes of this destiny.[39]

Horace See, who came to Brazil in 1816, observed the lack of unity and communication between the different Portuguese possessions on the American continent.[40] Ten years later, at the height of the First Empire, the British minister Chamberlain wrote to Canning expressing his grave misgivings about the indifference and disregard shown by the government in Rio de Janeiro toward the hardship and drought which had shaken the empire from Bahia northward, making ever more imminent and dangerous the sparking of a revolution which could sunder the empire.[41] Conscious of their internal weakness, Portuguese at the new court dedicated themselves to strengthening administrative centralization and the royal power which revolutionaries in Portugal wished to return to the old metropolis. Sierra y Mariscal summed up the situation in these words:

Brazil is a country being born, a settlement inhabited by peoples of different colors who have a mutual dislike for each other. The numerical strength of the whites is very small, and only Portugal could provide effective help in the event of any internal dissent or attack from abroad. The captaincies cannot help each other, as they are separated by enormous expanses so that that country does not yet constitute a single kingdom with unbroken territorial unity. In consequence, by means of the constitutional letter which will make both countries happy, Brazil is dependent on its union with Portugal.[42]

[37] *Ibid.,* p. 53.
[38] On the decreasing economic importance of Portugal in the eighteenth and nineteenth centuries, see A. K. Manchester, *British Preeminence in Brazil—Its Rise and Decline. A Study in European Expansion* (London, 1933); Stanley J. Stein and Barbara H. Stein, *The Colonial Heritage of Latin America (Essays on Economic Dependence in Perspective)* (New York, 1970); C. R. Boxer, *The Portuguese Seaborne Empire, 1415–1825* (London, 1969); K. Maxwell, "Pombal and the nationalization of the Luso-Brazilian Economy," *Hispanic American Historical Review* (hereafter cited as *HAHR*) 48, no. 4 (November 1968):608–31; Sideri, *Trade and Power,* chs. 3 and 6.
[39] Sierra y Mariscal, "Idéias gerais," p. 63.
[40] Sérgio Buarque de Holanda, "A herança colonial," p. 16.
[41] Letter of April 22, 1826, cited in C. K. Webster, *Great Britain and the Independence of Latin America* (New York, 1938), p. 308.
[42] Sierra y Mariscal, "Idéias gerais," p. 72.

Weakness and dispersion of authority, together with factional dissent, cast into even sharper relief internal social and racial contradictions identified, for contemporaries, with the danger of dispersion and political disunity among the various captaincies. For Sierra y Mariscal, writing in 1823, the South American possessions of the Portuguese afforded a distressing and wasteful picture of disunity. He wrote:

Pernambuco is already at odds with Rio de Janeiro. Bahia is destitute of income, and the basis of its prosperity is destroyed. Rio de Janeiro is on the point of bankruptcy because of the efforts and sacrifices which it has made and the losses it has suffered. The provinces of the south are restless. The provinces of the Maranhão and Pará are useless for the revolutionary party. Without exception they will all prove an embarrassment to the government in Rio de Janeiro by collapsing under the burden. Any hope that these provinces may reassert themselves in the future is in vain.[43]

The historian can glimpse the charisma of a prince regent and the strong appeal he held for the mass of half-castes and unemployed, incapable of acting on their own initiative and without means of political expression. Seething with discontent and frustration, conditioned by the paternalist surroundings in which they had evolved, they revolted against those monopolizing trade or engaging in a black market in foodstuffs but were fascinated by the court and royal authority. It was the faith which children have in a kind father who will come to their aid and attend to their wounds. Not even the fever of constitutionalism could have a drastic effect on their political conditioning.

The ruling classes also tended to attach themselves to the court. They were tormented by the lack of political prospects and by the wish to assert themselves against rival factions, their vanity was titillated by the princely nepotism, and they were attracted by the conferring of titles.[44]

[43] *Ibid.*, p. 74.

[44] It is interesting to note how curiously distorted by liberalism was the prism through which Pereira da Silva viewed critically what was a characteristic aspect of the internal equilibrium existing among the upper classes in Brazil. Pereira da Silva was here criticizing the civil service bureaucracy, one of the key features in his attack on the Joanine period. Although such persons were few and far between, some Brazilians did succeed in obtaining appointments in the governmental bureaucracy. Dazzled by the glamor and social importance attached to posts in the civil service, these Brazilians renounced their former lucrative positions, in which they had been respected and independent. All minds became obsessed with the attractions of administrative office. This tendency exerted, and exerted even in 1867, said Pereira da Silva, a deleterious influence on the independence of the individual and on the moral and material development of the country. The ambition to live within, and subordinate to, the action and control of the government deprives the individual of his liberty, while offering in exchange no guarantee of self-enrichment nor security for him or his family. Furthermore, Pereira da Silva pointed out, this obsession for public service milked the skilled trades, the arts, commerce, industry, and the worlds of letters and science of talented and intelligent citizens (*História* 2:46–47).

Above all else, they were anxious to guarantee their local autonomy by the protection and sanction of the central authority, which would confirm their position vis-à-vis the slave population or protect them against revolts by half-castes who were not landowners. Moreover, they needed the capital of the newly arrived Portuguese. They signed property contracts and entered into marriage ties with the newcomers. The Bank of Brazil offered advantages to those who knew how to seek political protection. Sierra y Mariscal observed: "Lack of financial means by this type of aristocracy deprives it of the wherewithal to gain clients and to become a party among the people, because they themselves are very weak and need the protection of businessmen, whom they venerate. If you like, it is commerce—and commerce alone—which is the sole aristocratic body." [45] A deeper study of the social predominance of the merchant and of the intimate interdependence between rural, administrative, and commercial interests gives the historian a clearer picture of the mechanisms of defense and cohesion among the elite, already a fundamental characteristic of the society of colonial Brazil. Guidelines for a revision of the European myth of the dual society have been established. Several available studies analyze from new perspectives the alleged dichotomy or opposition between urban and rural interests, identified and confused with each other and only finally to be reconciled by public administration, given the large social role it played in the colony. [46] The arrival of the court threw into relief characteristics already very apparent in the second half of the eighteenth century which tended to accentuate the predominance of the merchant. Because of these, Sierra y Mariscal had been alarmed by the revolution of Oporto and by displays hostile to Portuguese merchants:

Once the dike [commerce] which held back revolutions has been breached, there will be nobody to finance agriculture, and this will be paralyzed. One year of divinely assisted civil war, the very nature of agriculture, and the topography of the province have mitigated the severity of slavery. The sugar planters, having nobody to advance them capital, cannot feed the slaves. In this situation the slaves will revolt and the white race will perish immediately. [47]

Sierra y Mariscal reflected the thoughts of whites and landowners of Bahia and Pernambuco, but he generalized his apprehension to embrace the Portuguese empire in its entirety. It was the mission of the Portuguese monarchy to save the white race and to save itself because, if a revolt

---

[45] Sierra y Mariscal, "Idéias gerais," p. 72.
[46] C. R. Boxer, *The Golden Age of Brazil, 1695–1750* (Berkeley and Los Angeles, 1962), pp. 63–70; Boxer, *The Portuguese Seaborne Empire;* A. J. R. Russell-Wood, *Fidalgos and Philanthropists. The Santa Casa da Misericórdia of Bahia, 1550–1755* (London, 1968); S. Schwartz, "Magistracy and Society in Colonial Brazil," *HAHR* 50 (1970):715–30.
[47] Sierra y Mariscal, "Idéais gerais," p. 72.

should be hatched in the provinces of the north of Brazil, "dissolution and anarchy would spread to all the presently peaceful possessions west of the Cape [of Good Hope]. Nor would the Cape Verdes and Azores be immune, and in this terrible conflict the very foundations of the monarchy would be shaken." [48]

Conflicts generated by incompatibility between absolutism and the mercantilist policy of the crown and pressures of the new brand of economic liberalism born of the maturing of industrial capitalism in England were, without doubt, the master key to the forces of change in that period. However, given the characteristics of society in colonial Brazil, they were not immediately identified with a movement of national liberation. So great was the complexity of the internal conflicts and the heterogeneity of regionalisms that the events of the first decades of the nineteenth century, conventionally called the era of independence, indicate localist fragmentation on an even greater scale coinciding with the renewed presence of Portuguese nationals.[49] Unlike the situation in the majority of countries in Spanish America, where the "creoles" expelled and took away the possessions of Spaniards born in Spain, in Brazil we witness investment of new Portuguese capital and the establishment of commercial interests, stimulated by the presence of the court. Such initiatives were associated with the native ruling classes and were also centered on the struggle for the assertion of a central executive power to strengthen them against displays of insubordination by the less favored classes, frequently identified with factious nativisms or with regionalist forces hostile not only to each other but also, on occasion, to the new court. This had been the case in the northeast in the revolution of 1817 and in the Confederation of Ecuador.[50] So intense were the conflicts and the social and racial pressures against the Portuguese, depicted as rich men and monopolists of trade and public office, that they could not be resolved by the independence of 1822 or by the abdication of Dom Pedro in 1831. This attitude was no mere chauvinist prejudice related to separation from the mother country. It was an internal conflict, inherent to colonial society, which not even the empire would overcome. Lusophobia is continually evident in outbursts

48 *Ibid.*, p. 67.

49 Mareschal, the Austrian plenipotentiary at the court in Rio de Janeiro, noted that José Joaquim da Rocha, a prime mover behind the *Fico* and in whose house the manifesto of the *fluminenses* had been signed, refused to accept ministerial office because he believed that the Portuguese should be in the majority in the councils of Dom Pedro (Tobias Monteiro, *História do império*, p. 445). In the manifesto justifying their actions, the revolutionaries of Oporto cited the movement of population and of capital to Brazil and went on to deplore the effects of the treaty of 1810 and the loss of the monopoly on trade from Brazil (Pereira da Silva, *História* 2:46, 3:26).

50 Carlos Guilherme Mota, *Nordeste, 1817. Estruturas e argumentos* (São Paulo, 1972).

by the press throughout the entire nineteenth century, in the demands of the *praieiros* of the court and of Pernambuco in 1848, and in their struggle for the nationalization of retail trade. It surfaced repeatedly in many scattered violent incidents such as the events of 1873 in Macapá and Goiania and throughout the period of the First Republic.[51]

If the fundamental guidelines of Brazilian historiography are well defined, systematic studies of the characteristics of the colonial society are needed to elaborate the process of the establishment of the metropolis, which appears to be the key to an appreciation of the formation of Brazilian nationality. The fact is that the seed of "nationality" had absolutely no revolutionary content. The monarchy and the continuation of the status quo were the major preoccupations of the men forging the transition to empire. The *Correio braziliense* of April 1820 expressed the current attitude: "Moreover, we do not want a revolution, but a revolution it will be if the bases of the entire administrative and social structure of the monarchy are altered. Such a sudden revolution cannot take place without disastrous upheavals, and it is for this very reason that we do not wish it." [52] The seed of national integration was thus represented by the new court as a continuation of the administration and structure existing during the colonial period and an act of will by newly arrived Portuguese, strengthened by dependence and collaboration on the part of native Brazilians and forged by pressures exerted by the English, who wished to enjoy commercial benefits without the burden of administration. The union of native ruling classes was joined to that "will to be Brazilians" felt by the immigrant Portuguese who had come to establish a new empire in the tropics. Struggle between local factions led inevitably to a search for the more solid support afforded by the central authority. Conflicts inherent in Brazilian society were not seen in the light of events surrounding political separation from the mother country, and their solution continued, as before, to be relegated to posterity.

Participation by leading Brazilians in Portuguese public administration is a characteristic phenomenon of society in colonial Brazil, especially among the ruling classes.[53] "Bureaucratic elitism" afforded relief from the economic instability well expressed in the Portuguese proverb: "father a taverner, son a gentleman, and grandson a beggar." [54] Mechanisms were designed to help the impoverished and to maintain social harmony [55]—

[51] Paulo Cavalcanti, *Eça de Queiroz, agitador no Brasil* (São Paulo, 1966), p. 63.

[52] *Correio braziliense* 24:421.

[53] Maria Odila Silva Dias, "Aspectos da ilustração no Brazil," *Revista do Instituto Histórico e Geográfico Brasileiro* (hereafter cited as *RIHGB* 278 (1968):100–170.

[54] Boxer, *The Golden Age*, p. 12.

[55] Luiz dos Santos Vilhena, *Recopilação de noticias soteropolitanas e brasilicas contidas em XX cartas, que da cidade do Salvador Bahia de Todos os Santos escreve hum a outro amigo em Lisboa*, 2 vols. (Bahia, 1922), 1:43–45.

the charitable brotherhood of the Santa Casa da Misericórdia, convents, religious orders, and governmental bureaucracy in general.[56]

The role of bureaucratic elitism in colonial society should not be underestimated because it explains in large part the intimate collaboration between native ruling classes and Portuguese public administration which had its heyday with the arrival of the court and the founding of the new empire. At this time, absorbed by the wider issue of state policy, leading Brazilians strove to build up the new empire in the tropics. For this reason, the Brazilian situation can in no way be identified with anti-colonialism nor with the struggle of the colony against the metropolis.

Statesmen of the caliber of Dom Rodrigo de Souza Coutinho or the count of Barca regarded of paramount importance the task of establishing a new empire which would have Rio de Janeiro as its capital and which would govern the remaining captaincies. In this work they counted on the collaboration and backing of leading Brazilians. With the arrival of the court, for the first time since the beginning of the colonization of Brazil, there was an expression of concern appropriate to a colony in which human issues, and not merely commercial exploitation or the establishment of trading factories, were at stake.[57] The new arrivals recognized that they would have to live in Rio, that their survival depended on exploring the "enormous natural resources" and potential of the nascent empire, and that the well-being of the local population must be furthered. For this reason they favored signing the treaty of 1810 and opening of the ports so that, "by the promotion of commerce, the farmers of Brazil would be able to find the best market for their products, and would thereby ensure progress in the overall cultivation and peopling of this vast territory." [58] Settlers would be encouraged by "increased agri-

[56] For numerous examples see Boxer, *The Golden Age* and *The Portuguese Seaborne Empire;* Russell-Wood, *Fidalgos and Philanthropists,* provides a detailed study of one such institution.

[57] "One important factor contributing to an increase in population is the establishment of economic and political stability for the inhabitants of cities, towns, and villages and even of the most insignificant place where there is a settlement. It is essential that all their needs be satisfied. Failure to meet their needs can result in the lands being abandoned because people are reluctant to remain in a place where basic necessities are lacking. So that the relevant steps can be taken, it is essential to verify which commodities are indispensable for subsistence in any given area, and then to ensure that they are readily available. In every settlement manioc or wheat should be sown, slaughterhouses established, orchards planted, and pasturage made available for different types of animals. Furthermore, shops must be established for the sale of foodstuffs and merchandise most appropriate to the needs of the region. In each area of settlement there should be artisans versed in different skills and a doctor or surgeon. Any measure which will further the well-being of the community should be taken, in proportion to the size of the settlement and its prosperity. Unless such natural and human resources are available, government at any level is impossible" (António Luiz de Brito Aragão e Vasconcellos, "Memórias," p. 31).

[58] Pereira da Silva, *História* 3:274.

culture, plantations of hemp, spices, and other commodities of great importance and of recognized usefulness, both for internal consumption and for export, and the extraction of precious products, both mineral and vegetable," which were to be "encouraged and protected." [59] Enlightened despots and physiocrats deceived themselves by their exaggerated notions of the resources of the virgin territory and feverishly sought material improvements. They reserved numerous privileges for the central-southern region, where the court had been established. In order to meet the costs of installation of public works and the salaries of public servants, they increased existing taxes on exports of sugar, tobacco, cotton, and hides and imposed a new series of taxes directly affecting the northern captaincies, which the court continued to burden with the harsh task of supplying recruits and funds for wars in Portugal, Guiana, and the La Plata area. Governors and civil servants in the various captaincies drew no distinction between addressing themselves to Lisbon or to Rio de Janeiro. [60]

At least two ministers in the service of Dom João VI had had administrative experience during the colonial period. [61] The governors of the various captaincies continued to wield the same despotic powers which they had exercised before independence. Despite successful administrative terms by the count of Palma in Minas Gerais and the count of Arcos in Bahia, governors were not effective in establishing liaison or furthering unity among the different regions of the colony. Rather, within their respective areas of jurisdiction they committed excesses, acted in an arbitrary manner and disregarded the authority of the court on many occasions. [62] It is undeniable, however, that efforts were undertaken by the ministers of the prince regent to make the process of administrative centralization more efficient by the appointment of district judges (*juízes de fora*) representing central authority and responsible for the coordination of local interests with those of the new court.

Moreover, the court devoted itself to the opening of roads and to the almost unprecedented policy of improving communications between captaincies, encouraging settlement, and making land-grant concessions. The ministers were convinced, to the point of obsession, of the wisdom of the policy of taking advantage of the riches "in which this fortunate and opulent country abounds, especially favored in the concentration of riches otherwise scattered throughout the four corners of the world." [63]

[59] *Ibid.,* p. 283.

[60] Rocha Martins, *O último vice-rei do Brasil,* pp. 38–39.

[61] These were Fernando José de Portugal, viceroy in Rio de Janeiro from 1801 to 1806, and the count of Arcos himself (Oliveira Lima, *Dom João VI no Brasil* 1:171–73, 180).

[62] Pereira da Silva, *História* 3:156, 288–92.

[63] Decree of November 24, 1813, in Pereira da Silva, *História* 3:348–59.

To do so, trade had to be increased and means of communication and transportation established.[64] In addition to foreigners, Brazilian travelers and engineers continued to explore the interior of the country, making surveys and topographical maps; a special bureau was created for this purpose in Rio de Janeiro.[65] A hydrographic map was made of those captaincies comprising the region between the rivers Maranhão and Pará. Expeditions were sent to explore the tributary rivers of the Amazon. An attempt was made to gain access to the commerce of Mato Grosso by the Arinos, Cuiabá, and Tapajós rivers, thereby establishing a link by land and water between Mato Grosso and São Paulo.[66] A route was found across the Guaporé, Mamoré, and Madeira rivers which would put Amazonas in contact with the backlands of the interior of Brazil. Privileges, statutes, and fiscal exemptions were granted to a company for fluvial navigation.[67] The rivers Tocantins and Araguaia were explored, although a regular navigation company was not organized. In Goiás several "capitalists" joined together and began regular transport services on rivers in that captaincy. In Minas Gerais more systematic examinations were made of the rivers Doce, Belmonte, Jequitinhonha, and the Ribeirão de Santo António do Cerro do Frio. Roads were opened from the interior to Ilhéus and Espírito Santo and from Minas Novas to Pôrto Seguro.[68] The traditions of Portuguese colonization and the zest for integration and control of natural resources supported the picture of a strong central government, whose presence was essential to neutralize conflicts within society and internal forces of disunity.

This task of reform and construction absorbed the efforts of leading Brazilians in the service of the Portuguese court and was to mold the generation of independence. The consequences of this active participation for Portuguese official policy cannot be underestimated. It was to make a severe impression on the political elite of the First Empire and was to exert a decisive influence on the whole process of consolidation of empire in Brazil, especially in the area of organizing political forces, since the picture of the national state which was to impose itself on localist interests was largely born from that experience. In this light, a few decades after independence (1838–1870), leading Brazilians were to re-formulate their didactic,[69] unifying, and progressive brand of nationalism and their eminently elitist and utilitarian social conscience.

[64] Royal letter of December 4, 1813, in *ibid.*, p. 348.

[65] Oliveira Lima, *Dom João VI no Brasil* 1:255 et seq.

[66] *Ibid.*, 2:789.

[67] Pereira da Silva, *História* 3:133.

[68] António Luiz de Brito Aragão e Vasconcellos, "Memórias," p. 43.

[69] For didactic nationalism in the Brazilian literature, see Candido de Mello e Souza, *Formação da literatura brasileira*, 2:114–15; *Literatura e Sociedade* (São Paulo, 1967), pp. 93–94.

STANLEY E. HILTON

The United States and Brazilian Independence

The fact that the United States was the first country to recognize the independence of Brazil has nourished a myth, still fed by men of state for political convenience. According to that myth, from the very beginning of official contacts the two countries shared common ideals and values and were thus linked by mutual respect and sympathy. To speak of a "secular" or "traditional" alliance between the United States and Brazil, as government spokesmen in both nations have been wont to do, especially since the turn of this century, is seriously to distort that part of historical reality discernible from documents extant in both countries. Indeed, an examination of relations between Washington and the house of Braganza during the period that began with the transfer of the Portuguese court to its Brazilian colony in 1808 and ended with American recognition of Brazil's independence in 1824 reveals that the United States and Brazil had practically nothing in common other than their geographic location in the Western Hemisphere, and that their political intercourse was therefore characterized more by friction and divergence than by mutual understanding.

The attitude of the United States toward the movement for Brazilian independence is best understood when projected against the broader screen of American foreign policy vis-à-vis Latin America and Europe during the critical period following the Napoleonic invasion of the Iberian Peninsula.[1] American publicists and statesmen naturally viewed Brazilian developments as part of the general dissolution of colonial ties between the New World and the Old. They saw it as a question not only of relations between the two Americas, but one of triangular interaction.

[1] Standard general studies of American policy toward Latin America during the period are J. Fred Rippy, *Rivalry of the United States and Great Britain over Latin America, 1808–1830* (Baltimore, 1929); Charles C. Griffin, *The United States and the Disruption of the Spanish Empire, 1810–1822* (New York, 1937); and Arthur P. Whitaker, *The United States and the Independence of Latin America, 1800–1830* (New York, 1962; orig. pub. 1941). An indispensable book on American foreign policy in general during that era is Samuel F. Bemis, *John Quincy Adams and the Foundations of American Foreign Policy* (New York, 1949).

In Latin America, the interest of the United States was both economic and political. Commerce with the region had increased enormously after 1797, when Spain opened the ports of her New World colonies to neutral ships, and the prospect of those colonies becoming independent implied even greater trade opportunities.[2] Aside from commercial considerations the United States, itself still a young republic facing an essentially hostile monarchical Europe, had a political and strategic interest in seeing the Iberian monarchies lose their New World holdings and in seeing the latter split into separate nations. President Thomas Jefferson in 1808 privately summed up the American attitude toward the Latin American provinces. "We consider their interests and ours as the same," he explained, "and that the object of both must be to exclude all European influence from this hemisphere."[3]

The movements for emancipation that sprouted throughout Spanish America in 1810 naturally captured American sympathy. "This nation seems to rejoice over the revolutions that have taken place in some parts of Spanish America," observed a suspicious Portuguese consul in Philadelphia, "and in the gazettes they openly praise those events and express hope that all the colonies will become independent." A year later various American diplomats at European posts received instructions to do everything they properly could to promote recognition of the revolutionary juntas in Spanish America, but to take care "not to compromit the pacifick relations subsisting between the United States and other powers."[4] These instructions, together with Jefferson's earlier observation, constitute a succinct statement of what was to become official policy toward the Latin American struggle for independence. The United States would give moral support and would lend encouragement, in so far as this was legally permissible, to assist the rebels. But there would be no active intervention by the United States, nor would her representatives be allowed to assume any mediatory role to aid the two contenders in resolving their problems. As President James Monroe was to write a decade later, "With respect to the Iberian colonies, the object has been to throw into their scale, in a moral sense, the weight of the United States, without so deep a compromitment as to make us a party to the contest."[5] If, however, the independence of the Iberian possessions was

[2] Whitaker, *Independence of Latin America*, pp. 23–25.

[3] Thomas Jefferson to William Claiborne, October 29, 1808, *The Writings of Thomas Jefferson*, ed. Paul L. Ford, 10 vols. (New York, 1892–99), 9:213.

[4] Consul José Rademaker (Philadelphia) to count of Linhares, December 7, 1810, Arquivo Histórico do Itamaraty, Rio de Janeiro, folder 4, container 196; James Monroe to Minister Joel Barlow (France), November 27, 1811, *Diplomatic Correspondence of the United States Concerning the Independence of the Latin American Nations*, ed. William R. Manning, 3 vols. (New York, 1925), 1:12–13.

[5] Monroe to Minister Albert Gallatin (France), May 26, 1820, *The Writings of Albert Gallatin*, ed. Henry Adams, 3 vols. (Philadelphia, 1879), 2:142.

considered an important interest of the United States, how can North American reluctance to enter the lists boldly on behalf of the Latin Americans be explained?

For one thing, the United States was itself a new country, with serious internal problems still unresolved. When the general emancipation movement began in Latin America, the United States was completing only its third decade as an independent nation. Its governmental system had not been entirely defined. Several major constitutional issues, such as control of foreign policy, or federal powers versus states' rights, were still being debated. National boundaries were not definitively fixed and serious disputes were in progress with both Spain and Great Britain. The country was agrarian, the growth of the economy was unbalanced, and finances were disorganized and unstable. The nation emerged bankrupt from the War of 1812, and the shaky structure of postwar expansion was painfully revealed in the panic of 1819.[6]

National military weakness was also a significant determinant of American caution in foreign affairs. Europe after 1815 appeared to be united under the banner of the Holy Alliance and determined to stamp out liberal or revolutionary spirit wherever it raised its pernicious head. American policymakers saw serious consequences in any energetic intervention in favor of Latin American rebels. "I am satisfied," President Monroe remarked in 1820, "that had we even joined them in the war, we should have done them more harm than good, as we might have drawn all Europe on them, not to speak of the injury we should have done to ourselves." [7] With inadequate internal communications and no large standing army or navy, the United States was in no position to engage in foreign adventures. True, American forces had neutralized British regulars during the War of 1812, but the former had fought on native soil while the British faced serious logistical problems. At the same time, moreover, London had been compelled to keep an uneasy eye on Napoleon. Even so, American armies had not escaped embarrassing defeats, such as the humiliating capture of the national capital. Whatever disposition the United States might have felt to challenge a foreign power militarily over nonterritorial questions disappeared with the war, and the country entered a long period of absorption in domestic prob-

[6] George Dangerfield, *The Awakening of American Nationalism, 1815–1828* (New York, 1965), p. 8.

[7] Monroe to Gallatin, May 26, 1820, *Writings of Albert Gallatin* 2:145. For similar remarks, see Senator Rufus King to J. A. King, March 11, 1820, *The Life and Correspondence of Rufus King*, ed. Charles R. King, 6 vols. (New York, 1894–1900), 6:297; Secretary of War John C. Calhoun to Charles Tait, May 20, 1820, *The Papers of John C. Calhoun, Volume V, 1820–1822*, ed. W. Edwin Hemphill (Columbia, S.C., 1971), p. 132.

lems. Years of peace, said Jefferson in 1815, were now the *"summum bonum"* for the United States.[8]

The impact of elite "images" or perceptions on the formulation of foreign policy has in recent times received increasing attention from students of international politics who seek linkages between a policy-maker's perception of reality and his political reaction to that reality. It is interesting to note, with regard to the cautious official response by Washington to the Spanish American independence struggles, the extent to which the writings of major American leaders reveal a deeply ingrained prejudice toward Latin and Catholic societies and skepticism about the capacity and worthiness of the Latin American. In part that prejudice was a function of the exalted sense of mission that inspired the leaders of the republican, Protestant, anti-traditionalist nation.[9] The examples of three former presidents, men who continued to influence national policy after leaving office, indicate how pervasive that anti-Latin sentiment was. "Their people are immersed in the darkest ignorance, and brutalised by bigotry & superstition," wrote Jefferson scornfully of the Latin Americans in 1813; "their priests make of them what they please. . . ." John Adams went even further and confided in 1820, "I have long been decided in opinion that a free government and the Roman Catholick religion can never exist together in any nation or country. . . ." Reflecting in 1823 on the turmoil throughout the Iberian lands, James Madison concluded that the "people of Spain as well as of Portugal need still further light & heat too from the American example before they will be a match for . . . the treachery of their leaders, and what is most of all to be dreaded, their Priests & their Prejudices." Secretary of State John Quincy Adams revealed the same strong bias when he explained to a caller in 1821 why neutrality was the best policy for the United States in the Latin American question:

So far as they were contending for independence, I wished well to their cause; but I had seen and yet see no prospect that they would establish free or liberal institutions of government. They are not likely to promote the spirit either of freedom or order by their example. They have not the first elements of good or free government. Arbitrary power, military and ecclesiastical, was stamped upon their education, upon their habits, and upon all their institutions.

Portuguese America was not exempt from such deprecatory appraisals by American observers. A series of diplomatic agents sent back to Washington

[8] Jefferson to Pierre du Pont de Nemours, April 15, 1816, *Correspondence between Thomas Jefferson and Pierre du Pont de Nemours, 1798–1817*, ed. Dumas Malone (Boston, 1930), p. 172.

[9] For an insightful discussion of the American national temper in the period, see Russel B. Nye, *The Cultural Life of the New Nation, 1776–1830* (New York, 1960), pp. 3–53.

unflattering reports on Brazilian social and political institutions, although not all were as disdainful as Consul Henry Hill in Rio de Janeiro, who scorned the Brazilians as "immoral, ignorant and superstitious," and concluded that they were "wholly incapable of self Government." [10]

The connection between United States foreign policy and this unfavorable image of the Latin Americans is evident from the remarks of John Quincy Adams. The generalized nature of the prejudice and the policy judgment based in part upon it is revealed in the private admission in 1816 by Rufus King, an influential member of the Senate Foreign Relations Committee, that "whether those South Americans are capable and worthy of self gov[ernmen]t, one is embarrassed in determining." United States policy toward the ferment prevalent in the Iberian colonies should be, said King, "to let S[outh] America alone, and so long as other Powers do not meddle, to leave the struggle to those who are engaged in it." [11]

In contrast to the Spanish American provinces, the Brazilian situation during the greater part of the period did not require decisions on possible intervention or neutrality. The consequences of the Napoleonic invasion of the Iberian Peninsula were different for Spain and Portugal. In Spain, the monarchy fell under French domination, resistance formed in both the mother country and the New World colonies, and the latter gradually moved toward independence. American diplomacy thus had to confront opposing contenders for political control in Spanish America. When Napoleon's troops moved into Portugal, however, Dom João VI packed his court off to Brazil aboard British men-of-war. The transfer of the monarchy to Brazil was peaceful, and the absence of protracted civil conflict allowed Washington a more "normal" response to the new situation. [12]

Relations between the United States and Portugal-Brazil were tranquil until the War of 1812. President Jefferson, on learning of the arrival of Dom João VI in Rio de Janeiro, appointed Henry Hill as consul there and sent a cordial message to the Portuguese monarch expressing his

[10] Jefferson to marquis de La Fayette, November 30, 1813, Jefferson, *Writings* 9: 435; John Adams to Jefferson, February 3, 1821, *The Adams-Jefferson Letters*, ed. Lester J. Cappon, 2 vols. (Chapel Hill, N.C., 1959), 2:523; James Madison to Jefferson, September 6, 1823, *The Writings of James Madison*, ed. Gaillard Hunt, 9 vols. (New York, 1900–1910), 9:155; *Memoirs of John Quincy Adams*, ed. Charles F. Adams 12 vols. (Philadelphia, 1874–77), 5:324–25; Henry Hill to J. Q. Adams, May 1821, Manning, *Diplomatic Correspondence* 2:713, 716.

[11] King to Charles Gore, November 5, 1816, February 13, 1818, *Correspondence of Rufus King* 6:33, 116.

[12] On the removal of the Portuguese court to Brazil, see Alan K. Manchester, "The Transfer of the Portuguese Court to Rio de Janeiro," *Conflict and Continuity in Brazilian Society*, eds. Henry H. Keith and S. F. Edwards (Columbia, S.C., 1969), pp. 148–63.

interest in establishing a "system of intercourse between the different regions of this hemisphere." The following year the designation of a minister, Thomas Sumter, Jr., to represent the United States at the Portuguese court, and the sale of products worth an estimated $1 million, followed by a doubling of trade over the next two years, seemed favorable auguries for the future of relations between the United States and Portugal.[13]

Whatever enthusiasm those developments may have instilled in Yankee merchants was nonetheless of short duration. The War of 1812 had a disastrous effect on American commerce, which also began to feel the consequences of the tariff advantages conceded by Dom João VI to British exporters in 1810. The value of American shipments to Brazil declined from $1.7 million in 1811 to only $410.000 in 1816. Political relations between Washington and the Portuguese court also worsened in this period as a result of the incapacity or unwillingness of the court to make its neutrality respected during the war and the consequent damages suffered by American merchants at the hands of British raiders using Brazilian ports.[14] Furthermore, in the eyes of American ideologues, Brazil, with its apparent monarchical stability, did not awaken the same interest as certain areas of Spanish America where "republicans" were battling "royalists."

In a climate of deteriorating commercial and political relations, American acceptance of the elevation of Brazil to the status of joint kingdom with Portugal late in 1815 was cordial but unenthusiastic. Minister Sumter took advantage of the occasion to urge Dom João VI to improve relations with the United States, while in Washington Monroe, then secretary of state, expressed to the Portuguese chargé his interest in greater harmony with the royal government. But there was little sympathy in American official circles for the house of Braganza. Repeated complaints by the Portuguese minister in Washington, José Corrêa da Serra, concerning attacks made on Portuguese ships by Uruguayan corsairs fitted in American ports, and the counterprotests presented by the State Department over losses suffered during the War of 1812, did nothing to clear the air.[15]

It was in this atmosphere that word reached the United States late in April 1817 that a revolution against royal authority had taken place in Brazil's northeastern province of Pernambuco. For Americans, who tended to see any antimonarchist gesture as a sign of patriotism, the events were

[13] Lawrence F. Hill, *Diplomatic Relations between the United States and Brazil* (Durham, N.C., 1932), pp. 3–6.

[14] *Ibid.*, pp. 11–16; Whitaker, *Independence of Latin America*, p. 116.

[15] Thomas Sumter, Jr., to Monroe, December 29, 1815, Manning, *Diplomatic Correspondence* 2:699; Monroe to Rademaker, June 5, 1816, *ibid.*, 1:31; Hill, *United States and Brazil*, pp. 16–18.

regarded as the first manifestation of a truly "patriotic" reaction in Brazil. The news was accordingly received with undisguised glee by the press throughout the country. "Highly Important" was the headline of the first article to appear in the prestigious *National Intelligencer* (April 29) of Washington. The *Boston Patriot* (May 3) labeled the revolt an "Important Revolution." The press commentaries were based on two general assumptions. First, it was widely believed that the insurrection in Pernambuco was merely the initial spark of a conflagration that would ultimately sweep the whole country. "The residence of the Court of Portugal at Rio has . . . checked the revolutionary spirit which has been fomenting for several years, but which it will now be impossible to reduce," the *Boston Patriot* (May 3) affirmed with characteristic confidence.[16] The second general assumption was that the uprising was republican, that its objective was to establish a political regime molded on the American system, and that the new government would seek intimate ties with the United States. The *Boston Patriot* (May 3), for example, informed its readers that the "patriots" of Pernambuco were "entirely in favor of the United States," a judgment reiterated by the respected *Niles' Weekly Register* (May 10), which added that the Pernambucans "seem to possess very correct notions about the republican system." [17]

Rebel leaders in Recife had foreseen this reaction on the part of public opinion in the United States and hoped to use it as a lever to pry support from the American government. One of their immediate acts was to write a letter to their "Dear Brother," President Monroe, in which they argued that the Pernambucan cause was the same as that of the Americans in 1776 and held out the prospect of trade advantages in the event that their revolt was successful.[18] At the same time the revolutionary junta designated António Gonçalves da Cruz as special emissary to convey these greetings. Gonçalves da Cruz was a wealthy man whose republican sentiments had earned him the ill-will of the royal authorities before the revolt. He sold his belongings and was preparing to embark for New York when the uprising occurred. Persuaded to serve the cause, he sailed for the United States charged with the impossible task of securing formal diplomatic recognition, war supplies, and perhaps the services of exiled French officers. The junta reminded him that the "spirit of the American

---

16 Cf. *Niles' Weekly Register*, May 3, 1817; *Boston Patriot,* May 24, 1817. On the events in Pernambuco, see Francisco Muniz Tavares, *História da revolução de Pernambuco em 1817*, 3d ed. (Recife, 1917); Manoel de Oliveira Lima, *Dom João VI no Brasil, 1808–21*, 2 vols. (Rio de Janeiro, 1908), 2:785–828; and, for a recent and more analytical study, Carlos Guilherme Mota, *Nordeste, 1817. Estruturas e argumentos* (São Paulo, 1972).

17 Cf. *National Intelligencer* (Washington), April 29, 1817.

18 Governadores Provisórios da Província de Pernambuco to Monroe, March 12, 1817, *DHBNRJ* 101 (1953):18–19.

people is thoroughly mercantile" and instructed him to emphasize in his talks with American officials the unprecedented opportunity that the revolt afforded for commerce based upon "liberal principles of economy." [19]

The Pernambucan envoy met with a lively reception in the United States. His arrival flattered national pride and vanity and stimulated commercial appetites as well. "Hail, Pernambuco! Hail, the New Republic!" exulted the *Boston Patriot* (May 17). Seizing the occasion to attack monarchist principles, the *Patriot* praised the "wisdom, humanity, and moderation" of the rebel government, while other newspapers expressed pride in the fact that foreign patriots looked to the United States as their "guardian and natural protector." [20] But it was not solely a question of political sentiment. On hearing of the events in Pernambuco many observers had sensed a financial opportunity. Now, in the face of rumors that Gonçalves da Cruz would not be received officially by the administration, the *Patriot* (May 27) emphasized the potential commercial importance of Pernambucan goodwill. Because "any tendency to stimulate our commerce should be carefully cultivated," the Boston newspaper was convinced that the rebel delegate would be welcomed "by the President and by all the members of the government."

The *Patriot* was wrong. It was not that the developments in Pernambuco had not attracted official attention. On the contrary, they had sparked excited discussion in the diplomatic corps and influential political circles in Washington. Baron Hyde de Neuville, the French minister, for example, on the day that the news was received, noted worriedly that the movement in northeastern Brazil appeared to be "very menacing" to monarchical stability in that country.[21] Minister Corrêa da Serra was naturally alarmed, and he hastened to assure the State Department that it was a question of a "simple insurrection" that would be "as transient as it had been unjustifiable." The Portuguese diplomat, a man whom John Quincy Adams described as "quick, sensitive, fractious, hasty, and, when excited, obstinate," [22] subsequently delivered formal notes against the revolt and published an anonymous article in the *National Intelligencer* (May 12) minimizing the possibilities of rebel success. On May 14 he returned to the State Department to protest about arms allegedly shipped from American ports to the rebels. The United States, he complained in irritation, was regarded by European powers as the "great fomenters of rebellion." [23]

[19] Unsigned instructions for António Gonçalves da Cruz, March 27, 1817, Arquivo Histórico do Itamaraty, folder 5, container 195.

[20] *Philadelphia Weekly Aurora,* June 9, 1817.

[21] Baron J. G. Hyde de Neuville, *Mémoires et souvenirs,* 2 vols. (Paris, 1890), 2:269.

[22] *Memoirs of John Quincy Adams* 4:326.

[23] The activity of Corrêa da Serra is described in a letter from Acting Secretary of

National leaders of great influence sympathized completely with the Pernambucans. "Portugal . . . has lost her great northern province of Pernambuco," Jefferson wrote with premature satisfaction, "and I shall not wonder if Brazil should revolt in mass, and send their royal family back to Portugal." President Monroe himself, days before the revolt became a subject of public comment, had privately expressed his "well-founded hope" that the Spanish American provinces would be successful in their struggle to achieve independence.[24] The news of ferment in Brazil could thus only have pleased him. But it was impossible to think of deviating from the policy of neutrality. Relations with Spain were severely strained. Any official aid to the rebels in Recife would undoubtedly disrupt the already none too cordial relations with the Portuguese court, and the probable reaction of other European countries was disquieting to contemplate. The arrival of Gonçalves da Cruz, with the obvious intention of soliciting help from Washington, therefore placed Monroe in a potentially difficult position. He wanted to demonstrate unofficially his solidarity with the Pernambucans, but did not wish by so doing to encourage Cruz to make insistent overtures.

The president opted to send a personal representative, Caesar Rodney, to meet privately with Gonçalves da Cruz to explain the administration's dilemma. Monroe sent word that he and the American people hoped that the "cause of liberty and autonomy" would ultimately triumph in Brazil and that the United States would grant belligerent privileges to the rebel government. More than that he could not do. In Monroe's opinion, the United States would in fact best serve the Pernambucan campaign by remaining neutral. "That whilst they remain in their present neutral state," Rodney recalled the president as having said, "the [South American] provinces may be well supplied, without the interferences of England, who, if we were to take an active part would immediately cut them off." Indeed, said Monroe, American intervention might "provoke the enmity of the whole league [Holy Alliance]." The president, furthermore, did not believe that the executive branch of government possessed the constitutional authority to make decisions on foreign policy that could lead the country into war. For these reasons, Gonçalves da Cruz was to be informed that he should not request an official audience and should approach the government, if necessary, only through the official channels of the State Department.[25]

After conferring with the president on June 4, Rodney traveled

State Richard Rush to Madison, June 14, 1817, James Monroe Papers, Microfilm roll 6, Manuscripts Division, Library of Congress.

[24] Jefferson to La Fayette, May 14, 1817, *The Writings of Thomas Jefferson* 10:85, 15:117; Monroe to Joel R. Poinsett, April 25, 1817, Manning, *Diplomatic Correspondence* 1:39.

[25] Caesar Rodney to Monroe, June 6, 1817, Monroe Papers, roll 6.

the next day to Philadelphia, where the Pernambucan agent was lodged. In his conversation with the presidential emissary, Gonçalves da Cruz underscored the friendly disposition of the Pernambucans toward the United States, and compared their struggle with that of the Americans four decades earlier. He mentioned the letter he had brought for Monroe, and explained that he was also empowered to sign a commercial agreement that would be "highly advantageous" to the United States. American unwillingness to go further than allowing private shipments of supplies to Pernambuco was nonetheless clear, and Gonçalves da Cruz could only express satisfaction with Monroe's message and agree that caution was necessary because of European hostility. A talk with Secretary of State Richard Rush in Washington a few days later was equally discouraging. Rush recommended that the rebel delegate not even reside in the capital; declared emphatically, in response to an offer from Gonçalves da Cruz, that the United States could handle any difficulties with Great Britain without Pernambuco's aid; and brushed aside the idea of a "treaty of alliance" with Pernambuco. "He told me," Gonçalves da Cruz wrote, "that the matter could not be discussed at the present time." [26]

If the Pernambucan leaders based their revolt on the hope of gaining recognition from the United States, as has been suggested,[27] and that Gonçalves da Cruz could achieve this end, they committed a fatal error of judgment because his mission failed at the very outset. To be sure, American publicists continued to emphasize the possible commercial benefits that would result from more intimate ties with South America. Typical of such an attitude was a report in the *Philadelphia Weekly Aurora* (July 21): "We must look to the republics of the south, as our natural connexions, the entrepots of our particular commerce, the sources of that wealth and enterprise which the sordid selfishness of Europe really excludes us from. . . ." But in reality the probable fate of the Pernambucans suggested that there was little hope that those riches could be exploited. "If such a spirit [of liberty] is abroad [in Brazil], the king of Portugal cannot lay it," defiantly declared *Niles' Weekly Register* (June 28) but without its former enthusiastic conviction. In July, the well-known monthly *North American Review* sounded a pessimistic note regarding the attempt to overthrow royal authority in Recife, "a rotten branch of a decayed stock." [28] Later that same month the press announced that the Pernambucans had abandoned the fight. An eloquent plea for "aid of any kind" by Gonçalves da Cruz to the White House went unanswered. His subsequent efforts to enlist the assistance of French of-

---

[26] *Ibid.*; unsigned memorandum by Gonçalves da Cruz, n.d., Arquivo Histórico do Itamaraty, folder 5, container 195.

[27] Cf. Muniz Tavares, *Revolução de Pernambuco.*

[28] "Revolution in Pernambuco," *North American Review* 5 (1817):227–39.

ficers and Spanish-American revolutionaries were equally unproductive.[29]

The Pernambuco episode did stimulate the already keen interest of the Monroe administration in the progress of revolutionary movements in South America and accelerated the president's plans to send a special mission to the west coast of that region to gather information. The preparations were made even before the news of the rebels' defeat at Recife was received, but a series of events delayed the departure of the three commissioners—Caesar Rodney, Theodorik Bland, and John Graham—until the end of the year. Their initial instructions, drawn up in mid-June, charged the three agents with studying the political, economic, and military situation in South America. They were advised to pay particular attention to possibilities for commerce in South America and to current attitudes toward the United States and Europe. Reflecting the government's interest in Brazilian developments, the three men were originally instructed to visit Recife and Salvador, as well as Rio de Janeiro, Buenos Aires, and other major cities. The collapse of the revolt in Pernambuco, however, led the State Department to cancel the projected stopovers in northeastern Brazil.[30]

On arrival in Rio de Janeiro the special observers found an apparently tranquil situation. Dom João VI, perhaps because his current drive to establish Portuguese sovereignty over the Banda Oriental, or Uruguay, was arousing the opposition of European allies of the king of Spain, granted an audience to the captain of the ship carrying Rodney and his colleagues. The Portuguese monarch expressed "great respect" for the young republic in North America and said that he was "extremely desirous" of friendly relations with the United States. From Sumter the special envoys learned that the "spirit of revolt was by no means extensive through Brazil." The economic potential of Brazil made an indelible impression on the three visitors. Once back in the United States, Henry Brackenridge, the secretary of the mission, published a book in which he voiced sentiments shared by other Americans with experience in Latin American affairs:

The only empires that can be compared to the Brazil, in point of magnitude, are those of China, Russia and the United States; and although at present the least in point of population, the day will come, when it will be the greatest. Brazil is, in fact, the body and heart of South America. . . . It may seem pre-

---

[29] António Gonçalves da Cruz to Monroe, August 20, 1817, cited in Muniz Tavares, *Revolução de Pernambuco*, p. 199 (notes by Oliveira Lima). On the subsequent activities of Gonçalves da Cruz, see Corrêa da Serra to Governor Luiz do Rego Barreto (Pernambuco), December 15, 1817; José Carlos Mairink da Silva Ferrão to António Simões Roussado e Freire, December 20, 1817, *DHBNRJ* 107:173, 181.

[30] Rush to Rodney and John Graham, July 18, 1817, Manning, *Diplomatic Correspondence* 1:42–45; J. Q. Adams to Rodney, Graham, and Theodorik Bland, Nov. 21, 1817, *ibid.*, p. 47.

mature at this day to institute a comparison between the Brazils and our country; but the time will come, when such a comparison will appear natural, and even unavoidable. . . . Here, then, when we consider the vast capacities and resources of Brazil, it is not visionary to say, that this empire is destined to be our rival. If formed by the mighty genius of a Peter the Great, and developed on a scale commensurate with its extraordinary extent, resources, and advantages, it would not be long before the truth of these observations would be made evident.

Brackenridge's conclusions about United States interest in the Brazilian political system reflected the same prejudice that characterized North American observers in general. "Looking at the Brazils therefore as a rival, and in the nature of things she must be such," he wrote, "it may be well that she is placed under a race of kings, not likely to inspire the formidable energy of our republic; but rather to dissipate the force of the body politic, in childish projects, and royal extravagance." It was in the interest of the United States, however, to cultivate Brazil's goodwill: "With their monarchical government let them do as they please, we are not in search of proselytes to republicanism. . . ." [31] The fact that the value of American exports to Brazil increased progressively over the next five years—from $413,000 in 1817 to $1.38 million in 1821—although they did not reach the 1811 level, seemed to justify, in part, Brackenridge's optimistic assessment of Brazil's potential and his suggestions for American policy. [32]

Nonetheless, political relations between Washington and the house of Braganza remained precarious. The State Department was angered by the treatment given certain American citizens by Brazilian authorities, while the royal court was unhappy with the attitude of the United States during the Pernambucan episode. There was also the old problem of Uruguayan attacks on Luso-Brazilian shipping. The result of this diplomatic bickering was to envelop Luso-American relations in a cloud of intense acrimony. "News from Rio de Janeiro presents us with a very unfavorable view of the temper of the Portuguese government," Secretary of Treasury William Crawford privately commented in mid-1818. Early the following year, John Quincy Adams noted uneasily in his diary that the difficulties with Brazil had produced "so much ill blood between the two countries that it has festered into all but actual hostility." Matters appeared to reach a critical level that year when John Graham, one of the three commissioners who had visited Brazil in 1818, was appointed as the new minister to the Portuguese court. In conversation with Adams about his mission, Graham became "quite alarmed" with

[31] Henry M. Brackenridge, *Voyage to South America* . . ., 2 vols. (Baltimore, 1819), 1:125, 133–34, 155–57, 164.
[32] Whitaker, *Independence of Latin America*, p. 117.

the secretary's account of the state of American relations with the Luso-Brazilian empire. Graham gained from talks with Corrêa da Serra the definite impression, he told Adams, that the Portuguese envoy's dispatches to authorities in Rio de Janeiro tended to "inflame their animosity" against the United States. Adams reflected to himself that Graham's mission would hopefully "cool down all this inflammation, . . . [and] turn all this wormwood into balm." [33] His official instructions to Graham were to inform the Portuguese court that the United States was aware of the problem of violations of its neutrality laws by Uruguayan corsairs, and that it was its "sincere desire" to maintain Brazil's friendship. At the same time, recommended Adams, Graham should defend politely but "firmly and energetically" the right of the United States to a satisfactory resolution of its grievances. [34]

Graham's mission was destined to be unproductive. When he presented his credentials to Dom João late in July 1819, he spoke—in Spanish—of Washington's desire to improve relations with Portugal. Because he had difficulty in understanding Portuguese, he received the impression that the king had replied in like terms. Foreign Minister Tomás Vila Nova Portugal, however, had no problem in making himself understood. When Graham mentioned the possibility of mutual tariff reductions, the Portuguese official retorted "rather abruptly . . . that this was not the time to talk of commercial arrangements when the two countries were almost in a state of actual war." Vilanova brushed off Graham's inquiry about American seamen imprisoned in Brazilian jails, indicating that to him the question was insignificant. He also rejected Graham's suggestion that they have occasional "free and informal" discussions on the various issues straining relations between their governments. "This fact," noted Graham, "lessens my hopes of being able to do anything with him." Long weeks of fruitless negotiations left the American envoy totally disheartened and convinced that there was "little or no prospect of doing anything here." The house of Braganza, he glumly concluded, attributed "less importance to our Friendship than it would seem to merit," and appeared not to fear the consequences of an open break with the United States. [35]

The upshot of the failure of Graham's mission to establish a better understanding with Rio de Janeiro was to heighten American disenchantment with the ruling house there and to make even more difficult the elimination of the political differences between the United States and

[33] William Crawford to Gallatin, May 1, 1818, *The Writings of Albert Gallatin* 2:63; *Memoirs of John Quincy Adams* 4:341–42.

[34] J. Q. Adams to Graham, April 24, 1819, Manning, *Diplomatic Correspondence* 1:98–101.

[35] Graham to J. Q. Adams, August 7, 1819, October 26, 1819, Records of the Department of State, roll 5, microcopy 121, National Archives.

Brazil. Corrêa da Serra went so far as to warn Secretary of State Adams "that five or six years ago the people of the United States were the nation on earth for whom the Portuguese felt the most cordial regard and friendship. They were now those whom they most hated. . . ." The Portuguese diplomat also confided to Jefferson that his government had actually considered declaring war on the United States.[36]

Corrêa da Serra suggested that one solution to their strained relations would be for the United States and Portugal-Brazil to join together in an "American system of politics, in contradistinction to the European." This elaborately phrased notion amounted in practice to little more than joint action against pirates in the waters of the Western Hemisphere. It is not clear whether this proposal originated in Rio de Janeiro or whether it represented personal diplomacy. It was clear, however, that by "pirates," the Portuguese meant Uruguayans, and Washington staunchly resisted any measures that might hinder the movements for independence. "The idea has something imposing in it," Monroe admitted, "but I am inclined to think that the effect would be to connect us with Portugal in some degree against the revolutionary colonies." Secretary Adams, in a cabinet meeting, vigorously supported the president:

Portugal and the United States are the two great American powers much as a jolly-boat and the Columbus are two great line-of-battle ships. . . . So long as Portugal shall recognize the House of Braganza for her sovereign, so long the House of Braganza will be European, and not American—a satellite and not a primary planet. As to an American system, we have it; we constitute the whole of it; there is no community of interests or of principles between North and South America.[37]

Washington thus rejected Corrêa da Serra's curious proposal and even subsequently reaffirmed its "perfect and impartial neutrality" in the struggle between Brazil and the Banda Oriental.[38]

The tumult of 1820 in the Iberian Peninsula, with "liberal" uprisings first in Spain and then in Portugal, was to have a decisive influence on the course of Brazilian history. Summoned to Lisbon by the newly formed Côrtes, Dom João VI, in order to protect his throne, was forced to abandon Brazil in April 1821, leaving his son Dom Pedro as prince regent in Rio de Janeiro. Given the state of relations between Washington and the house of Braganza, it was natural that American observers should view with some satisfaction events which seemed likely to weaken the con-

---

[36] J. Q. Adams to Monroe, August 30, 1820, *The Writings of John Quincy Adams,* ed. Worthington C. Ford, 7 vols. (New York, 1913–17), 5:70.

[37] Monroe to J. Q. Adams, August 11, 1820, *ibid.,* p. 63; *Memoirs of John Quincy Adams* 5:176.

[38] J. Q. Adams to Corrêa da Serra, September 30, 1820, *Writings of John Quincy Adams* 7:74.

trol of that house over the Luso-Brazilian world. Jefferson spoke for many when he declared privately that to manifest support for the Portuguese liberals was one of the United States' "duties." [39] *Niles' Weekly Register* (October 28, 1820) referred optimistically to "considerable ferment" in Brazil, and thought a revolution probable. The *Register* hoped (January 20, 1821) that reports that Dom João VI would refuse to recognize the authority of the Côrtes in Lisbon were true because such a refusal, presumably by sparking a popular revolt, might lead to the downfall of the monarch, the "sort of animal that we are willing to get rid of, on very easy terms."

During the agitation of 1821–22, when Brazil moved rapidly toward independence, that marked antimonarchist sentiment found vigorous expression in the reports of American diplomatic agents, who continued to paint an unfavorable portrait of the royal government and the people it governed. Consul Hill, for example, commented in May 1821 that "this Government . . . has scarcely rested on any other foundation than the fears and supposed reverence of the people, for a superstitious religion and an antiquated Monarchy; and on the reliance which was placed upon their ignorance and inertness." [40] In following months the Brazilian situation captured the close attention of the American public. Because of delays in communications, news was always late and often confusing. But an unshakeable faith in the virtues and historical inevitability of "free" government led the American press to interpret practically all developments in Brazil as signs of a coming republic. Late in November *Niles' Weekly Register* confidently declared its "full expectation of a free and independent government" for Brazil. Although recognizing that events, as the momentous year 1822 wore on, did not permit precise evaluation of their probable outcome, the fact that Brazil seemed to be seeking "a total independence of Europe" was regarded as a positive sign—for might this not mean ideological as well as political separation? [41]

The ill-advised decision of the Côrtes to demand that Dom Pedro should also return to Lisbon greatly offended nativist sentiment in Brazil and gave powerful impetus to the embryonic independence movement. Ignoring the summons, the prince regent in mid-1822 called for the creation of a national assembly, an act "very pleasing" to North American observers. [42] Independence was now only a matter of time. In August and September 1822 the government in Rio de Janeiro, in a series of proclamations and acts, severed political ties with Portugal.

Such historic events did not prompt exuberant commentaries in the

[39] Jefferson to F. W. Gilmer, November 29, 1820, Thomas Jefferson Papers, roll 87, Manuscripts Division, Library of Congress.
[40] Hill to J. Q. Adams, May 1821, Manning, *Diplomatic Correspondence* 2:74.
[41] *Richmond Enquirer,* June 18, 1822.
[42] *New York Spectator,* August 13, 1822.

United States. Ample press coverage was given in the form of factual summaries of events and translations of various proclamations, manifestos, decrees, and letters exchanged between Dom Pedro and his father. But the euphoria of 1817 was lacking. Indeed, there was obvious disappointment that independence had been achieved under the aegis of a monarch. As long as the threat of Portuguese intervention to subjugate Brazil existed, said the *National Gazette* of Philadelphia (November 13, 1822), the new regime in Rio de Janeiro could suppress internal opposition to monarchical government. But once that threat was removed, "the principles of civil and political liberty which have been sown, will germinate and spread actively. A *constitutional* Emperor," the *Gazette* affirmed, "is a solecism which few will be at a loss to discern. No imperial or monarchical rule can be permanent on this Continent." Pointing to the language used by Dom Pedro in some of his public statements, the *New York Spectator* (November 1, 1822) warned that "some underhand plot is going on to play off a farce similar to that recently exhibited in Mexico," where Agustín Iturbide had been proclaimed emperor. Dom Pedro's words were "totally inconsistent with the rights of the people," the *Spectator* charged. In following weeks the New York newspaper continued its verbal onslaught on the domestic and foreign policies of the Brazilian monarch. "We do not think we exceed the bounds of common charity, when we express a wish, that these upstart Emperors were swept from the face of the earth," the *Spectator* editorialized (December 10) with regard to the clash between Brazil and the La Plata provinces. "They seem to be scorpions, who have placed themselves, by the turpidity of their conduct, and their hatred of liberty, beyond the pale of human tolerance." Some months later *Niles' Weekly Register* (May 3, 1823) was to sum up North American disillusionment when it branded the government in Rio de Janeiro as "stupidly monarchical."

Reports from diplomats in Brazil speaking of ties between Dom Pedro and European powers deepened the suspicions of American leaders toward the new order in that country. "There is little doubt but that France has made some promises to the Emperor," wrote the American consul in Rio de Janeiro, "and it is very clear that French influence now pre-dominates at this court." Some monarchist journals, the consul added, were openly calling Dom Pedro the *"point d'appui* upon which the Monarchs of Europe rely, regarding him as a 'counterpoise to the democracies of North and South America.'" Such reports made a deep impression in Washington, where the State Department utilized Dom Pedro's alleged pro-

European tendencies as an argument against recognition of the Brazilian monarchy.[43]

José Silvestre Rebello, sent to Washington as the first Brazilian chargé d'affaires, felt American distrust of his government on all sides. At the State Department the Brazilian diplomat argued that his people, like those of the United States, had a right to the form of government they wanted. The Brazilians, he said, desired a hereditary monarchy. This argument, however, had little impact, Rebello realized, since American leaders nourished a "dreadful antipathy" toward monarchies.[44] Indeed, "a king is today ill regarded merely for being a king, and monarchical governments are worthless, in the opinion of these people," he wrote.[45] So impressed did the Brazilian envoy become with the force of anti-monarchist sentiment in the United States that he became suspicious of all American intentions toward Latin America. "The idea that all America must be republican, since all Europe is royalist, has taken root [fez impressão]," he cautioned the court in Rio de Janeiro, "and in such a way that it serves as the basis for the conduct [of the United States] in politics. . . ." [46] It was known that an American congressman had visited Mexico on the eve of Iturbide's overthrow, "and I do not doubt that he spread antimonarchist ideas. . . ," he warned.[47] Although Rebello's fears of American policy were exaggerated, they serve as an interesting indication of the suspicion and mistrust with which American leaders and publicists reacted to the persistence of a monarchy in Brazil.

Despite these mutual doubts, there nonetheless were strong forces at work promoting normal diplomatic relations between the two countries. One such force was the prospect of commercial expansion. The vision of Brazilian potential carried back to the United States by the special commissioners of 1818 was reinforced by the increase in exports to Brazil and found echoes as that country moved toward independence. *Niles' Weekly Register,* though critical of Brazil's political system, recognized (November 10, 1821) its economic possibilities. In making the immodest suggestion that with wise rulers there was no reason why Brazil could not "advance almost as rapidly to greatness as we ourselves have done," the editors of the *Register* were at least implicitly calling attention to com-

---

43 Condy Raguet to J. Q. Adams, January 20, 1824, Manning, *Diplomatic Correspondence* 2:775; *Memoirs of John Quincy Adams,* 6:317.

44 José Silvestre Rebello to Foreign Minister Luiz Carvalho e Melo, May 26, 1824; *Archivo diplomatico da independencia,* 6 vols. (Rio de Janeiro, 1923), 5:107. For a detailed study of Rebello's mission, see Arthur P. Whitaker, "José Silvestre Rebello: The First Diplomatic Representative of Brazil in the United States," *HAHR* 20 (1940):380–401.

45 Rebello to Carvalho e Melo, June 26, 1824, *Archivo diplomatico* 5:118–19.

46 Rebello to Carvalho e Melo, June 5, 1824, *ibid.,* p. 117.

47 Rebello to Carvalho e Melo, May 26, 1824, *ibid.,* p. 107.

mercial opportunities. The consul in Rio de Janeiro agreed, observing in June 1822 that independence for Brazil could mean "great benefits" for American traders.[48] Shortly after receiving the news that Brazil had proclaimed its independence, the *Richmond Enquirer* (December 19, 1822) published a statement underlining these opportunities:

> The population of Brazil is now about that of the American colonies when they declared independence. . . . The commerce of this country is principally engrossed by the British, who have had a very beneficial Commercial Treaty with the Portuguese, and have almost glutted the country with their manufactures. Should a Brazilian government be permanently established, . . . preference will be given to the commerce of the United States; and a great market be found not only for several of our staple articles, but the surpluses of the products of our growing manufactures, and our ingenious handycraftsmen.

Within the cabinet itself there was opinion strongly in favor of protecting trade interests. Secretary of War John C. Calhoun argued forcefully at a meeting early in 1824 that "acknowledgment of the independence of Brazil was highly important, our trade thither being already very considerable, and promising to be more valuable than with all the rest of South America." [49]

Gonçalves da Cruz, who remained in the United States after his ill-fated mission on behalf of the Pernambucan rebels, and in 1823 was designated consul-general by Dom Pedro, saw the importance of such a current of public opinion and assured his government that the United States would not let republican scruples stand in the way of recognizing the Brazilian monarchy because it would be eager to share in Brazil's "exuberant riches." That the imperial government recognized the force of the commercial factor was made clear in instructions sent to Rebello: he was to impress upon the American authorities the fact that the possible trade advantages the United States would enjoy would be in proportion "to the enthusiasm that prompt recognition would arouse in Brazil." [50]

Another factor that cleared the way for Washington's acceptance of the new order in Brazil was a change in the political alignment of the European powers. The major shift was the growing split between England and the other powers, but there were also signs of discord between France and Spain, even before the so-called Riego Revolt of 1820. With the threat of European intervention lessened and the Spanish-American revolutionaries making military progress, in 1822 the United States had recognized "patriot" regimes in Colombia, Mexico, Chile, La Plata, and Peru.

---

[48] Acting Consul P. Sartoris to J. Q. Adams, June 13, 1822, Manning, *Diplomatic Correspondence* 2:737.

[49] *Memoirs of John Quincy Adams* 6:281.

[50] Cruz to José Bonifácio de Andrada e Silva, July 31, 1823; instructions to Rebello, *Archivo diplomatico* 5:73, 12.

The patent opposition of Great Britain to the French invasion of Spain in 1823 to restore the autocratic rule of Ferdinand VII was a prime consideration, of course, in Monroe's statements against European influence in the Western Hemisphere, contained in his message to Congress in December 1823 later known as the Monroe Doctrine.[51]

Concern over European activity and objectives in Latin America continued, however, to form part of the atmosphere in which American policymakers evaluated alternatives. Indeed, the Brazilian government regarded Washington's perpetual uneasiness over European intentions as its trump card, and Rebello was instructed to play it at the outset: "To convince that Government of the special interest it has in promptly recognizing our independence, it will suffice," said the minister of foreign affairs, "to recall what has so frequently been said and written about the danger that America faces if in its present position it does not look to itself and all of it unite, in order to create a barrier to the unjust schemes of old and ambitious Europe." If that reminder was not sufficient to obtain American diplomatic support, Rebello was to probe American sensitivity with less delicacy, making it known that Brazil, in the absence of such support, "would find itself forced to seek it from some power in Europe." Faithful to these directives, the Brazilian envoy delivered at least two notes to Secretary of State Adams in which he raised the specter of European influence in Brazil. Such admonitions undoubtedly fell on fertile ground. Monroe, at least, expressed privately the opinion that by recognizing a monarchy in Brazil, the United States might "come less in collision with the European powers." [52]

In assessing the reaction of the United States to Brazil's candidacy for recognition, it is important to recall that one of the Spanish-American governments recognized in 1822 was a monarchy. The American government, in the case of Iturbide's Mexico, overcame its ideological doubts and acted coldly in the national interest, perhaps largely because both the president and Secretary Adams were convinced that sooner or later all monarchies, particulary in the Americas, would disappear. Adams, in fact, expressed on one occasion his expectation that Brazil and Argentina would go to war "and then will soon be seen that the republican hemisphere will endure neither emperor nor king upon its shores." Distasteful as monarchies were, there nonetheless existed this precedent for their acceptance.

[51] On the influence of European events on American foreign policy, see Whitaker, *Independence of Latin America*, pp. 317–95; William S. Robertson, *France and Latin-American Independence* (Baltimore, 1939), pp. 178–225. The classic study of the Monroe Doctrine is Dexter Perkins, *The Monroe Doctrine, 1823–1826* (Cambridge, Mass., 1927).

[52] Instructions to Rebello, *Archivo diplomatico* 5:12; Rebello to J. Q. Adams, April 20, 29, 1822, Manning, *Diplomatic Correspondence* 2:788–89, 792; *Memoirs of John Quincy Adams*, 6:319.

Secretary of War Calhoun argued in a cabinet session of April 1824 that "to decline the recognition of the Empire of Brazil because it was monarchical, would be a departure from the policy hitherto observed, and would introduce a new principle of interference in the internal government of foreign nations." Monroe himself was certain by this time that recognition was the prudent course. "He said that the essential principle for us was the point of independence," Adams wrote after talking to the president early in May. "The form of government was not our concern." [53]

Three weeks later, on May 26, 1824, Monroe decided to receive Rebello formally, thereby acknowledging Brazil's independence. During his special audience with the president, Rebello assured him that "the government and people of Brazil will always remember," and Monroe in reply promised that the United States would always maintain the "most friendly relations" with Brazil. In Rio de Janeiro the news of recognition, according to the American consul, had a dramatic impact. Portuguese residents became "excessively enraged, for there is scarcely a native of Portugal here," the consul reported, "who has not been dreaming of a reunion with the Mother Country, and some of them indulged in bitter execrations, maintaining that it was a disgrace for a monarchy to solicit the patronage of a Republick, and of one so *insignificant* in the scale of nations." The emperor was said to have "rejoiced beyond measure" when he learned of Monroe's gesture. In a subsequent message to the American government he reiterated the promise never to forget Washington's attitude. [54]

Thus opened the first chapter in the history of diplomatic relations between the United States and independent Brazil. The American government had not recognized the Brazilian monarchy out of enthusiasm for the regime, which, in American eyes, had in its favor only the fact that it had severed political ties with a European power and that the nation it ruled was a potentially important market. The court in Rio de Janeiro retained dynastic ties with the king of Portugal, and in the recent past American leaders could find no reason for satisfaction over the prospect of continuing to deal with the house of Braganza in South America.

When Rebello early in 1825 proposed an "offensive and deffensive [*sic*] alliance" between the two countries to prevent Lisbon from undertaking the reconquest of Brazil, the State Department not only refused but declared that should Portugal forcibly occupy part of Brazilian territory the United States would remain neutral, "offering its friendship, and do-

<hr />

[53] Whitaker, *Independence of Latin America*, pp. 378–79, 554; *Memoirs of John Quincy Adams* 6:281, 319.

[54] Rebello to Carvalho e Melo, May 26, 1824; Carvalho e Melo to Rebello, September 13, 1824, *Archivo diplomatico* 5:23, 109; Raguet to J. Q. Adams, September 12, 1824, Manning, *Diplomatic Correspondence* 2:803–4.

ing equal justice to both parties." [55] Any such alliance for the United States in that epoch was clearly out of the question, but evident in the American reply was a distaste for the Brazilian monarchy that the polished language of diplomacy could not hide. The attitude of the government of the United States toward the new Brazil was cordial but suspicious and was still marked by ideological restrictions and a resolve to await the course of events. For North American leaders, only the future would tell whether or not the two countries would discover common interests and ideals.

[55] Rebello to J. Q. Adams, January 28, 1825; Secretary of State Henry Clay to Rebello, April 13, 1825, Manning, *Diplomatic Correspondence* 2:808–9, 1:233–34.

Social Aspects

STUART B. SCHWARTZ

Elite Politics and the Growth of a Peasantry in Late Colonial Brazil

Sometime toward the middle decades of the eighteenth century the Brazils, Portugal's New World colonies, underwent a series of changes which modified the nature of the society, the economy, and the colonial regime itself. Shifts in imperial policy, external political events, new philosophical tenets, and the internal dynamics of Brazilian polity and society all contributed to these new conditions. While scholars are generally agreed that the period after 1750 marked a new era in Brazilian history, there is no consensus as to the relative weight of the individual factors or the significance of any particular change. Traditionally, the late colonial era had been viewed as the prelude to independence, Brazil's preparation for nationhood.[1] Recently, some scholars of a more skeptical persuasion have argued that despite seeming changes, profound alterations in the nature of Brazilian society and politics were virtually impossible given the basic reality of Brazilian social life—slavery. They believe that in a society built on a foundation of slavery, the very men who most desired a break in the colonial relationship with Portugal or who were subsequently best able to profit from that separation were those who were often least interested in loosing the fetters of their bondsmen. Slavery therefore imposed severe limitations on the possibilities for social change in the late colonial and early national periods.[2] Still other authors claim that the political independence of 1822 was by itself relatively unimportant and that the period from 1750 to 1850 must be seen as a

---

[1] Francisco Adolfo de Varnhagen, *História da independência do Brasil,* published as vol. 6 of *História geral do Brasil,* 6 vols., 7th ed. (São Paulo, 1962); Manoel de Oliveira Lima, *O movimento da independência. O império brasileiro, 1821–1889,* 2d ed. (São Paulo, 1957).

[2] Emília Viotti da Costa, "The Political Emancipation of Brazil," in this volume; Kenneth Maxwell, "The Generation of the 1790s and the Idea of Luso-Brazilian Empire," in Dauril Alden, ed., *Colonial Roots of Modern Brazil* (Berkeley, Calif., 1973), pp. 107–44.

neocolonial epoch in which Brazil traded the sovereignty of Portugal for the economic dominance of Great Britain.[3]

It is not my intention to outline the political events that led to the declaration of Brazilian independence or to trace the economic conditions that underlay these events. Instead, I shall deal with a specific development in late colonial society: the rise of a rural peasantry and its impact on the social and political decisions of the Brazilian oligarchy. Basically, it is my contention that in the late colonial era the social structure of Brazil (which was never composed of masters and slaves alone) became increasingly complex as the population grew and the economy became more diverse. Although there were important regional variations, this process of economic, social, and racial diversification was general, and throughout the colony various interests, groups, and classes struggled to accommodate to these changing realities. The tension between merchants and planters or between the native-born and the metropolitan-born are well known, but there were others. As each group sought to adjust its position to the means of production and the political structure, a series of actual and potential conflicts emerged which contributed in a variety of ways to the movement for independence and the turbulence of Brazil's early national history.

While this process was general, the regional differences mentioned above cannot be forgotten. It is fair to say that late colonial Brazil was a series of relatively distinct colonies whose lack of political and economic integration was in part a result of Portuguese policy and in part a result of the human and economic geography of each region. The history of Brazil after 1822 was to a large extent the search for a formula of political integration among the disparate provinces, carried on by the colonial oligarchy and its descendants. At the same time, it was also a search to accommodate the social tensions created in the late colonial era. The conflict between landlord and peasant, engendered by the rise of a free rural population of mixed origin, signaled a potential threat to the social vision and economic position of the Brazilian landed oligarchy. Its ability to adjust to this situation both intellectually and politically provides a link between the colonial and modern eras of Brazilian history.

Raimundo José de Sousa Gaioso, Argentine by birth but a longtime resident in the Maranhão, presents in his informative *Compendio historico-politico* (1818) a vision of Brazilian society quite typical of the schema used by many Brazilians and foreigners in the late colonial era. He divided society into five "classes," but on closer analysis we shall see that his use of that term is deceptive, for what Gaioso had in mind was not "class" but caste or racial type. The most powerful class, by his

[3] Stanley Stein, *The Colonial Heritage of Latin America* (New York, 1970).

account, was that of the metropolitan-born Europeans who, he felt, monopolized the colony's high offices and honors. Beneath them was a second class composed of native-born Europeans who, despite their wealth, spent much time on their estates and had little interest in government and commerce. Gaioso felt that this aversion to public life could be attributed to the climate and to the inability of Americans to obtain honors and offices suitable to their position. He noted the rivalry between the two groups (more among the men than the women) but believed that it would cause no trouble. The third class were the *mestiços* and mulattos, and Gaioso included a chart giving the various degrees of racial mixture. This group, he felt, were the most active in society, performing all the mechanic arts and other occupations which the "superior classes" avoided either out of vanity or indolence. The fourth and fifth classes were composed of the black slaves and the Indians, who, along with the mixed bloods, said Gaioso, shared very bad habits, especially in their sexual predilections.[4]

The division of society employed by Gaioso and other authors of his day rested to a large extent on criteria other than income or occupation. Place of birth and color seem to be the most salient features of this schema, although it appears that economic position and degree of acculturation also enter into the gradient of rank. Admittedly, these elements closely corresponded to color in most cases. It is interesting to note that later in Gaioso's volume he undertook a description of certain parishes in the Maranhão. In his *Mappa da população da Ribeira do Itapucurú dos annos de 1803 a 1805* a quite different division of the population is made, based not on race but on occupation and civil state. Here we see the *"estados da população"* divided into such categories as clergy, agriculturists, artisans, day laborers, wives, children, and slaves.[5]

Gaioso's seeming inability to decide on a social gradient based on race, civil status, or occupation was shared by many contemporaries. Luís dos Santos Vilhena, the educated Bahian colonist, divided the population into the traditional corporate categories of medieval Europe.[6] Brazilian society, he thought, was composd of the bureaucracy, the ecclesiastical corporation, the military, the corps of merchants, and the people—noble, mechanic, and slave. Here is an almost classic description of a

---

[4] *Compendio historico-politico dos principios de lavoura do Maranhão* (1st ed., 1818; Rio de Janeiro, 1970), pp. 115–23.

[5] *Ibid.*, p. 164.

[6] Luís dos Santos Vilhena, *A Bahia no século XVIII*, 3 vols. (Bahia, 1969) 1:55–56. This is a new edition of the *Recopilação de noticias soteropolitanas e brasilicas* of 1802. See also Carlos Guilherme Mota, "Mentalidade ilustrada na colonização portuguêsa Luís dos Santos Vilhena," *Revista de história* 72 (1967); and his *Atitudes de inovação no Brasil, 1789–1801* (Lisbon, 1970).

society of estates and corporate privilege, and yet it was also Santos Vilhena who believed that, with the exception of the merchants and some planters, the population of Brazil was simply a "congregation of paupers." [7] The Brazilian historian Carlos Guilherme Mota has recently demonstrated in his brilliant essay *Nordeste, 1817* that the leadership in the Pernambucan revolt of that year displayed a similar inability to deal with a concept of society based on class. Instead, their discussions were usually couched in such terms as "orders" and "estates," a hierarchy based on ascribed status, corporate privilege, and juridical distinction which had grown out of the Portuguese medieval heritage and which remained closely associated with the ancient regime in general.[8]

This organic and static view of society, designed to create social cohesion and stability, persisted into the nineteenth century.[9] Even in the colonial era, however, it had been modified by American reality to include the *castas* or racial categories as part of the society of estates. Certainly, this was true of the Pernambucan leadership in 1817, whose racial perceptions imposed severe limitations on the nature of their republicanism. Nevertheless, this modification did not disrupt the traditional view. Political observers continue to see the social universe of Brazil as a functional-juridical hierarchy in which lineage and corporate privilege rather than wealth determined the individual's place. In late colonial Brazil this vision encountered a situation difficult to reconcile with the traditional categories.

During the course of the eighteenth century, the population had undergone considerable modification in size, composition, distribution, and structure.[10] By the end of the colonial regime the over four million inhabitants were dispersed to the farthest frontiers. The traditional population centers of Pernambuco and Bahia still contained over 30 percent of the total, but the captaincy of Minas Gerais now had over 20 percent and Rio de Janeiro was also growing at a rapid pace. Progressive miscegenation constantly increased the proportion of the *pardo* population, so that in areas like Minas Gerais and Bahia it constituted

[7] Santos Vilhena, *A Bahia* 3:915.

[8] Carlos Guilherme Mota, *Nordeste, 1817* (São Paulo,1972) , pp. 104–41. Cf. Vitorino Magalhães Godinho, *A estrutura na antiga sociedade portuguesa* (Lisbon, 1971).

[9] This was also true in France; see George Rudé, *The Crowd in History* (New York, 1964). For comparison, see L. N. McAlister, "Social Structure and Social Change in New Spain," *HAHR* 43 (1963): 349–71. Cf. Manuel Dugues Júnior, "Estrutura social brasileira: Aspectos do passado e transformações do presente," *Revista brasileira de estudos políticos* 33 (1972):31–62; João Camillo Oliveira Torres, *Estratificação social no Brasil* (São Paulo, 1965).

[10] Caio Prado Júnior, *The Colonial Background of Modern Brazil* (Berkeley, Calif., 1967) is the best survey of late colonial Brazil. See also Dauril Alden, "The Population of Brazil in the Late Eighteenth Century: A Preliminary Survey," *HAHR* 43 (1963): 173–205.

a large and volatile element. Minas Gerais in 1814 had 143,000 free people of color, 150,000 slaves, and 84,000 whites.[11] Many freedmen and free *pardos* performed a variety of artisan crafts in the growing urban centers of Minas Gerais, Rio de Janeiro, and the south. A glance at the published census of Vila Rica for 1804 indicates the role of the *pardo* and the slave in the urban life of the colony. The population of Rio de Janeiro, which counted perhaps 50,000 inhabitants in 1808, had more than doubled by 1822.

Despite this urban growth and the increase in the numbers of a petit bourgeoisie of artisans, mechanics, and small traders, the majority of the population remained in the countryside employed in agricultural or pastoral activities. Here the categories of master and slave still predominated, although in the later colonial era free rural agriculturists of various racial origins and various levels of economic position and integration had developed throughout the colony. Can we speak of a rural middle class? We shall confront this question subsequently, but whatever our conclusions, it is clear that the existence of these people upset the world view of those who would eventually lead the movement for independence.

For men in power a social vision based on legal inequality, stability, and cohesion presented definite advantages. During the colonial era the white agricultural, and later commercial, oligarchy had established control over the social and economic resources of the country. Planters, ranchers, miners, and traders dominated the internal life of Brazil with little interference from the crown. So long as they were able to maintain their position within Brazil and suffered no ill effects as colonials, the Brazilian oligarchy adhered to the metropolis.

One of the most curious aspects of late colonial Brazil is the tenacity with which the colonial elite clung to the Braganza regime and the monarchical form of government. In the period after 1750 the Brazilian oligarchy began to observe a real and eventually irreconcilable divergence of interest between themselves and the metropolis, especially in economic matters. At the same time, however, the reforms of Pombal, the "economic miracle" of the 1780s and 1790s, and the arrival of the court in Rio de Janeiro in 1807 presented distinct advantages to this stratum. Perceived advantage and Portuguese political measures combined to tie the Brazilian oligarchy to the crown. But even when the disadvantages of colonial dependency became painfully obvious, as they did in Minas Gerais after 1789 and in the Brazilian ports in 1821, the elite found its political and social options limited. The nature and composition of the

---

[11] Herbert S. Klein, "The Colored Freedmen in Brazilian Slave Society," *Journal of Social History* 3 (1969):30–52. See also Herculano Gomes Mathias, ed., *Um recenseamento na capitania de Minas Gerais. Vila Rica, 1804* (Rio de Janeiro, 1969).

colony's population and the threat of upsetting the established order impelled it to seek continuing accommodation with the colonial regime. When this became impossible, a political solution was sought that would not impair their social position. As Emília Viotti da Costa has observed, nationalism and liberalism in Europe were the expressions of a bourgeoisie which hoped to overturn a social order based on clerical and noble privilege; in Brazil a rural oligarchy that sought to maintain itself became the exponent of these principles and the architect of independence.[12] Its conservative social vision was based not only on the desire to maintain the line between slave and free, or the distinctions of racially segmented society but also on a recognition of potential class conflict. In the society of late colonial Brazil, however, race and class were not so different.

The period of the virtual dictatorship of Sebastião José de Carvalho e Melo, to whom we shall refer by the title conferred on him in 1770 as the marquis of Pombal, is a logical starting point for our discussion. From 1750 to 1777 Pombal ruled as an enlightened despot with a plan; he was an architect of national and colonial reform. In response to the economic dependency of Portugal on England and to a decrease in state revenues as Minas gold production began to fall off, he set out a series of measures designed to strengthen the Portuguese economy and to establish it on a basis of equality with its European neighbors.[13] Brazil by the mid-eighteenth century was the heart of the Portuguese empire, and the colony loomed large in Pombal's program. Administrative, social, and economic innovations and reforms were applied in Brazil with varying degrees of success. Monopoly companies were established for the development of Pernambuco and the State of Grão Pará and Maranhão;[14] experimentation with new agricultural crops was sponsored; Boards of Inspection were created to regulate the quality of agricultural exports. Pombal reformed the fiscal structure of the empire and in Brazil changed the system of taxation in the gold-producing area of Minas Gerais. He made a concerted effort to eliminate the extensive contraband gold trade in which Lisbon merchants, British traders, and colonial miners and officials were involved. Much of his effort was aimed at the defense of Brazil, and to that end he moved the capital to Rio de Janeiro in 1763 so that the viceroy might be closer to the theater of operations of the intermittent Luso-Spanish war in the Plata River area.

Moreover, Pombal was a firm believer in the policy, later expressed by

[12] See her essay in this volume.

[13] Kenneth Maxwell, "Pombal and the Nationalization of the Luso-Brazilian Economy," *HAHR* 48 (1968):608–31; Dauril Alden, *Royal Government in Colonial Brazil* (Berkeley, Calif., 1969), and the sources cited therein.

[14] Manuel Nunes Dias, *Fomento e mercantilismo: A companhia geral do Grão Pará e Maranhão (1755–1778),* 2 vols. (Belém, 1970).

Juan B. Alberdi, that *gobernar es poblar* ("to govern is to populate"). In hopes of populating the Amazon basin Pombal instructed his colonial administrators to sponsor the miscegenation of Europeans and Indians. In 1759 he expelled the Jesuits and placed their former Indian wards within a system of civilian control designed to turn them into productive subjects of the crown and possible defenders of the northern and western frontiers of the colony—in other words, to change the Indians from tribesmen to peasants by drawing them into the cash economy and the wage labor market. An increase in the flow of African slaves to Brazil and the settlement of Azorean couples in the colony were yet two more aspects of this policy of demographic and economic development.

Innovative and vigorous state intervention in a colony which by 1750 had been dominated for two and a half centuries by private influence and local interests disrupted existing patterns of patronage, profit, and power. Pombal did not seek to destroy existing interest groups but rather to protect those which he deemed necessary to the achievement of his goals. However, what benefited one sector usually worked to the detriment of another, and despite Pombal's attempts to ensure colonial cooperation in his program, his policies began to generate a series of sectoral clashes.

The unintended results of Pombaline policy can be seen in the colonial reaction to the Boards of Inspection (Mesas de Inspeção) created in 1751 in the major ports handling agricultural products—Rio de Janeiro, Recife, Salvador, and São Luís do Maranhão.[15] These boards were designed to stimulate agricultural production and to regulate the quality and price of exports, especially sugar and tobacco. Composed of a president, two sugar planters, two merchants, and two tobacco growers, as well as a clerk and inspectors, they came to be thoroughly disliked and resented by the agricultural interests of the northeast. Their ability to fix the price of sugar was an encroachment on the privileges of the municipal councils, which, in Salvador and Recife, had traditionally undertaken this duty.[16] The regulations which gave the boards the right to weigh, grade, and verify the contents of sugar crates were seen by the planters as sacrifice of their interests to those of the Lisbon merchants. Certainly, there was some truth in this. The planters' habit of placing rocks in crates of sugar to increase their weight had given Brazilian sugar a poor reputation in European markets; the Lisbon merchants hoped to eliminate this abuse and regain their foreign customers.

Complaints against the boards by the agricultural sector began almost

[15] Cf. José Honório Rodrigues, "Dois documentos sôbre açúcar no século XVII," *Brasil açucareiro* 20 (1942):159–69.
[16] Alden, *Royal Government,* p. 424.

immediately. In 1752 the sugar planters of Rio de Janeiro complained that poor harvests, high costs, and a lack of slaves placed them in conditions which the Board of Inspection only exacerbated.[17] The town council of Sergipe de-El Rey called the new institution "noxious" and extremely inconvenient to the planters of that region.[18] In general, sugar and tobacco planters felt that any advantages gained by state intervention in fixing a just price between agriculturists and merchants was negated by the costs and inconvenience of the forced inspection of their products.[19]

In the long run the Boards of Inspection probably contributed to the improving fortunes of Brazilian agriculture in the period after 1770.[20] Nevertheless, their creation aroused the latent hostility between the commercial and agricultural sectors. The former were identified with the metropolis, and the policy of the crown was seen as favoring their interests. In 1753 the planters of Bahia wrote to the crown in terms that merit repetition. They argued that

the misery of the state of Brazil should merit the most pious attention of Your Majesty since that state has been the most profitable to the Portuguese crown and since its subjects are no less Portuguese than those who live in the Kingdom of Portugal. The Brazilian subjects—if not themselves, then at least their ancestors—are those who at the cost of their blood and wealth conquered Brazil from the savage Indian and made it beneficial to the crown, and even today they continue settlement in the face of savage power for the greater benefit of the Portuguese scepter.[21]

The planters claimed that despite these inestimable services they, the

[17] *ABNRJ* 8 (1936), doc. 15513. See the discussion in José Honório Rodrigues, "Agricultura e economia açucareira," *Brasil açucareiro* 26.

[18] Câmara of Sergipe to governor of Bahia (April 30, 1753), AHU, Bahia, *pap. avul.*, box 64, 1st ser., noncatalogued.

[19] Wanderley Pinho, *História de um engenho no recôncavo* (Rio de Janeiro, 1964), pp. 186–87.

[20] Complaints continued into the 1790s. See "Representação dos cultivadores" (1772), BNRJ, II-33, 19, 27; Oficio de José Diogo de Bastos (1789?), BNRJ, II-33, 19, 27.

[21] AHU, Bahia, *pap. avul.*, box 63 (1753), 1st ser., noncatalogued. It is wrong to assume that sentiments of nationality or a sense of Brazilian-ness was limited to the white population of the colony. By the mid-eighteenth century such feelings could also be found among the free black and mulatto inhabitants of Brazil. In 1756, after a number of African-born freedmen had received commissions in the Henriques Regiment, the black militia unit of Bahia, a petition was forwarded to the crown from the officers of that body. These Brazilian-born blacks and *pardos* pointed out that in Pernambuco such appointments to that captaincy's Henriques Regiment were always limited to *crioulos* and that violation of this principle in Bahia was dangerous. The African-born freedmen, it was argued, were less than orthodox in their religion and were, for the most part, sworn enemies of the whites. Placing them in positions of authority and allowing them the use of arms gave them opportunities to lead insurrections, in which slaves and fugitives would surely join. See AHU, Bahia, *pap. avul.*, box 66 (December 8, 1756), 1st ser., noncatalogued.

"vasallos portugueses americanos," received less attention than the merchants of this or that trade.

Such complaints were obviously self-serving, but they do indicate a growing feeling of discontent, resentment of state intervention in colonial matters, and most of all, identification of the state with metropolitan groups in opposition to the colonial sons of Portugal. Nativist sentiments can be found earlier, but here in the 1750s Brazilians felt that their loyalty was not fully appreciated. By 1788 some even came to believe that it was misplaced. Intermittent feelings of discontent, however, were, for the most part, directed against specific policies in the defense of specific economic interests and did not generate a general movement for political separation.

Why? There is some advantage, I think, in viewing the Pombaline reforms in comparative perspective. Many of the goals of the Bourbon reforms in Spanish America and the techniques used to achieve them offer a striking parallel to Pombal's efforts, but there were differences as well, and one of them helps to explain the peculiar attachment of the Brazilian oligarchy to the colonial regime. It has been traditionally argued that both colonial regimes excluded colonials from high office in the New World as a way of maintaining metropolitan control. Recent research on Spanish America has clearly shown that despite royal prohibitions colonials had, by purchase, marriage, or kinship, obtained high bureaucratic office or created personal ties with metropolitan-born officers. The Bourbon reforms, especially the efforts of the active José de Galvez in the 1770s, were designed to eliminate these ties and end a situation in which local government had been "corrupted" by colonial self-interest. These measures were not equally effective throughout Spain's American empire. The great families of Chile, for example, demonstrated an ability to maintain their control of bureaucratic offices in the face of projected reforms. Despite the resiliency of the colonial elite in the face of royal attack, the attempt to exclude it was deeply resented. By the end of the century, critics of the colonial regime in Spanish America were virtually unanimous in their complaints against the exclusion of creoles from office.[22]

The monopoly companies, the Boards of Inspection, and the other reforms by Pombal elicited strong negative reactions from established agricultural and mercantile interests in the colony but were not designed as an attack on the colonial oligarchy. The bonds which tied the Brazilian elite to the metropolis were not, intentionally at least, dis-

---

22 Mark A. Burkholder, "From Creole to *Peninsular:* The Transformation of the Audiencia of Lima," *HAHR* 52 (1972):395–415; Leon G. Campbell, "A Colonial Establishment: Creole Domination of the Audiencia of Lima during the Late Eighteenth Century," *HAHR* 52 (1972):1–25; David Brading, *Miners and Merchants in Bourbon Mexico, 1763–1810* (Cambridge, 1971).

rupted. In another place we have tried to demonstrate the way in which the bureaucracy was linked by kinship and interest to the upper echelons of Brazilian society in a union of wealth and power. Not only did the colonial-born control most of the nonprofessional offices of justice and the treasury, but they had also penetrated into the ranks of the superior magistracy, the very core of supposedly impartial royal government. Clerks, notaries, tax collectors, customs officials, judges, and even governors were drawn from the colonial elite or joined to it by blood or interest.[23]

While the marquis of Pombal hoped to revitalize the colonial system, he, unlike his Spanish counterparts, did not make Brazilian officeholders his target. In fact, within the general lines of reorganization designed by Pombal, new opportunities were created for skilled Brazilians. The reorganized royal fisc, the newly created Boards of Inspection, and the expanded militia all recognized the participation of colonials in government. Even in the areas of mineral collection, the gold- and diamond-producing territories where the metropolitan interest was often enforced with a heavy hand, this was the case. The Junta da fazenda of Minas Gerais, created in the early 1770s to arrange the tithe contract and collect taxes, "contained and welcomed local participation." In the diamond district of the Serro do Frio the system of private contracts was ended in 1771 and replaced by direct royal control, but even here wealthy colonials were selected to serve as treasurers for the administrative boards.[24]

The failure of the crown to eliminate colonials from high office or from the control of much of colonial life tied the Brazilian oligarchy closely to metropolitan interests. Certainly the reward of office, titles, and military commissions became one of the most effective means used by Dom João VI to tie powerful colonials to the Braganza regime. The attraction of the elite of Minas Gerais and Rio to the "tropical Versailles" of the court in Rio de Janeiro was proof of its success.

While this policy had definite advantages for the maintenance of the colonial regime, it brought small benefits to the majority of Brazilians. It meant, in effect, that those families who controlled the economic resources of Brazil also had considerable influence on the implementation of policy and the operation of colonial administration. It also meant that colonial government was rife with corruption, but a corruption favorable to certain elements, usually the rural oligarchy.

It is important to see this situation in terms of the reciprocal relation-

---

[23] Stuart B. Schwartz, *Sovereignty and Society in Colonial Brazil: The High Court of Bahia, 1609–1752* (Berkeley, Calif., 1973).

[24] Kenneth Maxwell, "Conflicts and Conspiracies in Brazil and Portugal, 1750–1807," Ph.D. dissertation, Princeton University, 1970.

ship between local and "national" political control. The "bossism" of
sertão and plantation was intimately linked to the structure of the
colonial regime and, in fact, was the means by which the mass of the
rural population were tied to that regime.[25] The arrival of Dom João
and the transfer of the Portuguese court to Brazil created new opportunities for the use of bureaucratic employment as a tool of colonial
control. The demands of establishing both the organs of empire and
the royal household called forth a series of new appointments. By 1811,
425 appointments had been made to the royal household alone and the
bureaucracy in Rio de Janeiro had more than doubled, from 432 to 954
positions. While this growth was on a smaller scale in the other
captaincies, it was nonetheless to be seen there as well.[26]

The crux of the matter, however, was not the creation of new positions
but the background of the incumbents. As early as 1808 colonials and
men with previous Brazilian experience were complaining that recently
arrived Portuguese were receiving the bureaucratic plums, to their disadvantage. Although such complaints were loud, no scholar has ever
taken the yearly *almanaques* in hand and systematically attempted to
identify the origins and social class of the growing ranks of bureaucrats.
Until that is done we must proceed on the basis of contemporary observations. John Luccock, an English visitor to Rio de Janeiro in this
period, put the matter in these terms:

> By the arrival of the Court a new field was opened for the exercise and display
> of this favorite passion [intrigue]. Few as were the honors and emoluments which
> the Prince had to bestow, all sought them with eagerness, all endeavoured to
> supplant each other in the good graces of persons in power. Hence jealousies
> arose, and in between the old Courtiers and new, got to a high degree of viru-
> lence; hence frequent bickering and open dissention, until the parties gradually
> divided into Lisbonian and Brazilian.[27]

The Inconfidência Mineira of 1789, the unsuccessful republican plot
to free Minas Gerais from Portuguese control, is especially interesting
as one point at which the conflicting interests of the oligarchy clearly
emerged. In Minas Gerais many of the leading families were personally

[25] Shepard Forman, "Power, Ideology and National Integration: Rural Masses and
the Brazilian Political Process," paper read to the American Political Science Association, Washington, D.C., 1972; Maria Isaura Pereira de Queiroz, *O mandonismo na
vida política brasileira* (São Paulo, 1969); Raymondo Faoro, *Os donos do poder* (Rio
de Janeiro, 1958).

[26] Alan K. Manchester, "The Growth of Bureaucracy in Brazil, 1808–1821," *Journal
of Latin American Studies* 4 (1972):77–83. Cf. M. de Oliveira Lima, *Dom João VI no
Brasil*, 3 vols., 2d ed. (Rio de Janeiro, 1945), esp. vol. 1.

[27] Cited in J. F. Almeida Prado, *D. João VI e o início da classe dirigente do Brasil,
1815–1889* (São Paulo, 1968), p. 141. See John Luccock, *Notes on Rio de Janeiro and
the Southern Parts of Brazil* (London, 1820).

tied to the civil and religious government of the captaincy. Important administrators like Tomás António Gonzaga and Inácio José de Alvarenga Peixoto were educated colonials with personal and property ties to the region. However, these men, and others like them, when faced with the introduction of a punitive tax and a threat to their economic interest, were willing to participate in a plot to overthrow the colonial regime. The integration of the oligarchy and the colonial administration was a two-edged sword. As long as interests coincided there was little problem, but when colonials perceived some disadvantage they could strike out against the regime from high positions.[28] In their political discussions, however, the *inconfidentes* showed themselves to be fearful of the social consequences of their action. The problem of slavery could not be resolved in their minds. A number of authors have pointed out the far more radical nature of the Bahian revolt of 1798, staged by artisans, many of whom were free blacks and mulattos. Their social program was simple—liberty, equality, fraternity, and the total abolition of slavery.[29] The Brazilian oligarchy could not support such a program, and it was they who would bring independence.

The conservatism of the oligarchy was surely influenced by their vision of society, but it was not only St. Domingue and the spectacle of the violent dissolution of a slave regime and a racially segmented society which plagued their consciences and limited their actions. Increasingly, "enlightened" colonials perceived the emergence of a new series of social relationships which presented a threat to their position no less dangerous. It was not Karl Marx but Luís dos Santos Vilhena who wrote in 1799:

Political society is divided into proprietors and those who own no property; the former are infinitely fewer than the latter, as is well known. The proprietor tries to buy as cheaply as possible the only possession of the propertyless or wage earner, his labor. The latter in turn tries to sell it as dearly as possible. In this struggle the weaker contestant although greater in numbers usually succumbs to the stronger.[30]

Santos Vilhena's social world, despite his attempt to use the traditional categories of corporate society, had broken down into owner and laborer, rich and poor. In the agricultural world of colonial Brazil this meant, in effect, landlord and peasant as well as master and slave.

Matuto, caipira, caboclo—the terminology varied from region to region, but their presence was general. In the colonial era and especially in the later eighteenth century a free rural population had developed

[28] Maxwell, "Conflicts and Conspiracies."
[29] Maxwell, "The Generation of the 1790s"; Afonso Ruy, *A primeira revolução social brasileira 1798* (Bahia, 1951).
[30] Santos Vilhena, *A Bahia* 3:919.

throughout the colony. In Minas Gerais, for example, the decline of the gold washings after 1750 had led to a movement of the population toward the periphery of the captaincy and away from the older mining towns. Mixed farming developed in the southern region of Rio das Mortes. Here we find subsistence farmers alongside families with fifty or sixty slaves, all described by John Mawe as "the middling class." [31]

In São Paulo there was a long tradition of independent subsistence farming which persisted into the late colonial era alongside the growing plantation economies of coffee and sugar. Even in the cultivation of these crops, characterized by slave labor, free workers and farmers were to be found. In 1819 the fifty-four sugar estates of Campinas counted only thirty-two tenants (*agregados*), but there were surely other free men on the *Paulista* sugar plantations.[32] As in the northeast, the diversification of type and economic situation was found among the peasantry of the south. *Foreiros, agregados, cultivadores à favor, parceiros*—each term defined a different relationship of man to land or landowner to laborer. In São Paulo, however, most of the free agricultural population remained "farmers and inferior husbandmen" producing staple crops for their own consumption or for sale in local markets.[33]

The *caipira Paulista*, the peasantry of São Paulo, were usually *mamelucos*, the descendants of an Indian-European mixture. Travelers invariably commented on their rusticity, the isolation of their life, the poverty of their agricultural techniques, and the miserable condition of their lives. The rural backwoodsman of São Paulo, like his counterparts in the Brazilian northeast or far west, had little access to the social and political institutions of the colony. Many were self-sufficient, but even those whose surplus was sold in regional markets remained for the most part politically inert.[34]

In a recent study of ten rural *Paulista* communities, such as Itú, Areias, Taubaté, and Sorocaba, Emilio Willems has been able to establish, on the basis of colonial census data, the existence of a highly differentiated free rural population which is quite unlike the traditional model of large landowner and slave. Among this population was a significant proportion of small farmers who employed one to six slaves. Men of this category usually constituted over 70 percent of the slaveholding population. By 1822, however, in eight of the ten communities

---

[31] John Mawe, *Travels in the Interior of Brazil* (London, 1812), pp. 358–61; José Ferreira Carrato, *Igreja, iluminismo e escolas mineiras coloniais* (São Paulo, 1968), pp. 223–24.

[32] Maria Thereza Schorer Petrone, *A lavoura canaveira em São Paulo* (São Paulo, 1968), pp. 85–94.

[33] Mawe, *Travels*, pp. 70–72. See also Oliveira Viana, *Populações meridionais do Brasil*, 2 vols., 5th ed. (Rio de Janeiro, 1952), passim.

[34] António Candido, *Os parceiros do Rio Bonito* (São Paulo, 1964).

studied, nonslaveowning farmers constituted 40 to 70 percent of the total population, and a broad spectrum of artisan occupations led Willems to argue the existence of a "rural middle class in São Paulo." [35]

This segment of the population certainly constituted an intermediate category between master and slave, but it shared only some of the characteristics usually ascribed to a social class in a market economy. While the source of income and way of life of the *camponeses* was often similar, their income varied widely. Moreover, a sense of commonality, of class-consciousness, could not be found in this population. We might argue instead for the existence of a series of agricultural classes based on income distribution and shifting interests. The term "peasant" seems a justifiable description of some of this population if our definition is relational, that is, a rural worker "whose productive activities are influenced, shaped, or determined to a significant extent by powerful outsiders." Such a definition subsumes the varieties of types of peasant relationships to land and market and allows us to include not only subsistence farmers but laborers and tenants in a capitalist economy producing commercial crops for export.[36]

Perhaps nowhere in Brazil was the growth of a large, free peasantry as apparent as in the northeastern captaincies of Bahia and Pernambuco. In the coastal sugar-producing *mata*, in the intermediate *agreste* zone of cotton and subsistence agriculture, and in the arid stockman's country of the interior *sertão*, the free population had grown considerably during the eighteenth century. Comprised of poorer whites, Portuguese immigrants, mulattos, mixed-bloods, and free blacks, this element of the population was to play an ever greater role in the calculations of those who sought political or economic power.

The Englishman Henry Koster and the Frenchman Louis-François de Tollenare both left impressions of the rural conditions of Pernambuco in which the peasantry are described in some detail.[37] In the sugar-growing areas there were actually four distinct strata: the *senhores de*

[35] Emilio Willems, "Social Differentiation in Colonial Brasil," *Comparative Studies in Society and History* 12 (1970):31–49. Cf. Maria Luiza Marcilio, *La ville de São Paulo. Peuplement et population* (Paris, 1968), and her "Algunos aspectos de la estructura de la fuerza del trabajo en la capitania del São Paulo," *Anais de história* 3 (1971): 55–62.

[36] The definition is that of John Duncan Powell, "On Defining Peasants and Peasant Society," *Peasant Studies Newsletter* 1 (1972):94–99; see also Shepard Forman, "Bodo Was Never Brazilian: Economic Integration and Rural Development among a Contemporary Peasantry," *Comparative Studies in Society and History* 12 (1970):188–212.

[37] Henry Koster, *Travels in Brazil* (London, 1816); Louis-François de Tollenare, *Notas dominicais tomadas durante uma viagem em Portugal e no Brasil em 1816, 1817, e 1818* (Bahia, 1956). See also León Bourdon, "Un français au Brésil à la veille de l'independence: Louis-François de Tollenare," *Caravelle* 1 (1963):29–49. See also Luis Lisanti, "Quelques aspects des mouvements paysans et des problèmes agraires du Brésil du XVIIIe siècle à 1961," *Anais de história* 2 (1970):109–14.

engenho (plantation owners), the slaves, the intermediate categories of *lavradores,* and finally the *moradores* who, in a sense, comprised the rural peasantry.

The *lavradores de cana,* or cane farmers, who supplied cane to the sugar mills, were certainly the most prosperous of the rural middle class, and yet their story was a history of downward mobility. During the sugar boom of the seventeenth century many of the most distinguished colonists were willing to assume the burdens of cane farming as a necessary step toward eventual mill ownership. Although even at this time there were considerable variations within the group, the *lavradores de cana* held a relatively high social position as basically white proto-planters who simply lacked the capital needed to establish their own mills. The sugar crisis which began in the 1680s caused considerable changes in the structure of the northeastern sugar economy. The falling price of sugar through the next century drove many *lavradores* to seek their livelihood elsewhere, and those who remained were at a disadvantage.[38] A change in the fortunes of Brazilian sugar created by the elimination of St. Domingue as a competitor in the 1790s may have altered this situation to some extent, but in Tollenare's description of the Pernambucan *lavradores* we encounter a rural class without power tenaciously holding onto the vestiges of lost status.

As in the seventeenth century *lavradores de cana* were still predominantly white, although by 1800 they were almost invariably Brazilian-born. A cane farmer might own six to ten slaves, but he worked alongside them with hoe in hand. Such would not have been the case with many of his seventeenth-century predecessors. Perhaps the most significant modification of the *lavrador's* position lay in the insecurity of his tenure. Whereas written contracts between millowners and cane farmers were not uncommon during the sugar century, such was not the case in the late colonial period. *Lavradores* could be moved off the plantation land at will, and all their improvements (*bemfeitorias*) remained the property of the *engenho.* As soon as his property became productive, the *lavrador* could be moved to some other plot to clear and plant again, and the now producing cane field could be worked directly by the millowner. Thus *lavradores* tended to invest in moveable property—slaves and oxen. They did little to improve the soil; their fences were ramshackle and their houses miserable, for they knew that investment in such property would surely be lost to them when the plantation master so decided. The insecurity of their tenure placed them at the mercy of the sugar planters and reflected a social situation closely tied to the economic trend in the areas. There is something

[38] Stuart B. Schwartz, "Free Labor in a Slave Economy. The *Lavradores de Cana* of Colonial Bahia," in Alden, *Colonial Roots,* pp. 147–97.

pitiful in Tollenare's account of his reception in the houses of *lavradores*. Their cabins were humble but they received him with considerable pride. *Lavradores* labored with hoe in hand alongside their slaves, and yet when they went to hear mass or visit a nearby town they mounted a good horse and used spurs and stirrups of silver. We have here a class trying to maintain the social amenities of its former status in the face of an economic situation which has robbed them of it.[39] Their aspirations, however, joined them politically to the planter class.

It is the development of a Brazilian "plebe," the *moradores*, which marks the modification of the rural social structure in the eighteenth century. *Lavradores de roça* had existed in previous centuries, but the presence of large numbers of free agricultural workers, peasants living barely at the subsistence level, was a phenomenon which grew out of the economic and demographic realities of that century. In the coastal margins, and to some extent in the *agreste*, the rise of the *moradores* can be in part attributed to the vicissitudes of sugar.[40] From 1680 to 1770 the secular trend of sugar prices fell for Brazilian sugar, and Pernambuco, long the colony's major producer, was especially hard hit. By 1710 Pernambuco had lost its position as the largest exporter of Brazilian sugar. We may speculate that the industry's contraction in the northeast was accompanied by changes in the labor relations and organization of the plantations. It was also during the final decades of the seventeenth century and the opening years of the eighteenth century that the demand for slaves in Minas Gerais drove labor replacement costs beyond the reach of many planters.[41] The combination of rising slave prices and falling sugar prices led to a search for alternate types of labor and ways in which to maintain underused property.

Concurrent with these economic conditions was the growth of a free population of mixed origin, in general the result of white-black miscegenation but certainly including *mestiços*, free blacks, and acculturated Indians as well. Even in plantation regions such as the Maranhão, Bahia, and Pernambuco, the free population of color constituted 20 to 30 percent of the total population of the region in the late colonial era.[42] Whereas the *lavradores de cana* were almost invariably white, Tollenare noted that the *moradores* were generally mulattos, free blacks, and *caboclos*.

In conditions of declining profitability for the sugar industry, a con-

[39] Cf. Tollenare, *Notas,* p. 95; Santos Vilhena, *Bahia* 1:180.

[40] J. H. Galloway, "The Last Years of Slavery on the Sugar Plantations of Northeastern Brazil," *HAHR* 51 (1971):586–605; "The Sugar Industry in Pernambuco during the Nineteenth Century," *Annals of the Association of American Geographers* 58 (1968):285–303.

[41] See the tables in Schwartz, "Free Labor."

[42] Klein, "The Colored Freedmen," pp. 30–52.

traction of production, and an uncertain future, planters could turn to the growing *pardo* population as a means of maintaining and improving land while finding an alternate source of labor. In return for a minimal rent, landowners would turn over a small piece of land to a *morador* and his family. They would erect a small cabin, clear the land, plant some subsistence crops, and perhaps provide occasional wage labor to the *engenho*. Like the *lavrador,* their tenure was insecure and they lived at the whim of the *senhor do engenho*. Koster noted that the rent fee (*fôro*) was at times replaced by service or labor.[43] Writing in 1816, Koster noted that *cambão*, the serf-like labor of modern times, was already a feature of the rural northeast. It was not until the 1870s, however, that the *morador* class became a substitute for slave labor.[44]

The *moradores* constituted the vast majority of the free rural population. Tollenare claimed that *moradores* formed 19 to 20 percent of the free rural population. To give some idea of their distribution in the countryside, he cited one *senhor de engenho* in the district of Cabo who expelled all the *lavradores de cana* and *moradores* from his estate; they numbered over six hundred individuals.[45] An 1827 census from the northeastern province of Alagoas gives some idea of the size and importance of the free population. The document cited 37 *senhores de engenho,* 1,099 *lavradores de mandioca,* 348 *lavradores de lavoura,* and 333 day laborers, as well as 141 *lavradores de cana,* in one parish.[46]

The material life of the *morador* and his family was minimal. Their houses were poor cabins with hardly any furniture; their diet was the manioc and beans they grew themselves. Any surplus went to local markets, where, along with lace made by the women, it was traded for clothing or supplementary food items.[47] Dispersed along the margins and in the less productive lands of the large estates, they lived under the immediate authority of the planter and were isolated from the officers of state and church as well as from each other. "Servile, lazy, and suspicious" were the terms used by Tollenare to describe them. "This free class," he said, "is today the true Brazilian people—they are impoverished for they do not work."

There was hardly a colonial critic or foreign visitor to Brazil who did not comment with moral indignation on the slothful state of the rural

---

[43] Tollenare, *Notas,* pp. 94–96; Koster, *Travels,* p. 360.
[44] Galloway, "The Last Years," p. 602.
[45] Tollenare, *Notas,* pp. 94–97.
[46] Cited in Medeiros de Santana, *Contribuição à história do Açúcar em Alagoas* (Recife, 1970), p. 149.
[47] Tollenare, *Notas,* p. 96; Shepard Forman and Joyce Riegelhaupt, "Marketplace and Marketing System: Toward a Theory of Peasant Economic Integration," *Comparative Studies in Society and History* 12 (1970):188–212.

population and their seeming aversion to labor.[48] At the same time, however, these authors invariably noted the material poverty of the peasantry, the insecurity of their tenure and livelihood, and the maldistribution of land. Tollenare believed that land reform might help, but in last analysis he argued that "moral improvement" was necessary. It was Santos Vilhena, however, who came closest to the mark. He, too, complained of the bad character and degeneracy of the rural population but suggested other causes for their unwillingness to labor. The development of a free agricultural class in the midst of a slave system could not be accomplished, he said, without certain economic and psychological strains. Agricultural labor was associated with the slaves, and free men avoided the plantation if they could. Later in the nineteenth century, other critics of rural Brazil would postulate a "Gresham's Law" of labor: so long as slave labor was available, free men would not perform the same work. A second and related cause was the value of labor. Slave importations and the growth of the free population provided a large labor pool. The value of free labor, said Santos Vilhena, was therefore below the level of subsistence.[49] Even today plantation laborers in Ceará prefer working on their own small plots to working for wages, and, in fact, prefer indebtedness to paid labor. Calculations of the average cash value of a day's labor indicate that they are economically justified, for the cash value of a day's labor in one's own field is worth twice the average daily wage. Perhaps the colonial peasantry was making a similar calculation.[50] With land available on the frontier, we can speculate that the coercion used by landowners to control the rural population was in effect an attempt to prevent the development of an independent yeomanry and to maintain their attachment and service to the plantations and the export economy.

At the heart of the problem was land. Plantations in the late colonial period were not large according to modern standards but were certainly large for the time, incorporating hundreds of acres.[51] Invariably the land was underused. Tollenare reported that Engenho Salgado cultivated only 300 of its 700 *geiras* of land and that the Sibiró property planted only 180 of its 10,000 *geiras*. Within a twenty-league radius of Recife the ratio of unused to cultivated land was twenty-five or thirty to one.[52] These

[48] Santos Vilhena, *A Bahia* 3:926–27; Koster, *Travels;* Mawe, *Travels,* pp. 152, 360; Thomas Lindley, *Narrative of a Voyage to Brazil* (London, 1805), p. 268.
[49] Santos Vilhena, *A Bahia* 1:139–40, 3:919.
[50] Allan Johnson, *Sharecroppers of the Sertão* (Stanford, Calif., 1970), p. 83.
[51] A law of 1795 formalized the *sesmaria* system. See José Honório Rodrigues, "A concessão de terras no Brasil," in his *História e historiografia* (Petrópolis, 1970); Warren Dean, "Latifundia and Land Policy in Nineteenth Century Brazil," *HAHR* 51 (1971):606–26.
[52] Tollenare, *Notas,* p. 84.

observations were supported by Henry Koster, who, as a plantation manager, noted that sugar estates need more land than was planted in canes but that, even given this fact, most plantations held more land than could be put to use. He noted that generally agriculture was slovenly because landowners could continue to profit from extensive rather than intensive husbandry.[53] As the free and landless population grew, this situation became increasingly volatile and the question of land use and ownership rose again and again in the Pernambucan political crises of the following century. During the colonial regime, however, the proposals of land reform always insisted on the consent of the landowner and on the payment of an indemnity to him. They remained, therefore, unimplemented.[54]

The relation of the peasantry to the man who held the land was one of hostile subservience. The power of a *senhor de engenho* over his *moradores* was, in many instances, as absolute as that exercised over his slaves.[55] *Moradores* were asked to serve not only as tenants and workers, but as retainers as well, protecting the estate and acting as men-at-arms in the internecine family feuds of the rural northeast. Their women became the objects of the planters' escapades, and the result of these liaisons was often bitter and deadly vendettas.[56] Why did people choose to live under such conditions? In a world of limited economic opportunity, populated by rural potentates, corrupt judges, and tax collectors, an oppressive protector was better than none at all. *Moradores* were willing to accept the domination of a planter in return for his patronage and protection. Although various social mechanisms were used to reinforce this basically economic relationship, the result was a situation of tension between planter and tenant.

The planters looked down on, and took advantage of, the peasantry, but they lived in fear of it as well. Tollenare knew one *senhor de engenho* who lived in such terror of his *moradores* that he could not go half a mile from the big house. In Bahia the situation was similar. *Lavradores* dealt carefully with the *moradores*, each of whom was reputed to have a lance and a knife which they were known to use at least on the cattle they stole and killed for food.[57] Thus, despite the power of the planters and their ability to use violence almost indiscriminately, they lived in an uneasy truce with the peasantry. This situation was often hidden beneath social relations such as fictive kinship

---

[53] Koster, *Travels*, p. 67. For life in the *sertão* see Lycurgo Santos Filho, *Uma comunidade rural do Brasil antigo* (São Paulo, 1956).

[54] Tollenare, *Notas*, p. 94; Santos Vilhena, *A Bahia* 3:918–27.

[55] Koster, *Travels*, p. 224.

[56] Tollenare, *Notas*, p. 96.

[57] Santos Vilhena, *A Bahia* 3:927.

(*compadresco*) or an easing of social distinctions. Thomas Lindley observed in 1805:

> It is astonishing to see how little subordination of rank is known in this country: France in its completest state of revolution and citizenship never excelled it in that respect. You see here the white servant converse with his master in the most equal and friendly terms, dispute his commands, and wrangle about them if contrary to *his better opinion*—which the superior receives in good part and frequently acquiesces in.
>
> The system does not rest here; but extends to the mulattoes and even to the negroes.[58]

The conviviality and intimacy described here was a complex mixture of real sentiments as well as a mechanism for reducing potential hostility. Moreover, it may also represent the oligarchy's sense of patronship and noblesse oblige, accouterments of their traditional social vision.

Those peasants unwilling to accept the material and social conditions of colonial agriculture found their only recourse in banditry, vagabondage, and mendicancy. In the later eighteenth century these phenomena became common. In Minas Gerais bands of brigands under well-known leaders terrorized the countryside. This early manifestation of banditry (*cangaço*) could be found in the northeast as well, where throughout the eighteenth century attempts were made to control the growth and causes of banditry. Laws specifically aimed against highwaymen were accompanied by decrees against vagrancy. In 1704, 1729, and 1740, royal orders were sent to Pernambuco commanding the deportation of vagrants, gypsies, and others with no fixed residence. By the 1760s, the tactic had changed. In 1766, a royal effort was made to eliminate the vagrants' temporary camps (*sitios volantes*), over which local officials had little control. Rather than deporting the inhabitants to Angola, the crown now wished to place this itinerant population in towns of fifty or more families, where they would become part of "civil society." Such measures seem to have had little effect, and most European travelers in late colonial Brazil speak of the *bravos* and bandits of the road.[59]

Observers also complained continually of the beggars—poor whites,

---

58 Lindley, *Narrative,* pp. 68–69.
59 See the laws published in *Informação geral da capitania de Pernambuco (1749)* (Rio de Janeiro, 1908), pp. 228, 229, 340; king to count of Azambuja (June, 1766), BNRJ, 23–25, 32; Djacir Meneses, *O outro nordeste,* 2d ed. (Rio de Janeiro, 1966); bandits like Isidoro Manuel and Capitão Romão plagued the *sertão* of Minas Gerais and Goiás in the late colonial era. See AHU, "Brasil-Diversos," box 2 (1749–1824) (this document was made available to me through the kindness of Professor Luiz Mott of São Paulo). For an interesting overview of Brazilian banditry, see Amaury de Sousa, "The Cangaço and the Politics of Violence in Northeast Brazil," in Ronald Chilcote, ed., *Protest and Resistance in Angola and Brazil* (Berkeley, Calif., 1972), pp. 109–32.

mulattos, and blacks—seen everywhere on the city streets.[60] Santos
Vilhena indicated that in Salvador, at least, old and infirm slaves who
had been manumitted by heartless owners made up a major part of the
mendicant population. Certainly, this urban situation was exacerbated by
the conditions of life available to the free rural population. In 1774–75,
1791–93, and 1819–21, the *sertão* was struck by extreme droughts. In
Pernambuco and Ceará the rural population moved, as they have always
done, toward the cities. There the fortunate swelled the ranks of the
urban poor; the others died along the roadsides of the interior. Those
who reached the cities found conditions hard, especially in the 1790s.
Shortages had pushed commodity prices upward in the period after 1780.
Statistical data from Bahia shows this clearly, and the observations of
Mawe in Minas Gerais and Koster in Pernambuco support the impression
that food was scarce and expensive.[61] Whether in city or countryside, the
peasantry had gained little during the economic boom of the late colonial
era, and, in fact, the expansion of cotton and sugar agriculture in this
period had probably dislocated many.

The existence of a large and potentially dangerous population of
rural workers did not escape the notice of those men who sought
"liberty" from the restrictions of the colonial regime. Fear of the
canalha ("mob") certainly influenced the calculations of the commercial
bourgeoisie and rural oligarchy, leaders in the movement toward independence. Santos Vilhena's program of coerced settlement and deportation
was certainly an imaginative way of dealing with the social problem.
Social fears were still often expressed in racial terms. Justice officials
like the circuit judge (*ouvidor*) of Jacobina spoke of the "four infamous
nations of negros, *cabras, mulatos,* and *tapuyos,*" and Santos Vilhena's
complaints against Bahia's indigents border on racial paranoia. His ire
is chiefly directed against the "vagrant, insolent, uppity, and ungrateful"
mulattos, but it was increasingly apparent that the fear was not simply
racial.[62] The image of a barefoot mob of *pardos,* white and black
peasants and beggars with weapons in hand or the similar image of the
quilombo or slave rebellion were too much even for the liberal leadership
of the republican movement of 1817.[63] While the threat was still identified
in terms of the racial categories that had grown up within the traditional
vision of society, it was increasingly apparent that poverty and the

[60] Lindley, *Narrative,* p. 268; Santos Vilhena, *A Bahia* 3:926–27.

[61] Katia M. de Queirós Mattosa, "Conjoncture et société au Brésil a la fin du XVIIIe
siècle," *Cahiers des amériques latines* 5 (1970):33–53; Koster, *Travels,* p. 127; Mawe,
Travels, p. 169.

[62] Santos Vilhena, *A Bahia* 1:135–37. Forced enlistment in the militia became a common method for dealing with potentially dangerous "vagrants." See, for example,
Arquivo Público do Estado (Bahia), cartas do Governo 24, November 21, 1812.

[63] Mota, *Nordeste 1817,* passim.

plantation economy had worn away the significance of these distinctions.

The constitution of 1824 was a liberal document which established Brazil as a constitutional monarchy and guaranteed basic personal liberties.[64] It was at the same time formal recognition of a society which sought to reconcile the principles of the French Revolution with a colonial social structure. Liberty, equality, and fraternity were joined with the right of property, including the right of property in slaves. Indirect elections and a graduated system of property qualifications established for voters, provincial electors, and national representatives virtually excluded the peasantry and the urban poor from participation in the politics of the empire. These distinctions based on property and income rather than on estate, order, caste, or color were grounded in the concept of class. There was no longer need to create barriers based on color or *casta*. The legal exclusion of the poor had virtually the same effect.

[64] The nature and importance of the constitution of 1824 is pointed out in Viotti da Costa's essay in this volume.

RICHARD M. MORSE

Brazil's Urban Development: Colony and Empire

Precisely because the New World empires of Spain and Portugal displayed broad cultural and institutional similarities, scholars frequently accept the challenge to differentiate them. A point seized on by urban historians is the apparent contrast in urban form. Ricard makes a cautious distinction between the spacious *plaza mayor* of Spanish America and its Luso-Brazilian equivalents: the *rossio*, an outlying, generally communal piece of land lacking special architectural embellishment which the core city eventually absorbs, and the *largo*, a widened section of a street with no elevation of its central area.[1] Robert Smith makes the larger claim that urban form as a whole was different in Brazil and the Spanish Indies. To the elaborate colonizing ordinances and, more loosely, the influence of Renaissance design he attributes the prevalence of level sites, grid plans, and large *plazas* in the layout of Spanish American cities and Jesuit missions. He then asserts that the Portuguese never issued an urban code, that Brazilian cities grew in "picturesque confusion," and that their model (insofar as "confused" cities may have one) was the medieval acropolis form of Lisbon and Oporto. Hilltops, at first occupied for defense, were the favored sites for churches and convents, and from them narrow streets twisted down to the casually laid out commercial centers. Smith finds that Salvador and Rio de Janeiro followed this scheme and that many inland towns were sited on elevations. The earliest Brazilian grid plan he knows was used for a new quarter in Mariana, Minas Gerais, in 1745, antedating the spacious geometric reconstruction of Lisbon after the quake of 1755.[2]

An earlier version of this chapter has appeared in *Journal of Urban History* 1, no. 1. © 1974 Sage Publications, Inc.

[1] Robert Ricard, "La *Plaza Mayor* en Espagne et en Amérique Espagnole," *Annales, economies—sociétés—civilisations* 2 (1947):433–38.

[2] Robert C. Smith, "Colonial Towns of Spanish and Portuguese America," *Journal of the Society of Architectural Historians* 14 (1955):3–12.

In a still bolder analysis the Brazilian historian Sérgio Buarque de Holanda links the urban solutions of the Spaniards and Portuguese to the spirit and motivations of their respective colonizing enterprises. The Spaniards' zeal for detail and foresight, he suggests, their determination to reduce nature's whims to the abstract and rectilinear, their preference for high altitudes and clear air, all reflected a strenuous will to extend military, economic, and political control via stable and well ordered settlement nuclei. The Portuguese with their commercial interests, on the other hand, were Phoenicians, not Romans. Their settlements hugged the coast; social power flowed to the rural domain; city streets wound their way amid the accidents of topography; urbanism, like settlement itself, was marked by tropical abandon or *desleixo*. "The city the Portuguese built in America is not a mental product, it never manages to contradict the framework of nature, and its silhouette merges with that of the landscape." [3]

One cannot, of course, categorically differentiate Portuguese from Spanish urban form. The Portuguese did use geometric plans in India, where the slow Brazilian pace of settlement and conversion was not feasible and "it was necessary to move more swiftly and give monumentality to the public buildings, churches, and convents. The modest intentions of St. Francis Xavier, who wished the rapid expansion of Christianity but without ostentation or luxury, were soon set aside." [4] Even in Brazil the crown seriously attempted to control urban form in the royal domain, as distinct from the territories of donataries. The instructions of 1548 to Tomé de Sousa, first governor general, contain stipulations with respect to site selection and control of urban functions that recall the earlier Spanish instructions. [5] Early maps of Salvador, Rio de Janeiro, São Luís do Maranhão, and other coastal cities show a basic geometric design whose irregularities were scarcely less than those which topography and fortification imposed on many Spanish American ports. [6] The seventeenth century witnessed increasing use of level sites and semiregular street plans: Paratí, founded in 1660, is a notable instance of a near-grid pattern. [7] When the grid plan triumphed in the eighteenth

[3] Sérgio Buarque de Holanda, *Raízes do Brasil*, 5th ed. (Rio de Janeiro, 1969), pp. 61–66, 76.

[4] Mário T. Chicó, "A 'cidade ideal' do Renascimento e as cidades portuguesas da India," *Garcia de Orta*, special number (Lisbon, 1956).

[5] Thales de Azevedo, *Povoamento da cidade do Salvador*, 2d ed. (São Paulo, 1955), pp. 119–25.

[6] Luís Silveira, *Ensaio de inconografia das cidades portuguesas do ultramar*, 4 vols. (Lisbon, n. d.), vol. 4. See especially the map of late sixteenth-century Salvador in Teodoro Sampaio, *História da fundação da cidade do Salvador* (Salvador, 1949), facing p. 256.

[7] Nestor Goulart Reis Filho, *Evolução urbana do Brasil (1500–1720)* (São Paulo, 1968), p. 131.

century, the transition had not been as abrupt as is sometimes declared. Indeed, one might argue that the distinction between Spanish and Portuguese town planning in America was not so much a commitment to different principles as a differing pace of evolution—a reflection that may in some ways apply to the larger realm of institutions.[8]

Instead, then, of insisting on "Spanish" and "Portuguese" urban strategies, we might consider the urbanization of Brazil as representative of those regions of Ibero-America (such as northern Mexico, sub-Mayan Central America, the Spanish Antilles, or Paraguay) where there were no dense Amerindian populations organized for surplus production and no early mineral bonanzas to cause population concentration and to support elaborate urban services. In such regions the prospective Amerindian work force had to be "civilized" and made sedentary, or African slaves were imported, or the European himself was forced to wrest a living from the land. Under these conditions the claims of the soil and the neglect of the mother countries caused municipal life to be tenuous and weakly nucleated. Urban development in colonial Venezuela, for example, is more analogous to the Brazilian than to the central Mexican or Peruvian pattern. In each case discovery was followed by an extended period of extractive activity along the coast (pearls in Venezuela, dyewood in Brazil), and it was half a century before the settlement process gathered shape and momentum. Early towns were small and precarious, and the capitals were established late, Caracas in 1567 and Salvador in 1549. For a long time urban centers clung to the littoral and were scourged by foreign attackers. The gradual appropriation of the interior was greatly assisted by cattleraising, with its dispersive settlement pattern. For a lengthy period shifting cycles of agriculture and mining influenced the pace and distribution of town founding, and in both cases the creation of new towns accelerated during the seventeenth century. In Venezuela there were twenty-eight foundings in the first century of settlement and more than seventy in the second; in Brazil nineteen cities and *vilas* were established in the first and thirty-eight in the second century.

Colonial Latin America, then, was a congeries of diverse ecological zones in each of which the pattern of urbanization was determined by the dominant economic activity, and the external commercial relations

---

[8] Elsewhere I have explored similarities between Brazilian and Spanish American towns with respect to medieval antecedents, social organization, and relation to central power: see "A Prolegomenon to Latin American Urban History," *HAHR* 52 (1972): 378–91. Mario Góngora compares the way *Paulistas* organized for economic survival in *bandeiras* (sometimes called "towns on the move") with the earlier Spanish *cabalgadas:* see *Los grupos de conquistadores en Tierra Firme (1509–1530)* (Santiago de Chile, 1962), pp. 99–103. The Dutch urban experiment at Recife (1630–54) offers a useful contrast to the Iberian case and its variants: see José António Gonsalves de Mello Neto, *Tempo dos Flamengos* (Rio de Janeiro, 1947), pp. 35–149.

which it dictated, and by the character and organization of the labor force, as well as by Iberian institutions and traditions. Because they favor New Spain and the Andean area, studies of Spanish American cities tend to emphasize the corporate structure of the municipality: its function as outpost of empire, control center, and "civilizing" agent; its station in the hierarchical structure of the state; its service as an arena where imperial and ecclesiastical claims were mediated to those of local patriciates. In Brazil these considerations are germane to the analysis of important coast cities like Salvador and Rio.[9] Indeed, they pose questions appropriate to any impoverished hamlet possessed of a *câmara* on the *Paulista* plateau, in the Bahian *sertão*, or in distant Mato Grosso. The point is that beyond the limited radii of the few larger cities the efficacy of central power frequently evaporated. Although the forms prescribed by the Manueline or Philippine ordinances were observed and the minimal municipal offices were filled, the municipality itself might be virtually run by the private order. For centuries large parts of Brazil lived in a state of near-anarchy—not the turbulent anarchy of the young Spanish American republics but the anarchy of a society in which public power is closely insulated and reaches out only on the sufferance of the private domain.

Only when we have ranged Brazil's urban centers on a gradient along the public-private, corporative-familial, or municipal-clannish binomial can we properly formulate such important questions as how authority was maintained, how things got done, how local and imperial interests were accommodated in a society in which power was so widely disseminated. To address these questions leads us to review three successive institutional arrangements which mediated, or effected compromise, between private and public power: the *câmara*, whose golden age lasted from the period of early settlement to the mid-seventeenth century; the militia system of the late colonial period; and *coronelismo*, associated with the empire and the first republic. An examination of these systems helps one to reconstitute the trajectory of local government in Brazil and thus to define the institutional context within which occasional large cities grew and acquired hinterlands.

Brazil's first town council, or *câmara*, was established by Martim Afonso de Sousa at São Vicente in 1532. From then until 1650 some thirty-seven *vilas* and *cidades* were founded, only seven or so by the crown and the remainder by the donataries of the captaincies. The more important of the royal cities (*cidades reais*) such as Salvador and Rio were populous, exhibited modest occupational diversity, served distinctively

---

[9] Stuart B. Schwartz, for example, finds that Salvador and Mexico City functioned comparably as colonial capitals in many ways: see "Cities of Empire: Mexico and Bahia in the Sixteenth Century," *Journal of Inter-American Studies* 11 (1969):616–37.

urban functions (administration, coastal defense), and were in part laid out by military engineers. Their radii of control, however, were severely circumscribed, even that of Salvador, the governor's seat. Early colonial Brazil had only the rudiments of administrative structure. For the most part the colony was a loose assemblage of *vilas* that exercised sweeping powers by default. During the period of Spanish rule (1580–1640) Portugal's Manueline ordinances were replaced by the Philippine code of 1603. The new laws stripped away most of the judicial functions of municipalities and reduced them to uniform administrative units. The code was applied in the mother country but not in Brazil, where, lacking other authority, the *câmaras* continued to exercise comprehensive judicial and political functions at the margin of the law. The interesting issue, however, is not the one frequently raised in comparative discussions— namely, whether *câmaras* were more powerful, representative, or "democratic" than Spanish American *cabildos*—but rather how local government functioned when intermediate structures were tenuous, making the town council a miniature *audiencia*.

Evidence for municipal autonomy in colonial Brazil is abundant. *Câmaras* wrote freely to governors and other officials and to the king himself with complaints, proposals, or demands. Some royal governors ruled under the virtual sway of a *câmara;* some were expelled at the instigation of *câmaras*, as were circuit judges. The *câmara* of Belém do Pará seized and tried a governor's son, and in Pernambuco even a governor was jailed. The right to convoke assemblies of *câmaras*, legally reserved to governors, was appropriated by towns. The custom of "obeying without executing" orders from above, generally associated with high administrative levels in Spanish America, was frequent with *câmaras*. *Câmaras* might set the value of currency or determine whether transactions should be in specie or in kind. They could fix prices, levy taxes, and license businesses. In two areas particularly the *câmaras* asserted autonomy: Indian and ecclesiastical affairs. They authorized slavehunting expeditions in defiance of royal policy, and the São Paulo *câmara* once lifted the excommunications laid on *bandeirantes* who journeyed into the *sertão*. In 1639 the pope issued a brief at the Jesuits' instigation reaffirming the liberty of the Indians. When the Jesuits published it in Brazil they were expelled for years by the townsmen of São Paulo and, under their pressure, by those of Santos; in Rio they were spared the same fate only by the mediation of the governor, Salvador Correia de Sá. In 1662 the *câmara* of São Luís in the Maranhão followed the *Paulista* example.

Eulália Lobo takes issue with the opinion held by Nestor Duarte, Nunes Leal, Zenha, and others that the *câmaras* were mere creatures of the landed potentates: the sugar planters and cattle raisers.[10] Citing the municipal acts of São Paulo, Salvador, Belém, and São Luís, she maintains that the *homens bons* (literally, "good men") who voted in elections and occupied municipal posts were a "middle class" of artisans, merchants, and small farmers. It is difficult to believe that in the precarious, penurious, sparsely settled zones of the south, the north, and the *sertão* so clear a distinction existed. Municipal records monotonously register the lack of quorum for town meetings because councilors were engaged on their distant estates or in forays to the *sertão*. In 1676 São Paulo, the largest town of the *Paulista* region, had only 800 *vizinhos*, 3,000 fighting men, and 15,000 Indians. The figures for Santos were 250, 400, and 500 and for Parnaíba 180, 500, and 3,000. Six other nuclei had only 40 to 80 *vizinhos* each, 100 to 200 arms-bearing men, and 100 to 500 Indians. Buarque de Holanda, who gives these figures, reminds us that in these straitened, outlying Euro-Amerindian towns one cannot draw so neat a line as in Spain, Portugal, and Spanish America between propertied *vizinhos* and simple *moradores* who were excluded from municipal office.[11] Indeed, Zenha, who insists that the town was "an extension of the *fazenda*, the sugar mill, the ranch" and drew its strength from the patriarchy and the latifundia, also points out that legal prohibitions did not effectively bar artisans, deportees, or crypto-Jews from serving as municipal officers.[12] In a frontier society which linked its destiny to slaving and prospecting expeditions, mere knowledge of Amerindian tongues might be a strong qualification for public office.

In Salvador, seat of the governor general and leading seaport of a prosperous sugar zone, urban society was more diverse and differentiated. Here *câmara* officials were recruited principally from millowners and well-to-do tenant farmers. Since the personnel changed annually, town officialdom was not "a self-perpetuating oligarchy." In 1641 a *juiz do povo* (literally, "tribune of the people") and two representatives of the crafts and trades were added to the roster with rights to vote on matters concerning their professions and the economic life of the city, though in 1650 their bench was moved beyond earshot of the councilors' high table. This popular representation was abolished after a *juiz do povo* was accused of inciting street riots in 1710–11. Boxer concludes that the Salvador town council, though controlled by the plantocracy, often

[10] Eulália Maria Lahmeyer Lobo, *Processo administrativo ibero-americano* (Rio de Janeiro, 1962), pp. 344–69; Nestor Duarte, *A ordem privada e a organização política nacional*, 2d ed. (São Paulo, 1966); Victor Nunes Leal, *Coronelismo, enxada e voto, o município e o regime representativo no Brasil* (Rio de Janeiro, 1948); Edmundo Zenha, *O município no Brasil (1530–1700)* (São Paulo, 1948).

[11] Sérgio Buarque de Holanda, "Movimentos da população em São Paulo no século XVIII [*sic*; XVII]," *Revista do Instituto de Estudos Brasileiros* 1 (1966):85–86.

[12] Zenha, *O município no Brasil*, pp. 132–33.

spoke in the interests of the people, as when it opposed the monopolistic Company for the Brazil Trade.[13] In Rio a commission of three people's representatives (*procuradores do povo*), elected by three "estates" (nobility, trade, and industry), served as advisers to the municipal council.[14]

A geographer once proposed that, had the missions of the regular clergy prevailed as the principal instrument of colonization, Brazil might have acquired a true network of village settlements such as the ancient parish structure gave to France.[15] As it was, "the Brazilian nuclei and the organization of export agriculture were too complex to follow the pattern of subsistence agriculture and European villages, but too simple to follow the urban organization of the metropolis. As part of the colonizing process and as complementary to the urban markets of Europe, they did not manage to acquire equilibrium and complementarity among themselves, but only with the rest of the structure which contained them." [16] For matters of political, administrative, or military urgency *câmaras* might unite in assemblies to assume the powers of an absent governor, to allocate a tax, or to organize for defense. Some *câmaras* even maintained more permanent alliances. Political cooperation, however, could not ultimately avail against economic fragmentation. In the northeast, territorial expansion might occur in both the slave-based sugar economy and the cattle economy in quantitative, segmental fashion without causing structural changes affecting costs or productivity.[17] Comparable was the process by which older towns spun off new municipalities on the *Paulista* plateau during the seventeenth century. The multiplication of settlement nuclei responded not to economic development and specialization of subregions but to pressures that accumulated as lands reachable by primitive transportation from the older centers became pre-empted—a process of subnucleation hastened by clannish feuds and by emigration to escape retribution for acts of violence.[18]

The decline of the *câmaras'* power after the mid-seventeenth century coincided with commercial development and royal centralization. In northeast Europe one loosely associates royal interests with those of the landed aristocracy and thinks of urban commercial interests as posing a challenge to the old regime. This situation, granted that it is a stereotype,

[13] Charles R. Boxer, *Portuguese Society in the Tropics, the Municipal Councils of Goa, Macao, Bahia and Luanda, 1510–1800* (Madison, Wis., 1965), pp. 72–109; A. J. R. Russell-Wood, *Fidalgos and Philanthropists. The Santa Casa da Misericórdia of Bahia, 1550–1755* (Berkeley, Calif., 1968), p. 126.

[14] Zenha, *O município no Brasil,* p. 70.

[15] Pierre Deffontaines, "The Origin and Growth of the Brazilian Network of Towns," *Geographical Review* 28 (1938):179–81.

[16] Goulart Reis Filho, *Evolução urbana do Brasil,* p. 101.

[17] Celso Furtado, *The Economic Growth of Brazil* (Berkeley, Calif., 1963), pp. 55–71.

[18] Buarque de Holanda, "Movimentos da população em São Paulo," pp. 88–105.

was virtually reversed in Brazil. Here Portugal's increased economic dependence on the colony and, after 1660, the falling price of Brazilian sugar on the Lisbon market were leading factors in prompting the mother country to centralize the trading system, introducing convoys and chartered companies. These moves allied the crown with privileged merchant groups in the larger cities and expanded the size and power of urban elites. The number of whites living in Salvador and its environs had held steady at ten or twelve thousand during the first half of the seventeenth century, then doubled by the end of it. The city, rather than the Recôncavo, became the social and commercial center of the captaincy; and while sugar and cattle had hitherto offered the only avenues to wealth, now, in the eighteenth century, financial speculation and moneylending offered an attractive return.[19] Symptomatic outbreaks occurred against agents and allies of royal mercantilism: Barbalho's revolt in Rio (1660) against abusive taxation; Beckmann's revolt in São Luís (1684) against the Maranhão Company's exercise of its monopoly; and the War of the Peddlers (*Guerra dos Mascates*) (1710–11) over privileges which the often debt-ridden Olinda planters denied to the merchant creditors of neighboring Recife.

The decades of the gold rushes in Minas Gerais after the 1690s gave the crown both the cause and the wherewithal to strengthen its control over local government. In 1696 the High Court (*Relação*) and the governor general were given responsibility for selecting the municipal councilmen of Salvador. In this same period the number of circuit judges (*ouvidores*) was increased in each captaincy to tighten supervision of the *câmaras;* the crown appointed district magistrates (*juízes de fora*) to preside over the more important *câmaras;* and lucrative tax collections were shifted from the *câmaras* to the officers of the royal treasury.[20] Such measures, however, were not an unqualified success. Salvador's eighteenth-century town officers "displayed nearly as much initiative and independence as had their more freely elected predecessors"; [21] and *juízes de fora* who lacked authority or means to oppose the rural magnates (*mandões*) might ally with important landowners.[22] The formal autonomy of the *câmaras* was on its way to extinction, as indicated after independence by the 1828 law governing municipalities.[23] But this institutional eclipse did

[19] Russell-Wood, *Fidalgos and Philanthropists,* pp. 355.

[20] Dauril Alden, "The Colonial Elite and the Expanded Bureaucracy of Brazil during the Golden Age," paper presented at the annual meeting of the American Historical Association, 1965, and *Royal Government in Colonial Brazil* (Berkeley, Calif., 1968), p. 423.

[21] Boxer, *Portuguese Society in the Tropics,* p. 75.

[22] Maria Isaura Pereira de Queiroz, *O mandonismo local na vida política brasileira* (São Paulo, 1969), p. 25.

[23] João Martins de Carvalho Mourão, "Os municipios, sua importancia política no

little to strengthen the hand of the central government in dealing with regional patriciates—the millowners, ranchers, and magnates of the *sertão*.

The fresh energies of royal government not only met continuing grass-roots resistance but also were dissipated by rapid expansion of the settlement network. For the first two colonial centuries settlement gravitated along a series of weakly interconnected coastal centers. During the seventeenth century the pioneers, or *bandeirantes*, explored vast tracts of the continent but accomplished little colonization. One exception was the cattle ranches which *Paulistas*, advancing seaward from the interior, established along the São Francisco River and which came to form part of the extended cattle zone that lay adjacent to the sugar coast. Another was the founding of Laguna by *Paulistas* in 1684; it eventually became a beachhead for colonization in the far south. By the late seventeenth century Brazil had four sizable regions of stable settlement: at the mouth of the Amazon and penetrating inland along its banks and for short distances along its affluents; in an area radiating for appreciable distances from the northeast "bulge"; in an area radiating from the Rio-São Paulo sector with an overland connection to the northeast; in the Jesuit settlements of the extreme southwest.[24] These were, however, merely "settled" lands. Areas under effective control of *câmaras* were limited to the coastal strips from the Amazon to São Luís and from Paraíba at the bulge intermittently south to the *Paulista* area.

The opening of mines in the eighteenth century—first in Minas Gerais, then to the far west in Mato Grosso and Goiás—caused large inland displacements of population, attracted immigration from Portugal, and, by creating wealth and internal markets, hastened the interlinking of regions of conplementary production. Celso Furtado, who gives Brazil 100,000 inhabitants of European origin in 1700, estimates 300,000 immigrants for the eighteenth century, a number perhaps the same as or greater than the number of persons who went to Spanish America during the whole colonial period.[25] Tabulation of town foundings by decades makes clear how mining and its side effects accelerated the tempo of urbanization (table 1). A settlement map for the late eighteenth century shows an archipelago of a dozen or more inland clusters of *vilas* in the mining zones, the northeast *sertão*, and Amazonia.[26] But colonization still outraced the creation of municipal control centers, and by now almost half the country could be called settled—the northern and southern

Brasil-colonial e no Brasil-reino," *RIHGB*, special issue for the Primeiro Congresso de Historia Nacional, 3 (1916):299–318.

[24] Aroldo de Azevedo, *Vilas e cidades do Brasil colonial* (São Paulo, 1956), p. 26.

[25] Furtado, *Economic Growth of Brazil*, p. 81.

[26] Azevedo, *Vilas e cidades*, p. 39.

Table 1. Town foundings (*cidades* and *vilas* [a]) in Brazil by decades, 1530–1729

Decade	Foundings	Decade	Foundings
1530–39	7	1680–89	1
1540–49	2	1690–99	7
1550–59	2	1700–1709	5
1560–69	2	1710–19	11
1570–79	1	1720–29	10
1580–89	2	1730–39	5
1590–99	2	1740–49	5
1600–1609	2	1750–59	36
1610–19	4	1760–69	16
1620–29	2	1770–79	10
1630–39	9	1780–89	6
1640–49	2	1790–99	15
1650–59	4	1800–1809	12
1660–69	4	1810–19	31
1670–79	3		

[a] Occasional *vilas* which were later elevated to *cidades* are counted twice.

Sources: Nestor Goulart Reis Filho, *Evolução urbana do Brasil (1500–1720)* (São Paulo, 1968), pp. 84–88; Aroldo de Azevedo, *Vilas e cidades do Brasil colonial* (São Paulo, 1956).

cattle areas thinly but continuously, the mining areas in a clustered, discontinuous pattern.

Brazil's earlier municipalities developed at ports, Indian missions, military sites, agricultural centers, and finally mine sites. Now the economic articulation of the interior and the increasing interregional flow of people, mule-borne commodities, and cattle created a new type of settlement, located around facilities for travelers, at points of portage along rivers, and at places where cattle were rounded up, pastured, or sold—functions identified in such recurrent toponymy as *pouso, cachoeira, curral, rodeio, invernadas,* and *feira.* These points of transit or seasonal activity were long, however, in acquiring formal municipal structure. Even well-known Pôrto Feliz, embarcation point for the riverborne *moncões* (prospecting, trading, and settlement expeditions) of the early eighteenth century, did not become a *vila* until 1797. A traveler of the following century classified relay facilities into five evolutionary stages: the *pouso,* or camping ground, where a proprietor allowed mules to be watered and tethered; the *rancho,* an unfurnished "traveler's bungalow"; the *venda,* a small general store, still not "thoroughly respectable"; the *estalagem hospedaria,* or inn; and the hotel (a late introduction).[27]

[27] Richard F. Burton, *Explorations of the Highlands of the Brazil,* 2 vols. (London, 1869), 1:101–3.

These services have been linked to specific settlement types: *povoado* (*rancho*), *povoação* (*venda*), *vila* (*estalagem*) and *cidade* (hotel).[28]

With the exhaustion of many mines by 1760, new patterns of internal migration, shifting and somewhat confused, asserted themselves. The transition from mining to stock-raising, export agriculture, and subsistence farming exerted a centrifugal pull on the mining settlements and, in the view of Caio Prado Júnior, may have caused a reflux of population back to the coastal zones.[29] On the other hand, Singer, who estimates the population of Minas Gerais to have risen by an average of 1 percent annually from 1776 till independence, points out that even during the boom years mining utilized only one-fifth of the regional work force, with the rest largely dedicated to subsistence agriculture. This indicates that after the exhaustion of gold much of the displaced labor remained inland continuing the quest for minerals, settling new areas such as the upper São Francisco, and taking up cattle-raising along the valleys of the west and north, dairying in the south, and hog-raising in the west. Modest textile and metallurgical industries also appeared but were handicapped by the limited market and, from 1785 on, by the royal ban on manufactures.

The settlement of Minas Gerais stimulated Brazil's internal commerce, and by the late eighteenth century, the region could be described, according to Kenneth Maxwell, as having an "urban focus" uncharacteristic for colonial Brazil. The multiple local interests of the "plutocracy" linked it more to the regional than to the external economy, which allows one to interpret the Inconfidência of 1788–89 as an independence movement inspired by economic interests of the magnates rather than by the idealism of a few patriot intellectuals. Eventually, the urban focus weakened, and the Minas "plutocrats" gave way to "rural patriarchs." The spread of coffee and the modernization of the road system in the nineteenth century strengthened the region's external orientation and allowed Juiz de Fora to assert economic hegemony—comparable, on a small scale, to that of São Paulo—as an entrepôt and re-export center.[30]

---

[28] José Alípio Goulart, *Tropas e tropeiros na formação do Brasil* (Rio de Janeiro, 1961), 146.

[29] Caio Prado Júnior, *The Colonial Background of Modern Brazil* (Berkeley, Calif., 1967), pp. 73–89. (No such movement, however, can be detected for coastal Recife: see Bainbridge Cowell, Jr., "Cityward Migration and Urban Growth: Recife, Brazil, in the Nineteenth Century. Some Preliminary Findings," paper presented at the State University of New York Latin America Conference, State University College at Brockport, April 7, 1973).

[30] Paul Singer, *Desenvolvimento econômico e evolução urbana* (São Paulo, 1968), pp. 199–210; João Dornas Filho, "Povoamento do Alto São Francisco," *Sociologia* 18 (1956):70–109; Waldemar de Almeida Barbosa, *A decadência das minas e a fuga da mineração* (Belo Horizonte, 1971); Kenneth R. Maxwell, *Conflicts and Conspiracies: Brazil and Portugal 1750–1808* (Cambridge, 1973), pp. 90–91, 98.

The settlement pattern of central, western, and southern Brazil at the time of independence may be economically surveyed through the eyes of a perceptive traveler, the naturalist Saint-Hilaire. The dominant impression conveyed by his dozen or so volumes is that of a sparsely settled subcontinent, appreciably but not highly differentiated in terms of means of transportation, economic pursuits, social patterns, and attitudes toward authority. The reader is haunted by a montage of four scenes: the vast backlands with their isolated, impoverished dirt farmers sunk in lethargy and atony; the *fazendas*, islands of patriarchal authority, with their whitewashed, dilapidated, sparsely furnished big houses and seventeenth-century technology; the villages, often too dispersed to be recognized as settlement nuclei, virtually enfeoffed to *fazendeiros,* merchants, or priests—and to the raw elements of nature; and the towns (or ghost towns in the mining zone) with their clustered dwellings and commerce, their flamboyant and archaic civil-religious pageantry, their parochial, comfortless life, and their occasional priest or townsman who incongruously hungered for news of French politics. From time to time an Amerindian tribe or *aldeia* breaks the sequence, flashing us back to primeval times.

In the nineteenth century Saint-Hilaire found distinctions between village, town, and city to be less perceptible than in Europe, where urban populations were stationary except for the visits of the wealthy to their country houses and the occasional *fêtes champêtres* of the poor. In Brazil, one came to town to celebrate. At other times "the permanent population of towns and villages is extremely meager. Most of their houses belong to farmers who come there only on Sundays for divine services and keep them closed the rest of the week." [31] Paradoxically, the presence of a village signified more dispersed rather than denser settlement. Near Rio de Janeiro, where the land was well distributed and occupied, there was no need for villages. Few residences surrounded the churches because these were within convenient reach of rural dwellings. Commercial centers were unnecessary because stores (*vendas*) sold staples along all roads and at the doorstep of each *fazendeiro*. Only farther inland, where land holdings were more widely spaced, did farmers need a town house where their families might rest after a long trip, receive friends, and do business with their scattered neighbors. Such places attracted workmen, merchants, and innkeepers, "and this is generally the reason for the growth of those villages of the interior which do not trace their origin to the presence of gold." [32]

The small towns were not strong nodules of social energy, nor were

---

[31] Auguste de Saint-Hilaire, *Voyage dans les provinces de Saint-Paul et de Sainte-Catherine,* 2 vols. (Paris, 1851), 1:112–13.

[32] Auguste de Saint-Hilaire, *Voyage dans les provinces de Rio de Janeiro et de Minas Geraes,* 2 vols. (Paris, 1830), 1:53–54.

they woven into commercial networks or functional hierarchies. In much of the area Saint-Hilaire visited, each town was linked independently to Rio. Even Curitiba, seat of a *comarca*, had a short commercial radius. Its well-stocked shops were supplied directly from the capital, and the merchants "sold scarcely more than to the local landowners because the merchants of neighboring towns were also supplied from Rio." Similarly, the first French merchant to establish himself in Vila Rica do Ouro Prêto was forced to sell at retail for lack of wholesale customers, "wherein he merely imitated the regional merchants, not one of whom sells exclusively wholesale." [33]

Expansion of settlement and of informal rural command systems in the eighteenth century challenged governmental efforts at centralization. Relief was provided by the *ordenanças* (territorials or home guard), whose commanders mediated between crown officials and the parishes and small towns. The ranks of *capitães-mores* and *mestres do campo* were generally held by the largest landowners and local *poderosos*. In addition to military and police duties the territorials rendered a wide range of administrative services, gathered information from their districts, helped introduce agricultural innovations, and provided communications links.[34] Saint-Hilaire marveled at the ubiquity and resourcefulness of the *capitães-mores*, who lodged him, gave him orderlies, and alerted adjacent jurisdictions of his arrival. The *capitão-mor* of Curitiba determined how much land farmers should plant, required them to improve their preparation of *mate*, and introduced new crops. In Minas, *capitães-mores* appointed village commandants similar to mayors.[35]

Viceroy Lavradio (1769–79) is credited with having been the first official to appreciate fully the administrative potential of the militia. In his 1779 *relatório* he reflected on the growing masses of unschooled, undisciplined mixed bloods in the colony and saw the territorials as an instrument for dividing the inhabitants into small groups and subordinating them to qualified leaders.[36] Caio Prado Júnior finds it reasonable to affirm that "the *ordenanças* made possible the maintenance of law and order in this vast territory, with its scanty population and paucity of proper officials."[37] Concentrated in the capitals and larger cities, the authorities had no other means of control and surveillance.

---

33 Saint-Hilaire, *Saint-Paul et Sainte-Catherine* 2:120, and *Viagem pelo distrito dos diamantes e litoral do Brasil* (São Paulo, 1941), pp. 153–54.

34 Alden, *Royal Government*, pp. 443–446.

35 Saint-Hilaire, *Rio de Janeiro et Minas Geraes* 1:374–76, and *Saint-Paul et Sainte-Catherine* 2:48, 136–39, 155, 166.

36 "Relatorio do marquez de Lavradio, vice-rei do Rio de Janeiro, entregando o governo a Luiz de Vasconcellos e Sousa, que succedeu no vice-reinado," *Revista trimensal de historia e geographia* 4 (1842):424.

37 *Colonial Background*, p. 379.

The militia system was not imposed unilaterally but was mediated between central and local authority. Militia commanders, chosen from lists submitted by *câmaras*, were an independent source of authority and organization. Extension of the system had the effect of vesting with public authority the private command structures headed by *fazendeiros* and magnates. Centralization went hand in hand with delegation of authority. The earlier tension between the formal perquisites of municipal and of central government was resolved by accommodating both to "natural" systems of authority that intervened between them and served as an armature for the *câmaras*.

A more explicit analysis than Saint-Hilaire's of how such command structures inhibited urban growth was offered by another contemporary, Moniz de Souza. In explaining why the potentially prosperous *vila* of Campos remained stagnant he named several factors: bad administration of justice, lack of a free port and customhouse for heavy goods, and the planters' "lack of education and civilization," which infused the slave regime with ferocity and brutality. A final factor was the near-monopoly of land by five *senhorios* which, "joining hands with the *juizes de fora* and *ouvidores* of that *vila*, reduce a people of free condition to dependent, ignominious slavery." Except for a few small holdings, the rich sugar lands of the region were tributary to the *senhorios* and, instead of real sugar mills, supported only miserable "kitchens" (*pobres cosinhas de cosinhar assucar*). Small farmers (*lavradores*) were forced to sell their sugar at low prices to merchants from Salvador, who paid their bills late and kept their creditors in debt. On the Rio exchange the *lavradores'* names were unknown, and the persons who enjoyed the title of "planter" were the intermediaries (*traficantes*).[38]

Our discussion, which appears to be shifting from an urban to a rural focus, has in fact led us to examine the sociopolitical institutions of the whole nation which were to condition the process of urbanization as it gathered momentum in the late nineteenth century.[39] Urban historians may of course quite plausibly devote primary attention to the larger centers and to the commercial and industrial stimuli which produced them. Singer, who does precisely this in his study of five Brazilian cities, warns us, however, that for economic analysis "the social and political variables are 'givens' prior to the analysis. As such, these variables are

---

[38] António Moniz de Souza, "Viagens e observações de hum brasileiro," *RIGHBahia* 72 (1945):100–104.

[39] For succinct accounts of Brazil's nineteenth-century urban development see Emília Viotti da Costa, "Urbanização no Brasil no século XIX," paper presented at the Conference on Comparative Issues and Problems of Urbanization in Latin America, University of Wisconsin-Milwaukee, December 1971, and Bainbridge Cowell, Jr., "Brasil," in Richard M. Morse, ed., *Las ciudades latinoamericanas*, 2 vols. (Mexico City, 1973), 2:79–117.

'immobilized,' or become constants, with obvious impoverishment of the research results." [40] The institutional context of Brazilian urban development, then, deserves our further attention.

Saint-Hilaire's description of Brazil's stagnant, unarticulated settlement centers was reiterated in the twilight of the empire by Joaquim Nabuco in a penetrating chapter prophetic of the contemporary "internal colonialism" argument.[41] Almost all the interior cities he found to be "decadent." "The capital is the central supplier for the interior; the millowner and planter deal with the commission merchant of Recife, Bahia, or Rio, and thus commerce with the other towns of the province is nil." Much as Gilberto Freyre, fifty years later, was to make the intra-urban contrast of the *sobrado* and the *mucambo*, so Nabuco made an interurban one between the port cities with their mansions, palanquins, and liveried slaves and the "insignificant collections of houses" of the hinterland, their functions pre-empted by *fazendas,* their physical mass insufficient for a North American town of the tenth order. Small towns had no piped water or gas; "the municipality lacks the income of a moderately well-off private person; one finds no rudiment nor even a trace of the functional organs of a *city*."

The size and elegance of certain cities Nabuco attributed to ephemeral windfalls from sugar, gold, cotton, coffee, and rubber. Brazilians, however, were slaves to, not masters of, their vast territory. Coffee profits were shared by:

all the intermediate commercial groups, the factors, sackers, exporters, whose crumbs support an enormous clientele of all the professions from the henchman who serves as an elector to the doctor, lawyer, priest, and justice of the peace. Finally a portion of the total, and no small one, is absorbed by the treasury to hold up the colossal tail of our budget, namely, the public bureaucracy. From that same portion of the proceeds from slavery, the state guarantees a 7 percent return to the English companies who build railways in the country.

The parasitism of the large cities and the stagnation of small ones Nabuco ascribed to the historic nature of the labor system: slavery, in particular, but, more generally, a regime of dependency and intergroup hostility that failed to guarantee the wages required to maintain an effective labor market. Millions of Brazilians, lacking incentives for sustained work, were only half free. São Paulo province, though the bastion of slavery in the early 1880s, was something of an exception because its prosperity had come at the close of the slave era, and in a future crisis it would reveal "greater elasticity" than its neighbors. At the same time Nabuco felt *Paulista* enterprise to be overestimated. *Paulistas* were not

---

[40] Singer, *Desenvolvimento econômico,* p. 15.
[41] Joaquim Nabuco, *O abolicionismo* (London, 1883), pp. 147–70.

the "Yankees of Brazil, which has no Yankees, nor is São Paulo the most
advanced or most American or most liberal-spirited province of the
country." Then, in a flash of insight Nabuco wrote: "It may be the
Louisiana of Brazil, but not the Massachusetts."

In this remarkable chapter Nabuco raised a cluster of issues that
anticipate the concerns of today's urban historians, geographers, economists, and planners. A particularly inviting lead is his intimation that the
cases of Brazil and the United States merit comparative treatment. In
explaining urban growth and regional development in the northeast
United States, Jules Rubin stresses the fact that a commercial outlook
was shared by both townsman and farmer.[42] Unlike Brazil's Portuguese
merchants, who acquired lands to consolidate their social status, farmers
of New England and the Middle Colonies had often been urban workers
or craftsmen who were attracted by the personal independence and high
commercial returns of agriculture; characteristically they were healthier
and better educated than the average English farmer.[43] Their strong
market orientation made them regard subsistence agriculture as merely
an ephemeral frontier condition. The critical indicator for economic
change was therefore migration of people rather than movement of goods.
Such migrants, accustomed to a relatively high living standard, created
for inland regions what Rubin calls the "financial equivalent of the
modern mass tourist industry": a stream of consumers demanding varied
industrial as well as agricultural goods.

Commercialization of life in the northern colonies was abetted by the
diverse nature of the export commodities, which were "collected over an
extensive area, and shipped to many widely scattered home and foreign
markets." Thus commerce was ill-suited to monopolization or to domination by overseas merchants. Local traders developed leadership and
promotional techniques which went far beyond those of factors and
agents in other colonial empires and performed services that eventually
became specialized as marketing, insurance, and finance.[44] "It is clear
that the ability to organize commerce within, but partially autonomous
from, the British commercial structure contributed to urban and economic
development." [45] Humboldt's bare statistics that the Americas had six
cities of a hundred thousand inhabitants in about 1820—New York,

---

[42] Jules Rubin, "Urban Growth and Regional Development," in *The Growth of the
Seaport Cities 1790–1825,* edited by David T. Gilchrist (Charlottesville, Va., 1967),
pp. 1–21.

[43] George Rogers Taylor, "American Economic Growth before 1840: An Exploratory
Essay," *Journal of Economic History* 24 (1964):434.

[44] *Ibid.,* pp. 435–36.

[45] James T. Lemon, "Urbanization and the Development of Eighteenth-Century
Southeastern Pennsylvania and Adjacent Delaware," *William and Mary Quarterly* 24
(1967):507.

Philadelphia, Mexico, Havana, Rio de Janeiro, and Salvador—give no clue as to the vigorous and differentiated commercial institutions of the first two.[46] Nor do they convey the picture that the north Atlantic coast above Charleston was dotted with bustling ports of many sizes, while those of Brazil were widely spaced, had little intercommunication (causing disparities in the value of currency), and exported only the products of their own hinterlands. As an early French observer reported, "With respect to foreign trade, each province, or rather each zone of Brazil, can be considered as in some measure a distinct country." [47]

Indeed, it is misleading to classify New York, Philadelphia, Rio, and Salvador indiscriminately under the geographers' rubric of "port cities" insofar as the term implies a standard assemblage of functions and activities. In the northern colonies seaport-connected mercantile functions were widely replicated throughout the hinterland. Philadelphia's "port function was secondary to the commercial role in fostering growth." [48] The small population of an early western river town "could reproduce in microcosm some of the characteristics of the port cities of the period." [49] Nor did hubs of commercial subsystems require location on a waterway. In eighteenth-century Pennsylvania, merchants and agents left Philadelphia for background county towns to serve there as chief buyers, retailers, wholesalers, moneylenders, and creditors. They organized the sale of imports and local manufactures to farmers, handled outbound shipments of farm produce, occasionally owned flour mills, did the paperwork for the flour trade, and advanced credit to farmers and rural shopkeepers.[50] Thus Philadelphia's commercial hegemony had a broad radius but was pre-emptive for a distance of only thirty to fifty miles; beyond this its commercial influence was a stimulant.

In Latin America sociopolitical factors retarded the spread and differentiation of urban commercial functions. In Brazil, where leading cities were seaports, the role of these factors is somewhat masked, but the case is clear for colonial Mexico with its highland administrative capital. Here the maritime port, Veracruz, functional only episodically, and Mexico City, which had its own customhouse, controlled the handling and distribution of imports. Although this monopolistic structure was broken after independence, as late as 1873 merchants of the capital were demanding that their city be declared a "maritime port" and that Veracruz be

---

[46] Alexander von Humboldt, *Ensayo político sobre Nueva España*, 5 vols. (Barcelona, 1842), 2:179.
[47] Horace Say, *Histoire des relations commerciales entre la France et le Bresil* (Paris, 1839), p. 155.
[48] Lemon, "Urbanization and Development," p. 507.
[49] Rubin, "Urban Growth," p. 14.
[50] Lemon, "Urbanization and Development," p. 517.

restricted to a stevedore's function.[51] This same pre-emptive tendency of Mexico's highland "bureaucratic" city characterized the "port" city of Rio de Janeiro. And just as the liberal, developmentalist agenda for the Mexican nation was to decentralize mercantile functions from the capital to the ports, so a similar agenda for Brazil urged removal of central administration from its maritime location. In his plea that the capital be moved inland, first made in 1849–50, Francisco Adolfo de Varnhagen argued that this measure would transfer wealth and subsequently population to the *sertão*, create communications networks, establish centers of complementary economic production, force seaboard merchants to travel inland and become acquainted with the needs of the nation, and thus eventually enhance the prosperity of the maritime cities. What Varnhagen perceived, in other words, was that the expansionary potential for economic development lay in the politico-administrative, not the mercantile, institutions of Rio de Janeiro.[52]

Despite the differences indicated between the North American and Brazilian economies, both were heavily dependent on exports at the close of the eighteenth century. It was not till the decade of 1810-12, which George Rogers Taylor calls "the great turnabout" for the United States, that this similarity ended.[53] The two decades immediately previous had seen the peak of American export dependency. Thereafter the economy ceased facing seaward toward Europe and the West Indies and turned increasingly westward as business and political leaders directed attention to domestic trade and internal improvements. This turning point was the sole decade in United States post-colonial history to witness a relative decline in the urban population. It was merely a pause, however; a renewed surge of urbanization soon responded to the new directions of the economy. The sharpest increase in the incidence of urban growth in the 1820s and 1830s occurred in the eastern interior and the western cities. For Brazil, political emancipation confirmed its export dependency. Granted the unreliability of statistics, it does appear that the combined population of eight of the largest cities hovered at about 7.5 percent of the national population from the late eighteenth to the late nineteenth century (see table 2).

The ruralism of Brazilian society that persisted for a century or so after the mining boom ended had its counterpart in Spanish America. Institutionally it was expressed in the erosion or enfeeblement of corporate

---

[51] Alejandra Moreno Toscano, "Cambios en los patrones de urbanización en México 1810–1910," *Historia mexicana* 22 (1972):186.

[52] Francisco Adolfo de Varnhagen, *A questão da capital: marítima ou no interior?* (Vienna, 1877; reissued in Rio de Janeiro, 1935); Helmut Audrä, "Varnhagen e a idéia da mudança da capital brasileira," *Revista de história*, 39 (1969):139–54.

[53] George Rogers Taylor, "American Urban Growth preceding the Railway Age," *Journal of Economic History* 27 (1967):328.

Table 2. National and selected urban populations in Brazil, 1777–1920

Year	Brazil		Rio de Janeiro		São Paulo		Salvador		Recife[c]		Belém		Pôrto Alegre		Niterói		Curitiba		Manaus		Maceió		Fortaleza	
	pop.[a]	%[b]	pop.	%	pop.	%	pop.	%	pop.	%	pop.	%	pop.	%	pop.	%	pop.	%	pop.	%	pop.	%	pop.	%
1777	1,866		47		21		50		[15]d		[9]d		2				7							
1799	2,388	1.1	53	0.5	24	0.6	70	1.5			11	0.9					4	−2.7						
1808	2,861	1.8	65	2.3					25	1.6	[11]d		6	4.0									10	
1819	4,396	4.0	113	5.1	25	0.3	[78]d		50	5.5			12	5.9	5		11	5.8			5		16	4.4
1830	5,340	1.8									12	0.4					14	2.0						
1838			137	1.1	22	−0.6					20	6.6					16	1.9						
1854	7,678	1.5	[186]d	2.0	[26]d		[108]d	1.0	[86]d		41	3.7	30	2.4	[22]d		[15]d		29		[16]d		35	2.0
1872	10,112	1.5	267	2.0	31	1.0	129	1.0	117	1.7	62	1.9	44	2.8	48	4.5	13	−0.6	39	1.7	28	3.2	42	1.4
1890	14,334	2.0	523	3.8	65	4.0	174	1.7	112	−0.3	[82]d		52	0.9	34	−1.9	25	3.7	39	1.7	31	0.6	41	−0.1
1900	17,319	1.9	[688]d	2.8	240	14.0	206	1.7	113	0.1	166	16.5	74	3.6	53	4.5	50	7.2	61	4.6	36	1.5	48	1.6
1920	30,635	2.9	1,158	2.6	579	4.5	283	1.6	239	3.8	238	1.8	180	4.5	87	2.5	79	2.3	75	1.0	74	3.7	79	2.5

a In thousands.

b Average annual growth rate.

c N.71 below gives revised figures for Recife.

d Interpolation.

Source: Richard M. Morse, ed., Las ciudades latinoamericanas, 2 vols. (Mexico City, 1973), 2:82–85.

municipal structures and their replacement by paramunicipal, rural-based familistic or clientage structures. Examples are the consolidation of the regime of the *mantuanos* in Venezuela or the de facto assumption of local power in post-independence Argentina by *hacendados* and their militias.[54] In eighteenth century Chile *hacendados* concentrated their activities on their estates, leaving the small-town domain to shopkeepers and artisans. The officially sponsored "new town" movement of the period was never able to recapture the urban vitalities of the sixteenth century. Local economic initiative was largely monopolized by the landed aristocracy, who might own mule teams, have commercial involvements in the larger cities, and receive prebendary concessions from the state. Their outlook, Mario Góngora suggests, was not so much "mercantile" as it was *"negociante,"* a distinction which recalls our contrast between the expansionary, urbanizing nature of commercialism in the northern United States and its constrictive or pre-emptive effects in Latin America.[55]

In Brazil, as we saw, municipal structures were overlaid in the eighteenth century by the paramunicipal militia system. After independence, the 1824 constitution and the 1828 law of municipal organization centralized power in Rio and threatened to unilateralize the reciprocal channels which had joined the national and local command structures. In response to widespread protest, the Additional Act of 1834 reinforced the provincial governments, still leaving the municipal *câmaras* as mere administrative agents with paltry sources of revenue. This arrangement suited local patriciates because "once independent, Brazil was to be the Brazil of the rural *senhores*, and subordination of the municipal *câmaras* to the provincial assemblies would be of no concern, for it was the same as subordinating the rural *senhores* to themselves." [56] Moreover, had municipal revenues been increased in a nation whose most productive zones were increasingly being worked by slave labor—Brazil imported nearly a million slaves in three decades after independence [57]—the narrow tax base would have laid the aristocracy under heavy expenditures which, for political and economic reasons, it preferred to make irregularly in the form of private largesse. Finally, the *ordenanças* and militia were abolished in 1831 only to be replaced by a National Guard, nominally subject to the minister of the empire but in effect a municipally based police

[54] Carlos Irazábal, *Venezuela esclava y feudal* (Caracas, 1964); Tulio Halperín Donghi, "La expansión ganadera en la campaña de Buenos Aires (1810–1852)," *Desarrollo económico* 3 (1963):57–110.

[55] Mario Góngora, "Estratificatión social urbana en Chile (siglos XVI, XVII y primera mitad del XVIII)," paper presented at the Conference on Comparative Issues and Problems of Urbanization in Latin America, University of Wisconsin-Milwaukee, December 1971.

[56] Pereira de Queiroz, *O mandonismo local*, p. 39.

[57] Philip D. Curtin, *The Atlantic Slave Trade, a Census* (Madison, Wis., 1969), p. 234.

force controlled by the prestigious *chefes locais*, who became its *coronéis*.[58] "Thus, the apparent weakness of the municipal *câmaras* signified in fact an increase in the power of the rural *senhores* which reached beyond the local realms of administration, to which the metropolis had restricted them during the colony, and now controlled the whole province." [59] The significance of this functional reintegration of the municipality at the provincial level was obscured in the polemical and juridical literature that deplored the eclipse of "municipal autonomy" in nineteenth-century Brazil.[60] Though regional analyses of *coronelismo* in its golden age under the republic are now appearing, we still lack studies of the phenomenon for the empire, a time when, if Nunes Leal's general hypothesis is correct, extension of the suffrage and the expanding resources of the provincial and national governments did not so much sap the power of the *chefes locais* as enmesh them in a series of two-way compromises with the central authorities.

Our reflections so far confirm Nabuco's dichotomous picture of Brazil's small towns and large cities. Qualifications are needed, however, to guard against caricature. First, although the mass of the population was eliminated from effective political participation, municipal elections were still more lively and contentious than provincial and general ones, for it was in this arena that the political parties tested their strength and explored arrangements that would determine the eventual composition of legislative bodies at higher levels.[61] Second, in the zones directly linked to external markets the ascriptive, sharply stratified character of society was undermined by the intrusion of economic incentives, the instability of institutions, and multiplying possibilites for upward mobility. The *fazendeiro*, caught between the time-honored regime of personal domination and an impinging capitalist ethos, inhabited a fragmented world, could perceive only those realities close at hand, and had little capacity to unite with his peers in pursuit of broad common objectives.[62] Even patron-client relations could assume a makeshift quality. In an election incident in Rio province a planter who wished to deliver the votes of his freed men to a ministerial candidate of his acquaintance offered his men a lavish banquet, then tried to clinch the matter by giving 100 milréis to their self-appointed spokesman, a fast-talking mulatto. The latter then

---

[58] Nunes Leal, *Coronelismo, enxada e voto*, pp. 7–10; Lycurgo Santos Filho, *Uma comunidade rural do Brasil antigo (aspectos da vida patriarcal no sertão da Bahia nos séculos XVIII e XIX)* (São Paulo, 1956), p. 143.

[59] Pereira de Queiroz, *O mandonismo local*, p. 43.

[60] Reviewed in A. P. Canabrava, "Tendências da bibliografia sôbre a história administrativa do município," *Revista de administração* 1 (1947):80–87.

[61] Pereira de Queiroz, *O mandonismo local*, pp. 51–53.

[62] Maria Sylvia de Carvalho Franco, *Homens livres na ordem escravocrata* (São Paulo, 1969).

approached the opposition candidate, collected another 100 milréis, and delivered no one to the polls. Confronted by the furious planter, the mulatto explained that he could not have voted without betraying one of his benefactors, so as a man of honor he remained neutral. The planter "was above all a man of spirit; he couldn't refrain from laughing at this strange profession of faith, and the matter was closed." [63]

Further qualifications to the picture of small-town stasis arise when we examine the careers of specific municipalities. Two for which we have historical accounts are Feira de Santana (Bahia) and Guaratinguetá (São Paulo). Originating on a *fazenda* that was a site for worship and marketing, Feira de Santana prospered in the nineteenth century as a commercial and communications hub that linked a prosperous agropastoral hinterland to the city of Salvador. For decades after national independence the town was plagued by violence and lawlessness and was controlled by a planter group that showed little sense of civic responsibility. By 1860, however, the commercial class was infiltrating the elite, assuming municipal posts, and insisting on measures to suppress banditry and to capitalize upon the town's natural advantage as a communications center. Even a province usually dismissed as economically stagnant, then, had its points of commercial development with concomitant rationalization of urban services. [64]

Guaratinguetá in the Paraíba Valley underwent three economic reorientations from 1775 to the early twentieth century—transitions from subsistence farming to sugar, from sugar to coffee, from coffee to diversified agriculture—each accompanied by important social and political changes. In the early phase in-migrants went to rural zones; the town's commercial life was modest, and the artisans, rural and urban, were slaves. As sugar planting gathered momentum, the patriarchal millowners consolidated a position of authority and prestige which was no longer related, as in the days of the *capitães-mores*, to the rungs of the military hierarchy but was determined by possessions, production, and slave ownership. "The breakup of the former large administrative divisions into smaller ones, with a base more economic and demographic than military, weakened central control and led to the creation of powers dispersed through the rural areas in social and economic competition with the supreme power," Lucila Herrmann writes. The sugar planter used the *senado da câmara* to control the appointment of the *capitão-mor* and to curb external interference in the political and ecclesiastical spheres.

The coffee cycle hastened concentration of land ownership, the emerg-

[63] Adolfe Assier, *Le Brésil contemporain, races, moeurs, institutions, paysage* (Paris, 1867), pp. 231–38.

[64] Rollie Edward Poppino, "Princess of the Sertão: A History of Feira de Santana" (Ph.D. dissertation, Stanford University, 1953).

Table 3. Urban-rural distribution of population, municipality of Guaratinguetá

| | 1776 ← (transition → 1805 ← (transition → 1840 ← (apogee of → 1872 | | | | | | |
| | to sugar) | | to coffee) | | coffee) | | |
	Pop.	Index	Pop.	Index	Pop.	Index	Pop.	Index
Urban	1,413	100	1,088	77	1,275	90	9,750	690
Rural	2,432	100	5,506	226	5,624	231	11,044	454
Total	3,845	100	6,594	171	6,899	179	20,799	541

Source: Lucila Herrmann, "Evolução da estrutura social de Guaratinguetá num período de trezentos anos," Revista de administração 2 (1948):214.

ence of urban middle and commercial groups, the division of labor, and the articulation of the occupational structure. Although the coffee aristocracy maintained control of elective offices, the numerical growth of the elite, the incorporation of commercial, bureaucratic, and professional groups into politics, and the development of the party system complicated and broadened the political process. The ruralization of the sugar and early coffee periods finally reversed itself (table 3). During the first fifteen years of the republic, in the twilight of the coffee cycle, a plethora of improvements and innovations attested Guaratinguetá's rise to urban status: half a dozen churches built or repaired, three schools, two literary societies, two welfare associations, a bank, a new market, a slaughterhouse, a theater, trolleys, piped water, a new park, a new jail, electricity.[65]

It is clear, then, that Nabuco's description points not to a static tableau but to a sociopolitical field of force which conditioned the rhythms and patterns of urbanization. In explaining the slow pace of Brazilian urban development economists are wont to stress the narrow limits of the domestic market, which retarded commerce and industry. This consideration is essential for internal comparisons. For example, the fact that during the nineteenth century Brazil's southeast developed a strong advantage over the northeast as measured by per capita production and income clearly affected the rate and character of its urbanization.[66] Reflection on our earlier comparison between Brazil and the United States, however, suggests that the social ethic can be as important a variable as economics for understanding the Brazilian case.

Having made these caveats, we can still say that under the empire the larger cities, with their maritime location and separate hinterlands, perpetuated the colonial pattern. If the size distribution of Brazilian cities

[65] Lucila Herrmann, "Evolução da estrutura social de Guaratinguetá num período de trezentos anos," Revista de administração 2 (1948):3–326. Two M.A. theses for the Universidade Federal Fluminense provide case studies of small-town economies in the province of Rio de Janeiro: Ana Maria dos Santos, "Vida econômica de Itaboraí no século XIX," and Vânia Fróes Bragança, Município de Estrela—1846–1892 (Niterói, 1974).

[66] Nathaniel H. Leff, "Desenvolvimento econômico e desigualdade regional: Origens do caso brasileiro," Revista brasileira de economia 26 (1972):3–21.

falls into a pyramidal or lognormal pattern rather than the primate one of Mexico, Argentina, or Peru, this is because of the nation's immense size and the need for numerous points of entry. Primate distribution therefore characterized regions rather than the nation as a whole, and was perhaps accentuated by the advent of steamships, which circumvented the smaller ports. Rio, it is true, was a *primus inter pares,* a relay point for European fads and notions and the seat of national power. Spix and Martius observed at an early date that "even the more remote provinces of the infant kingdom, whose inhabitants . . . visited Rio de Janeiro, soon accustomed themselves to recognise that city as the capital, and to adopt the manners and modes of thinking, which, after the arrival of the court, struck them as European." [67] Walsh wrote that "old and respectable creole families" were losing the "rude" habits and outlook derived from "rustic seclusion" as they now "repaired to the capital, where frequent galas, levees, and birth-day ceremonies at court, attracted crowds together. Here, from mixing with strangers, both Portuguese and English, they soon rubbed off the rust of retirement, and returned home with new ideas and modes of life, which were again adopted by their neighbours, and so improvement and civilization spread through the country." [68]

Rio's cultural primacy rested on its political primacy. The meaning of Brazilian independence was not that a new nation had thrown off the shackles of colonial bondage but that the center of colonial control was shifted from Lisbon to Rio, where the structures of domination were re-elaborated in continuity with the earlier system. The "internationalization of the metropolis" had a commercial as well as politico-administrative dimension. Whereas in many of the new Spanish American republics, notably Mexico, Spaniards were displaced from privileged positions in urban commercial life, in Brazil the transplantation of the court caused "the installation of new Portuguese investment and interests linked to the dominant native classes and also polarized in the struggle to affirm a central executive power that they wished to reinforce against displays of insubordination by the underprivileged classes." [69] A series of outbreaks, from the Pernambucan revolt of 1817 to the Praieira revolts of the 1840s, had as a common theme the protest against this entente between the rural and urban-commercial elites. In this sense they were a reprise of the Barbalho and Mascate uprisings of the colonial period. By the mid-nineteenth century "popular" protest was defused, and the political history of the balance of the empire centers on conflicts within the

[67] Joh. Bapt. von Spix and C. F. Phil. von Martius, *Travles in Brazil, in the Years 1817–1820* 2 vols. (London, 1824), 1:143–44.
[68] R. Walsh, *Notices of Brazil in 1828 and 1829,* 2 vols. (London, 1830), 1:170.
[69] See the essay by Maria Odila Silva Dias in this volume.

burguesia itself.[70] Again, we have a reversal of the West European case, where citification and industrialization in this period increasingly elicited reaction, not acquiescence, from the proletariat.

Rio's political, fiscal, and cultural advantages were not matched in the economic realm. As national capital it exacted tribute, as it were, from regional centers. But the national hinterland was too immense and geographically fragmented, the buying power of its inhabitants too low, and the industrial productivity of Rio too weak for the capital to serve as a substantial force for economic integration. By the end of the empire five other leading cities served as outlets for regional hinterlands. The two largest after Rio, the traditional centers of Salvador and Recife, grew at modest rates, their fortune still tied to sugar.[71] The population of Belém, outlet for the Amazonian rubber trade, jumped from 62,000 in 1872 to 166,000 in 1890, and the city acquired the appurtenances of elegant life in the process.[72] At the southern extremity Pôrto Alegre was about to consolidate its dominance of the region. Historically, Rio Grande do Sul had been divided into two societies with few common ties: the latifundiary, pastoral zone of the southeast *serra* and the *campanha* and the diversified, farming zone worked by immigrant smallholders in the central depression. The dual railway system constructed after 1869 reflected this dichotomy. Under the early empire the commerce of Rio Grande, port for the southern cattle zone, greatly surpassed that of Pôrto Alegre. European colonization, commercial agriculture, and German entrepreneurship, however, began to shift the balance. When the empire fell, Pôrto Alegre was ready to industrialize for a statewide consumer market; its population would soar from 52,000 in 1890 to 180,000 in 1920.[73]

Of the six largest cities in 1890, São Paulo was the smallest and the fastest growing. Although one associates its rise with coffee, considerable infrastructure for regional urban development (transportation, port facilities, capital accumulation, credit mechanisms) had been laid during the

---

[70] Caio Prado Júnior, *Evolução política do Brasil e outros estudos*, 4th ed. (São Paulo, 1963), p. 82.

[71] Cowell's research shows that the census figures which give Recife a population decline for 1872–90 are probably erroneous (Bainbridge Cowell, Jr., "Migration to Recife, Brazil, 1790–1920," unpublished memo):

Year	Census Figures	New Estimates	
1872	116,671	100,000	
1890	111,556	150,000	(1893)
1900	113,106	200,000	(1910)
1920	238,843	330,000	

[72] António Rocha Penteado, *Belém, estudo de geografia urbana*, 2 vols. (Belém, 1968), 1:127–61.

[73] Singer, *Desenvolvimento econômico*, pp. 141–86; Francisco Riopardense de Macedo, *Pôrto Alegre, origem e crescimento* (Pôrto Alegre, 1968).

previous periods of mule trade and sugar production.[74] The coffee cycle itself had distinctive features. Initially slave-based, coffee planting attracted heavy European immigration, which soon provided both the market and the labor for industrialization. Further, coffee production in the *Paulista* West after midcentury was conductive to patterns of entrepreneurial rationalization that proved transferable to railroading, finance, and industry.[75] Coffee pioneering acted centrifugally on urban concentrations; the percentage of the provincial population living in the capital dropped from 11.6 percent in 1816 to 3.7 percent in 1872. Thereafter the trend reversed, with industrialization increasing the city's centripetal force. In the last decade of the century, São Paulo's population leaped from 65,000 to 240,000, back to 10.5 percent of the state total. By 1894 Santos had overtaken Rio in volume of exports, and twenty years later São Paulo was invading the consumer market of Rio's hinterland. The proximity of these two large cities created an industrial concentration so powerful that it eventually forced the integration of a national market.[76]

The cities of nineteenth-century Brazil are frequently seen as lightning rods for modernization, as transmission belts for the development process. This paper has tried to guard against a dichotomous view of the "two Brazils"—modern and traditional, urban and rural—by stressing that cities were embedded in larger social and institutional "fields" which conditioned the reception of innovations and in many ways shortcircuited their effects.[77] The intellectual progenitor of the "two Brazils" thesis is sometimes taken to be Euclides da Cunha, whose *Rebellion in the Backlands* seems to pivot on the antagonism between the citified, Europeanized coast and the atavistic savagery of the *sertão*. The author's dissatisfaction with so mechanistic a view, however, is apparent throughout, as when he describes the discomfiture of the government troops on hearing the mournful litanies, transfigured by religious faith, that arose at midnight from beleaguered Canudos. Euclides offered a pathology of Brazil, not

[74] Gilberto Leite de Barros, *A cidade e o planalto*, 2 vols. (São Paulo, 1967), 1:171–230; Maria Thereza Schorer Petrone, *A lavoura canavieira em São Paulo* (São Paulo, 1968).

[75] Fernando Henrique Cardoso, "O café e a industrialização da cidade de São Paulo," *Revista de história* 20 (1960):471–75; Warren Dean, *The Industrialization of São Paulo 1880–1945* (Austin, Tex., 1969).

[76] Only at this point can one speak, if one likes the charged phrase, of "internal colonialism." Under the empire the southeast was favored over the northeast in that the nation's foreign exchange rate favored coffee over sugar and cotton. But "the Southeast might have achieved the same pace of development without sacrifices by the northeast. In most cases, that is, the losses in northeast development were not *gains* for the southeast" (Leff, "Desenvolvimento econômico," p. 20–21). See, however, David Denslow's critique of Leff in: "As origens da desigualdade regional no Brasil," *Estudos econômicos* 3 (1973):65–88.

[77] Such a view of urban development is implicit throughout Gilberto Freyre's *The Mansions and the Shanties* (New York, 1963).

merely of the *sertão*. After describing a scene of mob looting in Rio he drove the point home:

The foregoing lines were written with one object in view, namely, to call attention in passing to a certain similarity between the scene in the Rua do Ouvidor and a disturbance in the *caatingas,* one equaling the other in savagery. Backlands lawlessness was precipitately making its entrance into history; and the Canudos revolt, when all is said, was little more than symptomatic of a malady which, by no means confined to a corner of Baía, was spreading to the capitals of the seaboard. The man of the backlands, that rude, leather-clad figure, had partners in crime who were, possibly, even more dangerous. Is it worth while to be more explicit? [78]

[78] *Rebellion in the Backlands* (Chicago, 1944), p. 279.

CULTURAL ASPECTS

MANOEL DA SILVEIRA CARDOZO

The Modernization of Portugal and the Independence of Brazil

When the Portuguese began their pioneer voyages of exploration, and established trading posts on several continents, an opportunity of universal dimensions presented itself to them: the conversion of heathens and infidels to the faith of Christ. The challenge was of surpassing magnitude, the like of which no Christian nation had faced before, but they accepted it, undaunted by the exiguousness of their material and human resources. Jorge Cardoso expressed the national mystique in these words: "the principal reason" why "the glorious kings of Portugal" spent much of their substance and the Portuguese endured "the immense labors" involved "in these discoveries and conquests" was to make possible "the preaching of the sacred Gospel, and the conversion of the heathen." [1]

In the euphoric, springtime days of the missionary enterprise, God was thought to be on the side of the people he had elected to spread the law of eternal life. Ecclesiastics of the gravity of Jerónimo Osório and Frei Luís de Sousa held this messianic view, as did Damião de Góis. In the sixteenth century, the Portuguese chronicler João de Barros wrote that the kingdom of Portugal was already "the grain of mustard seed . . . which has produced by itself a tree so large, that its size, power and doctrine embraces the larger part of the world." [2] Indeed, the harvest of conversions was very great, and there were those who looked forward to the time when there would be, as the Bible said, through the efforts of Portuguese missionaries, one shepherd and one flock.

[1] *Agiologio lusitano* 1 (Lisbon, 1652):28. This first section of my study, on the decline of religion before 1750, has not been developed more fully not only because of limitations of space but also because the subject is generally well known to scholars. Other sections have been given fuller treatment precisely because the subjects they talk about are less well known, not because they are more important, for my purposes, than the religious factor. See Manoel Cardozo, "The Idea of History in the Portuguese Chronicles of the Age of Discovery," *Catholic Historical Review* 49 (1963):1–19.

[2] Hernâni Cidade, *A literatura portuguesa e a expansão ultramarina: As idéias, os sentimentos, as formas de arte* (Lisbon, 1943) , 1:38.

Portugal had become the perfect training ground for the missionaries of Africa, Asia, and America, a fortress of faith in a Europe torn with religious dissension. "This kingdom," Friar Apolinário da Conceição, of the Franciscan province of Rio de Janeiro, observed during the reign of Dom João V (1706–50), "is a kind of emporium of faith and religion, being, among all the nations, the one with the greatest devotion." [3] "Among all the princes of the world," Diogo Guerreiro Camacho de Aboím declared, reflecting the views of his fellow countrymen, "none were more zealous in matters of religion than the princes of Portugal." [4] The loveliest tribute came from a foreigner, António Ardizone Spínola, a Neapolitan Theatine assigned to the India missions, in a sermon delivered in Goa cathedral on September 16, 1641, when he said that Portugal was, among the Christian nations of the world, the sight of the eyes of Christ.[5]

The grace of the Lord in inscrutable ways abided with the Portuguese who followed his commandments and kept them steadfast in their faith. Barlaeus, speaking of Brazil during the period of the Dutch invasions, still found the Old Religion strong among the papists, who stubbornly refused to accept the religion of their conquerors. The reason?—their "inveterate opinion of truth, which only with difficulty could be uprooted, since they hold that they must keep the religion and ceremonies received from their elders and that it would be an abomination to abandon them." [6] Unfortunately, after the heroic days came the evil days, the loss of the primitive evangelical spirit, the faltering in the conviction that the

[3] *Claustro franciscano, erecto no dominio da coroa portugueza, e estabelecido sobre dezeseis venerabilissimas columnas. Expoem-se sua origem e estado presente* (Lisbon, 1740), dedication.

[4] *Escola moral, politica, christãa, e juridica. Dividida em quatro palestras* (Lisbon, 1732), p. 36.

[5] *Cordel triplicado de amor a Christo Jesu sacramentado, ao encuberto de Portugal nacido, a seu reyno restaurado, lançado em tres livros de sermoens, da felis aclamaçam d'el rey Dom Joam IV. emparada do ceo: Da sagrada comumhaõ restaurada na India: Dos felices annos d'el rey, & saudosos nacimentos, natural, politico, & milagroso: com huma misteriosa declaraçam da arvore real de Christo Senhor nosso, debuxo, & pintura da decima sexta geraçaõ do sancto, & invicto rey, & senhor nosso Dom Joam IV. pregouos na India na see primacial de Goa, e em Lisboa na capella real, O M.R.P. Dom Antonio Ardizone Spinola, clergio regular, Theatino da Divina Providencia, Neapolitano por nacimento, Genoves por origem, Portuguez naturalizado por amor, doutor na sagrada theologia, & missionario apostolico, fundador dos conventos de Nossa Senhora da Divina Providencia da cidade de Lisboa, & da cidade de Goa, & das missoens, que tem na India sua religiaõ, vigario geral, visitador, preposito, & prefeito das missoens. Offerecido ao serenissimo senhor Dom Pedro principe, & regente da monarchia de Portugal* (Lisbon, 1680), p. 6.

[6] Gaspar Barlaeus, *História dos feitos recentemente praticados durante oito anos no Brasil e noutras partes sob o governo do ilustrissimo João Mauricio conde de Nassau etc., ora governador de Wesel, tenente-general de cavalaria das Provincias-Unidas sob o principe de Orange*, trans. from Latin by Cláudio Brandão (Rio de Janeiro, 1940), p. 136.

Portuguese were the elect of God. As the Portuguese became more corrupted by the blandishments of the world, the missionary mystique that had given a supernatural dimension to their lives, the respect for the clerical state, did not suddenly disappear, but the certainties of former times were less rugged.

The years that witnessed the decline of religion also witnessed a continuing reappraisal of the noble state. Moralists had traditionally been critical of a privileged class that was given every opportunity to do good but sometimes committed reprehensible deeds. The concerns of the moralists were essentially pastoral, and since the nobility served as examples to the rest of society, a noble sin was more heinous than a plebeian one. Yet the titled nobility of Portugal was not large. In 1751, there were three nonroyal dukes, eighteen marquises, forty-eight counts, three viscounts, and two barons.[7] Many other people enjoyed the privileges of aristocracy, and in time even professors were included, but the titled nobility, the core of the noble state, was hardly excessive for carrying on the business of government and the proper functioning of the court.[8]

The ideal *fidalgo*, or noble, was described by the ninth count of Vimioso in the instruction he wrote for his four-year-old son. "In these accounts of our ancestors," he said, "you will observe how valor is put before life, liberality before wealth, contempt of private interest before profit, courtesy before haughtiness, love of country before the greatest fortunes, and religion before everything."[9] The founder of the Vimioso line, who died in 1549, was a man of such integrity and conscience that Dom João III (1521–57) used to say of him that when he voted in council in the presence of the king of the world he always had present the King of Heaven.[10]

---

[7] Damião António de Lemos Faria e Castro, *Politica moral, e civil, aula da nobreza lusitana authorizada com todo o genero de erudiçaõ sagrada, e profana para a doutrina, e direcçaõ dos principes, e mais politicos; dividida em varios volumes, em que se dá noticia de todas as virtudes, e vicios moraes. De todas as sciencias, e artes liberaes. particularmente da astronomia, geografia, e chronologia. Das faculdades bellica, nautica, e equestre. Da historia sagrada, e ecclesiastica. De todas as religioens da Europe, e ordens militares, e regulares da Igreja. Da historia geral. Da fundaçaõ dos imperios, origem das monarquias, differenças dos governos, e razoens porque os estados crescem, se conservaõ, e diminuem. Da historia de Portugal. Da historia, e genealogia de Portugal. Das leys, e costumes, das batalhas, e tratados dos outros reinos. Da historia fabulosa. Dos interesses dos principes. Das maximas da corte, que ha de seguir, e dos livros necessarios, que deve ler o politico moral, e civil* (Lisbon, 1751), 4:522 et seq.

[8] See Luiz da Silva Pereira Oliveira, *Privilegios da nobreza, e fidalguia de Portugal* (Lisbon, 1806).

[9] *Instrucçam que o conde de Vimioso Dom Joseph Miguel Joam de Portugal, dá a seu filho D. Francisco Joseph Miguel de Portugal, fundada nas acçoens moraes, politicas, e militares dos condes de Vimioso seus ascendentes* (Lisbon, 1741), fol. 3v.

[10] *Ibid.*, p. 13.

There were others, in less cynical days, who sang the praises of the nobility of blood. "The grandees of the world," in the opinion of a Jesuit priest, "are instruments that God makes use of to carry out grand things." [11] The author of a book on the Brahmins, published during the last years of the reign of Dom Pedro II, believed that "hereditary nobility is always more illustrious, because it is natural; and if it is united with virtue, knowledge, and valor, these qualities acquire greater worth, and the possessor of them becomes endowed with greater glory." [12] But no words were more dithyrambic than those which flowed from the pen of Diogo Guerreiro Camacho de Aboím:

Nobility is a light inherited from our elders, a splendor derived from our ancestors, a paean of praise born of the merits of our parents, an honorable state issuing from our progenitors, an ancient virtue of our grandparents, . . . a quality, or dignity, that comes from the splendor of the blood; because just as the branches of the tree find sustenance in the humors that rise from the trunk, so the nobility of blood of our elders (as Vergil says) gives honorific being to their descendants.[13]

At the time of the Restoration, when the nation was being organized anew, and later, when the idea of aristocracy was openly criticized, the nobility was again and again reminded of its responsibilities, the raison d'être of its existence. The nobility had naturally changed, with changing and revolutionary times. Some, during the Restoration, were unsure of their national loyalties. Others cast in their lot with Castile. As the years went on, the austerity of former days gave way to high fashion, banqueting, dancing, gambling, and whoring. The exactions of factors, representatives of the noble houses, became more onerous as fortunes were tied up by law or, when free of legal restrictions, were dissipated. The elder count of Assumar, father of the governor of Minas Gerais, died penniless, ruined by the demands of his years of public service, yet surrounded by marks of opulence that under the law of primogeniture could not be alienated.[14] After pious legacies, the emancipation of a faithful slave, and the discharging of the other obligations that death imposed upon the nobility, there was often little left to maintain the dignity of one's house. Many a noble daughter was sent off to a convent because there was no money for her dowry.

[11] Alexandre Perier, *Desengano dos peccadores, necessario a todo genero de pessoas, utilissimo aos missionarios, e aos Prégadores desenganados, que só desejaõ a salvaçaõ das almas* (Lisbon, 1735), fol. 4.

[12] António João de Frias, *Aureola dos indios, & nobiliarchia bracmana: Tratado historico, genealogico, panegyrico, politico, & moral* (Lisbon, 1702), p. 19.

[13] Aboím, *Escola moral*, p. 221.

[14] Last will and testament of Dom João de Almeida, count of Assumar, Rilhafoles, April 19, 1731, Arquivo Nacional da Tôrre do Tombo, Registo Geral de Testamentos, bk. 204, fol. 118 et seq.

The general attitude toward nobility on the part of moralists was expressed very pithily by Dom João da Silva Carvalho in a letter to Cardinal Alencastre: "all the nobility of the world is vanity, shadow, wind." [15] Another moralist, Friar Amador Arrais, wrote that true nobility was "a perpetual tribute that we owe to virtue." [16] It was, in fact, generally held that "there is no nobility, where virtue is lacking; nor politeness, and urbanity, when the Christian law is not observed with special respect." [17] When the question of nobility was debated one day at the king's table, a courtier turned to Dom João III and said: "Sire, when Adam ploughed, and Eve spun, where was the nobility?" The prudent prince replied: "In virtue." [18] Put in another way and by another author: "True nobility does not consist in knowing who our parents were; but the works that we have fathered." [19]

The eighteenth century continued to say that virtue was the redeeming feature of nobility, but it also began to stress the equality of all men. Matias Aires Ramos da Silva de Eça, in a celebrated book on vanity which he published in 1752, was very blunt: "men were born equal." In another passage, he remarked that "the sun rises for everybody; the dawn awakens everybody for work; the silence of night announces the period of rest for everybody. . . . The world was not made for the greater benefit of some than of others." Men, in fact, were not born "wise, just, prudent, virtuous, good; and in the same way they are not born noble; it is here that they find nobility." [20] The censor, who was called upon to review the book, in turn wrote that vanity, "was a vice as old as the world itself, and as universal as mankind, which follows [men] in life, and ordinarily does not abandon them in death." [21] Diogo Borges Pacheco Pereira was not as plainspoken as Matias Aires, but he too castigated nobility. It was, he said, "the greatest vainglory of life, the fraud of reason, the life of remembrance, the changling of understanding, and the false witness of nature." [22] Friar Apolinário da Conceição

---

[15] The letter is undated and has no indication of place. Ajuda Library, manuscript division, 50-V-37, no. 34. Dom Veríssimo de Alencastre (or Lencastre) became cardinal in 1686 and died in 1692.

[16] Cited by Manuel Monteiro de Campos, *Academia nos montes, e conversações de homens nobres* (Lisbon, 1642), p. 32.

[17] *Ibid.*, pp. 45–46.

[18] Dom João Pinto Ribeiro, *Lustre ao Dezembargo do Paço, e as eleiçoens, perdoens, e pertenças de sua jurisdiçaõ* (Coimbra, 1729), p. 48. I owe this reference to the kindness of Profesor E. Bradford Burns.

[19] João de Medeiros Correia, *Perfeito soldado, e politica militar* (Lisbon, 1659), p. 7.

[20] *Reflexões sobre a vaidade dos homens, ou discursos moraes sobre os effeitos da vaidade* (Lisbon, 1752), pp. 117–18, 400.

[21] *Ibid.*, preliminary unnumbered pages 23–24.

[22] Diogo Borges Pacheco Pereira, *Espelho de hum peccador* (Lisbon, 1732), pt. 1, pp. 255–56.

remained faithful to his Franciscan training: "true nobility and wealth are those of the spirit." [23] People knew, they saw it before their eyes, that inherited nobility was everywhere prized, "but if actions belie the quality, nobility is the greatest of infamies." [24]

During the reign of Dom José I (1750–77), when the marquis of Pombal was the virtual ruler of Portugal, a number of massive attacks were leveled at the Church and the nobility, the two firmest pillars of the established order. Both were humbled, both were thenceforth unable to raise voices of protest against the power of the crown. In modernizing Portugal in this way, and to the extent that he did—there is no proof that Pombal thought out the broader implications of his actions—he weakened baroque society in its most vulnerable parts, and opened it, in effect, to ideas that the Enlightenment had given currency.

There was something in the old regime, as it reached its inglorious end, which justified, by its own shortcomings, the trauma of change. People who identified themselves with change were aware of the regime's deficiencies, but so were the traditionalists, men of the character of the Jesuit Gabriel Malagrida (1689–1761). Awareness of the situation was therefore not the problem; the issue was what to do about it, how to achieve reform. Should Portugal change or should it remain faithful to the dreams of the past? Those who cherished baroque values, as Malagrida did, wanted simply to return to the virtues of a bygone age.

Malagrida sounded the alarm when there was still time. His moral treatise on the true cause of the Lisbon earthquake of 1755, that most alarming of tremors that shook Enlightenment Europe out of its complacent theory of progress, published by the author on the heels of the great catastrophe, expatiates upon the ruin of "so rich, so beautiful, so flourishing a court," not by natural phenomena, as many people were already saying, but by the wrath of God, punishment for the sins of the city. The "sole destroyers of so many buildings and palaces, the levelers of so many churches and convents, the murders of so many of its inhabitants, the devouring flames of so many treasures . . . are not comets, not stars, not vapors or exhalations, not phenomena, not contingent happenings or natural causes, but exclusively our intolerable sins." [25] This was an unblushing statement of the granite faith of high baroque days,

---

[23] *Flor peregrina por preta ou nova maravilha da graça descuberta na prodigiosa vida de S. Philadelfio religioso leigo da Provincia Reformada de Sicilia, das da mais estreita observancia da religião serafica; vigario, e guardião, que foy do Convento de S. Maria de Jesus de Palermo* (Lisbon, 1744), p. 8.

[24] Castro, *Politica moral,* 1:iv.

[25] *Juizo da verdadeira causa do terremoto, que padeceu a corte de Lisboa no primeiro de novembro de 1755* (Lisbon, 1756), p. 3.

when religious conformity was the practice, blinded now by the Lights of the Century.

More than six months before the holocaust, a sister of a convent of the strictest observance, declared that Our Lord had revealed to her his "notable indignation" at the sins of Portugal and above all the sins of Lisbon.[26] This was proof of God's displeasure, proof enough for other more religious times, when people would have been provoked to an outpouring of works of penance. But no longer. In the midst of the destruction of Lisbon, nobody bothered because everybody believed "these pernicious doctrines, that all the desolation that we have experienced is the effect of natural causes and not the punishment of God for our offenses!"[27] There were at least two other pamphlets on the earthquake published in Lisbon in 1756, the year in which Malagrida's appeared, that hewed to the official line of the marquis of Pombal. They declared that the causes of the great earthquake were natural, not supernatural. One, the more solid scientific study, was from the pen of Veríssimo António Moreira de Mendonça, a study on the physical causes of the earthquake of November 1, 1755.[28] The other, without learned pretensions, by António dos Remédios, stressed natural causes in the form of a reply to a letter ascribed to José de Oliveira Trovão e Sousa.[29]

Who was this Malagrida, a priest who found himself catapulted to fame? Born in Menaggio, Italy, he entered the Company of Jesus in 1711, at the age of twenty-two. In 1721 he was sent to the missions of the Maranhão and Pará to work with the Amerindians. He returned to Lisbon in 1750 to get help, his reputation for sanctity having preceded him. When Dom João V, who was then on his deathbed, realized that Malagrida was in Lisbon, he asked the Jesuit to help him prepare for the last journey. In 1751, following the death of the king, Malagrida returned to the missions in the company of Francisco Xavier de Mendonça Furtado, Pombal's brother and the new governor of Grão Pará, who was not sympathetic to him. When the situation in the mission field became unbearable, the queen mother called him back to Lisbon, where he arrived in 1754. His missionary problems were never solved because Pombal sided with his brother against the priest. When the earthquake of 1755 occurred, and Malagrida published his piece on it, the final and tragic period of his life began.

The chief culprit in the loss of faith was the Lisbon establishment,

---

[26] *Ibid.,* p. 8.

[27] *Ibid.,* p. 11.

[28] *Dissertaçaõ philosophica sobre o terremoto de Portugal do primeiro de novembro de 1755. Expendem-se as suas causas physicas, as dos seus effeitos, e prognosticos* (Lisbon, 1756).

[29] *Reposta á carta de Jozé de Oliveira Trovam e Sousa, em que se dà noticia do lamentavel successo de Lisboa* (Lisbon, 1756).

already Enlightenment-minded enough to pay little attention to the theological implications of the earthquake; not the provinces, such as Coimbra, which carried out the penance that Lisbon found itself reluctant to do; and not Portuguese America, less sophisticated in its attitude toward religion, more willing to believe the pious explanations of a Malagrida. In a letter to the Jesuit moralist, Friar Dom Manuel da Cruz, the first bishop of Mariana, deep in the heart of Brazil, exclaimed that the earthquake was "the just punishment of God, especially because of the dissipation of the court." He praised the royal family for its religious exercises of reparation. What the royal family did was "the means more conducive to the reform of customs. Soon we shall see that Babylon of vices purified and as a consequence the kingdom as a whole, because *Regis ad exemplum totus componitur orbis.*" [30]

In São Paulo, the news of the destruction of Lisbon was received with tears. "His Excellency, the Most Reverend Bishop of this diocese, moved by love of country, and the fear that since the sins of America were greater than those of Portugal, his subjects might experience similar or worse destruction," placated God with eight days of public prayers in the parishes of his diocese, complete with exhortatory sermons for the mending of private lives. The penitential spirit of the provincial capital reached an extraordinary pitch of grief and repentance. When the last of the sermons was delivered, at the end of the octave, a procession of penitence began the solemn march through the streets of the city. Women were not allowed to join the marchers, by the bishop's special edict—they stayed indoors to give vent to lamentations as the procession passed by—but little boys, seven years of age, took a part in it, flagellating themselves for the edification of the faithful and carrying out other penitential acts. His Excellency brought up the rear, on foot, wearing *capa magna* but without a trainbearer, barefooted, with a rope about his neck to symbolize death, a crown of thorns on his head to symbolize the martyrdom of Jesus, and in his hands an image of Our Lord. There was a rush to the confessional as the result of the bishop's piety, and people who had not been absolved in thirty or forty years were reconciled with their consciences and the Church.[31] It was strange and revealing, a com-

[30] Raimundo Trindade, *Archidiocese de Marianna. Subsidios para a sua historia* (São Paulo, 1928), 1:154. The day was fast approaching when the king and queen no longer set the religious tone for the nation. The Castilian consort of Dom José I was observed by an Italian visitor in 1760 to have kissed her prayer book forty times at a ceremonial mass. An Irish official of the Royal Guard explained that Her Majesty customarily kissed the name of God, of Our Lady, of the saints, and of the blesseds every time they appeared in print. Giuseppe Baretti, *Viaggi di Giuseppe Baretti esposti in lettere familiari a suoi tre fratelli Filippo Giovanni e Amedeo* (Monza, 1850), 1:152.

[31] *Gazeta de Lisboa,* January 27, 1757, article dated São Paulo, July 15, 1756, in Manuel Lopes de Almeida, ed., *Notícias históricas de Portugal e Brasil (1751–1800)* (Coimbra, 1964), pp. 63–64.

mentary on the times, that what Lisbon had refused, through disinterest in religion, Brazil, firmer in the faith, accepted: the earthquake of 1755 spread its spiritual blessings not over the seat of the monarchy but over the provinces and the dominions beyond the sea.

If only Malagrida could have had the consolation of witnessing such marks of faith and devotion in the capital of empire! What he saw instead was that Lisbon was not able to maintain a single retreat house decently, at a time when the need was pressing, when people had forgotten how to confess their sins or how to prepare themselves for a fuller participation in the sacramental life. He found the churches solitary and empty, lovely shells (among those that had survived the earthquake), echoing eternal truths to unpeopled benches. Female convents with two or three hundred sisters were so lax in their liturgical observances that they were scarcely able to bring together five or six of their number for community prayers. The same relaxation of the rule was found among the male religious, among the beneficed clergy as among the clergy attached to collegiate and cathedral churches.[32] What a sad reality, the decline of faith in a country that for centuries had lived its spiritual life at the foot of the Cross!

The earthquake, Malagrida believed, bared the rottenness of the religious life of Lisbon. It was a sure sign from Heaven that the country had to repent for its sins, and repentance, as he saw it, could only mean going back to an earlier state of perfection, when religion flourished and the king basked in the virtue of his subjects. Dom José I attended masses of reparation, and repented as best he could in private, but neither he nor his principal minister, the future marquis of Pombal, did penance in the ostentatious public manner that Malagrida would have preferred, nor did they admit to the country, in a solemn pronouncement, that the earthquake was a warning from above. Actually, Pombal took advantage of the psychological moment that the earthquake afforded him by pushing forward the process of change that would leave baroque society a shadow of its former self. When doctrinaire liberalism later raised its head, threatening the stability of the established order, the baroque mind, by now buffeted and divided, was unable to meet the challenge, and in the upheavals that followed not only was the baroque conscience, as the guiding principle of society, irretrievably lost, but Brazil also.

During the "calamitous times" that followed the earthquake, "the affairs of Portugal," as a contemporary exclaimed, were "so prostrate, so depressed" that "the Afonsos, the Johns, not even all the Portuguese sovereigns that had flourished in the past" would have been enough to

---

[32] Malagrida, *Juizo da verdadeira causa do terremoto*, p. 13.

put things back in working order. It remained for Dom José and Pombal to achieve the impossible.[33] This was accomplished, as is obvious today, not so much by putting things in order as by creating elements of a new order. The heart of Lisbon, between Rossio Square and the Palace Yard and between Castle Hill and the Upper Town, was not rebuilt; it was built anew. New buildings, uniformly designed in a sober style, took the place of ancient structures, such as the Hospital of All Saints, humbled by the earthquake. Old thoroughfares were no longer recognizable, even hallowed names disappeared. The fame of Merchants New Street, the grandest shopping center of Europe during the time of Dom Manuel I (1495–1521), did not preserve it from the reforming zeal of the city planners. The new streets were built straight and wide, to the amazement of a Europe not yet accustomed to urban renewal on the grand scale. St. Petersburg, on the Gulf of Finland, and now Lisbon, on the great Atlantic routes, the extremities of Europe, the two planned cities of the Enlightenment, thus became sister cities.

At the same time, because of Pombal, the fortunes of the Jesuits and of Malagrida himself hung in the balance. There had been straws in the wind, irate criticisms of Jesuit unwillingness to cooperate with the boundary commissioners in Paraguay and on the upper Amazon valley and of Jesuit resistance in other ways to the boundary treaty of 1750. In 1755, Pombal sided with the Oratorians in their dispute with the Jesuits in the school question, thus limiting the extent of Jesuit control of secondary education in Portugal.

The worst, however, was still to come, a series of events that led to the expulsion of the Jesuits from Portugal in 1759, the death by garroting of a mad Malagrida in 1761, and the extinction by the Holy See of the Society of Jesus in 1774. No order with a more brilliant record of achievement was ever so treated at the hands of a Christian government. Thus was brought to a sudden end the Jesuit control of Portuguese education and of other aspects of Portuguese life that had lasted for two centuries; thus was wrecked a massive missionary enterprise, the most important single undertaking in the history of the Portuguese Church.

The Jesuits soon realized that they were no match for Pombal. He was in effect the ruler of Portugal, a man with hair on his heart, as Dom João V used to say, a hard, harsh man who brooked no opposition. And the king himself, though he suffered qualms of conscience, did nothing to mitigate the blows. Malagrida defied the all-powerful minister and personally took a copy of his tract to Pombal. A short time later he was

---

[33] Matias Pereira de Azevedo Pinto, trans., *Diario dos successos de Lisboa, desde o terremoto até o exterminio dos Jesuitas. Traduzido do idioma latino* (Lisbon, 1766), pp. 3–4.

exiled to Setúbal, where his devoted coterie, including members of the noble Távora family, attracted by his piety, followed him.

Meanwhile, reports on Jesuit machinations in Brazil and Maranhão continued to reach Lisbon, giving Pombal whatever excuses he may have needed to proceed against them. For their alleged insubordination, Pombal had the king sign the decree of 1755, published in Pará only in May 1757, by which, among other provisions, Jesuit control of the Jesuit missions was abolished. There were sporadic acts of violence against the Jesuits, and some members of the Society were expelled. In December 1757, a libelous pamphlet, purporting to be an abbreviated account of the republic which Jesuit religious of the Portuguese and Spanish provinces had established in the overseas dominions of the two monarchies, composed by officials of the secretariat of state, made its appearance. The pamphlet created an enormous stir; the papal nuncio was not willing to believe the charges against the Jesuits, yet he was unable to answer any of them.[34] The government printed perhaps as many as twenty thousand copies of the tract, in French, German, and Italian translations, distributed it widely in Europe, and added fuel to the flames of anti-Jesuit feeling everywhere.[35] Under such circumstances, it was clear that the days of the Jesuits as confessors of the royal family, a position of trust and influence they had long enjoyed, were numbered. On September 21, 1757, in the middle of the night, the Jesuit fathers were pulled out of bed and expelled in ignominious fashion from the palace. They would never return.[36]

In Rome, Portuguese diplomats importuned Benedict XIV, who died shortly thereafter, on May 3, 1758, for immediate disciplinary action against the Company. By a brief of April 1, in one of the last acts of his pontificate, Benedict bowed to pressure and appointed Cardinal Dom Francisco de Saldanha, Pombal's confidant and soon to become the third patriarch of Lisbon (1758–76), as apostolic visitor with authority to reform the Company of Jesus in Portugal, the Algarves, and the overseas dominions. The Portuguese had succeeded in convincing the Pope that the Jesuits were unscrupulously engaging in trade and commerce, at the expense of their vows and of the welfare of the Amerindians of South America, as the anonymous authors of the anti-Jesuit pamphlet had tried to show. About a month later the pope died, the victim, it was believed, of his remorse at having given in to the demands of the Portuguese.

Cardinal Saldanha, invested with the fullest apostolic authority and

[34] João Lúcio de Azevedo, *O marquês de Pombal e a sua época*, 2d ed. (Rio de Janeiro, [1922]), pp. 161 n, 162–63.

[35] *Ibid.*, p. 163.

[36] Azevedo Pinto, *Diario*, pp. 26–27.

not threatened with the immediate revocation of his powers because Benedict's successor would not be elected for some time, moved quickly against the Jesuits. He prohibited them from engaging in business, which was ostensibly the principal charge against them, and began taking an inventory of their properties. On June 7, 1758, because it was "convenient for the glory of God," he had the cardinal patriarch of Lisbon, Dom José Manuel da Câmara, a short time before he died, deny them the privilege of preaching and confessing in the Archdiocese of Lisbon (which included Setúbal, where Malagrida was then conducting spiritual retreats).[37] The irony of the spiritual sanctions was especially telling because the Company of Jesus had been founded in 1540 precisely *Ad majorem Dei gloriam,* and its history had always been, within the limitations imposed by the imperfections of man, a testimony to the zeal of its members.

Politics and religion had reached this nadir when an unexpected event took place, providential, as it turned out, for Pombal. On September 3, 1758, about 11 P.M., Dom José I was returning to the palace from a visit to his mistress, the handsome and elegant Dona Teresa de Távora e Lorena, sister of the elder marquis of Távora and wife of her brother's son, the younger marquis of the same title, accompanied by his trusted and dedicated pimp, Sergeant-Major Pedro Teixeira. On his way he was struck by shots fired by unknown assailants and was wounded in the arm. All Lisbon knew almost immediately what had happened, and rumors were widespread; yet the official announcement of the attack was made only by decree of December 9, 1758, published on December 13, at which point the persons supposedly involved in the shooting were arrested without warning and the Jesuit houses of study surrounded with security guards.[38]

During the intervening weeks a number of explanations of the attack on the person of the king were advanced. Some said it was a fabrication of Pombal's imagination as an excuse for doing away with his enemies; others, that the shooting was ordered by Pombal himself, for the same reason; still others, that the queen, whose jealousy was well known, had ordered it but wanted only to kill Teixeira and Dona Teresa and never intended that her husband be shot. Even the papal nuncio could report to Rome no more than idle rumor. In his dispatch of September 19, he could only say that the king was returning from an assignation with a plebeian, not his noble mistress, that Teixeira was shot also, and that

---

[37] *Ibid.,* p. 31.

[38] For my account of the regicide, I have relied heavily upon João Lúcio de Azevedo, cited above, and Guilherme G. de Oliveira Santos, *O caso dos Távoras* (Lisbon, [1958?]).

the queen was being advised in the crisis by the Jesuits.[39] A week later the nuncio was still in the dark, but nobody doubted, he said, the *"male del re,"* even though the extent of the injury was not publicly known because the king kept his arm bandaged. The current opinion, he went on, was that he was not returning from a visit to the marchioness.[40] On October 3 the nuncio told Rome that the king's health had worsened, that he had developed a fever that alarmed his attendants.[41] From the court record and sentence we get the official version, that the nobles and their plebeian underlings involved in the shooting fired with the intention of killing the king, and that the plotters were aided and abetted by the Jesuits.[42]

The special court of high treason set up to try the accused, presided over by Pombal himself and made up of magistrates whose loyalty to the minister was beyond question, interrogated all the defendants except the elder marchioness of Távora, the Jesuits, and a plebeian who had fled. Sentences were imposed on January 12, 1759. On the following day those found guilty were executed on a wooden platform in a public square of Belém. The first to die was the elder marchioness, who was beheaded.

A number of other alleged conspirators were first garroted, then their arms and legs broken: José Maria de Távora, younger son of the late marchioness; Dom Jerónimo de Ataíde, count of Atouguia, her son-in-law; Luís Bernardo, the younger marquis of Távora, husband of the king's mistress; Manuel Álvares, an employee of the duke of Aveiro; João Miguel, also an employee of the duke; and Brás Romeiro, a foot soldier belonging to the company commanded by Luís Bernardo. The elder marquis of Távora, Francisco de Assis de Távora, the former viceroy of India, was strangled and his arms and legs broken. The duke of Aveiro, the premier noble of Portugal, head of a house whose wealth was probably surpassed only by that of the house of Braganza, the chief steward and highest officer of the royal household, died from the blows of an iron mace.

The last to die was António Álvares, an employee of the duke, the man who fired the shot; he was burned alive. The wooden platform, scene of the executions, was then itself ignited and became a giant funeral pyre. What remained at nightfall to remind the people "of past miseries and past glories" were ashes of the dead, scattered to the wind.[43]

There were no Jesuits on that wooden platform, and not a single Jesuit was brought to trial before the special court for high treason, but

39 Letter of Pietro Acciaioli to Rome, September 19, 1758, Vatican Archives, Nunziatura di Portogallo, codex 117, fol. 96.

40 Letter of September 26, 1758, *ibid.*, fol. 99.

41 Letter of October 3, 1758, *ibid.*, fol. 102.

42 Oliveira Santos, *O caso dos Távoras*, p. 58.

43 *Ibid.*, pp. 44–45.

Jesuits were assumed, without evidence other than the fantasies of the judges, to have been at the root of the alleged conspiracy. The official reason given for the absence of Jesuits from the funeral pyre was that they, as priests, were protected by ecclesiastical immunity and were therefore beyond the control of the secular arm; the real reason may have been the scruples of the king.[44] Even so, many members of the Society were locked up in the infamous Fort Junqueira for eighteen years; those who still survived were released, as were other political prisoners, only after the fall of Pombal.

The conspiracy was the occasion for political terrorism. Between mid-December 1758, when the arrests began, and January, more than 1,000 persons were put in jail.[45] (Altogether, from 1750 to 1777, the years when Pombal was in power, an estimated 9,640 political prisoners were jailed in Portugal.[46]) When Dona Maria I became queen, the cells of Fort Junqueira were torn down to remove from sight the reminder of the suffering of so many innocent victims.[47]

Malagrida warned Pombal not to continue the persecution of his fellow Jesuits, pointing out to him that the vendetta would tax the conscience of the king and of the government too. But the warning did not deter Pombal. The law of 1759 banished them from Portugal and the dominions and confiscated their endowments—the story is too well known to require a retelling—and Pombal then moved against Malagrida. In 1760 he personally denounced him to the Inquisition as a false prophet and impostor. Once in prison, Malagrida's mind began to falter, and on the basis of his ravings and rantings he was condemned to death after a scandalous trial presided over by Paulo de Carvalho, Pombal's brother. Convicted of false prophesy and heresy, he was strangled on October 23, 1761, and his body burned. The execution of such a man caused a general revulsion of feeling, and even Voltaire was shocked by it.

The remainder of the century was characterized by the further desacralization of Portuguese life. Dona Maria I tried to turn the clock back with her honest piety, and make amends for some of the damage that Pombal had done to innocent persons, but it was too late. Even before she began to suffer from the insanity that led to her removal from power in 1799, the revolutions of France (not to speak of the reforming zeal of England, upon whom Portugal had to rely) made any return to a tradition-clad old regime out of the question.

Attempts to reform the religious houses proved generally unsatis-

[44] *Ibid.*, p. 112n.
[45] Azevedo, *O marquês de Pombal*, p. 181.
[46] Oliveira Santos, *O caso dos Távoras*, p. 111, n. 2.
[47] *Ibid.*, p. 112n.

factory, partly because of opposition from within them, partly because of government interference. (We should not forget that in the second half of the eighteenth century nothing could be done by the Church without the approval of the government.) One such attempt, which had achieved a certain vitality when the government put a stop to it, was the so-called Jacobeia, a widespread movement of reform designed to sanctify the lives of religious. Members of the Jacobeia, which was officially recognized in 1723, led frugal lives and, in their active apostolate, served as models of perfection to those who had strayed from the path of strict observance. They encouraged intensive and daily mental prayer, spiritual conversations and readings, austerity in living arrangements, the avoidance of religious who were lax in their vows, the penetrating study of ecclesiastical subjects, frequent recourse to the Eucharist and especially the Sacrament of Penance, examinations of conscience, and rigorous public penance.[48]

The zeal of the members of the Jacobeia did not sit well with many people, both inside and outside the religious houses, and in time the reforming priests were accused by their opponents of breaking the seal of the confessional, of obliging penitents at confession to reveal the names, addresses, etc., of their accomplices in sin.[49] The use of information received in the confessional, even when the purpose was to pressure sinners to mend their ways, was of course prohibited by the Church. The dispute became so intense that Benedict XIV, who admired the Jacobeia, on four occasions personally attempted to restore peace to the Portuguese Church.

So long as Dom João V lived, the Jacobeia could count on royal protection, but the death of the king in 1750 left its members at the mercy of their opponents. Even public opinion was against them and they were harassed and persecuted. Finally, on December 8, 1768, Dom Miguel da Anunciação, bishop of Coimbra, the most representative figure of the Jacobeia, was arrested in his palace on trumped-up charges and taken to Pedrouços, outside of Lisbon, where he was left to languish in prison for years.[50] Dom Frei Lourenço de Santa Maria, the archibishop-bishop of the Algarve, was appalled at Pombal's treatment of the hierarchy: "Never would the Catholic world see more infamed the Successors

---

[48] Frei António Pereira da Silva, O.F.M., *A questão do sigilismo em Portugal no século XVIII. História, religião e política nos reinados de D. João V e D. José I* (Braga, 1964), p. 529.

[49] *Ibid.,* p. 530.

[50] *Ibid.,* p. 397. The marquis of Lavradio, captain-general of Bahia, in a letter to the Reverend Paulo de Carvalho e Mendonça, Bahia, May 1, 1769, referred to the "pitiable bishop of Coimbra" and expressed the hope that Portugal would soon be free of "the abominable fanaticism." He reported that "this pest" had not yet reached his captaincy. Marquês do Lavradio, *Cartas da Bahia 1768–1769,* ANRJ publication series 68 (Rio de Janeiro, 1972), p. 170.

of the Apostles than at the present time, nor would one ever see the insolence against the most villainous petty king so unleashed as we have seen against the bishops." [51]

Before the century was quite over, a succession of events shook the old regime even more: the founding of the College of Nobles in Lisbon, the first properly secular school of Portugal; the overhauling of the University of Coimbra in 1772, which abolished the study of scholastic philosophy and put natural philosophy (or natural history) in its place (it is worth noting that those self-same men who were instrumental in bringing the baroque period to an end and welcomed the new liberal ideology were products of the new university); the founding of the Academy of Sciences, with its emphasis on technology; the establishment of a public school system to take the place of the Jesuit schools; the first restrictions against black slavery in Portugal, made by the law of 1761, which prohibited the importation of slaves; the severing of diplomatic relations with the Holy See, with the attendant dangers of the establishment of a national church; and the spread of Masonry, with its lack of patience with the established order.

With the growing secularization of life, a latitudinarian spirit developed on the upper levels of society. Religion was relegated to a position of diminished authority. At the threshold of the nineteenth century, the German traveler Link remarked that the Portuguese went to Mass only because they had no other promenade: "I will even go so far as to say that they love religious ceremonies as a form of entertainment." [52] In 1801, the diamond intendant of Tijuco was accused by the procurator of the people of showing little piety and Christianity and little regard for the Portuguese nation and monarchy. [53] These were but two examples, in two disparate parts of the Portuguese monarchy, of a larger reality.

Under these conditions, religious life in convents and monasteries lost its appeal to young men, creating a crisis of vocations at home and overseas and a consequent lack of personnel in the religious houses that seriously impaired their canonical functioning. In Brazil, where the needs were especially great, the decline was especially felt. The Discalced Carmelites of Olinda were obligated by wills and legacies to say 1,527

---

[51] Letter of the archbishop-bishop to an unknown person, without place or date of origin. Arquivo Histórico do Ministério das Finanças, Lisbon, Cartório da Casa Real, box 312, 1752–94.

[52] M. Link, *Voyage en Portugal, depuis 1797 jusqu'en 1799. Suivi d'un essai sur le commerce du Portugal. Traduit de l'Allemand* (Paris, 1803), 1:286.

[53] Petition of José Soares Pereira da Silva, Tijuco, July 9, 1801, "Administração diamantina. Traslado dos autos de inquirição, a que mandou S. Ex.ça proceder sobre as conductas do Intendente dos Diamantes João Ign.co do Amaral Silvr.a e do Fiscal João da Cunha Sotto Maior, assim como sobre a import.e administração q.e lhe está encarregada," *Revista do arquivo publico mineiro* 2 (1897):162.

masses every year, but in 1797 they had only nine priests left.[54] The convent of St. Anthony, of Paraíba, at one time had a community of thirty; in 1797 there were four priests, two of them over seventy years of age.[55] Some Carmelite convents were reduced to a single priest, the prelate. This was true of Nossa Senhora da Guia, Nossa Senhora da Piedade, and Nossa Senhora de Guadalupe.[56] In 1797, among the largest convents of Recife were the Calced Carmelites, with forty-eight religious (fifteen priests and thirty novices),[57] and St. Anthony's, with twenty-six religious, including fifteen priests, eight of whom were old and seven of whom were between the ages of thirty and fifty.[58] The Benedictine monastery of Olinda, with hallowed traditions, had a resident religious population in that year of only fourteen men, including the prelate and nine subject priests. Six more Benedictines were assigned to the farms and estates of Pernambuco.[59] Even the Oratorians, well known for their advanced ideas, had no more than thirty-three persons in their Recife house of studies, ten priests and fourteen students, among others.[60]

In Rio de Janeiro, the capital of Brazil, there were about two hundred religious in 1808, including some sixty female religious. The Franciscans of St. Anthony had a community of sixty, the Carmelites one of thirty, the Benedictines one of about thirty. Father Gonçalves dos Santos, who supplied these data, criticized foreign authors for exaggerating the size of the religious community of the city: "Behold the many convents and excessive number of regular clergy, and friars, in Rio de Janeiro that foreigners write about!" [61] The prevarications of badly intentioned outsiders were hardly consoling to those who knew that the Church of Rio de Janeiro was not in a healthy state.

By the beginning of the nineteenth century, the attacks on the established church were also directed by those who were influenced by, or were followers of, liberalism. The abbot of Medrões, Inocêncio António de Miranda, who wrote a liberal catechism for the indoctrination of his fellow Portuguese, suggested that what the faithful needed for salvation was an "essential" Christianity, divested of the accretions of tradition.[62]

---

[54] Letter of April 16, 1797, Arquivo Histórico Ultramarino, Pernambuco, box 11.
[55] Letter of April 15, 1797, *ibid.*
[56] Convento do Carmo do Recife, letter of June 6, 1797, *ibid.*
[57] *Ibid.*
[58] Letter of April 3, 1797, *ibid.*
[59] Letter of April 22, 1797, *ibid.*
[60] Letter of April 3, 1797, *ibid.*
[61] Luís Gonçalves dos Santos, *Memorias para servir á historia do reino do Brazil, divididas em tres epocas da felicidade, honra, e gloria; escriptas na corte do Rio de Janeiro no anno de 1821 e offerecidas a S. Magestade Elrei nosso senhor o senhor D. João VI,* I (Lisbon, 1825), LIV.
[62] *O cidadão lusitano breve compendio, em que se demonstrão os fructos da consti-*

He was against what he called the abusive veneration of saints.[63] "I would hope that every Portuguese would be a good Christian, but not foolish, and that he would convince himself once and for all that all images, be they of wood, stone, gold, silver, have the same virtue." [64] He was against *romarias,* the popular pilgrimages so close to the heart of the common people.[65] The expense of maintaining the religious establishment he considered socially unproductive. If the money thus spent had been spent instead on "bridges, public fountains, roads, and other public works, the people would be happier today." [66] He wanted the Portuguese to be good Christians but not "fanatics." [67] As to clerical celibacy, which he looked upon as evil, he would convoke a national council, with the approval of the pope, to discuss the matter. He himself would vote to abolish it.[68] He was also opposed to the plethora of religious houses in Portugal.[69]

The abbot of Medrões had equally harsh things to say in his book about the nobility, but this was nothing original with him. The flaying of the nobility, as we have seen, had a long tradition in Portugal, but the reasons for it had changed over the years. Earlier critics were moralists and had pastoral concerns in view. Later critics, such as the abbot, were influenced by the new egalitarianism, and were part of a movement that led eventually to the destruction of aristocratic privilege.

In 1806, almost on the eve of the departure of the prince regent for Brazil, Luís da Silva Pereira Oliveira published what must surely be the last compendium of the privileges of the nobility and aristocracy of Portugal.[70] Despite the title of his book, and its purpose, his sympathies were with the egalitarians, and because he wanted his position understood, he went out of his way to disavow his approval of the noble state. That is why he began by saying that nobles and plebeians were "equal by nature, and made out of the same mud and dust of the earth." [71]

On the edge of the liberal precipice Portugal stood before the world battered and buffeted. The French Revolution certainly exerted a dis-

---

tuição, e os deveres do cidadão constitucional para com Deos, para com o rei, para com a patria, e para com todos os seus concidadãos dialogo entre hum liberal, e hum servil —o Abbade Roberto—e D. Julio, rev. ed. (Lisbon, 1822), p. 50.

[63] *Ibid.,* p. 51.
[64] *Ibid.,* p. 52.
[65] *Ibid.,* p. 54.
[66] *Ibid.,* p. 55.
[67] *Ibid.,* p. 56.
[68] *Ibid.,* pp. 59–60.
[69] *Ibid.,* p. 70.
[70] Luís da Silva Pereira Oliveira, *Privilegios da nobreza, e fidalguia de Portugal* (Lisbon, 1806).
[71] *Ibid.,* p. 2.

ruptive influence in the long run, but the Portuguese had begun to modernize their society some time before 1789. In 1777, the year that Pombal fell from power, a caustic Englishwoman, Mrs. Nathaniel E. Kindersley, expressed the attitude of foreigners when she wrote that she saw no hope for Portugal, "now so sunk," and remarked that "the present race" of Portuguese could hardly have been descended from those "who lived some ages since." [72] Mrs. Kindersley shared the traditional English hatred of papists, and her words in their full meaning are nonsensical, but she was right in suggesting that something had gone wrong.

The marquis of Penalva tried to call the attention of the Portuguese to their ancient loyalties. In 1799 he published a "dissertation," as he dubbed it, in favor of monarchy, by "reason, authority, and experience . . . the best, and most just of all governments." [73] He hoped that the Portuguese would rally around their sovereigns, "the most absolute, and legitimate lords of their kingdoms." [74] In 1818, when the court was in Rio de Janeiro, the Royal Press of Lisbon issued a Portuguese translation of a book that had already appeared in six editions in France. It dealt with prophetic history, the precursors of Anti-Christ, or the French Revolution as prophesied by St. John the Evangelist, together with a discourse on the coming and future reign of Anti-Christ. [75] Such tracts did not stand in the way of the liberal revolution that would break out in 1820. By that time, the effectiveness of writings of this nature had been destroyed by the undermining of baroque society.

When the forces of Napoleon invaded Portugal, the ground had already been prepared for an ideological revolution. It should not surprise us, in view of what has been said, that a deputation of Masons met General Junot at the gates of Lisbon, or that there were Portuguese who were won over to the French side. The prince regent himself, when he moved the court to Rio de Janeiro, must surely have realized that the old regime was mortally wounded. Would he be able, under the circumstances, to save the monarchy as it was then constituted?

In 1808, two months after his arrival in Rio de Janeiro, the prince

---

[72] *Letters from the Island of Teneriffe, Brazil, the Cape of Good Hope, and the East Indies* (London, 1777), pp. 36–37.

[73] *Dissertação a favor de monarquia, onde se prova pela razão, authoridade, e experiencia ser este o melhor, e mais justo de todos os governos; e que os nossos reis são os mais absolutos, e legitimos senhores de seus reinos* (Lisbon, 1799).

[74] *Ibid.*

[75] *Os precursores do Anti-Christo; historia profetica dos mais famosos impios que tem havido desde o estabelecimento da igreja até aos nossos dias; ou a revolução franceza profetizada por S. João Evangelista; Com huma dissertação sobre a vinda e futuro reinado do Anti-Christo. Traduzida da sexta edição do original Francez* (Lisbon, 1818).

regent announced to the world, in a manifesto which also declared war
on the French, that he had come to the New World to create a new
empire.[76] Earlier, during his stopover in Bahia on his way from Lisbon
to the Brazilian viceregal capital, he had by a stroke of the pen brought
to an end the colonial system of mercantilism and established in its
place the *"systema liberal."* It was hardly an unexpected step for the
last uncontested absolute monarch of Portugal, in view of the secret
arrangement with England and, in a larger sense, in view of his upbringing in a court that, despite the fuzzy reactionary tendencies of
his mother, reeked with the modernization that the marquis of Pombal
had pushed forward.

During the next few months, the regent signed one decree after another
endowing Brazil with those agencies of royal government which it did
not have. According to an editorial of 1882: "When the court arrived
in Rio in 1808, those in charge of public affairs, and of the organization of the government, simply created there all those institutions that
they saw listed in the Lisbon *Almanac,* without considering whether or
not they were convenient, or superfluous, or ruinous." [77]

In 1815, the work of renovation having been substantially finished,
the former state of Brazil was raised in honor and dignity to the rank
of a kingdom, the dynastic coequal of the mother country. As an
exuberant Father Santos explained it, "Brazil had in a few years
reached such a height of prosperity that calling it the colony, and the
dominions, and conquests of America was no longer compatible with the
character of a Portuguese people, the progeny of the Portuguese, speaking the same language and having the same habits and customs of the
Portuguese of Europe." The time had come to put an end to the
absence of any reference to Brazil, "the most extensive, richest, and most
precious portion of the Portuguese monarchy in the title of the sovereigns." [78]

Was Father Santos, in his concern for equality, perhaps thinking that
this was the only way to put a stop to the agitation that rumbled
from the proponents of the new liberalism? We know that Masonry
flourished in the larger cities, and Masonry was opposed to the old
regime. We also know, in the words of Álvares Machado, delivered
before the Brazilian Chamber of Deputies on June 3, 1839, that "Brazil
already before the coming of King João VI professed liberal ideas; the
country was covered with patriotic societies, which aimed at establishing
the rule of law upon the ruins of absolutism. King Dom João VI came
to Brazil, and the Brazilians, always generous, decided that they should

[76] Gonçalves dos Santos, *Memorias,* 1:71.
[77] *Astro da Lusitania* (Lisbon), June 3, 1822.
[78] Gonçalves dos Santos, *Memorias,* 2:10–11.

not provoke our king, who, in search of asylum, threw himself into the arms of his American subjects." [79]

In 1821, two days before his return to Lisbon, the prince regent, now the twenty-seventh king of Portugal, Brazil, and the Algarves, told his son and heir, the future Dom Pedro I of an independent Brazil, "Pedro, if Brazil should separate itself [from Portugal], let it be for you, who will respect me, rather than for one of those adventurers." [80] By that time, after the liberal revolution had rocked Portugal and Brazil, Dom João must have felt that the independence of Brazil would soon be achieved. It is clear, from what he told Dom Pedro, that he was prepared to salvage what he could of the Portuguese monarchy through the establishment of another Braganza throne in the New World, separate yet tied to the mother country by family apron strings.

At the beginning of his Brazilian reign, Dom João could hardly have entertained the possibility of independence. He was most certainly aware of the stresses and strains of the Atlantic monarchy, which the Enlightenment and Napoleon Bonaparte had brought to the bursting point. He himself had left Portugal to avoid a confrontation with Junot's army and with Spain, and to keep Brazil from falling into the hands of the English. It could scarcely have occurred to him, as his ship sailed down the Tagus and out into the Atlantic, that the kingdom of Portugal would remain lost forever to the crown, or that the force of circumstance would oblige him to make Rio de Janeiro the permanent seat of his multicontinental nation. His declaration of war against France was assuredly not a last desperate measure, designed merely to cover up his real fears. And the record of his achievements in Brazil was not the record of a man who allowed himself to be carried by the current, pulled "by a blind fate over abysses" where nations, in the words of Mont'Alverne, "lose their grandeur and their glory." [81]

When he was able to overcome the threat to the monarchy as it was then constituted, posed by the Gomes Freire de Andrade liberal and Masonic conspiracy of 1817 and by its Brazilian counterpart, the Pernambuco uprising of the same year, Dom João may still not have realized that the end of political absolutism was near. (Could he have had a premonition that it was only the absolutism of the crown that held Brazil to Portugal, that the success of the liberal revolution would mean

[79] *Annaes da camara,* June 3, 1839.

[80] Augusto de Lima Júnior, ed., *Cartas de D. Pedro I a D. João VI relativas á independencia do Brasil* (Rio de Janeiro, 1941), pp. 65–66.

[81] Sermon delivered by Frei Francisco de Mont'Alverne, O.F.M., on March 25, 1831, in the Church of St. Francis de Paul, Rio de Janeiro, quoted in Fausto Barreto and Carlos de Laet, eds., *Anthologia nacional ou collecção de excerptos dos principaes escriptores da lingua Portuguesa do 20° ao 16° século,* 15th ed. (Rio de Janeiro, 1930), p. 227.

not only the death of the established order but also the independence
of Brazil?) The liberal revolution of 1820 in Portugal, following and
drawing strength from the Spanish revolution that broke out in Cádiz,
was a horse of another size and color, a massive revolt against the old
regime that shook Portugal to its foundations, with effects that elec-
trified Brazil and set it on the same course of action. With the revolution
of 1820, everything dramatically and suddenly changed.

The developments of that fearful year, and those that made themselves
felt in Brazil in 1821, were engineered on both sides of the Atlantic by a
vocal but influential minority, people influenced by revolutionary propaganda of the kind that Dom José Joaquim da Cunha de Azeredo
Coutinho, the last grand inquisitor of Portugal, had asked his fellow
Brazilians to guard against.[82] Over the sea routes that linked Lisbon to
northern Europe, and Brazil to Portugal, the propaganda of the Masons,
of the reforming clergy, of the Francophiles, of the intellectuals informed by the natural philosophy of the new school system, and of those
who, with no solutions of their own to the problems that faced them,
looked abroad for guidance and deliverance had a devastating effect
upon the larger Portuguese society.

Caio Prado Júnior's statement that the colonial period by the beginning
of the nineteenth century had reached a dead end is nonsense.[83]
Portugal and Brazil did not then become suddenly quiet and uncreative,
nor did marvelous progress take place, in the way that Prado insinuates,
after the unity of the Atlantic monarchy was severed. On the contrary,
the process of modernization was so massively encouraged at the highest
levels of church and state that what remained untouched of the old regime
by 1820 was in substance the absolutism of the crown. The liberals won
out, during those stirring months of 1820 and 1821, because the old
regime had already been weakened from within, had already been con-
sciously transformed by zealots who worked under the cover of modernization. The process would, in a sense, be repeated in 1889, when the
Brazilian Braganzas were overthrown. The pillars of monarchy, in 1821
as in 1889, had all been torn down or weakened. Without support, the
absolutist or liberal monarchy, as the case might be, like a house of
cards, came tumbling down.

There had never been a revolution like this one before. Neither the

---

[82] Manoel Cardozo, "Azeredo Coutinho and the Intellectual Ferment of His Times,"
in Henry H. Keith and S. F. Edwards, eds., *Conflict & Continuity in Brazilian Society*
(Columbia, S.C., 1969), p. 96.

[83] Caio Prado Júnior, *The Colonial Background of Modern Brazil* (Berkeley, Calif.,
1967), pp. 2–3. I agreed with Caio Prado before I began to study the old regime more
deeply. See my "The Modernization of Brazil, 1500–1808: An Interpretative Essay,"
in Eric N. Baklanoff, ed., *The Shaping of Modern Brazil* (Baton Rouge, La., 1969),
pp. 17–18.

revolution of 1383, which destroyed the old nobility and ushered in the trading bourgeoisie, nor the revolution of 1640, which restored the independence of the nation, were truly ideological.[84] Following his victory at Aljubarrota, Dom João I had wanted to be an idoneous monarch, free from Castilian imperialism. Dom João IV with the outbreak of the Restoration had symbolized the feelings of the Portuguese people, determined as they were, after a subjection of sixty years, to rid themselves of Castilian control.

The developments of 1820, long after Napoleon and the French Revolution had been put to rest, were of a different order. What had caused the Portuguese crisis when Europe was already consolidating the law and order of Prince Metternich? Why was the mother country to be an exception to the uniformity of Europe? Dom João may have believed that the answer was to be found in the last years of his absolutist reign, but how could it have been more than a rhetorical answer when the realities of the moment of his return were such that the independence of Brazil was in his mind? Could he, at that final moment of high drama and political tragedy, have suddenly realized that everything that over the centuries had held the Portuguese together, that sent them around Africa to conquer India, that caused them to swarm over the Dark Continent, that made them cross the Atlantic to found the "new Lusitanian empire," that gave them the strength to keep the Castilians away from their doors—could he now have realized that what had created the greatness of his country in the past would no longer be able to sustain it in the present? No longer sustain it because those ancient qualities had disappeared, or been made to disappear?

Upon his return to Portugal, Dom João VI heard blunt words from his faraway son: "Portugal is today a fourth-class state and needful, therefore dependent; Brazil is of the first class and independent." [85] Was the answer perchance better understood, at least in part, by the president of the province of Piauí, as expressed on July 11, 1846, in his report at the opening session of the provincial legislature? "Formerly, even in this province, beautiful churches were built: today the maintenance of those that remain is so difficult, and the construction of new ones seems impossible. What are the reasons for this difference? Is it the lack of means? No, gentlemen: public and personal wealth has not decreased; rather it has grown. But the olden times were rich in faith, and in piety, our [times] in selfishness and sordid self-interest." [86]

---

[84] See the tendentious essay by António Borges Coelho, *A revolução de 1383 tentativa de caracterização, importância histórica* (Lisbon, 1965).

[85] Augusto de Lima Júnior, *Cartas*, p. 66.

[86] *Relatorio do presidente da Provincia do Piauhy na abertura da Assemblea Legislativa Provincial no dia 11 de julho de 1846* (from a copy in the BNRJ), p. 16.

What had happened to the traditional loyalty of the Portuguese, the marvelous bond that united the throne and the nation? To the reverence for the sanctity of an oath (which the Brazilian delegates to the Lisbon Constituent Asser₄bly flagrantly flouted)? To the reverence for one's plighted word? As late as the seventeenth century, the fidelity of the Portuguese to their sovereigns was unique. "The bad king they love," Faria e Sousa wrote, "and the good ones they adore." [87] The Abbé de Pradt, the French priest-journalist who was paid by Simón Bolívar to spread the glad tidings of the redemption of Spanish America and who, like a chameleon, changed color with every changing regime, compared a colony to a ripe fruit: when it reaches its appointed time, it will fall naturally, without anybody being able to hold back the biological process.[88]

In the case of Brazil, it is impossible to carry out the analogy and say that the country was ripe for independence when it did come, symbolically, on September 7, 1822. On the eve of the separation from Portugal, when the Portuguese were nervously aware of the probability of a break, Portuguese newspapers spoke in favor of a continuing union, expressing doubts about the viability of a Brazil no longer tied to the mother country. One remarked on April 16, 1822, that Brazil "has no shipping, no commerce, no industry, no population, and only a kind of fictitious and precarious wealth, consisting of abundant products obtained by means of a relative agricultural system founded upon slavery; this [situation] thus demonstrated . . . we shall conclude that not only the independence but also the separation of Brazil would be in opposition to its interests, and bring about its ruin." [89] Another newspaper, also in 1822, upbraided Brazilians for believing the prophecies of the Abbé de Pradt, reminding them that a country without people and without agriculture could hardly aspire to the status of an independent power even in the span of a century.[90] The abbot of Medrões, who as a delegate to the Lisbon Constituent Assembly was later to vote in favor of forcing Brazil to remain in the Portuguese union, once believed that "in Brazil's present state it was physically impossible to maintain that independence. In the course of time it may perhaps be possible, [but] at this moment I do not look upon the Brazilians as being foolish enough to try such a thing." [91]

---

[87] Manuel de Faria e Sousa, *Europa portuguesa. Segunda edicion correta, ilustrada, y añadida en tantos lugares y con tales ventajas, que és labor nueva* (Lisbon, 1680), 3:408.

[88] See Manuel Aguirre Elorriaga, S.J., *El Abate de Pradt en la emancipación hispanoamericana (1800–1830)*, 2d ed. (Buenos Aires, 1946).

[89] *Jornal da Sociedade Literaria Patriotica* (Lisbon), 1st quarter, no. 1, April 16, 1822.

[90] *Astro da Lusitania* (Lisbon), no. 57, April 19, 1822.

[91] *O cidadão lusitano, breve compendio*, p. 45.

The theory of dependence in which some Portuguese put their faith was to prove just as foolhardy as De Pradt's facile political biology. One might stretch a point and say that Dom Pedro did in fact pick the fruit of independence at the appropriate time, yet it was a strange fruit, from a strange tree—not the fruit of the ancient tree that had been planted when the monarchy was founded, but a tree onto which other fruits had been grafted by the liberals. Perhaps the lesson to be learned is not that colonies obey a biological process, as the abbé said, but that they are lost to their mother countries when the society that first called them into being is rapidly and thoughtlessly changed. In the case of Portugal, the humanistic and baroque social structures of earlier times were replaced by an untried constitutional liberalism that depended for its success not only upon needed reforms but also upon a relentless and naive attack upon the old regime. By throwing out the baby with the bath water, the liberals alienated people who might have been their cowed and unsure supporters and, through political verbiage and maladroit measures, paved the way for civil war in Portugal and in Brazil, for independence.

During the full flush of the liberal victory, the abbot of Medrões held a contrary view. Liberalism, not "despotism," would keep Brazil united to Portugal. He wrote, before the awful events of September 7, 1822:

Who in his right mind will hold that Brazilians want their independence under present conditions? I do not doubt that they should have wanted it in the immediate past, because the prisoner wants to get out of jail, and the slave works to be free. But he who is out of jail and free, why will he struggle to break the irons that he sees are already broken? . . . Today, when they are free, now that they have broken the irons of their slavery, and removed so heavy a yoke from their necks, what purpose would be served by struggling for their independence? Their independence could not bring them greater advantages than those of the new constitutional system.[92]

The abbot, like so many converts of liberalism, had faith in the liberal way as a panacea for the problems of Portugal. If constitutionalism, not despotism, had been the rule at the time of the French invasion, the government would have moved to Madeira, never to Rio de Janeiro. Indeed, with a constitutional regime in power, Napoleon might not have invaded Portugal at all.

Unfortunately for the abbot's political convictions, liberalism did not save the Portuguese union. One reason for his lack of realism must surely have been his espousal of the new ideology, which gave him a distorted view of the past; he could not see that liberalism, far from being a force that bound together, was in fact a force that fragmented. Marius André, writing about Spanish America, put the blame for the success of the movement for independence among Brazil's geographical neighbors on the parliamentary system and liberalism as set up and practiced in Spain.[93] We might apply the André thesis to Brazil and say that its separation from the Atlantic monarchy was the immediate result of the liberal revolution. Yet a political break, after a union of three centuries, however sudden it may appear, has a history too. To express it another way, we might suggest that the independence of Brazil was an inevitable result of the breakup of the Portuguese baroque structures. When these were weakened or destroyed, the society that they held together and directed acquired another face, and the loyalties that kept it whole were either severed or shaken. Brazil's separation from the Atlantic monarchy took advantage of the liberal revolution, and the new nation was informed by the new ideology, but independence would not have been achieved so readily if the old regime had been vital and strong, if it had not been torn apart by the modernization of Portugal.

[93] *La fin de l'empire espagnol d'Amérique* (Paris, 1922), esp. ch. 2. See in this connection Federico Suárez, "El problema de la independencia de América," *Estudios americanos. Revista de la Escuela de Estudios Hispano Americanos* (Seville), 1 (1949): 229–44.

E. BRADFORD BURNS

The Intellectuals as Agents of Change and the Independence of Brazil, 1724–1822

This paper will consider some of the roles played by the intellectuals in the development of Brazil at the end of the colonial era. The period embraces those years between the establishment of the Brazilian Academy of the Forgotten (Academia dos Esquecidos) in 1724 in Salvador and the declaration of Brazilian independence in 1822. To appreciate fully the activities of the intellectuals, it is necessary to look briefly first at the urban growth of Brazil after 1695 and second at the construction of a secular intellectual infrastructure, beginning in 1724. Within the cities, and facilitated by the secular intellectual infrastructure, the intellectuals contributed significantly to accelerating change in the colony and eventually to the declaration of Brazil's independence.

The discovery of gold in 1695 in the interior of Brazil, with subsequent increased commercial activity and bureaucratization, initiated a long period of change in Portuguese America. Slowly the colony broke with some traditions which were forged in the sixteenth century and were strengthened throughout the seventeenth century by a rural patriarchal society based primarily on sugar production and cattle raising.

During the eighteenth century, Brazil became territorially formed, a fact recognized by the Treaty of Madrid in 1750. The Brazilians as a people—a racial composite of Europeans, Amerindians, and Africans—already existed. Indeed, certain basic types—the *gaúcho, vaqueiro, tropeiro, bandeirante, senhor do engenho*—were evident. Before mid-century, land and water routes linked together, however imperfectly, the vast reaches of the sprawling and underpopulated colony. Politically, the colony consolidated: the states of the Maranhão and Brazil merged and the remaining hereditary captaincies disappeared. After 1720, the Portuguese king's representative in the New World bore the title of "viceroy," and viceroys were, as a general rule, more effective executives than their predecessors.

Visions of reaping a golden harvest enticed tens of thousands of immigrants to Brazil. The population of European origin jumped ten-fold in the eighteenth century. Internal migration shifted the population focus from the northeast to the southeast, where the newly arrived immigrants also congregated. The population of gold-producing Minas Gerais grew from thirty thousand in 1709 to approximately six hundred thousand by 1820, to make it the most populous of the captaincies.[1] The new economic activity also raised the demand for African slaves, a demand which did not go unheeded by the slave traders. One authority asserts that the increase in the slave population in the eighteenth century was twelvefold.[2]

To fiscalize closely the mining, minting, and transportation of gold, and later the diamond mining, the crown dispatched larger numbers of civil servants, military officers, and soldiers to Brazil. Intensifying royal absolutism as the century progressed required still more bureaucrats. Commerce became increasingly complex, more merchants, middlemen, and agents appeared, and for the first time a vigorous mercantile class developed.[3] All these groups lived in urban areas. If Brazil had been overwhelmingly rural prior to the eighteenth century, it became urban thereafter, a demographic characteristic particularly applicable to the southeast. The crown chartered 3 cities and 118 towns, as contrasted with 4 cities and 37 towns in the previous century.[4] Some of the Brazilian cities boasted impressive populations.[5] By the opening of the nineteenth century, both Rio de Janeiro and Salvador were reputed to have populations in the vicinity of 100,000, making them far larger than New York City, Philadelphia, or Boston in that period.[6] They surpassed

[1] C. R. Boxer, *The Golden Age of Brazil, 1695–1750. Growing Pains of a Colonial Society* (Berkeley, Calif., 1962), p. 49; José Ferreira Carrato, *Igreja, iluminismo e escolas mineiras coloniais*, Brasiliana 334 (São Paulo, 1968), p. 246. It is estimated that Brazil had a population between 2,188,596 and 2,387,559 in 1798 (p. 195), growing at an annual rate of 1.18 percent (p. 194); Minas Gerais was the most populous captaincy (p. 191) (Dauril Alden, "Population of Brazil in the Late Eighteenth Century: A Preliminary Survey," *HAHR* 43 [1963]:173–205).

[2] Rollie E. Poppino, *Brazil. The Land and the People* (New York, 1968), p. 170.

[3] These administrative and social developments are described in Dauril Alden, *Royal Government in Colonial Brazil with Special Reference to the Administration of the Marquis of Lavradio, 1769–1779* (Berkeley, Calif., 1968), pp. 296–97ff.; Gilberto Freyre, *The Mansions and the Shanties. The Making of Modern Brazil* (New York, 1963), p. 15; and A. J. R. Russell-Wood, *Fidalgos and Philanthropists. The Santa Casa da Misericórdia of Bahia, 1550–1755* (Berkeley, Calif., 1968), pp. 354ff.

[4] Richard M. Morse, "Recent Research on Latin American Urbanization: A Selective Survey with Commentary," *Latin American Research Review* 1 (1965):40.

[5] For a florid description of the Minas Gerais urban elite in the eighteenth century, see Elysio de Carvalho, *Esplendor e decadência da sociedade brazileira* (Rio de Janeiro, 1911), pp. 103–38. Further information on the eighteenth-century urban environment of Minas Gerais can be found in Carrato, *Igreja, iluminismo*, pp. 13–21ff.

[6] The population figures are at best educated guesses, and they vary widely. Thomas Lindley, who knew Salvador well, in 1803 estimated the city's population "at upwards of a hundred thousand" (*Narrative of a Voyage to Brazil* [London, 1805], pp. 252–53);

Oporto in size and ranked, after Lisbon with its 180,000 inhabitants in 1800, as respectively, the second and third largest cities of the empire.[7]

The invigorated urban areas challenged the once dominant countryside. In fact, the struggles between planters and merchants, so well illustrated in the bitter War of the Peddlers in Pernambuco (1710–11), troubled the colony throughout the century. The cities triumphed.

By contrast with the static countryside, fluidity characterized urban society, where merchants came into prominence.[8] They governed Recife after their victory over the planters of Olinda. In 1740, Dom João V ordered that in Salvador the names of prominent businessmen be included in the electoral rolls for the posts of aldermen, thus confirming that the merchant class was well established and qualified to hold public office.[9] There were even instances when the lower classes challenged the *homens bons* for power.[10] Service as a militia officer offered another opportunity for the Brazilian male to ascend socially.[11] In Minas Gerais, where acquisition of land, discovery of gold, or trade served as the means of improving one's status, the frontier society witnessed an unusual degree of social mobility. Social distinction, intellectual achievement, and economic affluence characterized the new *mineiro* bourgeoisie, a predominately urban-oriented group.[12] As the evidence is slowly gathered, it seems to indicate that members of the petite bourgeoisie could transcend social barriers and join the more privileged classes.[13]

The increased number of merchants, professionals, and bureaucrats concentrated in a few strategic cities receptive to change gave the initial impetus to modernization. In Brazil, as in many other areas of the world, the complex process of modernization began through greater commercialization and bureaucratization, rather than through industrialization. Modernization took various forms. To improve bureaucratic efficiency,

Fernando de Azevedo estimated the population of Rio de Janeiro in 1800 as one hundred thousand (*Brazilian Culture. An Introduction to the Study of Culture in Brazil* [New York, 1950], p. 78). For smaller estimates see Richard M. Morse, ed., *The Urban Development of Latin America, 1750–1920* (Stanford, Calif., 1971), p. 37.

[7] A. H. de Oliveira Marques, *History of Portugal*, vol. 1: *From Lusitania to Empire* (New York, 1972), p. 380.

[8] Russell-Wood, *Fidalgos and Philanthropists*, pp. 354–55. On the other hand, the traditional and conservative nature of the countryside is emphasized by José Fernando Carneiro, "Fazendeiros na história do Brasil," *Província de São Pedro. Revista de difusão cultural* 21 (1957):35–52.

[9] Russell-Wood, *Fidalgos and Philanthropists*, p. 64.

[10] Affonso Ruy, *Contribuição ao estudo das manifestações corporativas na Bahia do século XVIII*, Publicação do Centro de Estudos Bahianos 41 (Salvador, 1960).

[11] A. J. R. Russell-Wood, "Mobilidade social na Bahia colonial," *Revista brasileira de estudos políticos* 27 (July, 1969): 187.

[12] Carrato, *Igreja, iluminismo*, pp. 183–84.

[13] Carlos Guilherme Mota perceptively discussed the changing social structure of eighteenth-century Brazil in *Atitudes de inovação no Brasil, 1789–1801* (Lisbon, n.d. [1970?]), pp. 32–34.

the marquis of Pombal reformed bookkeeping methods in 1764 in imitation of the system "presently followed by nearly all the genteel nations [nações polidas] of Europe." [14] The physicians of Bahia introduced Jenner's method of vaccination into Brazil in 1804.[15] The botanists adopted the classification methods of Linnaeus.[16] The merchants agitated for better roads and bridges as well as less governmental control.[17] These real or suggested changes help to indicate the new spirit apparent in Brazil in the last half of the eighteenth century and the first decade of the nineteenth. Brazil, after all, simply echoed those momentous changes which were shaking and altering the Western world at that time.

· The trends toward bureaucratization, urbanization, and modernization coupled with a desire to expand commerce intensified during the Joanine period.[18] A respected and influential professor of the period, José da Silva Lisboa, hailed the arrival of the Braganzas in Brazil as the beginning of a new era.[19] He was correct. The thirteen years 1808–21, in which the Braganzas resided in Brazil and ruled their global empire from Rio de Janeiro, constitute the most intensive period of change in Brazil's history.

Prince-Regent Dom João, after 1816 King João VI, opened the ports to world trade in 1808, ending the colony's economic and cultural isolation. Trade increased immediately, particularly with Great Britain. The crown rescinded all prohibitions on manufacturing and a tentative attempt at industrialization began. The steam engine appeared for the first time. In 1815, Bahia boasted its first steam-driven sugarmill; two years later Pernambuco also possessed one. In Bahia de Todos os Santos, the first steamboat plied Brazilian waters in 1819. Rio de Janeiro grew in size and prosperity.[20] Salvador, too, was "taking on a new aspect." [21] Returning to Recife in late 1811 after an absence of only fourteen months, the traveler Henry Koster marveled, "I perceived

[14] Quoted in Alden, Royal Government in Colonial Brazil, p. 287.

[15] Luiz Monteiro da Costa, "A introdução da vacina jeneriana na Bahia," Anais do Arquivo do Estado da Bahia 39 (1970):145–48.

[16] Carrato, Igreja, iluminismo, p. 203.

[17] João Rodrigues de Brito, Cartas económico-políticas sobre a agricultura e commércio da Bahia (Salvador, 1924), pp. 27–28, 49, 78, 84–85.

[18] Azevedo, Brazilian Culture, p. 82. One recent study affirms: "In the space of thirteen years, from 1808 to 1820, the measures and acts put into effect by Dom João cause one to recall one of our modern plans of integrated action." The author then lists some of the more outstanding accomplishments of the Joanine period (José Bonifacio de Souza, Associação Comercial do Ceará, memória história, 1868–1968 [Fortaleza, n.d. (1969?)], pp. 9–12). The Joanine period is well described in Manoel de Oliveira Lima's Dom João VI no Brasil, 2 vols. (Rio de Janeiro, 1909).

[19] José da Silva Lisboa, Memória dos benefícios políticos do governo de El-Rei Nosso Senhor D. João VI (Rio de Janeiro, 1818), p. 66.

[20] Descriptions of the changing Rio de Janeiro are many. An excellent example of them is Johan A. Kantzow, "Correspondência diplomática do ministro da Suécia no Rio de Janeiro, 1806–1811," RIHGB 276 (1967):179–222.

[21] Idade d'ouro (Salvador), no. 35, September 10, 1811.

a considerable difference in the appearance of Recife and of its inhabitants, although I had been absent from the place for so short a period." The city visibly grew and some of its twenty-five thousand inhabitants shed their traditional habits to experiment with innovation. Koster attributed some of the changes to the influence of the Europeans who had recently settled in the Pernambucan capital and then concluded, "The time of advancement was come, and men, who had for many years gone on without making any change either in the interior or exterior of their houses, were now painting and glazing on the outside, and new furnishing within; modernizing themselves, their families, and their dwellings." [22]

Brazil witnessed a surge of bureaucratization. The crown brought with it a huge and complex court. [23] Governmental offices with which the Brazilians were acquainted by name and reputation but which they had never dreamed of seeing in operation in their midst were set up in Rio de Janeiro. Perhaps as many as twenty thousand people eventually followed the court from Lisbon to Rio de Janeiro. How many of those were bureaucrats is unknown, but it would not be unreasonable to guess that they constituted a sizeable proportion. Portuguese officials surrounded Dom João. No Brazilian served as minister, nor was any chosen to sit on the Council of State, although they held posts on the secondary level and below. The metropolitans monopolized the government while the colonials financed it.

The court fomented cultural changes as monumental as the economic and bureaucratic developments. An increasing number of foreigners entered Brazil. Between 1808 and 1820 more than 300 Frenchmen lived in Rio de Janeiro alone. An impressive number of English merchants resided there too. Officials registered 601 foreigners living in Maranhão, Pernambuco, Minas Gerais, São Paulo, and Rio Grande do Sul in the period between 1777 and 1819. [24] Many of them brought new ideas, insights, and methods which contributed to the renovation of Brazil.

Foreigners who knew Brazil during the first decade of the monarch's

[22] Henry Koster, *Travels in Brazil*, edited with an introduction by C. Harvey Gardiner (Carbondale, Ill., 1966), pp. 88–89.

[23] See also Alan K. Manchester, "The Transfer of the Portuguese Court to Rio de Janeiro," in Henry H. Keith and S. F. Edwards, eds., *Conflict and Continuity in Brazilian Society* (Columbia, S.C., 1969), p. 156.

[24] Arquivo Nacional, *Os franceses residentes no Rio de Janeiro, 1808–1820* (Rio de Janeiro, 1969); Anyda Marchant, *Viscount Mauá and the Empire of Brazil. A Biography of Irineu Evangelista de Sousa 1813–1889* (Berkeley, Calif., 1965), p. 23; B. W. Clapp, *John Owens, Manchester Merchant* (Manchester, 1965), the biography of an English merchant who began to trade with Brazil in 1812; Herbert Heaton, "A Merchant Adventurer in Brazil, 1808–1818," *Journal of Economic History* 6 (1946):1–23 (the "merchant adventurer" is John Luccock); Arquivo Nacional, *Registro de estrangeiros nas capitanias, 1777–1819* (Rio de Janeiro, 1963).

residence there, such as Henry Koster, John Luccock, J. B. von Spix, K. F. P. von Martius, and Johan A. Kantzow, commented on the salutary effect that the presence of the crown exercized.[25] Typifying the elation of the Brazilians, Ignácio José de Macedo rhapsodized:

In its colonial status, from which it has just emerged, Brazil was known only because of the products of an abundant nature; and now with its new status within the empire, it begins to be admired for its political products which foretell its future elevation and long life. The unexpected transference of the monarchy brought a brilliant dawn to these dark horizons, as spectacular as that on the day of its discovery. The new day of regeneration, an omen of brighter destinies, will bring long centuries of prosperity and glory.[26]

The *Idade d'ouro*, Salvador's first and Brazil's second newspaper, thanked and congratulated Dom João for initiating needed change in Brazil.[27]

The cities along the coast and in the interior of Minas Gerais seethed with intellectual activity. The growing urban centers brought together ever larger numbers of people, exposing them to wider varieties of experiences, life styles, and opinions. Such a milieu encouraged the introduction, discussion, and circulation of ideas.[28]

During the decades in which he dominated the Portuguese government, the marquis of Pombal helped to prepare the Brazilians for the acceptance of new ideas by expelling the Jesuits in 1759 and reforming some of the empire's educational institutions, most notably Coimbra University in 1772.[29] For more than two centuries, the Jesuits had dominated intellectual life and education in Brazil (and, for that matter, throughout the empire) and imposed scholasticism and classical texts on their students.[30] In the mid-eighteenth century, they stood accused

[25] Koster, *Travels in Brazil;* John Luccock, *Notes on Rio de Janeiro and the Southern Parts of Brazil Taken During a Residence of Ten Years in That Country from 1808 to 1818* (London, 1820); J. B. von Spix and K. F. P. von Martius, *Travels in Brazil in the Years 1817–1820,* 2 vols. (London, 1824); Kantzow, "Correspondência diplomática."

[26] *Oração gratulatória ao príncipe regente* (Salvador, 1811), p. 1.

[27] *Idade d'ouro,* no. 43, May 29, 1812.

[28] Nelson Omegna, *A cidade colonial* (Rio de Janeiro, 1961), pp. 98–99 et passim. Carlos Guilherme Mota dwells on the increasing complexity of Brazilian society at the opening of the nineteenth century in his perceptive and highly informative *Nordeste 1817. Estruturas e argumentos* (São Paulo, 1972), pp. 69–71.

[29] For the intellectual history of eighteenth-century Portugal there are at least three excellent studies: Hernâni Cidade, *Lições de cultura e literatura portuguesas,* vol. 2: *Da reacção contra o formalismo seiscentista ao advento do romantismo* (Coimbra, 1968); José Augusto França, *Lisboa pombalina e o iluminismo* (Lisbon, 1965); and António Alberto de Andrade, *Vernei e a cultura do seu tempo* (Coimbra, 1966).

[30] An English missionary who visited Rio de Janeiro in 1718 noted with some disgust that Jesuit discussions there were phrased in "a scholastic manner" (*Propagation of the Gospel in the East: Being a Collection of Letters from the Protestant Missionaries and Other Worthy Persons in the East Indies* [London, 1718], pt. 2, p. 6).

of—among other things—retarding intellectual development. With their influence removed, a major cause for the consequent decline of the intellectual influence of the Roman Catholic Church in the Portuguese empire, Pombal hoped to modernize education following the recommendations of Luís António Vernei and António Nunes Ribeiro Sanches, among others.[31] He implemented many of their suggestions in his reforms at Coimbra. Thereafter some of the philosophy associated with the Enlightenment radiated outward from the ancient university to distant parts of the far-flung Portuguese empire.[32] The university trained many of the Brazilians who participated in and contributed to the Enlightenment in Brazil, to the accelerating change, and eventually to independence.[33]

Meanwhile, in the Brazilian cities, the Luso-Brazilians were constructing a new secular intellectual infrastructure, which renovated intellectual life by facilitating the introduction and discussion of ideas. That infrastructure consisted of such formally organized institutions as academies, schools, and public libraries and of less formal but equally significant ones such as private libraries, bookdealers, and literary gatherings. The formal and informal institutions interconnected frequently, buttressing and strengthening each other. The same intellectuals participated in all of them.

The foundation stone of the intellectual infrastructure rested on the various academies which sprang up and flourished briefly in Salvador and Rio de Janeiro throughout the eighteenth century. Six of them can be identified: Academia Brasílica dos Esquecidos (Salvador, 1724–25), Academia dos Felizes (Rio de Janeiro, 1736–40), Academia dos Selectos (Rio de Janeiro, 1751–52), Academia Brasílica dos Renascidos (Salvador, 1759–60), Academia Scientífica (Rio de Janeiro, 1772–79), and Sociedade Literária (Rio de Janeiro, 1786–90, 1794).[34] The academies provided the

---

[31] Lúis António Vernei, *Verdadeiro método de estudar* (Lisbon, 1746); António Nunes Ribeiro Sanches, *Cartas sobre a educação da mocidade* (Paris, 1760).

[32] Manoel Cardozo, "Azeredo Coutinho and the Intellectual Ferment of His Times," in Keith and Edwards, *Conflict and Continuity in Brazilian Society*, p. 79.

[33] From the time of the reform in 1772 to 1820, 755 Brazilians studied at Coimbra (Ministério da Educação, *Estudantes brasileiros na Universidade de Coimbra, 1772–1872* [Rio de Janeiro, 1943]). Approximately 1,750 Brazilians studied at Coimbra in the eighteenth century (Francisco Morais, *Estudantes da Universidade de Coimbra nacidos no Brasil* [Coimbra, 1949]; Divaldo Gaspar de Freitas, *Paulistas na Universidade de Coimbra* [Coimbra, 1958]). Sylvio de Mello Cahú pointed out that the educated class posed the most dangerous threat to established order in Brazil in the eighteenth and early nineteenth centuries (*A revolução nativista Pernambucana em 1817*, Biblioteca do Exército 165 [Rio de Janeiro, 1951], p. 6).

[34] There is some published material on the academies, but superficiality characterizes it. A general conclusion easily deduced after reading the material is that original research has been kept to a minimum and that what has been done has not been di-

perfect forum to ventilate the thoughts wafted westward from Europe. With a baroque flourish, the academicians introduced and discussed a wide variety of ideas in their sessions. Devoting much of their time to environmental and botanical studies, they put considerable emphasis on improving agriculture and exploiting the natural wealth of Brazil, thereby demonstrating their endorsement of the physiocrat doctrines gaining popularity in Portugal.[35] In general, the Brazilian academies, like their counterparts throughout the Western world during the eighteenth century, sought and examined that practical knowledge which promoted man's fuller utilization of, and adaptation to, his surroundings. In doing so, they understood as had never before been understood the potential wealth of Brazil; and in their fulsome praise of that potential, many of the savants contributed significantly to a spirit of

gested. See J. Lúcio de Azevedo, "A Academia dos Renascidos da Bahia e seu fundador," *Revista de língua portuguesa* 14 (1921):17–29; Moreira de Azevedo, "Sociedades fundadas no Brasil desde os tempos coloniaes até o começo do actual reinado," *RIHGB* 48 (1885):265–322; "Estatutos da Academia Brazílica dos Académicos Renascidos," *RIHGB* 45 (1882):49–67; José Vieira Fazenda, "Academia dos Felizes," *RIHGB* 149 (1943):433–37; Max Fleiuss, "As principaes associações literárias e scientíficas do Brasil (1724–1838)," in *Páginas brasileiras* (Rio de Janeiro, 1919), pp. 381–456; Barão Homen de Melo, "O Brasil intelectual em 1801," *RIHGB* 64 (1901):i-xxxi; Augusto da Silva Carvalho, *As academias científicas do Brasil no século XVIII* (Lisbon, 1939); J. C. Fernandes Pinheiro, "A Academia Brasílica dos Esquecidos. Estudo histórico e literário," *RIHGB* 31 (1868):5–32, and "A Academia Brasílica dos Renacidos, estudo histórico e literário," *RIHGB* 32 (1869):53–70—both essays are reprinted in his *Estudos históricos* (Rio de Janeiro, 1876), 2:235–300; Visconde de São Leopoldo, "O Instituto Histórico e Geográfico Brasileiro he o representante das ideas de illustração que em differentes épocas se manifestarão em o nosso continente," *RIHGB* 1 (1839):66–86; Lycurgo Santos Filho, "Sociedades literárias do século XVIII," *RIHGB* 267 (1965):43–60; José Joaquim Norberto de Souza e Silva, "Litteratura brasileira; as academias litterárias scientíficas no século décimo octavo. A Academia dos Selectos," *Revista popular* (Rio de Janeiro) 15 (1862):363–76; Alexandre Passos, "Academias e sociedades literárias nos séculos XVIII e XIX. Sua influencia na vida cultural bahiana," *Anais do primeiro congresso de história de Bahia* (Salvador) 5 (1951):7–51; Joaquim Jozé de Atahide, "Discurso em que se mostra o fim para que foi estabelecido a Sociedade Literária do Rio de Janeiro . . . ," *RIHGB* 45 (1882):69–76; Mário Ferreira França, "A Arcádia Ultramarina," *Anais do Museu Histórico Nacional* 22 (1971):63–86. There is only one book on the subject, Alberto Lamego de Campos' brief *A Academia dos Renacidos, sua fundação e trabalhos inéditos* (Paris, 1923). Fidelino de Figueiredo treats the academies at some length in his *Estudos de história americana* (São Paulo, 1927), and most literary historians discuss them, some in considerably more detail than others. Alexander Marchant discusses them briefly in English in his "Aspects of the Enlightenment in Brazil," in Arthur P. Whitaker, ed., *Latin America and the Enlightenment*, 2d ed. (Ithaca, N.Y., 1961), pp. 95–118.

[35] Moses Amzalak, "Les Doctrines physiocratiques au XVIIIe et au début du XIX siècles au Portugal," in René Gonnard, ed., *Mélanges économiques* (Paris, 1946), p. 1 et passim; António Alberto de Andrade, "O Cartesianismo em Portugal nos séculos XVII e XVIII," *Proceedings of the International Colloquium on Luso-Brazilian Studies, Washington, October 15–20, 1950* (Nashville, Tenn., 1953), p. 272; Thales de Azevedo points out the acceptance of physiocrat doctrine in Bahia in his *As ciências sociais na Bahia, notas para sua história* (Salvador, 1964), p. 35.

nativism which cities nourished. Indeed, in the speeches made and poems recited in the academies, it is possible to trace the development of a new Brazilian mentality, a profound psychological change from a feeling of inferiority to Europeans to one of equality or even superiority.[36]

Libraries, both private and public, were mighty pillars supporting the intellectual infrastructure. Books facilitated the introduction and circulation of ideas, thus contributing fundamentally to the shaping of a new mentality. At least on two occasions, the *Idade d'ouro* emphasized to its readers the importance of books "to acquire enlightenment" and knowledge.[37] Information on the book trade remains scarce and vague. Some of the earliest data concern the bookdealer Manuel Ribeiro Santos, who imported books from Portugal and sold them in Vila Rica, Minas Gerais, between 1749 and 1753.[38] He ordered works on medicine, law, literature, history, geography, and classics. Apparently his service was fast (the imprint date on the book and its date of arrival in Minas Gerais were sometimes only one year apart) and frequent (he spoke of books arriving with every fleet). To avoid the disapproval of the censor and the Inquisition and the consequent confiscation of books by customs officials, the Brazilians imported their forbidden books in false covers.[39] It was a method the Portuguese bibliophiles had perfected, and apparently it worked.[40]

[36] An ambitious project is under way to publish the proceedings of the academies. The first five volumes, all concerned with the proceedings of the Academia Brasílica dos Esquecidos, are available. See José Aderaldo Castillo, ed.; *O movimento academista no Brasil, 1641–1820/22,* vol. 1, bks. 1–5 (São Paulo, 1969–71). For studies of changing Brazilian attitudes, see João Capistrano de Abreu, *Capítulos de história colonial (1500–1800),* 4th ed. (Rio de Janeiro, 1954), p. 248–68; José Honório Rodrigues, *The Brazilians, Their Character and Aspirations* (Austin, Tex., 1967), pp. 37–144; José Honório Rodrigues, *Teoria da história do Brasil (introdução metodológica)* (São Paulo, 1957), 1:168–69. That the Brazilian elite had a parochial rather than an imperial view is one of the main theses in Allan K. Manchester, "The Rise of the Brazilian Aristocracy," *HAHR* 2 (1931):145–68. In the *senados da câmara,* Brazilian voices favoring local interests and points of view were clearly heard throughout the colonial period; see C. R. Boxer, *Portuguese Society in the Tropics, the Municipal Councils of Goa, Macao, Bahia and Luanda, 1510–1800* (Madison, Wis., 1965), pp. 85–88. Cf. João Capistrano de Abreu, *O descobrimento do Brasil* (Rio de Janeiro, 1929), p. 135.

[37] *Idade d'ouro,* no. 92, November 17, 1812. Cf. *ibid.,* no. 91, November 13, 1812.

[38] Sílvio Gabriel Diniz, "Um Livreiro em Vila Rica no meiado do século XVIII," *Kriterion* (Belo Horizonte) 12 (1959):180–98.

[39] "Notas colhidas em conversa com Joaquim J. de Sequeira sobre a entrada clandestina, no Brasil, de obras probidas e reuniões de conspiradores no tempo do conde de Resende. . . . Rio de Janeiro, 27 Nov. 1848," BNRJ, Manuscript Section, Coleção Freire Alemão, I-28, 9, 51. There is ample evidence of customs refusing to admit certain books. As late as 1821(?), a governmental secretary, António Marquês da Costa Soares, was refused permission to import a copy of Rousseau's *Social Contract* into São Luís do Maranhão (Jerônimo de Viveiros, *História do comércio do Maranhão, 1612–1895* [São Luís, 1954], 2:339–340).

[40] The bookdealer Jorge Rey ordered books from France in the 1770s and on his

The *Almanaques* for Rio de Janeiro prepared by António Duarte
Nunes reveal that in 1792 and 1794 there was a bookdealer in the
vice-regal capital. In 1799, there were two. The American visitor H. M.
Brackenridge reported the existence of two bookstores in 1817–18, and
Robert Walsh spoke of twelve booksellers in the 1820s, all of whom
were French.[41] Salvador boasted of two bookdealers in 1812, one of
whom published a catalog of his books.[42] Nine years later the city still
supported two bookdealers.[43]

Private libraries existed in the major Brazilian cities.[44] A recent study
explores the library of Canon Luís Vieira da Silva, a participant in
the Inconfidência Mineira. His magnificent collection of nearly 800
volumes and 270 titles represented all of Europe's foremost thinkers of
the seventeenth and eighteenth centuries.[45] The implication was—and
the Portuguese government did not hesitate to draw it—that he was
influenced enough by what he read to conspire for Brazil's independence.
The remarks of foreign travelers shed additional light on the reading
preferences of the Brazilians. Thomas Lindley remembered Father
Francisco Agostinho Gomes, whose library in Salvador in 1803 was
"very complete" in English and French works. The Englishman mentioned by name Buffon, Lavoisier, and d'Alembert. Andrew Grant
spoke of private libraries in Rio de Janeiro and Salvador which contained books by "d'Alembert, Buffon, Adam Smith, Thomas Paine,
etc." In Pernambuco, L. F. de Tollenare commented on the literary
preferences before the revolution of 1817: "The French works are
the most sought after and among those all the writers . . . of the
philosophy of the eighteenth century." John Luccock mentioned a brisk

order marked with an asterisk works prohibited by the Inquisition so that they
could be shipped to him in false covers (Angela Maria do Monte Barcelos da Gama,
"Livreiros, editores e impresores em Lisboa no seculo XVIII," *Arquivo de bibliografia
portuguesa* 13 [1967]:59). See also Georges Bonnant, "Les Libraries du Portugal au
XVIIIe siècle vus a travers leurs relations d'affaires avec leurs fournisseurs de Genève,"
ibid., 6 (1960):195–200.

[41] H. M. Brackenridge, *Voyage to South America, Performed by Order of the American Government in the Years 1817 and 1818* (Baltimore, 1819), 1:154; Robert Walsh,
Notices of Brazil in 1828 and 1829 (London, 1830), 1:469–70.

[42] The Loja da Gazeta advertised its books frequently in the *Idade d'ouro*. On
March 13, 1812, the *Idade d'ouro*, no. 21, mentioned another: "The new shop of
Angelo Pinto de Souza, No. 4 on Rua direita da Misericórdia, has various books for
sale." The new shop also sold the *Correio braziliense*. The catalog was published in
various issues of *Idade d'ouro*: August 18, 25, 28, September 1, 4, 8, 11, 1812.

[43] Maria Dundas Graham, *Journal of a Voyage to Brazil and Residence There, During Part of the Years, 1821, 1822, 1823* (New York, 1969), pp. 137–38.

[44] E. Bradford Burns, "The Enlightenment in Two Colonial Brazilian Libraries,"
Journal of the History of Ideas 25 (1964):430–38; Sílvio Gabriel Diniz, "Biblioteca se-
tecentista nas Minas Gerais," *Revista do Instituto Histórico de Minas Gerais* 6 (1959):
333–34; "Sequestro feito em 1794 nos bens que forão achados do Bacharel Mariano
José Pereira da Fonseca extrahido do respectivo processo," *RIHGB* 63 (1901):14–18.

[45] Eduardo Frieiro, *O diabo na livraria do Cônego* (Belo Horizonte, 1957).

book trade in Rio de Janeiro in 1818, where "French books are in demand." In 1823, Maria Graham visited the private library of a *carioca* judge. Examining the books, she observed, "Of course the greater part is law; but there are history and general literature, chiefly French, and some English books."[46]

The first public libraries date from 1810. On June 4, the library of the Coast Guard Academy (the predecessor of the Naval Academy) was opened to "the elites of the realm [*grandes do reino*] and naval officers."[47] On October 29, Dom João opened to the public the Royal Library, a rich collection of about sixty thousand volumes, although apparently it contained few recently published works. The city of Salvador inaugurated a public library on August 6, 1811, in the former library of the Jesuit College, "with the hope of spreading enlightenment." The *Idade d'ouro* editorialized, "Knowledge of all things put within reach of the curious ought to awaken talents hitherto asleep." The library depended on contributions, both of money and books, from public-spirited citizens.[48] The local inhabitants, including the governor and foreign consuls, responded. By 1818, the library contained between five and six thousand books.[49] The library subscribed to English newspapers and received Hipólito da Costa's *Correio braziliense,* a monthly journal published in London but intended to keep Brazilian readers abreast of world events.[50]

Essential to the strength of the intellectual infrastructure was the effort made to improve the few schools in the colony after the expulsion of the Jesuits, but progress appears to have been painfully slow and spotty. Critical of scholasticism, in 1776 the Franciscans in their province of the Immaculate Conception of Rio de Janeiro updated the curriculum and put a new emphasis on geometry, natural history, and experimental physics.[51] The professor of rhetoric, Manoel Ignácio

46 Lindley, *Narrative,* pp. 66–67; Andrew Grant, *History of Brazil* (London, 1809), p. 230; L. F. de Tollenare, "Notas dominicaes tomadas durante uma viagem em Portugal e no Brasil em 1816, 1817, e 1818," trans. Alfredo Carvalho, *RIAHGP* 11 (1904):436; Luccock, *Notes on Rio de Janeiro,* p. 575; Graham, *Journal of a Voyage to Brazil,* p. 231.

47 Augusto Zacarias da Fonseca e Costa, *Esboço histórico da Academia de Marinha* (Rio de Janeiro, 1873), 225.

48 *Idade d'ouro,* no. 25, August 6, 1811; no. 60, December 6, 1811. For further information on the library see nos. 27, August 13, 1811, and 43, May 29, 1812.

49 Maria Beatriz Nizza da Silva, "A livraria pública da Bahia em 1818: Obras de história," *Revista de história* (São Paulo) 43 (1971):225–39.

50 For an indication of the significance of the *Correio braziliense* see Jane Herrick, "The Reluctant Revolutionist: A Study of the Political Ideas of Hipólito da Costa, 1774–1823," *The Americas* 7 (1950):171–81.

51 *Estatutos para os estudos da província de N. Sra. da Conceição do Rio de Janeiro, ordenados segundo as disposições dos estatutos da nova universidade* (Lisbon, 1776). Cf. Cardozo, "Azeredo Coutinho and the Intellectual Ferment of His Times," pp. 87–88.

da Silva Alvarenga, a graduate of Pombal's reformed Coimbra, came to the attention of crown officials investigating the "Conspiracy of the Intellectuals" in the viceregal capital in 1794, partly because they disapproved of some of his teaching. His library contained a copy of Gabriel Bonnet de Mably's *Direitos do cidadão* (to use the title in the court testimony), a book which seemed to particularly upset the viceregal bureaucrats. His own notes expressed ideas similar to those of the Frenchman, and what seemed even more dangerous to the officials was the fact that he had explained such ideas to at least one student. According to one judge, Professor Alvarenga was too much a Francophile for the public good.[52] At the end of the century in Salvador, in teaching philosophy the Benedictines were using, among others, texts by Antonio Genovesi, Johann Gottlieb Heineccius, and Pieter van Musschenbroeck. António Joaquim das Mercês, a sort of itinerant philosophy professor between 1818 and 1823, lectured in Bahia, Alagoas, and Paraíba, where he too used Genovesi and Heineccius, in addition to Etiene Bezout and Rousseau's *Social Contract* (the latter he used apparently only in Paraíba).[53] A Portuguese disciple of Condillac, Silvestre Pinheiro Ferreira, lectured in Rio de Janeiro in 1811 and 1812.[54] His lectures appeared in book form in 1813 under the title *Preleções filosóficas*.

Bishop José Joaquim da Cunha de Azeredo Coutinho introduced some of the Pombaline reforms of Coimbra into the seminary he established in Olinda in 1800.[55] The curriculum put a new emphasis on the sciences; the bishop persuaded a number of outstanding teachers to accompany him to Pernambuco to teach; and he shunned pedagogic methods based on Aristotelian theory in favor of innovations influenced by Cartesian doctrines.[56] The staff of the seminary seemed well aware of its own novel role. Professor Father Miguel Joaquim de Almeida e

[52] António Diniz da Cruz e Silva to count of Rezende, Rio de Janeiro, June 18, 1797, reprinted in *RIHGB* 28 (1865):159; "Devassa ordenada pelo vice-rei conde de Rezende," *ABNRJ* 61 (1941):239–523.

[53] António Joaquim das Mercês, "Do archivo do instituto. Carta escripta na Bahia, em 12 de Agosto de 1851, pelo Cônego Dr. António Joaquim das Mercês ao Padre Mestre Amaral a respeito dos primeiros professores da philosophia da Bahia, Alagoas, e Parahiba," *RIGHBahia* 58 (1932):84–87.

[54] Miguel Reale, *Filosofia em São Paulo* (São Paulo, 1962), pp. 19–20.

[55] The growing interest in Azeredo Coutinho is reflected in recent studies: see E. Bradford Burns, "The Role of Azeredo Coutinho in the Enlightenment of Brazil," *HAHR* 44 (1964):145–60; Cardozo, "Azeredo Coutinho and the Intellectual Ferment of His Times," and "Dom José Joaquim da Cunha de Azeredo Coutinho, governador interino e bispo de Pernambuco, 1798–1802," *RIHGB* 282 (1969):3–45. Sérgio Buarque de Holanda has re-edited four of the bishop's major essays on Brazil (*Obras economicas de J. J. da Cunha de Azeredo Coutinho* [São Paulo, 1966]) and has written a superb introductory essay.

[56] Manoel de Oliveira Lima, *Pernambuco e seu desenvolvimento histórico* (Leipzig, 1895), p. 216.

Castro, at the solemnities accompanying the opening of classes, delivered an impassioned address in which the evoked a new enlightened age of glorification of the sciences and arts to supplant the "dark centuries" of the past. Drawing on a wide variety of European, particularly French, authorities to substantiate his thesis, he asserted that only the sciences could "illuminate the darkness" and dispel ignorance and superstition.[57] The speaker reminded his audience that science eschewed the blind acceptance of life and encouraged man to explore the world around him. The students seemed to welcome those remarks. As one of those attending the seminary remembered, "most of the students of the Seminary of Olinda were liberals in that period around 1800. . . . They possessed a liberal spirit which they maintained thereafter."[58]

During the Joanine period, educational institutions multiplied. The crown established naval and military academies, both of which offered courses in engineering, two medical schools, and courses in economics, agriculture, and chemistry. An admirer of French civilization, Dom João invited a French cultural mission to Rio de Janeiro in 1816 to staff the new Academy of Fine Arts. Primary and secondary schools received needed attention and improvement. In 1812, the Colégio da Boa Sorte was offering a modern curriculum in Salvador, placing a new emphasis on geography, history, mathematics, French, and English. The *Idade d'ouro* reported with obvious satisfaction that scholasticism, superstition, and fanaticism had been banished in favor of practical knowledge. "Bahia has never had such a well-organized and directed school," the newspaper concluded proudly.[59]

The printing press arrived very late in Brazil, but once installed it too contributed to the dissemination and discussion of ideas. The first printing establishment, the Régia of Rio de Janeiro, was set up in 1808. The second, the press of Manuel António da Silva Serva, began to function in Salvador in 1811. Both presses published some foreign authors in translation, although the Régia did so with greater frequency than did Silva Serva. A press began operation in Recife in 1817, and both Belém and São Luís do Maranhão had presses by 1821.[60]

Finally, mention should be made of the private gatherings, salons,

[57] Miguel Joaquim de Almeida e Castro, "Orasam Académica," *RIAHGP* 35 (1937–38):180, 174.

[58] José Melquíades, *Padre Francisco de Brito Guerra, um senador do império* (Natal, Rio Grande do Norte, 1968), pp. 68–69.

[59] *Idade d'ouro*, no. 64, August 11, 1812.

[60] For a history of early Brazilian printing see Carlos Rizzini, *O livro, o jornal e a typografia no Brasil, 1500–1822* (Rio de Janeiro, 1946), pp. 309–426. Also useful is Renato Berbet de Castro, *A primeira imprensa da Bahia e suas publicações* (Salvador, 1969).

and clubs, which served as a forum for diffusing ideas and debating new concepts. During the closing decades of the eighteenth century in Minas Gerais, the *tertúlias literárias* served as effective means of gathering together the local intellectuals to discuss the current topics of the day. Strictly speaking, the famous Inconfidência Mineira was hardly more than a succession of such *tertúlias*.[61] Perhaps the *oiteiros*, which epitomized the intellectual life of Fortaleza in 1813, exemplified similar activities elsewhere. Governor Manuel Inácio de Sampaio invited the local intellectuals to his residence to participate in literary discussions and poetical contests.[62] The salons were not always the exclusive domain of the male. The diary of Maria Graham provides a unique look into the habits of upper-class women at the time of Brazilian independence. Herself well educated and extremely intelligent, she admired the wit and conversation of many of the Brazilian ladies she met in Recife, Salvador, and Rio de Janeiro. Some knew English and most spoke French. In contrast to the silent, shrouded, secluded females mentioned by most nineteenth-century travelers—who happen to have been men— the women Ms. Graham found frequented drawing and dining rooms, contributed to the conversation, and were aware of what was going on in the world.[63]

The secular intellectual infrastructure took shape slowly after the establishment of the first academy in 1724. It grew more rapidly during the last decades of the century, and the pace accelerated markedly during the first decades of the nineteenth century. The flow of new ideas into Brazil increased as the intellectual infrastructure expanded. The input of new ideas and the construction of the infrastructure buttressed each other. The more ideas that entered, the stronger the infrastructure became; and as the infrastructure strengthened, it became easier for ideas to migrate. The entire progress of intellectual change from more traditional ideas to acceptance of much of the thought associated with the Enlightenment took generations; the slowness of the process was by no means peculiar to the Luso-Brazilians but was rather a testimony to the fact that people are more creatures of habit and tradition than of innovation and change.

Obviously, in the process of intellectual change intellectuals themselves figure predominantly. It is difficult to define them precisely. We can use the term "intellectuals" in a general sense to refer to all the educated elite, the teachers, doctors, lawyers, bureaucrats, some military

---

[61] António Candido, *Formação da literatura brasileira (momentos decisivos)*, 2d ed. rev. (São Paulo, 1964), 1:239–41; Carrato, *Igreja, iluminismo*, p. 196.

[62] José Ramos Tinhorão, *A província e o naturalismo* (Rio de Janeiro, 1966), p. 34; Dolor Barreira, *História da literatura cearense* (Fortaleza, 1948), p. 69.

[63] References to her encounters with female elites are frequent; see *Journal of a Voyage to Brazil*, p. 224 and elsewhere.

officers, merchants, and priests, those who engaged in literary conversations, read European authors, exposed themselves to new ideas or methods emanating from Europe, and concerned themselves with the world around them. A tiny group, their importance lay not in their size but in their ability to articulate and in their location. They lived in the cities, near the decisionmaking process. Their skill in expressing their ideas cogently in public oratory, in the classroom, in conversation, and later in books and newspapers made them influential. Unlike their counterparts before the eighteenth century, they were increasingly less associated with the church, more secular in origin and orientation, and above all else, in their professed devotion to reason they were prone to question some of the ideas and institutions which their predecessors had not only accepted but defended.[64]

At the very core of the intellectual elite were the university graduates, or in some cases the ablest graduates of seminaries, colégios, and military schools.[65] That group began the construction of the secular intellectual infrastructure, and as it grew it recruited more diverse elements into the intellectuals' ranks. The intellectuals seem a group when they are contrasted with the rest of the population, but among themselves they held diverse opinions and manifested different life styles. They became increasingly divorced from the traditional rural patrician class; of course they were not associated with the slaves or peasants who made up the vast majority of the population. They occupied, then, a middle position between the two extremes of Brazilian society.[66]

The intellectuals of the period understood, perhaps better than

[64] I am indebted to the following essays for my definition and description of intellectuals: John Friedman, "Intellectuals in Developing Societies," Kyklos, International Review for Social Sciences 13 (1960):520; Frank Knopfelmacher, Intellectuals and Politics (Melbourne, 1968), pp. 3–4; Franklin L. Baumer, "Intellectual History and Its Problems," Journal of Modern History 21 (1949):192; and Edward Shils, "The Intellectuals in the Political Development of the New States," World Politics 12 (1960):329–68.

[65] Carrato draws a significant conclusion about the different generations of mineiros who studied at Coimbra in the eighteenth century. During the first half of the century, the Brazilian graduates tended to remain in Portugal. In the latter half of the century, most returned to Brazil eager to solve some of the colony's outstanding problems (Igreja, iluminismo, p. 181). Louis Bodin flatly states, "The intellectual is born with the universities" (Los Intelectuales [Buenos Aires, 1965], p. 21).

[66] It might be of interest to follow the parallel development of the Russian intelligentsia, who in the nineteenth century were considered to be the "raznochintsy" and occupied a social position between the gentry and the masses (Martin Malia, "What Is the Intelligentsia?" in Richard Pipes, ed., The Rusian Intelligentsia [New York, 1961], pp. 1–18). Both Brazil and Russia borrowed heavily from western Europe, and in both cases as the intellectuals became more like their European counterparts they became more distant from the masses in their own countries (Leo Weiner, An Interpretation of the Russian People [New York, 1915], p. 147). Bodin emphasizes that intellectuals frequently came from the middle class, rarely from the popular class (Los Intelectuals, pp. 40–41).

anyone else, the conditions of Brazil. They also knew, either through reading, conversation, or travel, about other areas of the world, particularly western Europe, whose progress and achievements they admired, envied, and hoped to emulate. Partial toward the "progressive" countries, they freely drew their ideas from them. The vast difference between reality (Brazil as it was) and desire (Brazil as they wished it were) frustrated them and heightened their advocacy of change.[67] Indeed, by the opening of the nineteenth century, the intellectuals allied with the commercial class—both urban groups—were the foremost partisans of innovation.[68] A convincing case can be made that those two groups were fundamental in bringing about Brazil's nominal independence in 1822.[69]

The intellectuals played a number of significant roles in the late colonial period by ushering new ideas into the country, creating a flattering image of Brazil which was the basis of nativism, and voicing in a cogent and often literary fashion some of the major complaints of the colonials. Likewise, they suggested and championed some major reforms in the imperial system; and they provided much of the leadership for the independence movement.

The intellectuals introduced new ideas into Brazil as a result of their studies and travels in Europe, their reading of books, and quite possibly their encounters and conversations with North Americans, Portuguese, and other Europeans in Brazil.[70] Greater tolerance on the

[67] Knopfelmacher dwells on the extreme frustration of the intellectuals in under-developed countries (*Intellectuals and Politics,* p. 16). An excellent study of the frustrations of Brazilian intellectuals in the early twentieth century is Carlos Steven Bakota, "The Search for Brazilian National Consciousness: A Middle Class Perspective, 1916–1922" (Ph.D. dissertation, University of California, Los Angeles, 1972).

[68] António Gramsci emphasizes the concern of urban intellectuals with change in "A formação dos intelectuais," in Romeu de Melo, ed., *Os intelectuais e a política* (Lisbon, 1964), pp. 260–62. Friedman proposed the idea that, in developing societies, the intellectuals and business leaders are really the foremost advocates of changes; see "Intellectuals in Developing Societies," p. 514 et passim, and cf. Shils, "The Intellectuals in the Political Development of the New States," pp. 329–30.

[69] In *Locubrações* (Lisbon, 1874), António Henriques Leal wrote one of the most perceptive and concise discussions of the causes of Brazilian independence that I have read in nineteenth-century Brazilian historiography. He placed an unusual—for the century—emphasis on the role of ideas (pp. 114–28). For a reaction to the usual political and economic causes for the independence movement, see Mário Ypiranga Monteiro," The Influence of Intellectuals in the Evolution of Brazil," in Edward Davis Terry, ed., *Artists and Writers in the Evolution of Latin America* (University, Ala., 1969), p. 114.

[70] The *Idade d'ouro,* for example, noted that the physician Dr. Vicente Navarro de Andrade of Rio de Janeiro had written and sent to the library in Salvador a pamphlet entitled "Plano d'organização d'huma Escola Medico-Cirurgica." It was "the result of his studies and work in foreign nations," said the newspaper, "and we have reason to hope that he will continue to instruct us" (no. 47, June 12, 1812). See also Manoel Cardozo, "The Internationalism of the Portuguese Enlightenment: The Role of the

part of royal officials facilitated travel abroad and contact with foreigners. By the end of the eighteenth century, the stern countenance of the Inquisition was relaxing.

It is significant that among the educated much emphasis was placed on the mastery of foreign languages, which provided direct access to European thought. English was known to some degree, but French was especially valued as the language in which all the modern discoveries and ideas were set forth. *Arte de língua franceza* was specifically mentioned as one of the works sold by the bookdealer in Vila Rica in the mid-eighteenth century.[71] As one of its first titles, the press in Salvador published *Principaes geraes ou verdadeiro methodo para se aprender a ler, e pronunciar com propriedade a língua francesa.*[72] The viceroy, the count of Rezende, in 1793 authorized the teaching of French to military officers in Rio de Janeiro.[73] Apparently the students at the seminary of Olinda appreciated their instruction in French. One remarked in a public oration in 1801:

It is extremely useful to study French. . . . If some reject Latin as a dead language, how practical they find the French language, which is spoken throughout the world. One would have to be blind or hopelessly behind the times to doubt its usefulness. Written in that language are all the discoveries of medicine and philosophy . . . the treasures of the sciences too. Therefore you can conclude that French is not only useful but necessary for those seeking knowledge and the glory of the Fatherland.[74]

In that same year, the seminary of São José in Rio de Janeiro began to teach French.[75] The higher schools established during the Joanine period seem to have required not only French but other languages as well. The Military Academy taught French, German, and English. Medical students had to pass French and English examination. The newspapers in Rio de Janeiro and Salvador contained numerous advertisements offering the services of French and English teachers.[76]

Estrangeirado, c. 1700–c. 1750," in A. Owen Aldridge, ed., *The Ibero-American Enlightenment* (Urbana, Ill., 1971), pp. 141–207; E. Bradford Burns, "Concerning the Transmission and Dissemination of the Enlightenment in Brazil," *ibid.,* pp. 256–81.

71 Diniz, "Um livreiro em Vila Rica," p. 196.

72 A pamphlet of twenty-two pages published in 1811. It is believed that Diogo Soares da Silva was the author; see Berbet de Castro, *A primeira imprensa da Bahia,* pp. 68–69.

73 Manoel Duarte Moreira de Azevedo, "Instrução pública nos tempos coloniais de Brasil," *RIHGB* 55 (1892):150.

74 "Oração Academica diante do Exmo Sr. D. José Joaquim Coutinho . . . por Francisco de Brito Guerra, aluno do mesmo seminário, no dia 5 de dezembro de 1801," in Melquíades, *Padre Francisco de Brito Guerra,* p. 162.

75 Delso Renault, *O Rio antigo nos anúncios de jornais* (Rio de Janeiro, 1969), p. 8.

76 These examples represent dozens of other similar ads which appeared: "A person who spent some years studying in France is available to teach the French language"

Books in French—as well as representatives of works in other languages—filled the shelves of private and public libraries.[77] The comments of foreign visitors further testified to the widespread use of French among the Brazilian elite.

This concentration on foreign languages signified that Brazilians preferred to draw from a large European reservoir of ideas. By the end of the eighteenth century, Portugal no longer served as the colony's intellectual mentor. Not surprisingly, French influence dominated. Primarily that influence was exerted through the large number of French books eagerly imported, but by the end of the century, more Brazilians were also visiting and even studying in France.[78] The arrival of the French cultural mission in 1816 consolidated the French intellectual domination. Although disturbed by its excesses, Brazilians followed the developments of the French Revolution with fascination. Indications are that information on the causes, course, and consequences of that revolution circulated widely in Brazil.[79]

(*Gazeta do Rio de Janeiro*, December 2, 1815); "Whoever wants to learn English, French, or German should seek Henrique Hull, who lives in João Homem Street (*ibid.*, May 15, 1813). Even night classes were offered: "Courses in French and English for the convenience of people employed in business during the day, from 6 to 8 at night in the *caza do Alfaiate*" (*ibid.*, November 8, 1817). Renault's *O Rio antigo* catalogs numerous such advertisements. In Salvador, one person sought work as a translator, giving French, English and Portuguese as the languages he knew (*Idade d'ouro*, no. 45, October 15, 1811); another ad requested an English teacher for one of the local schools (*ibid.*, special suppl., no. 8, June 8, 1811).

[77] About three-quarters of the books in the Salvador public library in 1817 were in French; see L. F. de Tollenare, *Notas dominicais tomadas durante uma viagem em Portugal e no Brasil em 1816, 1817, e 1818* (Salvador, 1956), p. 320.

[78] On Brazilian students at Montpellier, see Robert Reynard, "Recherches sur quelques brésiliens étudiants en médecine à Montpellier à la fin du XVIIIme siècle," *Languedoc médical* (Faculty of Medicine of Montpellier) 98 (1954):162–66; Xavier Pedrosa, "Estudantes brasileiros na Faculdade de Medicina de Montpellier no fim do século XVIII," *RIHGB* 243 (1959):35–71; Carlos da Silva Araújo, "Médicos brasileiros graduados em Montpellier e os movimentos políticos da independência nacional," *Revista do Instituto Histórico e Geográfico de Minas Gerais* 8 (1961):125–41.

[79] The conspirators in Rio de Janeiro in 1794 apparently approved the revolution. According to one judge, they had "approved and praised the French republic and had demonstrated an unusual passion for it" (Diniz da Cruz to Rezende, June 18, 1797, *RIHGB*, p. 159). Throughout the 1790s, Manuel António Leitaõ Bandeira, a crown judge and member of the Junta de Comércio in São Luís do Maranhão, spent long hours writing essays on the French Revolution and its meaning for Europe and Portugal. His correspondence is scattered through boxes 60–72 (boxes pertaining to Maranhão) in the Arquivo Histórico Ultramarino, Lisbon. Of particular interest is box 64, which contains a group of ten documents. One foreign visitor observed of the Brazilians in 1792, "They seem to enquire, with an uncommon degree of interest, into the progress of the French Revolution, as if they foresaw the possibility of a similar event among themselves" (G. Stanton, *Authentic Account of an Embassy from the King of Great Britain to the Emperor of China . . . Taken Chiefly from the Papers of His Excellency the Earl of Macartney*, 2 vols. [London, 1797], 1:181). A decade later, Thomas Lindley detected a similar fascination (*Narrative of a Voyage to Brazil*, p. 154 et passim); cf. Andrew Grant, *History of Brazil*, p. 144.

English influence also burgeoned, partially as a result of the commercial dominance Great Britain exerted over Brazil after 1808. Growing numbers of British merchants, diplomats, and visitors entered Brazil after the opening of the ports, and their presence facilitated the circulation and acceptance of Anglo-Saxon ideas.[80] The works of John Locke may have been the first of any English thinker to be introduced into Brazil, where Locke enjoyed considerable respect among intellectuals. In fact, the constitution of 1824 had its roots in the ideas of Locke.[81] The Brazilians translated and published extracts from the works of Edmund Burke in Rio de Janeiro in 1812, and the *Idade d'ouro* recommended his ideas to its readers.[82] However, Adam Smith was the most influential intellectual from the British Isles. We can get some notion of the impact of the Scottish economist when we look at the impressive number of outstanding Brazilian intellectuals, such as José Joaquim da Cunha de Azeredo Coutinho, José da Silva Lisboa, João Rodrigues de Brito, Hipólito da Costa, and José Bonifácio de Andrada e Silva, who cited, praised, and quoted from him.[83] Two editions of *The Wealth of Nations* issued from the new Brazilian presses: the Régia Press brought it out in 1811 and Silva Serva published it the following year.[84] Analyzing Smith's theses, the *Idade d'ouro* applied them favorably to Brazil.[85] On a subsequent occasion, the newspaper returned to his ideas, assuring its readers that their implementation would guarantee Brazil's prosperity.[86] Thus Britain seems to have exerted greater intellectual influence over Brazil during the waning years of its colonial status than has been ordinarily recognized.

[80] For a full discussion of the growing English influence in all aspects of Brazilian life after 1808, see "A presença inglesa," in Sérgio Buarque de Holanda, ed., *História geral da civilização brasileira*, vol. 2(1): *O processo de emancipação* (São Paulo, 1962), pp. 64–69. The *Idade d'ouro* announced on various occassions the arrival of English books and newspapers for the public library; see nos. 52, November 8, 1811, 47, June 12, 1812, and 62, August 4, 1812.

[81] One of Locke's Portuguese disciples, Martinho de Mendonça de Pina e de Proença, was sent to Brazil (circa 1730) as a tax collector. See C. R. Boxer, *The Golden Age*, p. 209; M. M. de Carvalho, "A Philosophia no Brasil," *Minerva brasiliense* 1 (1844): 226 ("The philosophy of Locke and Condillac . . . continue being propagated among us"); the preface by Afonso Arinos de Melo Franco, in Arquivo Nacional, *O constitucionalismo de D. Pedro I no Brasil e em Portugal* (Rio de Janeiro, 1972), unnumbered pp. 1–3.

[82] José de Silva Lisboa, *Extractos das obras de Burke* (Rio de Janeiro, 1812); *Idade d'ouro*, no. 91, November 13, 1812.

[83] J. F. Normano, *Brazil, a Study of Economic Types* (Chapel Hill, N.C., 1935), pp. 86–88; Moses Amzalak, *Economistas brasileiros: D. José Joaquim da Cunha Azeredo Coutinho* (Porto, 1942), p. 33.

[84] *Compêndio da obra da Riqueza das Nações de Adam Smith* (Rio de Janeiro, 1811); *Compêndio da obra de Adão Smith a Riqueza das Nações* (Salvador, 1812).

[85] No. 43, May 29, 1812.

[86] *Idade d'ouro*, no. 61, July 31, 1812.

German, Italian, and North American intellectual influences could be discerned as well. In his lectures on philosophy in Rio de Janeiro in 1811 and 1812, Silvestre Pinheiro Ferreira, who had travelled extensively in the German states, outlined the thought of Immanuel Kant, Johann Gottlieb Fichte, Friedrich Wilhelm Joseph von Schelling, and Georg Wilhelm Friedrich Hegel.[87] Beginning with Friedrich Wilhelm Sieber in 1801, an impressive number of German naturalists, explorers, geologists, geographers, and zoologists descended on Brazil. The arrival of Austrian Archduchess Leopoldina, the young bride of Dom Pedro, in Rio de Janeiro in 1817, accompanied by a retinue of distinguished intellectuals, further exposed the Brazilians to German thought. The Italian Antonio Genovesi ranked as one of the most widely read European philosophers, and apparently his books circulated among most Brazilian intellectuals.[88] The botanist Alexandre Rodrigues Ferreira was one of his most notable Brazilian disciples.[89] The appearance of works by Thomas Jefferson, Benjamin Franklin, and Thomas Paine in Brazilian libraries indicated curiosity about the United States as well as interest in the intellectual currents there.[90] Apparently Tiradentes possessed copies of laws passed in North America as well as of the Declaration of Independence.[91] Hipólito da Costa, one of the few Brazilians to visit the United States, later commented at length on his impressions.[92] Increasing trade between the United States and Brazil brought Brazilians into closer contact with North Americans and their ideas.[93]

[87] Reale, *Filosofia em São Paulo*, pp. 19–20; Miguel Reale emphasized the growing popularity of Kant in *Momentos decisivos e olvidados do pensamento brasileiro* (Porto Alegre, n.d. [1958?]), p. 19.

[88] Reale, *Momentos decisivos*, p. 20; João Cruz Costa, *A History of Ideas in Brazil* (Berkeley, Calif., 1964), pp. 40–41; several copies of Genovesi's works were found in the libraries of Cipriano José Barata de Almeida and Hermógenes Francisco de Aguilar, both implicated in the Bahian conspiracy. Kátia M. de Queirós Mattoso noted about the author, "an Italian philosopher and economist whose work enjoyed wide circulation during that period" (*Presença francesa no movimento democrático baiano de 1798* [Salvador, 1969], p. 22).

[89] Glória Marly Duarte Nunes de Carvalho Fontes, *Alexandre Rodrigues Ferreira (aspectos de sua vida e obra)* (Manaus, 1966), p. 10.

[90] The United States consul in Salvador, Henry Hill, donated books in English to the Salvador public library (the titles are not known to me) (*Idade d'ouro*, no. 31, August 27, 1811). Thomas Lindley noted in 1803 that Francisco Augustinho had "Paine's works; and seemed to lay stress on some of his null opinions" (*Narrative of a Voyage to Brazil*, p. 68). See also Burns, "The Enlightenment in Two Colonial Brazilian Libraries," pp. 434–35.

[91] David Carneiro, *Tiradentes* (Curitiba, 1946), p. 64.

[92] Mecenas Fourado, *Hipólito da Costa e o Correio brasiliense*, Biblioteca do Exercito 234 (Rio de Janeiro, 1957), 1:43–58.

[93] Between 1792 and 1805, eighty-three U.S. ships called at Brazilian ports (C. L. Chandler, "List of United States Vessels in Brazil, 1792–1805," *HAHR* 26 [1946], 599–617); North American whalers occasionally appeared in Brazilian ports (Dauril Alden,

Drawing from a wide variety of sources, the intellectuals imported those ideas which pleased them most into Brazil, where they were discussed, in some cases Brazilianized, in some cases implemented. Exposure to them prompted a more thorough questioning than ever before of concepts long held sacrosanct. Thus skepticism and inquiry challenged the more traditional and less rational aspects of a colonial system which was proving to be less and less satisfactory to the colonials.

As one result of the influx of new ideas, the Brazilians more sharply focused attention on their own land, its problems as well as its potential. Physiocrat doctrines in particular impelled them to investigate their surroundings, an activity which accelerated the growth of the nativism already manifested. Love of, devotion to, pride in Brazil constituted the cult for which the intellectuals served as high priests.

That cornerstone of the secular intellectual infrastructure the Brazilian Academy of the Forgotten established a nativistic pattern which intellectuals would follow and build on. Throughout the prolix prose and poetry of the Academy's sessions, the Luso-Brazilian literati wove abundant references to the beauty, importance, and wealth of Brazil. Nativistic pride reached a climax of sorts in the "Dissertação terceira" of Caetano de Brito e Figueiredo, which describes the bounty of Brazilian geography. In part the judge mused: "Golden Brazil is the depository of the most priceless metal, fertile producer of the sweetest sugar canes, and generous cultivator of the most useful plants. Let me say it boastfully: Brazil is the most precious jewel of the Lusitanian scepter, the most valuable stone in the Portuguese crown, which of itself possesses much majesty and beauty." [94]

The "Forgotten" elected Brazilian history as their subject of study, a theme which lent itself to expressions of nativism. The topic obviously inspired one of the academicians, Sebastião da Rocha Pita. In 1730 he published the best history of Brazil written during the colonial period. His florid *História da América portuguesa* stands out as one of the classic statements of nativistic sentiment. Rocha Pita also penned a baroque poetic gem entitled "The Shift of the Sunrise," in which he proclaimed that the sun "is born with greater brilliance in the west." [95] During the following century, Brazilian literature repeated

---

"Yankee Sperm Whalers in Brazilian Waters and the Decline of the Portuguese Whale Fishery [1773–1801]," *The Americas* 20 ([1964]:267–88).

[94] Castillo, *O Movimento academicista* 1:5, 167.

[95] Péricles Eugenio da Silva Ramos, ed., *Poesia barroca. Antologia* (São Paulo, 1967), p. 104. The role of the Brazilian intellectuals in encouraging nativism can perhaps be better understood by comparing it with that of intellectuals elsewhere in the hemisphere. For the Chilean example, see Simon Collier, *Ideas and Politics of Chilean Independence, 1808–1833* (Cambridge, 1967). Gabriel Careaga noted the important contri-

that symbolic allusion to a new sunrise in the west.

Some remarkable poets raised their voices to praise Brazil. Few were more nativistic than José Basílio da Gama and José da Santa Rita Durão. Basílio da Gama's epic poem *O Uraguai* glorified the heroic resistance of the Indians of the seven missionary villages of southern Brazil to Spanish and Portuguese incursions. It painted an alluring picture of the Brazilian landscape. In his exaltation of the noble qualities of the Indians, Basílio da Gama proved to be a precursor of the nineteenth-century romantic Indianist movement. The Indian emerged for the first time as the symbol of what was truly Brazilian. Later the nationalists seized on that convenient symbol and carried the glorification of the Indian to more exaggerated extremes. Santa Rita Durão's epic *Caramurú* traced the history of the colony from discovery to the expulsion of the last foreign invader, mixing political insights with descriptions of lush vegetation.

The theater contributed to nativism as well as to intellectual change. It may be difficult to assess its exact influence in eighteenth-century Brazil, but let us consider its important social function in a society which had no press and high illiteracy rates and in which books were expensive and secular amusements few. It exposed relatively large numbers of people to new ideas, customs, or influences. It was a convenient place to gather and converse as well as to view a spectacle. The audiences of the eighteenth century attended plays written by foreigners and translated into Portuguese. In fact, Spanish, Italian, and French plays proved more popular than those of Portuguese writers to the audiences of Salvador, which applauded the works of Molière, Voltaire, Carlo Goldoni, and Matastasio. One can speculate on the impact those plays might have had on the people in the audience. For example, António Rodrigues Machado, arrested and implicated in the Bahian conspiracy of 1798, frequented the theater constantly.[96]

The Brazilians themselves wrote and produced theatrical pieces reflecting nativist themes. One delightful example was *A Felicidade no Brasil,* presented in the Teatro Público of Belém in 1808. The author, Bento de Figueiredo Tenreiro Aranha, a singular figure, lived his entire life (1769–1811) in the Amazon region and had only a rudimentary formal education. Self-taught, he wrote poems, plays and orations. The cast of his one-act drama consisted of the Grande Génio

---

butions of the Mexican intellectuals to national independence, as well as the significant role they played in national life. He saw their mission as twofold: "One of them is to serve as a critic; the other is to describe and explain the reality which surrounds us" (*Los intelectuales y la política en México* [Mexico City, 1971], pp. 47–61).

[96] Affonso Ruy, "Aspectos teatrais da Bahia do século XVIII," *Universitas* (University of Bahia) 3–4 (1969):103–7; Sábato Magaldi mentioned a tragedy by Voltaire presented in Salvador in 1790 (*Panorama do teatro brasileiro* [São Paulo, 1962], p. 29).

Tutelar e Superior, who presided over the destinies of all Brazil, the Génio Tutelar do Cabo Frio, and a nymph of the Amazon River leading a chorus of other undines. As the curtain rises, the Grande Génio do Brasil promises a bright future for the land, indeed *"hum novo Sol."* He salutes the fabulous richness of the land, predicting, "You will see your name and commerce flourish." Throughout the short drama, essentially celebrating the arrival of the royal court in the New World, the potential wealth and promising future of Brazil are his themes.[97]

Not content just to sing Brazil's praises, the intellectuals industriously probed their surroundings—with the blessing and encouragement of Portuguese officials, whose motives, however, were quite different from theirs. They produced a remarkably varied series of monographs on Brazilian flora, fauna, geography, minerals, and agriculture.[98] Their authors, more often than not recent graduates of Coimbra, were, in the words of a student of their activities, "the first men of this country who had an objective view of the need for national development." [99] Their conclusions, as well as their pride, can be summed up in the results of a debate held in the Academia dos Felizes on the question, "Was Portuguese America the best part of this continent?" They unanimously concluded that it was. Later the *Idade d'ouro* concluded that it was superior to Europe as well![100]

Although the physiocrat urge to know Brazil, if anything, intensified in the early nineteenth century, the *Idade d'ouro* claimed that Brazilians paid far too much attention to what was going on elsewhere in the world when, according to the editor, they should be concentrating on Brazil: "It is a disgrace that there are those among us who know more about the geography of China than they do about the land they inhabit." The newspaper went on to exhort its readers: "Let us study our territory, let us explore its possibilities, let us see what it can provide us. Following this method constantly for a period of thirty years, we will see Brazil rise from poverty to become one of the richest and

[97] My source is João Baptista de Figueiredo Aranha, ed., *Obras do litterato amazonese Bento de Figueiredo Tenreiro Aranha*, 2d ed. (Lisbon, 1889).

[98] Fidelino de Figueiredo, *Estudos de história americana* (São Paulo, n.d.), pp. 109–10. Revisionist studies of the Enlightenment claim that those who opened the windows to its breezes also threw open the door to the winds of "nationalism:" "further research may show that . . . one result of the Enlightenment's transmission overseas was to sow the seeds of the rudimentary nationalism that soon cropped up in the new Spanish American states" (Arthur P. Whitaker, "Changing and Unchanging Interpretations of the Enlightenment in Spanish America," *Proceedings of the American Philosophical Society* 114 [1970]: 269).

[99] José Ferreira Carrato, "Uma primeira tomada de consciência do desenvolvimento brasileiro," *Revista de história* (São Paulo) 44 (1972):263.

[100] No. 43, May 29, 1812.

most respected nations of the universe." [101] The newspaper seemed particularly annoyed that an Englishman, Robert Southey, was the successor to Rocha Pita. It chided the Bahians for letting foreigners show "greater curosity about our affairs, what we have, and what we need than we ourselves do." [102] Obviously the appearance of the first volume of Southey's elephantine history in 1810 had wounded Brazilian pride.

One does not have to look far in the early nineteenth century for evidence of that pride. Whereas formerly the Brazilians had only compared their land to paradise, Francisco de São Carlos published a long poem, A Assunção, in 1819 in which he pictured paradise as remarkably similar to Brazil. The Brazilian deputies to the Portuguese Côrtes in 1822 voiced their nativistic pride repeatedly with a frankness which widened the gap between themselves and the Portuguese. As one deputy reminded the assembly, "There is not a Brazilian who does not boast of the great resources of his land; there is not a Brazilian who is not proud of the potential which Brazil has to be one of the first nations of the universe." [103] The resources and potential of Brazil provided the leitmotif of nativism.

Among the elite and in some vague way among large numbers of the urban masses as well, the intellectuals inspired an awareness that Brazil not only differed from Portugal and the rest of the world but that it was superior. While eroding confidence in the motherland, they created a flattering self-image which was the nucleus of national consciousness. In short, they promulgated the idea of the nation and instilled a sense of nationality in their fellow countrymen. Taking the longest possible historical view, the colonial intellectuals in the eighteenth century accelerated a movement of "Brazilianization" which reached its climax with the proclamation of the majority of Dom Pedro II in 1840.[104]

Growing pride in Brazil, coupled with a knowledge of the enlightened thinking of the eighteenth century, prompted the intellectuals to criticize those aspects of the Portuguese imperial system which they believed inimical to Brazil's wellbeing. Criticism, after all, was and is one of the principal activities of intellectuals. Of course, by later standards their criticism would seem mild: indeed, the majority of the intellectuals appear to be moderates. Hipólito da Costa repeatedly emphasized in his Correio braziliense the need for reform, not revolu-

---

[101] No. 92, November 17, 1812.

[102] No. 51, November 5, 1811.

[103] Diário das Côrtes Geraes, Extraordinárias, e Constituintes da Nação Portugueza, sess. of July 1, 1822, 6:630.

[104] Shils, "The Intellectuals in the Political Development of the New States," pp. 330, 342–43; Afonso Rui de Souza, Páginas de história do Brasil (Salvador, 1955), pp. 86–89.

tion, an observation in which succeeding generations of intellectuals concurred.[105] However, moderate as the intellectuals were in their suggestions and aspirations, they proved to be instrumental, given the climate of opinion favoring change, in discrediting some traditional ideas so that it could take place.

Scattered and oblique at first, the criticism did not become really pronounced until the closing decades of the eighteenth century. It intensified during the early years of the nineteenth century and was directed at many targets, economic, political, and social, although perhaps economic complaints have been most familiar to subsequent generations.

Early political criticism tended to be theoretical and idealistic, not directed toward specific issues. The *Paulista* Matias Aires da Silva de Eça, in his major work, *Reflexões sobre a vaidade dos homens,* published in 1752 in Lisbon, where he lived, discoursed on the equality of man. "Men are born equal. . . . The world was not made for the greater benefit of some than of others," he concluded. That novel idea found scant acceptance in a hierarchical society. Eça's sister, Teresa Margarida Silva e Otra, denounced absolutism in her own book, *Aventuros de Diófanes* (Lisbon, 1753). Praising liberty and reason, scoffing at the divine right of monarchs, she advocated a government of law to which all, the king not excluded, were obedient and responsible.[106] In his "Instrucção para o governo da Capitania de Minas Gerais," an essay on political philosophy composed in 1780, José João Teixeira Coelho, reflecting on eleven years of experience in Minas Gerais, held that a worthy government was one established for the good of the people, one of laws, not of the whims of the executive.[107] In a polite way these writers were questioning the Portuguese political system.

The *inconfidências* of Minas Gerais (1789), Rio de Janeiro (1794), Bahia (1798), and Pernambuco (1801) and the rebellion in Pernambuco (1817) expressed in dramatic form and somewhat more precise language festering political grievances.[108] Unlike the critics before them, the

---

[105] Herrick, "The Reluctant Revolutionist," p. 176. Some years later Evaristo da Veiga stated the prevalent moderate view of the intellectuals: "Let us have no excesses. We want a constitution, not a revolution" (*Aurora fluminense* [Rio de Janeiro], no. 59, June 25, 1828). Carlos Guilherme Mota emphasized the moderation of the intellectuals in "Mentalidade ilustrada na colonização portuguesa: Luís dos Santos Vilhena," *Revista de história* (São Paulo) 72 (1967):405.

[106] Matias Aires Ramos da Silva de Eça, *Reflexoēs sobre a vaidade dos homens* (Lisbon, 1752), pp. 117–18, 400; see Cardozo, "Azeredo Coutinho and the Intellectual Ferment of His Times," p. 75. For a fuller discussion of *Aventuros'* contents consult Cardozo, "The Internationalism of the Portuguese Enlightenment," pp. 197–99.

[107] *RIHGB*, 3d quarter of 1852, 15:257–58.

[108] Documentary sources for the *inconfidências* are *Autos de devassa da Inconfidência*

participants in the *inconfidências* and the rebellion were specific: they decried the Portuguese imperial system as repressive, preferred republican to monarchical institutions, and in general subscribed to the political doctrines popular at the time in France and the United States. The extent of republican sentiment has never been adequately measured, and assessments of it range broadly. During his enforced stay in Salvador da Bahia in 1802–3, Thomas Lindley observed that such sentiment was spreading. He concluded:

This partiality for the new republicans and their principles, I have long observed very general both here and in other parts of Brazil, among the younger branches of society; who have imbibed such notions so effectually, that I should not wonder at this circumstance eventually causing a total change in their political situation. They already ridicule their subjection, and seem to be conscious that they possess the most desirable country in the world, sufficient of itself to supply all the wants of man.[109]

In the long political discussions filling its pages, the *Correio braziliense* mixed general and specific criticism of the Portuguese system. Believing that government was a contract between the governor and the governed, the editor favored a written constitution to limit the powers of government. He argued that the government of Brazil did not conform to enlightened principles. Such political views motivated most of the Brazilian deputies to the Portuguese Côrtes in 1822, whose speeches expressed some of the most important attitudes of the Brazilian elite on the eve of independence. José Lino Coutinho, one of the Bahian representatives, emphasized to the Portuguese deputies the many differences between the kingdoms of Portugal and Brazil, pointing out that laws appropriate for one did not necessarily fit the other. He asked them to recognize those differences in considering legislation. On other occasions, he advocated the separation of powers, autonomy for the courts, a military responsible to the legislature instead of to the executive, and the franchise for freed slaves.[110] The debates of the Côrtes reveal the degree to which the Portuguese political system displeased the new generation of Brazilian spokesmen, who eventually participated in the breaking of ties with Portugal.

In addition to their political complaints, the intellectuals voiced frequent economic criticism, prompted in part by the economic dol-

---

Mineira, 7 vols. (Rio de Janeiro, 1936–38); "Devassa ordenada pelo vice-rei conde de Rezende," *ABNRJ* 61 (1941):239–523; "Autos de devassa do levantamento e sedição intentados na Bahia em 1798," *Anais do Arquivo Público da Bahia,* vols. 35–36 (Salvador, 1959, 1961); "Devassa de 1801 em Pernambuco," *DHBNRJ* 90 (1956).

[109] Lindley, *Narrative of a Voyage to Brazil,* p. 154.

[110] *Diário das Côrtes,* sess. of February 1, 1822, 5:68; sess. of January 11, 1822, 4:3669; sess. of April 3, 1822, 5:711; sess. of April 17, 1822, 5:839.

drums of the late eighteenth century. Bewilderment over the wide-spread poverty in Brazil in the midst of potential wealth was best expressed in the pertinent question of Luís dos Santos Vilhena, a Portuguese who lived for twelve years in Bahia: "Why is a country so fecund in natural products, so rich in essence, so vast in extent, still inhabited by such a small number of settlers, most of them poor, and many of them half-starved?" He laid the blame on slave labor, latifundia, and obsolete agricultural methods.[111] In doing so, he castigated the fundamental economic institutions of colonial Brazil. His discussions of the need for greater economic freedom and reform, of "hunger," "shortages," and "poverty" indicated the crisis into which the imperial system had plunged. An anonymous manuscript written in Bahia at the same time, but unpublished until recently, examined at length the colony's economic problems. Critical of Portuguese policies, it voiced the economic complaints of the Brazilians.[112] At the same time, Manoel António Leitão Bandeira, writing to the crown from São Luís do Maranhão, spoke out in favor of relaxing restrictions on commerce and in support of free trade.[113]

From Lisbon, the Brazilian José Joaquim da Cunha de Azeredo Coutinho commented on the imperial economy.[114] His three economic essays, all of which were published, were widely circulated and became the focus of considerable comment. They suggested some far-reaching adjustments in the Brazilian economy but did not imply that they should be instituted by means other than reform within the empire. Like most of his contemporaries, he preached neither revolution nor independence. Undoubtedly the importance of his three essays lay in the fact that for the first time a series of basic economic reforms highly desired by Brazilians had been classified and clarified. Azeredo Coutinho wanted them to be carried out within the empire, but when they were not forthcoming from Portugal, Brazilians came to realize that only by taking control of their own destiny could change come about. Hence, by indicating a path to economic reform, Azeredo

111 Luís dos Santos Vilhena, *Recopilação de notícias soteropolitanas e brasílicas*, 2d ed. (Salvador, 1922), 2:926.
112 The manuscript bore the title "Discurso preliminar, histórico, introdutivo, com natureza da descrição econômica da comarca e cidade da Bahia." Edited by Pinto de Aguiar, it was published under the title *Aspectos da economia colonial* (Salvador, 1957). Another example of the economic criticism of the eighteenth century is José Gregório de Morais Navarro, *Discurso sobre o melhoramento da economia rústica do Brazil, pela introducção do arado, reforma das fornalhas, e conservação de suas mattas, etc.* (Lisbon, 1799).
113 Letter dated October 30, 1792, Arquivo Histórico Ultramarino, Lisbon, Maranhão, box 64.
114 Burns, "The Role of Azeredo Coutinho in the Enlightenment of Brazil," pp. 147–53.

Coutinho's essays had the unexpected effect of increasing the Brazilians' desire to be economic masters in their own house.

In his first essay, *Memória sobre o preço do assúcar*, published in 1791, Azeredo Coutinho argued that any governmental regulation of the price of sugar would thwart the natural economic order, harming not only Brazil but, in the long run, Portugal itself. The second essay, *Ensaio económico sobre o commércio de Portugal e suas colónias*, first published in 1794, was destined to have great importance to Brazilians. Some have heard it as one of the first notes of a hymn to Brazilian independence.[115] Following both nativistic and physiocrat traditions, it first analyzed the rich resources and potential of Brazil and then proceeded to recommend policies which would permit the best utilization of them. Azeredo Coutinho emphasized frequently the physiocrat doctrine that agriculture was the true source of wealth. Gold, a false wealth, instead of enriching the empire had impoverished it. Greater liberty, he reasoned, would help Brazilians tap their potential wealth. He called specifically for the abolition of the salt monopoly and the restrictions on forest industries, permission to manufacture in Brazil, and freer trade outside the empire. A third essay, *Discurso sobre o estado actual das minas do Brasil*, published in 1804, correctly attributed Brazil's economic distress to overemphasis on mining and the consequent neglect of agriculture. He urged the Luso-Brazilians to take advantage of the new European technology in order to increase their economic efficiency. In the depressed economy of the period, the Brazilians were receptive to the new economic ideas.

Other critics of the economy joined Azeredo Coutinho, one of the most enlightened being the Bahian João Rodrigues de Brito. Writing in the first decade of the nineteenth century, he lamented the backward state of Brazilian agriculture, advising an end to monopolies and restrictions, which, he argued, only inhibited growth. He prescribed "the liberty to think freely and to publish those thoughts by all the means known, principally the press." [116] The Brazilians' criticism of the economic policies of Portugal seemed to mount in proportion to their optimism about the potential of their land.

A third aspect of the intellectuals' criticism focused on pressing

---

[115] "That work [the *Economic Essay*] had a great influence in disseminating the doctrines of economic freedom, and thereby it mentally prepared the Brazilians for independence" (Francisco Muniz Tavares, *História da revolução de Pernambuco em 1817* [Recife, 1917], p. 34). "Azeredo . . . was preparing us with his books and his action for our political and spiritual separation and autonomy" (Heliodoro Pires, "Azeredo Coutinho," *RIAHGP* 18 [1916]:381).

[116] Brito, *Cartas economico-políticas*, pp. 28, 85; the Brazilian experience may be compared with similar events in other parts of the hemisphere. For the Chilean example, see Collier, *Ideas and Politics*, p. 40.

social problems. Slavery aroused some concern, although few advocated the outright abolition of the institution. The Bahian conspirators of 1798 seem to have been the only ones to favor so dramatic a remedy. The *Paulista* judge António Rodrigues Veloso de Oliveira, writing in 1810, supported the manumission of children born of slave women.[117] In that same year, far to the northeast in Recife, Manoel de Câmara summed up his thoughts on the social iniquities of Brazilian society:

The benightedness of the colored people must be done away with. This must come to an end so that when later men are needed to fill public positions they will be ready, for Brazil will never progress unless they can play their part in its affairs; never mind that degraded and absurd aristocracy which will always try to create obstacles. With a monarchy or without it, the colored people must share in Brazil's prosperity.[118]

An impressive, albeit limited, criticism of the harsh treatment of the slaves appeared.[119] The *Idade d'ouro*, published in a heartland of the slave system, editorialized in 1812 on the necessity of eventually ending the slave trade.[120]

Many of the deputies representing Brazil in the Côrtes in 1822 expressed strong opinions against slavery.[121] Notably effective in his efforts to protect the nonwhite from discrimination—as well as nativistic in his defense of the Brazilian "family"—Cipriano José Barata de Almeida,

[117] The manuscript did not reach print until twelve years later (*Memória sobre o melhoramento da Província de S. Paulo, applicável em grande parte a todas as outras províncias do Brasil* [Rio de Janeiro, 1822]).

[118] Freyre, *The Mansions and the Shanties*, pp. 362–63.

[119] "This growth in humanitarian feeling was presumably a reflexion of the ideas fostered by the movement known as the Enlightenment" (C. R. Boxer, *Race Relations in the Portuguese Colonial Empire, 1415–1825* [Oxford, 1963], p. 104). There was a small but impressive body of eighteenth-century Luso-Brazilian literature concerned with the slave's welfare: Jorge Benci, *Economia christãa dos senhores no governo de escravos* (Rome, 1705); André João Antonil, *Cultura e opulência do Brasil* (Lisbon, 1711); Manuel Ribeiro Rocha, *Ethiope resgatado, empenhado, sustentado, corregido, instruido, e libertado* (Lisbon, 1757); an anonymous pamphlet, *Nova e curiosa relação de um abuzo emandado, ou evidencias da razão; expostas a favor dos homens prêtos em hum diálogo entre hum letrado e hum mineiro* (Lisbon, 1764) (for an English translation see C. R. Boxer, "Negro Slavery in Brazil: A Portuguese Pamphlet of 1764," *Race* 5 [1964]:38–47); Santos Vilhena, *Notícias soteropolitanas*, which frequently denounces the harsh treatment of slaves. Although Azeredo Coutinho rationalized the slave trade, at the same time he preached humane treatment of slaves: "God did not create mankind to be servants, or slaves; . . . it is a brutal error to believe that some people are born to flatter the laziness and the pride of others; . . . we are all brothers and children of the same Father" (*Estatutos do recolhimento de N. Senhora da Gloria do lugar da Boa-Vista de Pernambuco: Ordenados por D. Jozé Joaquim da Cunha de Azeredo Coutinho, bispo de Pernambuco do Conselho de S. Magestade Fidelíssima* [Lisbon, 1798], p. 90, quoted in Cardozo, "Azeredo Coutinho and the Intellectual Ferment of His Times," p. 91).

[120] No. 48, June 16, 1812.

[121] See particularly the debates for April 17, 1822, in *Diário das Côrtes* 5.

a deputy from Bahia, reaching an emotional apogee in his oration before the Côrtes, declared:

Mulattos, *cabras*, and *crioulos*; Indians, *mamelucos*, and mestizos are all our people; they are Portuguese; they are honorable and valuable citizens. Throughout history they have proven their value to Brazil, defending it, working for its prosperity whether it be in agriculture, commerce, or the arts. Those races have provided great heroes. . . . They are Portuguese citizens, the sons of Portuguese or Brazilians, even if they are illegitimate. Whatever their color, whatever their status, they were born in Brazil.[122]

Much to its credit, the Côrtes voted unanimously to extend the suffrage to all *libertos*.[123]

The harsh treatment accorded the Indians awakened the social conscience of some intellectuals. José Bonifácio, for one, defended the remaining original inhabitants. The ode he published in 1820 testified to his social concern. At one point, he demanded "quick and certain aid to the unlettered Indian, the Negro, and the hapless poor."[124] Some observed that the Roman Catholic Church had failed to help the Indians because it had neither properly civilized them nor integrated them into the colony. Criticism of the Church's missions, the Church's Indian policy, and even the "indolent clergy" appeared in print.[125]

A long editorial commentary appearing in the *Idade d'ouro* in 1812 in many ways summed up the criticism of the Brazilian intellectuals.[126] Labeling the Portuguese "inert," it said, "the three centuries since discovery have not been well employed to construct the strong foundation Brazil now needs." The editor counseled the building of roads and increased immigration in order to improve conditions in the colony. The newspaper thanked Prince-Regent Dom João for the salutary reforms he had instituted and intimated that they should be expanded.

Throughout the criticism—for that matter throughout all the activities of the intellectuals—it is easy to detect the influence of the Enlightenment. The philosophies of all the European thinkers associated with the Enlightenment are visible, and the intellectuals looked increasingly to reason and science to find solutions for the problems they discussed. Once again it is possible to refer to the Brazilian Academy of the Forgotten to see the establishment of a pattern which would characterize the intellectual activity of the ensuing century. In his address in 1724 inaugurating the Academy, José da Cunha Cardoso paid

[122] *Ibid.*, sess. of August 13, 1822, 7:139.
[123] *Ibid.*, sess. of April 17, 1822, 5:840.
[124] Candido, *Formação da literatura brasileira* 1:235.
[125] *Idade d'ouro*, no. 43, May 29, 1812.
[126] *Ibid.*

tribute to some of the tenets of the Enlightenment by recognizing that man's search for knowledge was natural, appropriate, and rational.[127] His fellow academicians echoed that opinion. One reminded his peers that "science is the fundamental base" of their work.[128] For the remainder of the final colonial century speeches and orations resounded with denunciations of scholasticism and superstitution and with praises of science, inquiry, and reason. The Luso-Brazilians, then, offered their criticism within the accepted framework of *o século das luzes*.

The criticism provided the explanation for as well as the justification of change. The intellectuals suggested those reforms they felt would benefit Brazil. Implied in their criticism or accompanying it, as the discussion above indicates, was a program of reform, most of it based on ideas emanating from those few nations whose government, culture, and/or economic success they most admired.

At this juncture, it is tempting to oversimplify, to point to one current of criticism and one program of reform and show how the one intensified, while the other gained popularity over the course of a century. Events and emotions were far more complex, however. Varying intellectual trends moved forward and backward, intersected, and contradicted one another. Some intellectuals simply sought change within the system; others questioned the system itself and saw change as altering it. On one issue the intellectuals seemed unanimous. They insisted that Brazil's status within the empire be improved. They felt it imperative that the kingdom's overwhelming importance be recognized.[129] After all, at the beginning of the nineteenth century, Brazil had a population larger than the metropolis, furnished approximately three-quarters of the empire's exports, and boasted an economic potential far superior to that of any other part of the empire.[130] In size, Brazil dwarfed the motherland. The inevitable clash between metropolis and colony on the issue of the colony's rising importance was postponed by the un-

[127] "Oração com que da dominica in Albis e vinte, e tres de abril deste ano de 1724 abriu a Academia Brasílica o Doutor José da Cunha Cardoso," in Castillo, *O movimento academicista* 1:13.

[128] "Oração acadêmica," *ibid.*, p. 254.

[129] Some few Portuguese statesmen were all too aware of the importance of Brazil. See the remarks of Tomás António de Vila Nova Portugal in Francisco Adolfo de Varnhagen, "História da independência do Brasil," *RIHGB* 79 (1916):50. The contemporary Portuguese historian A. H. de Oliveira Marques asserts that Brazil was the basic element of the Portuguese empire (*History of Portugal*, p. 431); C. R. Boxer affirms that Brazil was more prosperous than Portugal by the mid-eighteenth century (*The Golden Age of Brazil*, pp. 323, 325).

[130] Oliveira Marques gives the population of Portugal in 1820 as 3,100,000 (*History of Portugal*, p. 379). The official census ordered by Dom João VI in 1817–18 recorded 3,817,900 inhabitants over ten years of age in Brazil (Poppino, *Brazil*, p. 170). Economic progress is described in Caio Prado Júnior, *The Colonial Background of Modern Brazil* (Berkeley, Calif., 1967), p. 274.

expected transfer of the court to Rio de Janeiro in 1808. The return of the king to Lisbon in 1821 projected the issue to the forefront again.

To summarize the political reforms most frequently advocated, it can be said that on more than one occasion over this long time span, intellectuals suggested the integration of the Indians and manumitted blacks into society, the unification of the sprawling territory by means of better roads, a constitution based on the concept of government as a social contract, a stronger Brazilian voice in the imperial government, and the enhancement of the roles of the legislature and judiciary. A few spoke out for the establishment of a republic. As for the economic aspects of their reforms, they favored free trade, industrialization, modernization of agriculture and mining, and an end to burdensome restrictions, monopolies and taxes. Their social statements were much more nebulous. They paid lip service to the concept of the equality of all men and talked in vague terms of improving the conditions of the Indians and the slaves; a few even spoke of ending the slave trade. They wanted personal liberties, civil freedom, and religious tolerance. Most emphatically, however, they proposed ambitious plans to reform and expand education. Such, then, in composite was the ideology of change espoused by the intellectuals. It has never been fully implemented, but it provided the goals of the reformers throughout the nineteenth century.

From the small group of intellectuals writing and speaking of reform came an important segment of the leadership of the independence movement. Apparently despairing of seeing the Portuguese officials enact the reforms they wanted, they resolved to take matters into their own hands. Hipólito da Costa, always the quintessence of the moderate, eventually came to believe that revolution was inevitable since the necessary reforms which could have diverted it were not forthcoming.[131] Graduates of Coimbra played a significant role in the *inconfidências* of Minas Gerais and Rio de Janeiro.[132] Graduates of the Seminar of Olinda headed the revolution of 1817. It seems that the order from the Côrtes in late 1821 for Dom Pedro to return forthwith to Europe spurred the intellectuals to action. That humiliating command

[131] Herrick, "The Reluctant Revolutionist," p. 180.

[132] Freyre, *The Mansions and the Shanties*, p. 361. The viscount of Barbacena wrote to Minister Martinho de Melo e Castro on July 11, 1798, "I cannot help believing that the ideas [of the conspiracy] came from Coimbra, whether the conspiracy of the students is certain or not, because in that matter I found very dangerous the sentiments, opinions, and influence of the Brazilian university graduates, who have returned to their own land, especially those who have studied public and international law, to the self-interests of Europe and in their knowledge of the natural products [of Brazil]. Even more dangerous were those who studied in foreign universities, as some have done without sufficient reason." Quoted in José Camillo de Oliveira Tôrres, *História de Minas Gerais* (Belo Horizonte, n.d. [1961?]), 3:685.

transformed moderates into revolutionaries—at least for the moment. When Dom Pedro appointed José Bonifácio de Andrada e Silva in January of 1822 to the key post of minister of the kingdom, the first Brazilian to hold such an exalted position, the course toward independence was charted. Unlike the prince and the Portuguese functionaries surrounding him, Bonifácio possessed a clear vision of what lay ahead. He guided the prince and Brazil toward independence.

A stellar example of the Brazilian intellectual of the period, the patriarch graduated from Coimbra in 1787 and went on to continue his studies in Italy and Germany.[133] He traveled extensively in Europe and met some of the Continent's outstanding intellectuals. Scholarly institutions in France, Germany, and England elected him to membership. He observed the French Revolution at first hand during his residencies in Paris for parts of the years 1790, 1791, 1793, 1794, and 1799. An avid reader of the *philosophes*, he particularly admired Rousseau, all of whose works he owned.[134] In short, he immersed himself totally in the European Enlightenment. He returned to Brazil in 1819, intent upon applying the knowledge gained from his studies, travels, and experience.

Few Brazilians could exhibit such a distinguished and extensive education as José Bonifácio, but if we examine the biographies of the leaders of the independence movement, one salient characteristic emerges: a majority of them were educated abroad. To celebrate the centenary of the Grito de Ipiranga, Affonso de Taunay published *Grandes vultos da independência brasileira* (São Paulo, 1922), biographical sketches of men and women who in one way or another were considered to be major contributors to the 1822 movement. Of the twenty-four born in Brazil, fourteen, roughly 60 percent, had studied at Coimbra University. Looking into the biographies of the Brazilians active in politics in the decade of the 1820s, one is impressed with the large number of unversity graduates among them, a further indication of the leadership the intellectuals provided in Brazil's transition from a kingdom within the Portuguese empire to an independent empire. The contribution of the intellectuals to change in Brazil and to independence was considerable. Yet one final aspect of their role remains to be examined.

Confronting his judges in Salvador at the close of the eighteenth cen-

---

133 The standard biography of Bonifácio is Octávio Tarquinio de Sousa, *José Bonifácio, 1763–1838* (Rio de Janeiro, 1945). A bibliography of works by and about José Bonifácio, is *Bi-Centenário do nascimento do patriarca da independência do Brasil. José Bonifácio de Andrada e Silva, 1763–1963* (Brasília, 1964), pp. 103–42.

134 Godin da Fonseca, *A revolução francesa e a vida de José Bonifácio* (São Paulo, 1968), 57, 2, 130, 144.

tury, the twenty-three-year-old soldier Lucas Dantas do Amorim Tôrres stated, "We want a republic in order to breathe freely because we live subjugated and because we're colored and we can't advance and if there was a republic there would be equality for everyone." [135] More than boldness was notable in his statement. Obviously, the young soldier had imbibed the thoughts of the Enlightenment; the revolution of ideas had reached him. Dantas was but one of a larger group of conspirators arrested in Salvador in 1798 for plotting against the crown. By and large those conspirators were simple folk: soldiers, workmen, artisans, and so large a number of tailors that the movement sometimes bears the name of the "Conspiracy of the Tailors." The statistics tell the tale. Of the forty-nine arrested, forty-six were male, forty were freedmen, almost all were literate, all were between seventeen and thirty years old, all had modest backgrounds, and all were mulattos.[136]

As in the case of Dantas, the testimony of the other defendants at the trial revealed that those representatives of the lower classes were acquainted with current European thought. They made accusations against Portugal similar to those of the intellectuals of the time. In general, the conspirators favored independence, a republic, the equal treatment of all men, the abolition of slavery, and free trade.[137] The Bahian rebels proposed far more profound changes than the other colonial dissidents before and after them. They were the only ones to strike at slavery, that institution which was the sinew and muscle of colonial Brazil. In some ways their desires harmonized more with the Enlightenment than did the programs of the intellectuals, who were

[135] Quoted in Braz do Amaral, *Fatos da vida do Brasil* (Salvador, 1941), p. 28.

[136] *Ibid.*, pp. 10, 23. There are two editions of the *devassas*, Biblioteca Nacional, *A inconfidência da Bahia. Devassas e sequestros*, 2 vols. (Rio de Janeiro, 1931), and the edition brought out by the Arquivo Público da Bahia mentioned in n. 108. The pioneer study of the Bahian conspiracy would appear to be José Carlos Ferreira, "Princípios jacobinos, sedição de 1798 na Bahia," *RIGHBahia* 26 (1900):371–411. Basic studies are Amaral, *Fatos da vida do Brasil*, pp. 5–71; Affonso Ruy, *A primeira revolução social brasileira, 1798*, 2d ed. (Salvador, 1951); Luís Henrique Dias Tavares, *Introdução ao estudo das idéias do movimento revolucionário de 1798* (Salvador, 1959); Kátia de Queirós Mattoso, *Presença francesa*. It is significant to note that the works on the Bahian conspiracy were all published in Salvador. Brazilian historians have displayed an overwhelming preference for the Inconfidência Mineira and Tiradentes. In fact, the bibliography on Tiradentes, in addition to being extensive, contains works published in all parts of Brazil, principally by the major presses in Rio de Janeiro and São Paulo, ensuring national circulation. Two traditional histories of Brazil widely used for decades in the public schools do not even mention the Inconfidência Bahiana. João Ribeiro, *História do Brasil*, 17th ed. (Rio de Janeiro, 1960), devoted ten pages to Tiradentes and the Inconfidência Mineira, as much space as he gave to the *bandeirante* movement and much more than he gave to the abolitionist movement. Rocha Pombo, *História do Brasil* 10th ed. (São Paulo, 1961), devoted eighteen pages to Tiradentes and the *mineiros*, more than was allocated to either the First Empire or the abolitionist movement.

[137] Dias Tavares, *Introdução ao estudo das idéias*, pp. 7–34.

compromised by their aspirations or association with the interests of the upper class or the Portuguese.

The first signs of the impending rebellion appeared in the form of handwritten posters affixed to public walls on August 12, 1798. One announced, "Courage Bahian People, the happy day of Liberty is at hand, the time when we will all be brothers, the time when we will all be equal." Another affirmed, "Each soldier is a citizen, particularly the brown and black men who are abused and abandoned. All are equal. There is no difference. There will only be liberty, equality, and fraternity." [138] References to "liberty, equality, and fraternity" abounded, as did praises of the French Revolution and the French republic. The plot had its picturesque aspects. A letter addressed to one priest informed him that the conspirators had named him "Future General-in-Chief of the Bahian Church." Another, to the governor, addressed him as "President of the Supreme Tribunal of Bahian Democracy." The entire affair prompted one exasperated Portuguese official to lament that the Bahians "for some unexplained madness and because they did not understand their own best interests had become infected with the abominable French ideas and shown great affection for the absurd French constitution." [139]

A major significance of the Bahian *inconfidência* lay in the revelation that the new ideas had reached the masses as well as the educated elite.[140] Somehow the intellectuals communicated to the lower strata of urban society those ideas of which they were the brokers. Perhaps the transmission testifies to the social fluidity of the Brazilian city by the close of the eighteenth century, which was sufficiently in flux to facilitate interchange between various classes. Francisco de Assis Barbosa has hypothesized about Brazil in general during that period that ideas were probably passed on by word of mouth, since books were expensive and illiteracy predominated.[141] Speaking of the Bahian case in particular, Luís Henrique Dias Tavares also stressed conversations as the major means by which the lower classes might have picked up their notions of the philosophy of the Enlightenment.[142] Some testimony in the trial of the conspirators mentioned word of mouth as the means by which they might have gathered their ideas. In his defense, Cipriano José Barata de

---

[138] Queirós Mattoso, *Presença francesa*, pp. 148, 157.

[139] Letter from Minister Rodrigo de Souza Coutinho to Governor of Bahia Fernando José de Portugal, October 4, 1798, quoted in Amaral, *Fatos da vida*, p. 12.

[140] The full significance of the Bahian *inconfidência* has yet to be examined. Reasons for its importance are advanced by Braz do Amaral in his *Fatos da vida* and by Kenneth R. Maxwell, "The Generation of the 1790s and the Idea of Luso-Brazilian Empire," in Alden, *Colonial Roots of Modern Brazil*, pp. 119–22.

[141] *Alguns aspectos da influência francesa no Brasil* (Rio de Janeiro, 1963), p. xxi.

[142] *Introdução ao estudo das idéias*, pp. 50–54.

Almeida admitted a penchant for discussing "the state of politics in Europe without any reference to Brazil" and allowed that some dissatisfied members of the lower classes might have heard and misunderstood his remarks.[143] However, since most of the Bahian conspirators, despite their lowly status, seem to have been literate, they could have formed their views at least partially from reading, perhaps borrowing books from intellectuals sympathetic to the cause of rebellion. A few intellectuals, among them João Ladislau de Figueiredo e Melo, Francisco Agostinho Gomes, Cipriano José Barata de Almeida, and Francisco Moniz Barreto de Aragão, have already been identified as sympathetic. Careful scholarship has traced some of the ideas of the conspirators to two French sources, *L'Orateur des États-Généraux pour 1789* and *Séance du 11 pluviose: discours de Boissy d'Anglas,* both of which had been translated into Portuguese and were circulating from hand to hand in manuscript form prior to August of 1798.[144] There may also have been contacts between the soldiers who participated in the plotting and a few junior officers well acquainted with European thought and also implicated in the *inconfidência.* For example, Lt. Hermógenes Francisco de Aguilar Pantoja, who was known to Lucas Dantas, possessed a private library containing French books. The court testimony pointed out that the young lieutenant would bring his books to the barracks and read aloud from them to his troops.[145] At any rate, by whatever means, the intellectuals did transmit ideas to the masses.

The Bahian conspiracy added the dimension of the common person, almost always overlooked, to the history of ideas in colonial Brazil.[146] As a historian of Bahia, Dias Tavares, noted, "The Brazilian people rarely appear in the histories of Brazil, but in the revolutionary movement of 1798 they are the principal actors." [147] Awareness of that popular dimension in intellectual history is an incentive to broaden future studies of Brazil to encompass wider segments of the population. The urban masses also acted on the ideas of the times. The influence of the intellectuals extended beyond the narrow confines of the elite.

[143] Quoted in Ruy, *A primeira revolução social,* p. 82.

[144] Queirós Mattoso, *Presença francesa,* pp. 50–129.

[145] *Ibid.,* pp. 28–33; Dias Tavares, *Introdução ao estudo das idéias,* p. 38; Ruy, *A primeira revolução social,* pp. 81, 83.

[146] In his provocative essay "Intellectual History: Its Aims and Methods," Felix Gilbert notes that "the interaction which continuously takes place among the various levels of intellectual life might lead to modifications of each of them through interpenetration, or it might have the opposite effect of hardening each group in its own position" (*Daedalus* 100 (1970):88). Franklin L. Baumer advises that one of the most important questions the intellectual historian can ask is "to what extent and precisely how do ideas affect the majority of nonintellectual people?" ("Intellectual History and Its Problems," p. 200).

[147] One of the few examples I know of the Brazilian intellectual historian trying to incorporate the thinking of the "common man" into his studies is the outstanding work of Carlos Guilherme Mota, *Nordeste 1817.*

Chronological Table

Sovereigns of Portugal and Brazil

1706–50   Dom João V.

1750–77   Dom José I.

1777–92   Dona Maria (deposed; died, 1816).

1792–1816 Dom João, prince-regent.

1816–26   Dom João succeeds to the throne as Dom João VI.

Significant Events

1660   Barbalho's revolt, Rio de Janeiro.

1684   Manuel Beckmann's revolt, São Luís do Maranhão.

1693–95   The discovery of gold in Minas Gerais.

1703   The Methuen Treaty, whereby the exchange of port wine for English woolens became the basis of Anglo-Portuguese trade.

1708–09   Guerra dos Emboabas in Minas Gerais.

1710–11   Guerra dos Mascates in Pernambuco.

1720   Uprising in Vila Rica do Ouro Prêto against the establishment of foundry houses in Minas Gerais.

1724   Establishment of the Academia dos Esquecidos in Salvador (–1725).

1736   Establishment of the Academia dos Felizes in Rio de Janeiro (–1740).

1746   Luís António Verney publishes his *Verdadeiro Método de Estudar*.

1750   Treaty of Madrid between Spain and Portugal adopts the principle of *uti possidetis* for establishing boundaries between the two empires in South America; publication of *Discours sur les sciences et les arts* by Jean Jacques Rousseau; Sebastião José de Carvalho e Melo (later Marquis of Pombal) comes to power.

1751–72   Publication of the 28 volumes of the *Encyclopédie*.

1751   Establishment of the Academia dos Selectos in Rio de Janeiro (–1752); creation of Boards of Inspection in Rio de Janeiro, Recife, Salvador, and São Luís do Maranhão.

1755   Lisbon devastated by earthquake.

1756   Pombal establishes the Junta de Comércio, or Board of Trade.

1759   Establishment of the Academia Brasílica dos Renacidos in Salvador (–1760) ; expulsion of the Jesuits from Portugal and her dominions.

1761   Treaty of Pardo annuls the Treaty of Madrid.

1762   Publication of *Du Contrat Social* by Jean Jacques Rousseau.

1763   Transfer of the capital from Salvador to Rio de Janeiro.

1771   Pombal places diamond mines in Brazil directly under crown control.

1772   Extinction of the state of Maranhão; Pombal reforms the University of Coimbra; Academia Científica established in Rio de Janeiro (–1779) .

1776   The British colonies in North America gain their independence; publication of Adam Smith's *Inquiry into the Nature and Causes of the Wealth of Nations.*

1777   Dismissal of the marquis of Pombal; the Treaty of San Ildefonso marks the limits of the Spanish and Portuguese empires in South America.

1786   Establishment of the Sociedade Literária in Rio de Janeiro (–1790, 1794) .

1789   French revolution; Inconfidência Mineira in Minas Gerais.

1791   General slave revolt in Haiti.

1794   Plot in Rio de Janeiro; publication of José Joaquim da Cunha de Azeredo Coutinho's *An Economic Essay on the Commerce of Portugal and Her Colonies.*

1797   Establishment of the Masonic lodge Os Cavaleiros da Luz in Salvador.

1798   Revolt of the Tailors in Salvador.

1800   Bishop José Joaquim da Cunha de Azeredo Coutinho establishes the seminary of Nossa Senhora da Graça in Olinda.

1801   Conspiracy of the Suassuna brothers in Pernambuco.

1804   Jenner's method of vaccination introduced into Brazil.

1807   Secret Franco-Spanish Treaty of Fontainebleau; General Andoche Junot invades Portugal; November 27, prince-regent and the royal court leave Lisbon for Brazil.

1808   January 28, royal order opening the ports of Brazil to foreign trade; April 1, decree permitting the establishment of factories and manufacturing concerns in Brazil, lifting restrictions imposed in 1785; Régia Press established in Rio de Janeiro; naval academy established in Rio de Janeiro; Bank of Brazil established in Rio de Janeiro, with branches in São Paulo and Salvador; School of Medicine established in Salvador; October 11, law exempting textiles made in Portugal from customs due on entering Brazil.

1810   Treaties signed with Great Britain, giving England dominance over Brazilian foreign trade; military academy established in Rio de Janeiro; March 27, royal decree authorizing the sale in Brazil of any commodity on the streets and at doors of households.

1811   Dom João sends troops into the Banda Oriental of Uruguay, withdrawing them in 1812; September 28, revocation of decree of December 6, 1755, and henceforth Portuguese subjects free to trade in any commodity except those forbidden by law; inauguration of the Public Library in Salvador.

1813   January 21, decree exempting from import duties at Brazilian ports all merchandise and manufactured goods from Portugal.

1814   May 5, resolution that import duties on British woolen cloth entering Brazil be reduced to 15 percent; July 18, Portuguese ships allowed to sail for foreign ports without restriction and ships of any nation allowed to enter any port of the Portuguese empire; National Library inaugurated in Rio de Janeiro.

1815   August 11, decree allowing goldsmiths to work and deal freely in works of gold and silver in Brazil; first steam-driven sugar mill in Bahia.

1815   December 16, the state of Brazil raised to the status of a kingdom.

1816   Luso-Brazilian troops reoccupy Uruguay; French artistic mission arrives in Brazil.

1817   Republican revolution in Pernambuco; António Gonçalves da Cruz, special emissary of the revolutionary junta in Pernambuco, goes to the United States.

1817–18   United States mission of Caesar Rodney, Theodorik Bland, and John Graham visits the west coast of South America.

1819   First steamboat in Brazilian waters; July, John Graham presents his credentials as U.S. minister to the Brazilian court.

1820   August 24, outbreak of the Constitutionalist revolution in Oporto; August 30, decree exempting all hardware made in Portugal from import duties at Brazilian ports.

1821   Dom João annexes the Banda Oriental of Uruguay as the Cisplatine Province; April 22, Dom João VI appoints Dom Pedro as regent; April 24, Dom João VI leaves Brazil for Lisbon, arriving July 4; April 24, decision by the Portuguese Côrtes to make the provincial governors in Brazil subordinate to the Côrtes and not to the court in Rio de Janeiro; July 16, Côrtes revokes the resolution of 1814 and henceforth woolen cloth and other woolen products from Great Britain imported into Portugal liable for 30 percent duties.

1822   January 9, Dom Pedro's famous pronouncement *Fico* ("I shall remain") ; José Bonifácio de Andrada e Silva appointed as minister of the kingdom by Dom Pedro; February 16, decree convoking the Council of Procurators-General of the provinces of Brazil; February 17, resolution forbidding the disembarkation in Brazil of troops from Portugal; May 13, Dom Pedro accepts the title "Perpetual Defender of Brazil"; June 2, initiation of Dom Pedro into the Apostolado; June 3, installation of the Council of Procurators-General.

1822   September 7, Dom Pedro proclaims the independence of Brazil in São Paulo with the "Cry of Ipiranga"; September 14, Dom Pedro made Grand Master of the Great Orient; December 1, Dom Pedro crowned as Dom Pedro I, emperor of Brazil.

1823   May 3, first session of the Constituent Assembly, Rio de Janeiro; November 12, dissolution of the Constituent Assembly; December, President James Monroe's message to the U.S. Congress, later to be known as the "Monroe Doctrine."

1824   March 25, Liberal constitution for Brazil promulgated by Dom Pedro; May 26, José Silvestre Rebello, first Brazilian chargé d'affaires to Washington, finally received by President Monroe.

1825   August 29, Portugal recognizes Brazil as an independent nation.

Glossary

agreste	The bleak and rocky zone in the northeast of Brazil between the coastal plain and the arid *sertão*.
alqueire	A grain measure varying regionally between 13 and 36 liters.
bandeirante	Explorer, frontiersman, or slaver, often of Amerindian-Portuguese extraction.
caboclo	White-Amerindian crossbreed; pejorative term for a low-class person.
cabra	crossbreed of black and mulatto parentage; a pejorative term.
caipira	Country bumpkin or yokel.
Câmara municipal	Municipal council.
cangaço	Banditry.
charque	Jerked beef.
Côrtes	Portuguese parliament.
cruzado	Monetary unit worth 400 réis.
Emboaba	Pejorative term used by the natives of São Paulo to describe Portuguese and Brazilian born "outsiders."
engenho	Sugar mill and, by extension, a sugar plantation; hence *senhor de engenho*.
fazenda	Ranch or large property; the crown treasury.
fôro	Land rent.
gaúcho	Cowboy of southern Brazil and the pampas.
inconfidência	A conspiracy for independence, especially referring to that occurring in Minas Gerais in 1789; hence *inconfidentes*, conspirators.
juiz de fora	Crown district judge.
juiz do povo	People's tribune.
largo	Widened section of a street.
lavrador	Smallholder, tenant-farmer, sharecropper, peasant; hence *lavrador de roça, lavrador de cana*.

251

mameluco	Crossbreed with a white father and Amerindian mother.
mandão	Rural magnate.
mascate	Peddler; pejorative epithet for a merchant.
matuto	A backwoodsman.
mestiço	Crossbreed of white and black or Amerindian parentage.
Mesas de Inspeção	Boards of inspection.
milréis	Monetary unit, comprising 1,000 réis, usually written 1$000.
mineiro	A miner; a native of Minas Gerais.
monção	Riverborn prospecting, trading, or colonizing expedition.
morador	Settler, head of household, or share-tenant.
ordenança	Militia company.
ouvidor	Crown judge.
pardo	A person of color; often replaces the more pejorative *mulato;* literally, "brown."
Paulista	White or Amerindian inhabitant of the town or region of São Paulo.
Praieiro	Participant in the Praieira revolt of 1848, suppressed 1850.
prensário	Literally, "squeezer," hence extortionists.
procurador do povo	People's representative.
quilombo	Community of runaway slaves.
rossio	Public square; outlying and often communal piece of land.
senhor de engenho	Sugar plantation owner.
sertão	Desolate and arid hinterland of Brazil.
sobrado	Town house of more than one story.
tropeiro	Drover or dealer in pack animals.
vaqueiro	Cowboy.

Notes on Contributors

E. BRADFORD BURNS is a member of the Department of History at the University of California, Los Angeles. He has traveled extensively throughout Brazil and was guest lecturer at the University of Paraná in 1963 and at the University of Brazil in 1965. A specialist on the history of Latin America, his *The Underwritten Alliance, Rio Branco and Brazilian-American Relations* won the Herbert E. Bolton Prize in 1967. His most recent study is *A History of Brazil*. Professor Burns was awarded the Order of Rio Branco by the Brazilian government in 1966 and is a member of the Instituto Histórico e Geográfico Brasileiro.

MANOEL DA SILVEIRA CARDOZO is curator of the Oliveira Lima Library and has been a member of the Department of History at the Catholic University of America since 1940. Author of numerous learned articles and monographs, Professor Cardozo has lectured widely in Portuguese and Brazilian universities. In 1958 he was the Smith-Mundt lecturer to Portugal. His contributions to the history of Portugal and Brazil received official recognition in 1945, when the Brazilian government awarded him the Rio Branco Medal, and in 1958, when he was made a Knight of the National Order of the Southern Cross.

EMÍLIA VIOTTI DA COSTA is a member of the Department of History at Yale University. A specialist on Brazilian history, with an emphasis on slave systems, she published *Da senzala à colônia* in 1966 and has written many articles on nineteenth-century Brazilian social and economic history. She is currently at work on a study of slavery in Brazil.

MARIA ODILA SILVA DIAS is a member of the Department of History at the University of São Paulo. A wide-ranging student of Brazilian history of the eighteenth and nineteenth centuries, she has published monographs on the Enlightenment in Brazil and historiography. Her most recent book is *André Rebouças. Diário. A guerra do Paraguai (1866)*; her book on Robert Southey, *O fardo do homen branco*, is scheduled for publication in 1975.

253

STANLEY E. HILTON is a member of the Department of History at Louisiana State University. He has undertaken extensive research in Brazilian archives and from 1972 to 1974 served as director of the Center of Contemporary History at the National Archives in Rio de Janeiro. He is the author of several studies of diplomatic and political events in modern Latin America; his *Brazil and the Great Powers, 1930–1939: The Politics of Trade Rivalry* will appear in 1975.

RICHARD M. MORSE is a member of the Department of History at Yale University. He served as director of the Institute of Caribbean Studies at the University of Puerto Rico from 1958 to 1961. A sometime consultant on Latin American Affairs for the Ford Foundation, a past fellow of the Guggenheim Foundation and the Center for Advanced Study in the Behavioral Sciences, Professor Morse was chairman of the Conference on Latin American History in 1969. His publications include *From Community to Metropolis: A Biography of São Paulo, Brazil; the Bandeirantes: The Historical Role of the Brazilian Pathfinders;* and other investigations of Latin American urban history.

A. J. R. RUSSELL-WOOD is a member of the Department of History at The Johns Hopkins University. His interests are reflected in articles on race relations, colonial society, local government, and ethnicity. His *Fidalgos and Philanthropists. The Santa Casa da Misericórdia of Bahia, 1550–1755* was the co-recipient of the Herbert E. Bolton Prize and was commended by the Albert J. Beveridge Award Committee as the best book on Latin American history published in 1968. He is a corresponding member of the Instituto Geográfico e Histórico of Bahia and a fellow of the Royal Geographical Society.

STUART B. SCHWARTZ is a member of the Department of History at the University of Minnesota. His wide-ranging research interests have been reflected in numerous articles on Portuguese and Brazilian history, based on extensive research in the libraries and archives of Brazil and Portugal. His most recent publication is *Sovereignty and Society in Colonial Brazil: The High Court of Bahia and Its Judges, 1609–1751.* He is now engaged on a social and economic study of the plantation society of Bahia during the colonial period.

Index

Aboím, Diogo Guerreiro Camacho de, 186, 188

Academia Brasílica dos Esquecidos (Salvador), 211, 217, 231, 240–41

Academia Brasílica dos Renascidos (Salvador), 217

Academia dos Felizes (Rio de Janeiro), 217, 233

Academia dos Selectos (Rio de Janeiro), 217

Academia Scientífica (Rio de Janeiro), 217

Academy of Fine Arts (Rio de Janeiro), 223

Academy of Sciences (Lisbon), 200

Adams, John, 112

Adams, John Quincy: attitude toward Latins, 113; cited, 112, 116, 120, 121, 122, 127

Afonso VI, King Dom, 33

Africa: Dutch in, 20; source of slaves, 8, 11, 19; trade to Brazil from, 8, 28

Agregados, 145

Agriculture: crown policy, 24–25, 29, 30, 55–56, 237–38; in Brazilian northeast, 24–25, 146–53, 176; impact on migration, 153, 165; in Minas Gerais, 165; in Paraíba Valley, 176–77. *See also* Boards of Inspection

Ajuda palace (Lisbon), 98

Alagoas, free rural population in, 149

Alberdi, Juan B., 139

Albuquerque, António Coelho de Carvalho de, 15–16, 27, 32

Alembert, Jean le Rond d', 58, 220

Alencar, José Martiniano de, 65

Alencastre, Dom Veríssimo de, 189

Aljubarrota, battle of, 207

Almanaques (Rio de Janeiro), 143, 220

Almeida, Cipriano José Barata de, 239, 245–46; cited, 240

Almeida, Dom Lourenço de, 27

Almeida, Dom Pedro de (Count of Assumar), 27

Almeida e Castro, Miguel Joaquim de, 222–23

Alvarenga, Manoel Ignácio da Silva, 221–22

Alvarenga Peixoto, Inácio José de, 67, 69, 144

Álvares, António, 197

Álvares, Manuel, 197

Álvares Cabral, Pedro, 7

Álvares de Almeida, José Egídio (Marquis of Santo Amaro), 85, 99

Álvares Machado, 204–5

Amador Arrais, Friar, 189

Amazonia: colonization of, 163; communications in, 22, 108; free labor pool in, 10; Jesuits in, 194; population policy for, 139; rubber production in, 179; territory disputed, 21. *See also* Amerindians

American Revolution, 39; impact elsewhere in Americas, 3, 59; impact on Brazil, 27, 32, 34, 59, 92

Amerindians: Amerindians in North America, 10; in Spanish America, 9, 10, 157; in Brazil, 8, 11, 160; *aldeias* of, 139; and Brazilian nationalism, 232; enslavement of, 159; as free labor pool, 10, 139, 148; intellectuals defend, 240, 242; measures against enslavement of, 10; miscegenation of, 9, 19, 139, 145, 148; in North America, 10; Pombaline policies toward, 10, 19, 20, 139; position in society, 8, 19, 135; source of literary inspiration, 232, 240; in Spanish America, 9, 10, 157; warrior nature of, 10–11

Amorin Tôrres, Lucas Dantas do, 244, 246

Andarati, palace at, 98

Andrada e Silva, José Bonifácio de, 37, 62, 66, 74, 82, 83, 84, 85, 229, 243; and freemasonry, 69, 84; cited, 72, 100

André, Marius, 209–10
Angola, 15, 17
Anunciação, Dom Miguel da, 199
Apostolado lodge (Rio de Janeiro), 69, 84–85
Aragão, Francisco Moniz Barreto de, 246
Araguaia river, 108
Aranha, Bento de Figueiredo Tenreiro, 232
Araújo, António de (Count of Barca), 98, 99, 106
Arcos, Count of, 62, 107
Areias, 145
Areopago, 60, 61
Argentina, 174, 178
Arinos river, 108
Artisans: free black and mulatto, 68, 69, 135, 137, 144, 244; as municipal officers, 160; privileges of, 25, 50, 57, 87; role in Revolt of the Tailors (q.v.), 69, 244
Assis Barbosa, Francisco de, 245
Assumar, Count of: elder, 188; younger, 27
Ataíde, Dom Jerónimo de (Count of Atouguia), 197
Atlantic islands, 6, 9, 19
Atouguia, Count of, 197
Aveiro, Duke of, 197
Avila, Dias d', 29
Avilez, General, 80
Austria and Brazilian independence, 37, 83
Azeredo Coutinho, José Joaquim da Cunha de, 50, 206, 222, 229, 237–38
Azeredo Coutinho, José Mariano de, 74, 81
Azevedo, José Joaquim de, 98
Azores, 53: migration from, 9, 139

Badaro, Libero, 88
Baependi, Marquis of, 85
Bahia: agriculture in, 8, 153; Amerindians in, 8, 9, 10; black and mulatto population in, 136–37, 148; cattle ranching in, 8; economic decline of, 102; gold discoveries in, 8, 13; "Haitianism" in, 100, 103; peasantry of, 146–49, 151, 153. *See also* Revolt of the Tailors; Salvador
Banda Oriental, 114, 119, 120, 122
Bandeira, Manoel António Leitão, 237
Bandeirantes, 9, 159, 163. *See also* Paulistas
Banditry, 152
Bank of Brazil, 103

Barata de Almeida, Cipriano José, 239, 240, 245–46
Barbacena, Count of, 33
Barbalho uprising (Rio de Janeiro), 162, 178
Barca, Count of, 98, 99, 106
Barlaeus, Gaspar, 186
Barreto de Aragão, Francisco Moniz, 246
Barros, João de, 185
Beckmann uprising (São Luís do Maranhão), 48, 162
Belém do Pará: municipal council, 159, 160; population of, 173, 179; printing press in, 223; theater in, 232
Belmonte river, 108
Benedict XIV, Pope, 195, 199
Benedictines, 201, 222
Benin, Gulf of, 28
Bernardo, Luís, 197
Bezout, Étienne, 222
Bland, Theodorik, 119
Board of Trade (Lisbon), 17
Boards of Inspection (Mesas de Inspeção): Brazilians appointed to, 30, 142; colonial reaction against, 29, 139–41; creation of, 17, 138, 139
Bolívar, Simón, 208
Book trade: from Europe to Brazil, 58–61, 63, 219–21, 227, 245–46; restrictions on, 31, 61
Boston, 212
Boston Patriot, 115, 116
Botocudos, 10
Boxer, C. R., 160
Brackenridge, Henry M., 220; cited, 119–20
Branco, Alves, 84
Brazil: changing role in Portuguese empire, 7–8, 12–13, 20–21, 76, 81, 99, 103–4, 138, 214, 241–42; "melting pot," 9–12; raised to status of kingdom, 35, 51, 114, 204; settlement of, 8–10, 22, 163–67; territorial consolidation of, 18, 21, 22–23, 211. *See also* Independence of Brazil; Society and social structure; Urbanization and cities in Brazil
Brazilian Academy of the Forgotten (Salvador), 211, 217, 231, 240–41
Brazilians: hostility to *reinóis*, 23–24, 25, 26, 31–32, 33, 60, 104–5, 134, 141, 143 (*see also* War of the *Emboabas*; War of the Peddlers); participation in government, 22, 25, 30, 31, 105–6, 108, 141–43; pride in being, 31–32, 35, 96, 105, 219, 233–34
Brazilwood, 51, 52

Brésilianité, 35. *See also* Brazilians: pride in being

Brígido, João, 71

Brito, João Rodrigues de, 229, 238

Brito e Figueiredo, Caetano de, 231

Brotherhoods, lay, 24, 30

Buarque de Holanda, Sérgio, 90, 92, 156, 160

Buenos Aires, 119

Buffon, Georges-Louis Leclerc de, 220

Burke, Edmund, 229

Cabildos, 19, 159–60. *See also* Câmara Municipal

Caboclo, 19

Cabugá, António Gonçalves da Cruz, 60, 62

Cacao, 17

Cachaça, 17

Cádiz, 206

Caio Prado Júnior, 44, 48, 89–90, 165, 167, 206

Cairú, Viscount of, 55–56

Caldeira Brant Pontes, Felizberto, 37

Calhoun, John C., 126, 128

Camacho de Aboím, Diogo Guerreiro, 186, 188

Câmara, Dom José Manuel da, 196

Câmara, Manoel de, 239

Câmara, Manuel Arruda, 60

Câmara Municipal (Senado da Câmara), 13, 71–72: and collection of fifths, 27; compared to *cabildo*, 19, 159–60; correspondence of, to crown, 25, 28, 31; crown curb on autonomy of, 19, 161–63; and electoral abuses, 19, 175–76; functions of, 158–60, 163; historiography of, 159–60; and landed oligarchy, 24, 30, 159–60, 174; merchants on, 160, 213; municipal officers, 24, 30, 159–60, 162, 174, 213; popular representation on, 160–61; post-independence, 174–75; privileges of, 19, 25, 30, 139, 140

Cambão, 149

Campinas, 145

Campos, 168

Campos, Joaquim Carneiro de (Marquis of Caravelas), 85

Caneca, Friar, 65, 84

Cangaço, 152

Canning, George, 37, 77, 101

Cantagalo, Marquis of, 85

Canudos revolt, 180, 181

Cape Verdes, 21, 53

Capitalism, commercial vs. industrial, 45–47

Capitão-mor: authority of, 167, 176; mulatto, 68

Caracas, 157

Caravelas, Marquis of, 69, 85

Cardoso, João Lopes, 67–68

Cardoso, Jorge, 185

Cardoso, José da Cunha, 240–41

Carlos, António, 62

Carlota, Dona, 98

Carmelite Order, 200–201

Carneiro de Campos, Joaquim (Marquis of Caravelas), 69, 85

Carneiro Leão, Fernando, 98

Carvalho, Dom João da Silva, 189

Carvalho, Paulo de, 198

Carvalho e Melo, Sebastião José de. *See* Pombal, Marquis of

Casa da Índia, 12

Cattle: industry developed, 8, 22, 163; and labor, 11; ranchers, 23, 160; and settlement patterns, 22, 157, 163–64, 165

Cavalcante de Albuquerque, Francisco de Paula, 61, 62

Caxias, Duke of, 97

Ceará, 66, 71, 150, 153

Cesar de Menezes, Vasco Fernandes (Count of Sabugosa), 28

Chacim, 75

Chamberlain, Sir Henry, 101

Charleston, 171

Charque, 97

Chartered trading companies. *See* Monopoly companies

Chile: oligarchy in, 141, 174; patriot regime in, 126

China, 53

Church: attacked in Portugal, 190–92, 193; in Brazil, 18, 240. *See also* Jacobeia; Jesuits; Religious orders

Cities. *See* Câmara Municipal; Society and social structure; Urbanization and cities in Brazil

Coast Guard Academy, 221

Cochrane, Thomas (Lord Dundonald), 37, 86

Cocoa, 8

Coelho, José João Teixeira, 235

Coffee, 8, 145, 165, 169, 176, 177, 179–80

Coimbra University: Brazilian students at, 20, 23, 32, 85, 217, 242, 243; Pombaline reform of, 200, 216, 217, 222; "purity of blood" criterion, 69

Colégio da Boa Sorte (Salvador), 223

College of Nobles (Lisbon), 200

Colombia, 126

Colonial pact, Luso-Brazilian, 11–14: and colonialism, 3–7; characteristics of, 3–7; colonial response to, 21–22, 26–33; increasing regalism of, 14–21; rupture of, 33–40, 44–47, 49–50, 74–88

Communications, in Brazil, 22, 23, 107–8, 165

Compadresco, 152

Company for the Brazil Trade, 161

Conceição, Friar Apolinário da, 186, 189–90

Condillac, Étienne Bonnot de, 222

Confederation of Ecuador, 84, 104

Constancy masonic lodge, 62

Constitutional Assembly, Brazilian, 37, 50, 82–83, 86, 87

Constitution of 1824, Brazilian, 83, 86–88, 154, 174, 229: popular misunderstanding of term, 71

Contraband, gold, 15, 16, 21, 31, 138

Contracts. *See* Monopolies

Coronelismo, 29, 158, 174–75

Corrêa da Serra, José, 114, 121, 122

Correio braziliense, 58, 105, 221, 234, 236

Cortés, Hernán, 6

Côrtes Gerais (Portuguese parliament): abolition of, 37; Brazilian deputies at, 35, 55, 66, 77, 79, 83, 234, 236, 239–40; Brazilian loyalty to, 73; British attitude toward, 94; colonial reaction against measures of, 35, 36, 38, 72, 74, 77–81, 83–84, 90; dispatches troops to Brazil, 36, 79, 84; grants suffrage to *libertos*, 240; orders Dom João's return, 122; orders Dom Pedro's return, 4, 123, 242–43; policies for Brazil, 13, 36, 56, 78–79, 81, 83–84; seeks to recolonize Brazil, 35–36, 37

Costa, Emília Viotti da, 90, 92, 138

Costa, Hipólito da, 58, 93, 221, 229, 230, 234, 242

Costa Rica, 3

Cotton: as export crop, 8, 17, 57, 107; factories in Portugal, 75; and labor, 11, 146

Council of Procurators-General of the Provinces of Brazil, 80, 81

Council of State (Brazil), 74, 82, 84, 85, 86

Court (in Rio de Janeiro): Brazilian antagonism toward, 38, 143; bureaucratic aspects of, 143, 215; cost of, 94, 107; cultural impact of, 178, 215–16; financial investment in Brazil, 97–99, 103–4; fiscal policies toward north and northeast, 94, 95, 99, 101, 107; French influence at, 124; popular attraction of, 102; relation to central-southern region, 94, 97–99, 107; relation to colonial oligarchies, 102–3, 105, 137–38, 142–43; represents strong centralized government, 101, 104–8, 178, 204; stimulates Brazilian economy, 33, 106–8, 214–16; transfers from Lisbon to, 33, 34, 35, 74, 92, 97, 109, 113, 203, 209, 241–42; U.S. minister to, 114, 120–21

Coutinho, Domingos de Souza, 100

Coutinho, José Lino, 236

Coutinho, Rodrigo de Souza, 94, 106

Covilhã, 75

Crato, 71

Crawford, William, 120

Cruz, Friar Manuel da, 192

Cuiabá, 8

Cuiabá river, 108

Cunha, Euclides da, 180–81

Cunha Barbosa, Januário da, 84, 85

Curitiba, 167, 173

Declaration of the Rights of Man, 87

Democratic University masonic lodge, 61

Derrama, 28, 33. *See also* Fifths, Royal

Deus, João de, 68–69, 70

Diamonds: and contract system, 28, 142, 200; discovery of, 8, 14, 25; export of, 21; fiscal measures regarding, 16, 28, 212

Diderot, Denis, 59

Doce river, 14, 108

Donatories, 8, 158

Douro Wine Company (Companhia dos Vinhos do Douro), 57, 84

Duarte, Nestor, 159

Dundonald, Lord, 37, 86

Dutch: in Brazil, 8, 9, 14, 20, 31; commercial dominance of, 20; manufactured goods, 21, 28; piracy, 48

Dutch West India Company, 8

Edinburgh University, 20

Education: in Brazil, 221–23; learning of foreign languages, 227–28

Ellis, Myriam, 49

El-Mina (São Jorge da Mina) fortress, 20

Emboabas, 26, 31–32

Encyclopédie, 59

Engenho Salgado, 150

England: active in Brazilian contraband, 21, 48, 101, 138; book trade to Brazil, 59–61, 220–21; and Brazilian independence, 4, 37–38, 83, 86; dominance of Brazilian commerce, 34, 39, 86, 88, 90, 134, 229; impact of theories of economic liberalism, 50, 55–56, 91; industrial capitalism in, 34, 47, 104; intellectual influence on Brazil, 32, 59–61, 220–21, 223, 227, 229; pressure for abolition of slave trade, 37, 91; role in transfer of court, 113; trade with Brazil, 75, 77, 105, 214. *See also* Independence; United States of America

English-Portuguese relations: tariff treaties, 52, 54, 55, 75–76, 78, 93, 106; trade, 75, 94–95

Enlightenment: in Europe, 63; impact on Brazil, 20, 27, 32, 58–61, 224, 240–41, 244–46

Espírito Santo, 9, 10, 108

Falmouth packet, 21

Faria e Sousa, Manuel de, 208

Feijó, João da Silva, 66

Feira de Santana, 176

Ferdinand VII, King, 127

Ferreira, Alexandre Rodrigues, 230

Ferreira, Silvestre Pinheiro, 73, 222, 230

Ferreira França, Clemente (Marquis of Nazareth), 85

Fichte, Johann Gottlieb, 230

Fifths, Royal (*Quintos Reais*): evasion of payment of, 15, 16, 31; forms of collection of, 15, 16, 17, 27–28, 138; smelting houses, 16, 27–28

Figueiredo e Melo, João Ladislau de, 246

Foreigners: commercial concessions to, *see* England; denied ballot in Brazil, 82; hostility toward, 56; resident in Brazil, 61, 215; support Brazilian independence movement, 76; trading restrictions on, 53

Fortaleza, 173, 224

Fort Junqueira, 198

Foundry houses. *See* Fifths, Royal

France: book trade to Brazil, 220–21, 222, 223, 227, 228, 246; Brazilian students in, 228; cultural mission to Brazil, 223, 228; ideological impact on Brazil, 32, 58–61, 69, 227–28, 236; influence at Brazilian court, 124; invasion of Iberian Peninsula, 34, 35, 94, 95, 113; invasion of Rio de Janeiro, 21, 32, 48; officers assist Brazilian independence, 37, 86; prose and drama in Brazil, 232; residents in Rio de Janeiro, 215. *See also* French Revolution

Francis I, King, 37

Franciscans, 201, 221–22

Franklin, Benjamin, 230

Freemasons and freemasonry: closure of lodges, 62; lodges established, 61–62; membership of, 62–63, 84–85; revolutionary activities of, 32, 60, 65, 69, 200, 203, 205, 206

Freire de Andrada, Gomes, 19

French Revolution: impact on Brazil, 32, 59–60, 87, 154, 228, 245–46; impact on Portugal, 92–93, 202–3

Freyre, Gilberto, 169

Frias, António João de, S.J., 188

Furtado, Celso, 163

Furtado, Francisco Xavier de Mendonça, 191

Gaioso, Raimondo José de Sousa, 134–35

Galvez, José de, 141

Gama, José Basílio da, 232

"General Mines." *See* Minas Gerais

Genovesi, Antonio, 222, 230

Germany and Brazil, 230

Goa, 7

Goiania, 105

Goiás: Amerindians in, 9; captaincy created, 18; fluvial navigation in, 22, 108; gold mining in, 8, 13, 16, 21, 163

Góis, Damião de, 185

Gold and gold mining: contraband, 15, 16, 21, 31, 138; crown fiscal measures, 14–16, 27–28, 31, 33, 138, 142; decline of production, 8, 33, 138, 145, 165; discovery of 8, 13, 24, 26; effect on Brazilian demography, 49, 163–65, 211–12; gold rush, 14, 162; labor, 10–11; socioeconomic repercussions of, 8, 13–16, 24, 25, 148, 211, 238

Gold Coast, 20

Goldini, Carlo, 232

Gomes, Friar Francisco Agostinho, 220, 246

Gonçalves da Cruz, António, 115-16, 117–18, 126

Gonçalves dos Santos, Friar Luís, 201, 204

Gonçalves Lêdo, Joaquim, 74, 81, 82, 83, 84, 85

Góngora, Mario, 174

Gonzaga, Tomás António, 144

Graham, John, 119, 120, 121

Graham, Maria, 221, 224

Grande Oriente, 84

Grant, Andrew, 220

Grão Pará and Maranhão monopoly company, 17, 19, 138, 162

Great Orient masonic lodge (Rio de Janeiro), 84

Grenfell, John Pascoe, 86

Grito de Ipiranga, 36

Guadeloupe, 47
Guaporé river, 108
Guaratinguetá, 176–77
Guatemala, 3
Guedes de Brito family, 29
Guerra dos Emboabas, 26, 31–32
Guerra dos Mascates, 23, 26–27, 31, 48, 162, 178, 213
Guiana, 95, 107
Guilds. *See* Artisans

"Haitianism," 67, 68, 69–70, 82, 103–4, 153, 155; defined, 100–101
Havana, 47, 171
Hegel, Georg Wilhelm Friedrich, 230
Heineccius, Johann Gottlieb, 222
Herrmann, Lucila, 176
Hides tax, 107
High Court *(Relação)*, 12, 31, 162
Hill, Henry, 113, 123, 124
Holy Alliance, 37, 97, 111, 117
Humboldt, Alexander von, 170
Hyde de Neuville, Baron, 116

Idade d'ouro, 216, 219, 229, 239; cited, 221, 223, 233–34, 240
Iguape, Baron of, 91
Ilhéus, 108
Inconfidência. See Inconfidência Mineira; Revolt of the Tailors
Inconfidência Bahiana. *See* Revolt of the Tailors
Inconfidência Mineira: as expression of political grievances, 235–36; influenced by European Enlightenment, 32, 58–59, 220, 224; localized support for, 26, 66; racial aspect of, 67, 69; social profile of participants in, 64, 143–44, 165, 242
Independence in the Americas, 3–7, 39. *See also* United States of America
Independence of Brazil: attitude of rural oligarchy toward, 137–38; British diplomatic role in, 4, 37–38, 86; course taken by independence movement, 35–37, 89, 92 *et seq.,* 105–6, 209; declaration of independence, 4, 34, 77, 83–84, 123; differing concepts of "independence," 66, 72–74, 81–82, 84–85, 88, 92, 105; elitist tone of, 84–85, 86, 88; foreign forces participate in, 36–37, 86; and freemasonry, 60, 61–63, 69, 84–85; historiography of, 89–92, 99–100, 103, 105, 133–34; hope of foreign support, 79, 80; monarchical aspects of, 137–38; policy of Great Britain toward, 77, 86; racial aspects of, 67–70; reaction by Côrtes

Gerais toward, *see* Côrtes Gerais; recognition by Portugal, 4, 37–38, 39, 86; recognition by U.S., 4, 109, 125–28; role of intellectuals in, 211, 217–43; role of populace in, 67–71, 80, 243–46; U.S. policy toward, 37, 109 *et seq. See also* American Revolution; Enlightenment; French Revolution
Indigo, 17
Intellectuals, in Brazil: active in *inconfidências,* 32, 242 *(see also* Inconfidência Mineira); as advocates of reform, 234–42; alliance of, with commercial class, 226; attitudes toward slave trade and slavery, 88, 239–40, 242; clubs, 223–24; "conspiracy" of, 222; contact with populace, 245–46; European influences on, 217–30, 240–41; female, 224; interest in U.S., 230; as leaders of independence movement, 211, 217–43; as supporters of Amerindians, 240, 242
Irigoyen, Matias, 62
Italian influence in Brazil, 230, 232
Itapocara, Baron of, 85
Itú, 145
Iturbide, Agustín, 124, 125, 127

Jacarepagua, Marquis of, 85
Jacobeia, 199–200
Jacutinga, Baron of, 85
Janeiristas, 98
Jardim, 71
Jefferson, Thomas: anti-Latin sentiments, 112; encourages independence movements in Brazil, 117, 123; influence of, in Brazil, 230; on Latin American independence, 110; overtures to Dom João VI, 113–14; cited, 122
Jenner, Edward, 214
Jequitinhonha river, 108
Jesuits: alleged role in regicide attempt, 196, 197, 198; college in Salvador, 221; and education, 20, 216–17, 221; expulsion from Portugal and Brazil, 20, 139; missionary activity of, 10, 21, 139, 155, 191, 194, 195; opposition to enslavement of Amerindians, 159; Pombaline persecution of, 29, 194–96, 216
Jews: Pombal's legislation against antisemitism, 20; service as municipal officers, 60. *See also* "Purity of blood"
João I, King Dom, 207
João III, King Dom, 8, 187, 189
João IV, King Dom, 207
João V, King Dom, 29, 33, 186, 191, 194, 199, 213: fiscal policies for Brazil, 15–16,

27–28; promotes territorial expansion of Brazil, 18

João VI, King Dom: and administrative reform in Brazil, 99–100, 101, 106–8, 204, 240; arrives in Brazil, 33, 113, 143, 203, 204–5; assessment of reign, 58; Brazilian loyalty toward, 72–73, 83; commercial policies of, 36, 50–54, 75–77, 90–91, 114; declares war on Amerindians, 10; declares war on France, 204, 205; diplomatic relations with U.S., 119–21; dispenses privileges and titles, 33, 64, 142–43; and fiscal reform in Portugal, 94–95; and freemasonry, 62; opens Brazilian ports to international trade, 13, 34, 50, 51, 52, 55, 61, 75, 90, 214; opposition to policies of, 55–58; popular appeal of, 101, 102; promotes education, 221, 223; returns to Portugal, 34, 62, 76, 77, 100, 122, 205, 242

José I, King Dom, 19, 190, 193: colonial policies of, 15, 16–17; regicide attempt against, 196–98

Juiz de Fora, 165

Juiz do povo, 160

Juízes de fora, 19, 162, 168

Junot, Andoche, 93, 203, 205

Kant, Immanuel, 230

Kantzow, Johan A., 216

Kindersley, Mrs. Nathaniel, 203

King, Rufus, 113

Knights of Light masonic lodge, 61

Koster, Henry: on agriculture, 151; on modernization of Recife, 214–15; on peasantry, 146, 149, 153; on race relations, 68

Labatut, Pierre, 37, 86

Labor pool, free, 24, 137, 139, 150. *See also* Peasantry

Lago dos Siganos, 98

Laguna, 163

Lahmeyer Lobo, Eulália Maria, 159–60

La Plata river: scene of Luso-Spanish disputes, 19, 21, 95, 107, 138

Lavoisier, Antoine, 220

Lavradio, Marquis of, 167

Lavradores de cana, 147–48, 151, 168. *See also* Peasantry

Leiria, 75

Lemos Sampaio, Manuel Vieira de, 65

Lencastre, Dom Veríssimo de, 189

Leopoldina, Princess, 84, 230

Lesírias, 95

Liberalism: in Brazil, 32–33, 58–61, 63–66, 91–92, 223; social impact of, 70–72 (*see also* Pernambuco Revolt of 1817; João VI, King Dom: commercial policies of); in Portugal, 50–51, 122, 209–10. *See also* Oporto: liberal revolution in

Libraries, in Brazil, 219–22, 228, 246

Lindley, Thomas, 220; cited, 152, 236

Link, M., 200

Linnaeus (Carl von Linné), 214

Lisbon: acropolis form of, 155; as commercial entrepôt, 15, 17, 18, 21; moral impact of earthquake in, 190–93; population, 213; reconstruction after earthquake, 17, 194; as seat of government of empire, 12, 35

Literary academies, in colonial Brazil, 20, 211, 217–19, 231, 233

Locke, John, 229

Louis, XIV, King, 15

Luccock, John, 216, 220–21; cited, 143

Lusophobia, 104, 105. *See also* Brazilians: hostility to *reinóis*

Mably, Gabriel Bonnet de, 58, 60, 222

Macaé, Viscount of, 85

Macapá, 105

Macedo, Ignácio José de, 216

Macedo, Jorge de, 47

Maceió, 173

Machado, António Rodrigues, 232

Madeira, Island of, 53

Madeira river, 108

Madison, James, 112

Madrid, Treaty of, 18, 21, 211

Mafra, 18

Maia, José Joaquim de, 59

Malagrida, Friar Gabriel, 190–95, 198

Malapá river, 105

Mamoré river, 108

Manaus, 173

Manuel, António, 71–72

Manuel I, King Dom, 7, 12

Manumissions, 11–12, 153, 239

Maranhão: Amerindian population of, 9; Beckmann uprising in, 48, 162; black and mulatto population of, 19, 67, 148; economy of, 8, 17, 39; foreign residents in, 215; Jesuit missions in, 191, 195; monopolistic trading company for, 17, 19, 138, 162; opposition to independence in, 37, 83, 86; social structure of, 135; and territorial expansion, 18

Maranhão river, 108

Maria I, Queen Dona, 16, 198

Mariana, 155, 192

Martins, Domingos José, 62, 68
Martius, C. F. Phil. von, 178, 216
Masonry and masonic lodges. *See* Freemasons and freemasonry
Mataporcos, 98
Mato Grosso: Amerindians in, 9; captaincy created, 18; fluvial communications in, 22, 108; gold strikes in, 13, 16, 21, 163
Mawe, John, 145, 153
Maxwell, Kenneth, 165
Medrões, Abbot of, 201–2, 208, 209
Mercês, António Joaquim das, 222
Merchants in Luso-Brazilian world: antagonism toward planters, 26–27, 48, 134, 139–41, 162; crown's protectionist policy toward, 28, 36, 78, 90–91, 139–41; English, 29, 77; hostility toward, 103; loyalty to crown, 64, 85–86; position in society, 26–27, 212–13; and revolutionary movements, 64; threatened by economic liberalism, 45–47, 49–58. *See also* Boards of Inspection; Monopolies; Monopoly companies; War of the Peddlers
Merchants in Mexico, 171
Merchants in Philadelphia, 171
Mercure, Le, 60
Mesa de Consciência e Ordens, 78
Mesa do Bem Comum, 29
Methuen Treaty, 21
Metternich, Prince Klemens Wenzel von, 37, 207
Mexico: authority of viceroy in, 18; independence in, 4; Mexico City, 171–72; U.S. reaction toward, 124, 125, 126, 127; urban development in, 157, 171–72, 178
Migration: to Brazil, 8–9, 19, 163, 211–12, 215; within Brazil, 14, 145, 163, 165, 212
Miguel, João, 197
Military Academy (Rio de Janeiro), 227
Militia: in Argentina, 174; in colonial Brazil, 30, 142, 158, 167–68, 174, 213
Minas Gerais: agriculture in, 145, 165; Amerindian population in, 9, 10; authority of *capitães-mores* in, 167; banditry in, 152; cattle industry in, 8; cost of living in, 33; crown fiscal policy in, 14–16, 27–28, 31, 138, 142; diamond extraction in, 14, 24; electoral irregularities in, 19; fluvial navigation in, 108, 163; foreign residents in, 215; free blacks and free mulattos in, 136–37; "French faction" in, 58; gold mining in, 8, 13–16, 21, 24, 33, 138, 145; as independent captaincy, 16; intellectual life in, 31, 224; population trends in, 136–37, 145, 163–65, 212; republican senti-

ment in, 35; social structure of, 24, 213. *See also* Inconfidência Mineira; Vila Rica do Ouro Prêto; War of the *Emboabas*
Minas Novas, 108
Mining, impact on settlement patterns, 157, 163–65
Ministry of Conciliation, 97
Ministry of the Empire, 84
Mints, 30, 31. *See also* Gold and gold mining
Miranda, Inocêncio António de, 201–2, 208, 209
Miranda Montenegro, Caetano Pinto de, 82
Miscegenation: Amerindian and white, 139, 145, 211; black and white, 68, 136–37, 148, 211
Monções, 22, 164
Monopolies: as part of colonial system, 17–18, 45–47; on commodities, 17, 49, 57; deterioration of, 49–58, 66, 90–91, 238
Monopoly companies, 17, 19, 29, 57, 84, 138, 141, 162. *See also* Pombal, Marquis of
Monroe, James: and independence movements in Latin America, 110, 111, 115, 117, 118, 122; recognizes Brazilian independence, 4, 128; relations with Dom João VI, 114, 119, 122
Monroe doctrine, 127
Mont'Alverne, Friar Francisco de, 205
Monteiro, Tobias, 43
Montesquieu, Charles Louis de Secondat, 58
Montpelier University, 20
Moradores, 147–52
Moreira de Mendonça, Veríssimo António, 191
Mosqueira, José de Oliveira Pinto Botelho, 74
Mota, Carlos Guilherme, 136
Mulattos, in colonial Brazil: as artisans, 135, 137, 144; as free labor pool, 137, 148–49, 153; granted suffrage, 239–40; hostility toward blacks, 24; increase in, 136, 137; in revolutionary movements, 67–70, 144, 244; social position of, 11–12, 68, 135; as soldiers, 30, 33
Musschenbroeck, Pieter van, 222

Nabuco, Joaquim, 169–70, 175, 177
Napoleon I, Emperor: invades Portugal, 93, 109, 111, 113, 203, 205, 209
National Gazette, 124
National Guard, 174

National Intelligencer, 115, 116
Nationalism: in Europe, 63, 91–92; revolutionary content of, 96–97, 105; and revolutionary movements in Brazil, 26–27, 31–32, 60, 65–66, 72. *See also* Brazilians: pride in being
Nativism in Brazil: championed by intellectuals, 218–19, 226; and criticism of colonial system, 238; literary manifestations of, 231–34; social aspects of, 239–40
Nazareth, Marquis of, 85
"New Christians," 20, 24, 26
New York, 170, 171, 212
New York Spectator, 124
Neves, Acúrcio das, 93
Niles' Weekly Register, 115, 118, 123, 124, 125
Niterói, 173
Nobility in Portugal: ideal of, 187–90; under attack, 190, 202
Nogueira da Gama, Manuel Jacinto (Marquis of Baependi), 85
North American Review, 118
Nunes, António Duarte, 220
Nunes Leal, Victor, 159, 175
Nunes Viana, Manuel, 29

Obes, Lucas José, 74, 81
Occident of Pernambuco (Pernambuco do Ocidente) masonic lodge, 62
"Old Christians," 24. *See also* "Purity of blood"
Olinda: religious orders in, 200–201; seminary of, 222–23, 227, 242. *See also* War of the Peddlers
Olive oil, 17
Oliveira, Luís da Silva Pereira, 202
Oliveira Lima, Manoel de, 43, 62
Oporto, 155, 213: liberal revolution in, 34, 54, 64, 75, 76, 78, 90, 92, 96, 100, 103, 206–7
O prêto e o bugio de mato, 61
Oratorians Order, 201
Orient of Pernambuco (Pernambuco do Oriente) masonic lodge, 61
Os Cavaleiros da Luz, 61
Osório, Jerónimo, 185

Padroado Real, 65
Paine, Thomas, 59, 220, 230
Palma, Count of, 107
Pamplona, David, 88
Pantoja, Hermógenes Francisco de Aguilar, 246

Pará: economy of, 8, 39; Jesuits in, 195; loyalist forces in, 37, 86; settlement of, 9; and territorial expansion, 18
Pará river, 108
Paradise masonic lodge, 61
Paraguay, 157, 194
Paraíba do Norte, 66, 72, 201
Paraíba river, 176
Paraná, Marquis of, 97
Paratí, 156
Pardo, Treaty of, 21
Paris, Treaty of, 3
Parnaíba, 160
Paulistas, 26, 163, 169–70; apathy to independence movement, 70–71. *See also* São Paulo; War of the *Emboabas*
Peasantry: as political factor, 153–54; rise of, in Brazil, 134, 137, 139, 144–46; socioeconomic conditions of, 146–53
Pedro I, Emperor Dom, 74, 76, 122, 205, 207, 230; abdicates, 104; declares Brazilian independence, 4, 84; diplomatic overtures of, 37–38, 126; given title of "Perpetual Defender," 81, 83; orders Portuguese troops out of Brazil, 80, 83; refuses to return to Portugal, 13, 73, 79–80, 123, 242; support for, 25, 33, 36–37, 78–81; U.S. attitudes toward, 123–29
Pedro II, Emperor Dom, 234
Pedro II, King Dom, 14, 21, 188
Pedrouços, 199
Penalva, Marquis of, 203
Pereira, Clemente, 73, 80
Pereira, Diogo Borges Pacheco, 189
Pereira da Silva, João Manuel, 93
Pereira de Faro, Joaquim José (Baron of Rio Bonito), 85
Pereira Filgueiras, José, 71
Perier, Alexandre, S. J., 188
Pernambuco: agriculture in, 57, 148; foreign residents in, 215; land usage in, 150–51; peasantry in, 146–49; population changes in, 136, 148; vagrancy in, 152–53
Pernambuco do Ocidente, 62
Pernambuco do Oriente, 61
Pernambuco Revolt of 1817, 33, 58, 104, 178, 235: English influence in, 60–61; fear of masses in, 67–70, 103, 136, 153; French influence in, 60, 220; masonic role in, 60, 61, 65; planter class support for, 70, 72; popular view of, 70; role of merchants in, 64; role of priests in, 65; U.S. reaction toward, 59, 114–19. *See*

also Monopoly companies; Olinda; Praieira revolts; Recife; War of the Peddlers

Peru, 18, 126, 157, 178

Philadelphia, 110, 171, 212

Philadelphia Weekly Aurora, 118

Philanthropic masonic lodge, 62

Piauí, 207

Pindamonhangaba, Baron of, 85

Poderosos do sertão, 29, 31

Pombal, Marquis of (Sebastião José de Carvalho e Melo): Amerindian policy of, 10, 19–20, 139; commercial policy of, 15, 16–17, 28–29, 34, 47–48, 138, 141–42; defence policy of, 138–39; education reforms of, 200, 216–17, 222; establishes monopoly companies, 17, 29, 138, 141; fiscal reforms of, 214; harassment of Jacobeia, 199–200; impact on baroque society, 190–93; and legislation against anti-semitism, 20, 24; and persecution of Jesuits, 20, 139, 191, 194–96, 198, 216; promotes colonization, 139; and reconstruction of Lisbon, 194; and regicide attempt, 196–98; and slavery measures, 20, 139, 200; stimulates agriculture, 29, 138–42

Ponte, House of, 29

Ponte do Cajú, palace at, 98

Pôrto Alegre: Brazil, 173, 179; Portugal, 75

Pôrto Feliz, 164

Pôrto Seguro, 9, 10, 108

Portugal: agriculture in, 75, 94; Anglo-Portuguese trade, 29, 55, 75, 78, 93; decline of religion in, 187, 190–93, 198–203; domestic unrest in, 92–95; economy of, 15, 21, 74, 75, 78, 93–94, 95; education in, 200, 216–17, 222; foreign policy of, 19, 20, 21; French invasion of, 21, 34, 35, 113; impact of French revolution in, 202–3; industry in, 75, 93; liberal revolution in, *see* Oporto; overseas empire of, 7–8, 12, 20–21, 53; position of nobility in, 187–90; under Spanish rule, 159, 207; weakening of baroque society in, 190–210

Portuguese crown: administrative policy of, 7–8, 12–13, 18–19; agricultural policy of, 24–25; attitude of, toward blacks and mulattos, 10–12, 68, 69; attitude toward Brazilians, 22, 25, 26, 30, 143; colonial policy of, 21–33, 45–51, 55–58, 74–76, 89–91; and colonization, 7–9; commercial policy of, 24–25, 28–29, 48–54, 162; ecclesiastical policy of, 12, 14, 18; eco-

nomic policy of, 8, 13–18, 30; increasing regalism of, 13–21, 162–63; judicial policy of, 12, 18; and mining, 14–18, 27–29, 31; military policy of, 19; treatment of Amerindians, 9–10, 19–20

Prądt, Abbé de, 208, 209

Praieira revolts, 105, 178

Príncipe, Island of, 21

Printing presses, 12, 31, 223, 229

Privileges: divisive social impact of, 25–26; municipal, 19, 30; as part of colonial system, 33, 45–47; reaction against, 30, 47–51, 63; seekers of, 64, 102. *See also* Monopolies; Monopoly companies

"Purity of blood," 11, 20, 24, 25, 69

Quixeramobin, Marquis of, 85

Race relations in Brazil, 19, 144, 153. *See also* "Haitianism"; Miscegenation; Mulattos, in colonial Brazil; "Purity of blood"

Raynal, Guillaume Thomas François, 58, 60

Recife: Board of Inspection, 29, 139; city council, 25, 139; described by Koster, 214–15; economy of, 63; freemasonry in, 61; intellectual life in, 224; population of, 173, 179, 215; printing press in, 223; religious orders in, 201; society of, 24, 26, 64, 213. *See also* Olinda; Pernambuco; War of the Peddlers

Recôncavo, 8, 22, 162

Redondo, 75

Régia Press (Tipografia Régia): Lisbon, 203; Rio de Janeiro, 229

Regionalism in Brazil, 22–25, 33, 35, 38–39, 66–67, 90, 94, 96, 100–102, 104, 107, 134

Reinóis, 23, 24, 25. *See also* War of the *Emboabas;* War of the Peddlers

Relação, 12, 31, 162

Religious orders, 200–201. *See also* Jesuits

Remédios, António dos, 191

Republican sentiment, 33, 35, 70–72, 80. *See also* Pernambuco Revolt of 1817

Resende, Count of, 59, 227

Resende, Estevão de, 74, 85

Resende, Marquis of, 62

Resgates, 10

Revolta dos Alfaiates. See Revolt of the Tailors

Revolt of the Tailors, 26, 32–33, 58, 61, 64, 235: French influence on, 58, 60, 69, 232, 245–46; intellectuals' role in, 243–

44, 245–46; issue of slavery in, 239; racial aspects of, 32–33, 68–70, 144, 244–45

Revolts and *inconfidências*. *See* Enlightenment; Inconfidência Mineira; Liberalism; Oporto; Pernambuco Revolt of 1817; Revolt of the Tailors; Suassuna conspiracy

Ribeirão de Santo António, 108

Ribeiro, João, 61

Ribeiro de Andrada, António Carlos, 61

Ribeiro Sanches, António Nunes, 217

Ribeiro Santos, Manuel, 219

Ricard, Robert, 155

Rice, 17

Richmond Enquirer, 126

Riego Revolt, 126

Rio Bonito, Baron of, 85

Rio das Mortes, 14, 145

Rio das Velhas, 14

Rio de Janeiro, 31, 34, 155–56, 158–59; Board of Inspection, 29, 139–40; city council, 73–74, 79–80, 81, 159, 161; commerce in, 63, 97, 171, 180, 214; foreign residents in, 215; freemasonry in, 61–62, 69, 84; French invasion of, 21, 32, 48; and hinterland, 22, 178, 179; intellectual and cultural life in, 98, 217–19, 220–22, 223–24; lotteries in, 98; population of, 136–37, 173, 212; religious orders in, 201, 221–22; as seat of government, 35, 106–7, 138, 166–67, 172, 174–75, 178, 179; seminary of São José at, 227; U.S. consul at, 113, 124, 126; U.S. mission to, 119–20; unrest in, 58, 62, 64, 235, 242. *See also* Court

Rio Grande do Norte, 66

Rio Grande do Sul, 9, 21, 179, 215

Rio Pardo, Count of, 85

Rio Seco, Baron of, 98

Rocha Pita, Sebastião da, 231, 234

Rodney, Caesar, 117–18, 119

Romeiro, Brás, 197

Rousseau, Jean Jacques, 60, 222, 243

Royal Library (Rio de Janeiro), 221

Rubber trade, 179

Rubin, Jules, 170

Rush, Richard, 118

Sá e Benavides, Salvador Correia de, 159

Sabará, 16

Sabugosa, Count of, 28

Sacramento, Colônia do, 21

St. Benedict, Order of, 201, 222

St. Christopher, palace of, 98

St. Domingue, 69, 144, 147. *See also* "Haitianism"

St. Francis, Order of, 201, 221–22

Saint-Hilaire, A. Prouvensal de, 70–71, 166–69

St. Petersburg, 194

Saldanha, Cardinal Dom Francisco de, 195–96

Salt: monopoly contract of, 17, 49, 50, 238; tax on, 54

Salvador, 22, 119, 155: archbishopric, 12; Board of Inspection, 29, 139; as capital, 8, 10, 19, 24, 138, 156, 157, 158–59, 160; city council, 24, 25, 139, 160–61, 213; commerce in, 28, 63; cultural and intellectual life in, 216, 217, 220, 221, 223, 224, 232, 246; freemasonry in, 61; High Court, 12, 162; population of, 162, 171, 173, 179, 212, 214; Portuguese garrison in, 36–37; religious orders in, 222; vagrancy in, 153. *See also* Bahia; *Idade d'ouro*; Revolt of the Tailors

Sampaio, Manuel Inácio de, 224

San Ildefonso, Treaty of, 18, 21

Santa Casa da Misericórdia, 13, 25, 30, 106

Santa Catarina, 9

Santa Cruz, palace of, 98

Santa Maria, Dom Lourenço de, 199–200

Santa Rita Durão, José da, 232

Santo Amaro, Marquis of, 85, 99

Santos, 22, 159, 160, 180

Santos, Felício dos, 48

Santos Marrocos, Luiz dos, 98–99

Santos Vilhena, Luís dos, 135–36, 150, 153; cited, 144, 237

São Carlos, Francisco de, 234

São Francisco river, 22, 163, 165

São Gonçalo, Baron of, 85

São João d'El Rei, 16

São João Marcos, Baron of, 85

São João theater (Rio de Janeiro), 98

São Jorge da Mina (El-Mina), 20

São José seminary (Rio de Janeiro), 227

São Luís do Maranhão: Board of Inspection, 29, 139; city council, 159, 160; city planning in, 156; printing press in, 223. *See also* Beckmann uprising

São Paulo, captaincy of, 16: Amerindians in, 9, 10; communications in, 108; Dom Pedro's visit to, 84; economy of, 8, 145, 169; foreign residents in, 215; peasantry in, 145–46; reaction to independence movement in, 70–71. *See also* Paulistas; War of the *Emboabas*

São Paulo, city of: city council, 159–60; population of, 160, 173, 179–80; provincial junta of, 79; religious fervor in, 192–93
São Tomé, 21
São Vicente, 158
Sartoris, P., 126
Say, Horace, 171
Say, Jean Baptiste, 47
Schelling, Friedrich Wilhelm Joseph von, 230
Secret societies. *See* Freemasons and free-masonry
See, Horace, 101
Senado da Câmara. *See* Câmara Municipal
Senhores de engenho, 151 et seq.
Separatist sentiment in Brazil, 26, 35, 38, 55, 72–74, 79–81, 83, 90–91, 208, 242–43
Sergipe de-El Rei, 140
Serra, José Francisco Corrêa da, 116, 121
Sesmarias, 29, 31
Setúbal, 195
Sibiró, 150
Sieber, Friedrich Wilhelm, 230
Sierra y Mariscal, 100, 101, 102, 103, 104
Silva, António Teles da (Marquis of Resende), 62
Silva, Luís Vieira da, 220
Silva de Eça, Matias Aires Ramos da, 189, 235
Silva e Otra, Teresa Margarida, 235
Silva Lisboa, José da, 50, 55–56, 214, 229
Silva Serva, Manuel António da, 223, 229
Silva Xavier, Joaquim José da, 59, 230
Silvestre Rebello, José, 125, 127, 128
Singer, Paul, 165, 168–69
Slaves and slavery: abolished in Portugal, 20, 200; abolition sentiment, 239–40; in agriculture, 8, 10–11, 24, 39, 86, 169; Amerindian, 10, 159; attitude of revolutionary movements toward, 38–39, 64, 66, 67, 86, 88, 133, 144, 242; manumission of, 11–12, 153, 239–40, 242; in mining, 11, 14, 16, 17, 24, 25, 148, 212; Negro, 10–11, 135, 137. *See also* "Haitianism"; Peasantry; Revolt of the Tailors
Slave trade, African, 8, 11, 139, 212: pressure to end, 37, 91, 239
Smelting houses, 27, 28, 30
Smith, Adam, 47, 50, 220, 229
Smith, Robert C., 155
Sociedade Literária (Rio de Janeiro), 217
Society and social structure, 9–12, 19–20, 23–24, 29, 38, 66–71, 134–38, 211: compared with Spanish America, 104, 141–

42, 172–74; rural oligarchy, 23, 24, 102–4, 137–38, 141–44, 158, 159–60, 167–68, 174, 175, 176; social mechanisms, 105–6, 151–52; social mobility, 11–12, 23, 136–37, 213, 245; tensions and antagonisms, 22, 23–24, 25–27, 30, 33, 38, 57, 69, 90, 100–105, 134, 140–41, 151–52, 196. *See also* Amerindians; Brazilians: pride in being; "Haitianism"; Merchants; Miscegenation; Mulattos; Peasantry; Sugar: planters
Sodré, Nelson Werneck, 44, 45
Soldiers: black and mulatto, 30, 33; Portuguese, in Brazil, 36–37, 77, 80–81, 83, 85–86. *See also* Militia
Sorocaba, 145
Sousa, António Moniz de, 168
Sousa, Friar Luís de, 185
Sousa, Martim Afonso de, 158
Sousa, Tomé de, 156
Southey, Robert, 234
Spain: liberal uprisings in, 122; Napoleonic invasion of, 113; proponent of colonialism, 47
Spanish America: independence movements in, 3–4, 35, 39, 104, 209–10; society of, 104, 141, 172–74; U.S. policy toward, 109–13, 117, 126; urban planning in, 155–58, 178
Spínola, António Ardizone, 186
Spix, Joh. Bapt. von, 178, 216
Stuart, Sir Charles, 37–38
Students, Brazilian, in Europe, 12, 20, 23, 32, 61, 217, 228
Suassuna conspiracy, 58, 60, 61, 62
Suffrage, in Brazil, 82, 86–87, 154, 175, 239–40
Sugar: industry, 8, 10, 24, 47, 107, 162, 176–77, 214; planters, 23, 26–27, 62, 146–52, 160. *See also* Boards of Inspection; Society and social structure
Sumter, Thomas, Jr., 114, 119

Tagus river, 21, 80
Tapajós river, 108
Taubaté, 145
Taubaté, Marquis of, 85
Taunay, Affonso de Escragnolle, 243
Tavares, Luís Henrique Dias, 245, 246
Távora e Lorena, Dona Teresa de, 196
Távora family, 195–97
Taxation: in Brazil, 17–18, 94, 95, 107, 142; "extraordinary," 15, 17–18, 94; import-export dues, 52–54, 74–75, 107; in Portugal, 94–95. *See also* Derrama; Fifths, Royal; Monopolies

Taylor, George Rogers, 172
Teixeira, Pedro, 196
Theater and drama, 232–33
Tijuco, 8, 200. *See also* Diamonds
Tipografia Régia, 203, 229
Tiradentes (Joaquim José da Silva Xavier), 59, 230. *See also* Inconfidência Mineira
Tobacco, 8, 11, 17, 107. *See also* Boards of Inspection
Tocantins river, 108
Tollenare, Louis-François de: on 1817 revolution in Pernambuco, 60, 65, 67, 220; on peasantry, 88, 146–51
Tomar, 75
Tôrre, House of, 29
Tôrres, Lucas Dantas do Amorim, 244, 246
Trade. *See* Monopolies; Monopoly companies; Pombal, Marquis of
Tribunal of Conscience and Orders, 78
Trovão e Sousa, José de Oliveira, 191
Turgot, Anne Robert Jacques, 58

United States of America: anti-Latin prejudice in, 112–13; antimonarchical sentiment in, 124–25, 127–28, 129; commercial relations with Brazil, 113–14, 119–20, 125–26, 230; diplomatic relations with House of Braganza, 113–14, 120–22, 123, 125; economy, 172; ideological influence in Brazil, 230, 236; mission to Brazil, 119–20, 125; policy toward independence movements in Brazil, 37, 59, 122, 124–25, 127–29; policy toward Latin America, 34, 109–13, 117, 126; reaction to Brazilian independence, 123–24, 126; reaction to Pernambuco revolution, 114–19; recognizes Brazilian independence, 4, 128; urban growth in, 170–72
Universidade Democrática masonic lodge, 61
Urbanization and cities in Brazil: commercial radius of, 166–67, 172, 180; compared with Spanish America, 155–58, 171–72, 177–78; compared with U.S., 170–72, 212; demographic growth of, 30, 136–37, 160–72, 173, 180, 211–13; described by Joaquim Nabuco, 169–70; factors determining development, 157–58, 161, 177–78; historiography on, 155–56, 168–69, 180; model for, 155–56;

numbers established, 157, 158, 212; "port cities," 63, 158, 169, 172, 178; public libraries in, 219, 221; and rural hinterland, 180–81, 213; Saint-Hilaire (q.v.) on, 166–67; small town stasis, 169–70, 175–76; sociopolitical aspects of, 168, 180, 213, 245. *See also* Câmara Municipal; Intellectuals; Society and social structure
Urbanization in Portuguese India, 156
Uruguay: piracy in, 114, 120, 121, 122
Uruguay river, 21
Uruguay, Viscount of, 97

Valença, Marquis of, 85
Varnhagen, Francisco Adolfo de, 43, 172
Vasconcelos, Bernardo de, 97
Veloso de Oliveira, António Rodrigues, 239
Venezuela, 157, 174
Veracruz, 171–72
Vernei, Luís António, 217
Viceroys, 18–19
Vieira da Silva, Luiz, 58
Vila do Príncipe, 28
Vila Nova Portugal, Tomás António de, 54, 121
Vila Real, Count of, 77
Vila Real da Praia Grande, 81
Vila Rica do Ouro Prêto, 16, 63, 137, 167, 219, 227: 1720 revolt in, 26, 27, 28, 48. *See also* Gold and gold mining; Inconfidência Mineira
Vimioso, Count of, 187
Voltaire, 198, 232

Walsh, Robert, 178, 220
War of Divine Liberty, 31
War of 1812, 111, 113, 114
War of the *Emboabas* (*Guerra dos Emboabas*), 26, 31–32
War of the Peddlers (*Guerra dos Mascates*), 23, 26–27, 31, 48, 162, 178, 213
Weech, J. Friedrich von, 58
Willems, Emilio, 145–46
Williams, Eric, 91
Wine, 17, 57, 84

Xavier, Francis, S.J., 156

Zenha, Edmundo, 159, 160

THE JOHNS HOPKINS UNIVERSITY PRESS

This book was composed in Baskerville type by Port
City Press, Inc. It was printed on 60-lb. Warren 1854
paper and bound in Holliston Roxite cloth by
Universal Lithographers, Inc.

Library of Congress Cataloging in Publication Data

Russell-Wood, A. J. R. 1939–
    From colony to nation.

    (The Johns Hopkins symposia in comparative history)
    Includes bibliographical references and index.
    1. Brazil—History—1763–1821—Congresses.
I. Title. II. Series.
F2534.R87   981'.03   74-24381
ISBN 0-8018-1665-3